Sustainable Tourism:
A Marketing Perspective

2

2

By the same author

Joint Industry Committee for Tourism Statistics (JICTOURS)
Marketing in Travel and Tourism (two editions)
Measuring the Local Impact of Tourism
New Visions for Independent Museums in the UK
New Visions for London Museums
Review of Museums and Cultural Centres in the South Pacific
Review of Tourism Studies Degree Courses in the UK
Tourism Policy in Britain—The Case for a Radical Reappraisal
Tourism in Context (two editions)
Travel & Tourism and the Environment (with R. Hawkins)

Sustainable Tourism:
A Marketing Perspective

*Victor T. C. Middleton with
Rebecca Hawkins*

BUTTERWORTH
HEINEMANN

Butterworth-Heinemann
Linacre House, Jordan Hill, Oxford OX2 8DP
225 Wildwood Avenue, Woburn, MA 01801-2041
A division of Reed Educational and Professional Publishing Ltd

ℛ A member of the Reed Elsevier plc group

OXFORD   BOSTON   JOHANNESBURG
MELBOURNE   NEW DELHI   SINGAPORE

First published 1998

British Library Cataloguing in Publication Data
A catalogue record for this book is available from the British Library

ISBN 0 7506 2385 3

Typeset by David Gregson Associates, Beccles. Suffolk
Printed and bound in Great Britain by Martins The Printers Ltd., Berwick-upon-Tweed

Contents

About the authors

Professor Victor T. C. Middleton has had some thirty years' international experience of marketing practice covering most of the private and public sectors of travel and tourism. With a commercial background prior to involvement in the tourism industry, his career spans marketing planning and research for a national tourist board (British Tourist Authority), research and teaching as a full-time academic (University of Surrey to 1984), and independent international management consultancy in tourism since then. He was appointed Visiting Professor at Oxford Brookes University in 1990 and at the University of Central Lancashire in 1997. At Oxford he was the first Director of the World Travel and Tourism Environment Research Centre funded by the World Travel and Tourism Council, where he developed and communicated best practice analyses of sustainable tourism with Rebecca Hawkins. Widely known as an author and lecturer on the international conference circuit, he has produced nearly one hundred published articles, reports and books over the last two decades. His interests link visitor management, sustainability and heritage issues from a thoroughly practical industry and marketing perspective.

Rebecca Hawkins completed her PhD at Bournemouth University in 1992, analysing tourism management in the coastal zone, and went on to work in the regional tourist boards in the UK. She was subsequently appointed as Senior Researcher and later Deputy Director of the World Travel and Tourism Environment Research Centre where she played a key role in the development of good practice guidance for the travel and tourism industry. She also played a primary role in the development of WTTC's Green Globe environmental management programme for travel and tourism companies. Recently she established her own business specializing in environmental aspects of tourism projects and has undertaken a number of pioneering programmes in this role. In 1997 she completed a major research programme to enable the International Hotels Environment Initiative and British Airways Holidays establish benchmarks for the environmental performance of hotels. Rebecca has written a wide range of technical and academic papers and publications, including most of the Green Globe series of environmental management guides (with Jo Lloyd), HCIMA technical briefs, Inter-Continental Hotels and Resorts Environmental Review and the WTO/ WTTC/Earth Council interpretation of the implications of AGENDA 21 for travel and tourism companies.

Foreword

Over the last twenty-five years, as this book reveals, travel and tourism has been a remarkable economic success story driven largely by marketing initiative and energy working in favourable market conditions. On the other hand, despite the many obvious warning signs that poorly managed tourism around the world damages the environment and undermines business prosperity, most businesses in what can now be identified as the world's largest industry have yet to come to terms with the environmental consequences of their actions.

Since 1990, however, in common with leading players in other sectors of the world economy, enlightened companies in travel and tourism have formally adopted environmental ethics at the core of their business interests and future prosperity. As an industry leader with some 40 000 staff in 200 properties in over seventy countries around the world, Inter-Continental Hotels and Resorts has positioned itself with the World Travel & Tourism Council at the forefront of implementing the principles of sustainable development.

Inter-Continental launched a major environmental initiative in 1990 to ensure that each of our hotels makes a positive contribution to improving the quality of the environment in its locality. That initiative led to a comprehensive environmental manual providing detailed guidelines on environmentally sound products and procedures which we shared with our competitors in 1991 to form the International Hotels Environment Initiative (IHEI). By the late 1990s eleven international hotel companies controlling some 2 million rooms (approaching 1 billion guest nights a year by the new millennium) were being operated in accordance with guidelines pioneered by Inter-Continental. This is just the beginning of new corporate attitudes to the environment.

Looking ahead, to achieve the goals of sustainable development we must have the right mix of private sector initiative, economic tools, incentives and regulation. This means we need new public sector–private sector delivery mechanisms and we must have industry participation in order to translate global principles into local action. I recommend this important new book to practitioners as well as students, and commend its authors for their contribution to a better understanding of environmental impacts and the new partnership delivery mechanisms that are needed. In particular they have stripped the subject of many of the myths and prejudices that continue to surround it, setting out practical proposals for achieving local solutions within a marketing perspective that are at the leading edge of industry thinking.

Robert Collier
Vice-Chairman, Saison Overseas Holdings B.V.
(The parent Company of Inter-Continental Hotels and Resorts)

Preface

In the run-up to the United Nations Earth Summit at Rio de Janeiro in 1992, general public and industry awareness of the ideas of *sustainable development* were fuelled by massive media coverage and doomsday/eco-disaster scenarios that coincided with the late 1980s economic boom in many countries. *Sustainable tourism* subsequently became a buzzword for many in travel and tourism. It is a useful sound-bite; a mantra for politicians, NGOs and many academics around the world; an aspiration with which all can agree – until aspiration has to be turned into practice. The aim of this book is to communicate meaning to three overall concepts relevant to tourism and to outline methods of implementation, illustrated by international good practice involving partnerships between the private and public sectors:

- Sustainable tourism means achieving a particular combination of numbers and types of visitors, the cumulative effect of whose activities at a given destination, together with the actions of the servicing businesses, can continue into the foreseeable future without damaging the quality of the environment on which the activities are based.
- For all practical decisions in tourism, environment means the *'quality* of natural resources such as landscape, air, sea water, fresh water, flora and fauna; and the *quality* of built and cultural resources judged to have intrinsic value and be worthy of conservation' (Middleton and Hawkins, 1994).
- Sustainability for tourism requires that 'the cumulative volume of visitor usage of a destination and the associated activities and impacts of servicing businesses should be managed below the threshold level at which the *regenerative resources* available locally be-

come incapable of maintain the environment' (Middleton and Hawkins, 1994). Regenerative resources are part natural and part managed by human intervention.

The balances implied between environmental quality and tourism activity in each of these linked concepts are never static. They are infinitely susceptible to the influence of human behaviour and management decisions as well as to the natural processes of ecology and the emerging science and technology of measuring environmental impacts and responding to them. Although the words are modern, there is nothing new in the concepts; in principle they have been relevant in tourism for at least a century. What gives the debate its modern context is the increasing awareness of tourism impacts as part of the overall pressure on the quality of the global environment exerted by a combination of a growing world population, growing expectations for economic development, and the industrial and other technology used to supply population needs. From farming and fishing to the extraction of minerals and other finite resources such as timber, the impact of human economic activity generally, and the many forms of pollution to which it gives rise, has been pushing the limits of environmental tolerance at an accelerating rate. Defined in *Beyond the Limits* (Meadows *et al.*, 1992) as 'exponential growth' leading to 'overshoot', the process has been lurching out of control, since the 1950s.

The Rio Earth Summit brought to a head influential global environmental processes, such as the United Nations Environment Programme (UNEP – established in 1972), and concerns such as the Club of Rome's *Limits to Growth* (1972), and the Brundtland Report, *Our Common Future* (1987). The main international action follow-up programme was drawn up and published as AGENDA 21. Often perceived as an agenda for governments, what is implied in the follow-up is far more than a regulatory programme to be enacted and implemented by governments and their agencies. It is a global action plan laying out the requirements for achieving more sustainable forms of living in the twenty-first century for all nations. Changing individual behaviour and consumption patterns for all types of product is the first aim of AGENDA 21, but in practice this has usually to be initiated by government agreements in developed countries where the major environmental problems lie. It also requires a fundamental change in corporate behaviour in the private sector, especially multinational companies, recognizing the environmental mistakes that have been made in the last fifty years in all sectors of economic activity. Companies' economic rationale for this is to protect their resource or asset based in the short run, and ensure profitability in the long run.

International shifts in behaviour of this magnitude do not occur in a matter of months or even a decade. This is a long-term agenda. It has already begun with a growing understanding and continuous media exposure of the impacts of human actions on the environment and a shift in the attitudes influencing corporate and personal behaviour. However long it takes to convince the majority of businesses and the general public, environmental recognition is growing strongly now and it is reflected in the emergence of more sustainable policies around the world by governments, local authorities and public sector agencies, by commercial organizations and their trade associations, and in the development of *green policies* by political parties and pressure groups dedicated to sustainable environmental goals. Whatever the rights or wrongs of the case, when a major multinational oil corporation such as The Royal Dutch Shell Group can be obliged by pressure groups (1995) to abandon its declared policy for disposing of an oil platform, negotiated in agreement with governments over a two-year period, neither governments nor their agencies can consider themselves immune

from a process which already commands widespread public backing. The BSE crisis for British beef arising from ecologically unsound feeding practices for cattle is another clear indication of massive consumer backlash against perceived environmental risks. It is a major international task to persuade more businesses, customers/users and local authorities to recognize that the quality of the environment is a core part of product quality created by producing all types of manufactured and service products. But the signs of progress are already clear in direction if not yet in adequate volume.

In the early 1990s there were high but implausible hopes that the politics of exhortation backed by media campaigns would shift attitudes towards sustainability. By 1996 it was clear that entrenched attitudes, economic systems and human behaviour patterns, will not change solely as a result of appeals to common sense. The threats appear too remote and the science of environmental monitoring and prediction, on global warming for example, remains imprecise. So much depends on scientific interpretation and media reporting. Economic recession in Europe and elsewhere pushes economic growth and employment up the political agenda, and environmental concerns go down. Sustainability also requires seriously unpopular decisions, for example on personal mobility and levels of energy consumption, and partial denial of traditionally free access to attractive destinations. There is little evidence that politicians in government have the resolve to pursue such measures in any country until disaster appears imminent, when it may be too late. Interestingly, while concepts of sustainability have apparently lost popular appeal in the 1990s, issues of personal health and safety, especially through air and water quality and when cancer risks and other diseases seem likely, have gained enormously in perceived importance. The tunes of public health and safety are far more powerful and immediate and force governments and businesses into urgent action. Deaths from asthma, for example, are quantifiable and may be directly linked to measurement of air pollution, while sanctimonious appeals to 'safeguard the birthright of future generations' can safely be ignored as sound-bite claptrap. Sustainable programmes generally appear more likely to be achieved on the back of health and safety lawsuits and associated financial and political penalties, than by appeals to care for the Earth.

Compared with most other large industries, the consumers and the products of travel and tourism, increasingly identified as the 'world's largest industry', are highly visible. In democratic societies the products created and their impacts on the environment can only continue with the support or acceptance of the residents of visited destinations. Most leisure tourism is about visiting places with residents who are, or could be, vocal and proactive about the quality of their environment as they perceive it. Commercial operators in the tourism industry are, therefore, more vulnerable to changes in attitudes and perceptions of impact and damage than most industries.

Few doubt that international, national and especially local regulations for environmental protection will set the overall climate for attitude change in travel and tourism, as for all other forms of industry. In many popular destinations the introduction of controls to limit the scale of tourism activity and set quotas for development are inevitable over the next decade. But tourism is a highly competitive industry and consumers have many choices as to how and where they allocate time and money to their preferences. Many tourism businesses also have a wide choice of location. The process of understanding and managing voluntary transactions for consumers and businesses with choices in a rapidly developing international market, such as tourism, cannot safely be left to lawyers and civil servants; they do not understand it. It is the business primarily of private sector management, especially marketing management. Regulation can, at best, establish the ground rules for competition and aim to penalize individuals and organizations flouting the rules. But it is a blunt instrument for persuasion in a free market and it can be bypassed, especially where the points of

sale and consumption may be thousands of miles apart.

Modern marketing, which is as much concerned with communicating the benefits of ideas, people and places as about selling products in the high street, is the only proven set of continuously developing management techniques for influencing behaviour, designing and communicating product benefits, and ensuring high quality and value for money in the delivery of products. These techniques are global and they represent a massive, continuous outpouring of management energy that can be harnessed to achieve environmental goals. This energy can also be used to help regulators understand, formulate and monitor ground rules that are sensitive to changing demand.

International and domestic travel and tourism has a quite remarkable record of successful economic growth over the last thirty years, and excellent prospects for further development into the twenty-first century. Historically much of this growth has been achieved at an increasing cost to the environment of popular destinations that is now undermining the quality of life of resident populations in some areas, and jeopardizing the future profitability of tourism businesses. We believe that encouraging, analysing, and communicating best practice in visitor management techniques developed especially for local destinations provides the logical focus and practical way forward for achieving sustainability in tourism. Overall, in all forms of destination, tourism management is always likely to comprise a mix of regulatory and self-regulatory techniques. Our experience and judgement lead us to believe, however, that innovative marketing, not regulation, provides the vital *management insight and knowledge* for understanding, communicating, and delivering sustainable tourism in visitor destinations over the coming decades. Marketing is the business of asset management for the long run as well as designing and delivering products of increasing quality to targeted customers in the 'world's largest industry'. That energy can, and it must, be harnessed to sustainable goals.

The aim of the book and its intended market

This book aims to provide, using illustrations and case material drawn from recent practice:

- A basic text about the particular environmental threats and opportunities arising from global travel and tourism, as part of the overall impact of human population growth and economic activity.
- A cohesive set of international management principles and techniques available specifically for controlling the negative impacts of travel and tourism and achieving its benefits, set within an underlying theme of marketing and the principles of AGENDA 21.
- A particular focus on the growing role of partnerships between the private and public sectors in tourism, especially at local destinations, and especially to manage the environmental problems resulting from the very high ratio of small to large businesses in tourism –

the dominant supply-side characteristic of a highly diverse and fragmented 'industry'.

The authors are well aware of the extensive outpouring of books on all issues of sustainability and of marketing in the last five years and we make no attempt to replicate them. Our aim is to provide a structured way of thinking about the impacts of travel and tourism, and how in practice to harness the energy that exists in the industry to achieve more sustainable economic growth in all parts of the world. This book is written to meet the needs both of students and teachers on tourism, hospitality and leisure management courses, and of managers at all levels in the private and public sectors of tourism. Of all the issues on which existing and potential managers in the world's largest industry need knowledge and support for the next decade, a better understanding of how to manage visitors to achieve more sustainable futures is surely the primary concern. They cannot afford to fail.

Victor T.C. Middleton
Rebecca Hawkins

The structure of the book

Part One

The six chapters in Part One introduce the key environmental issues and aspects of travel and tourism addressed in this book. It is assumed that all readers, whether practitioners or students, will be at least broadly familiar with the concepts of tourism, on the one hand, and of marketing, on the other. To establish the authors' view, and because their stance is not the same as that of the majority of writers on sustainability in tourism, the world's largest industry is defined with reference to internationally agreed concepts, not restricted solely to holidays and leisure. These chapters identify tourism issues for the environment in an overall context of global threats from all sources of human activity. They introduce our view that sustainability must be approached from two different but related dimensions. The first is *tourism management* at local destinations and the second is the *management of business operations* by commercial and other enterprises.

Part Two

The four chapters in Part Two deal with the processes of managing tourism to achieve sustainable development at local destinations. Sustainable policies and management approaches operate on supply and demand and involve the public and private sector both separately and especially in partnership. We stress that such policies can best be understood and effectively targeted at the local level rather than the national or regional level, but that existing levels of management information for supply and demand are woefully inadequate.

Part Three

The five chapters in Part Three switch the focus from tourism management at the destination to the management of business operations in the sectors of the tourism industry that provide, market, or otherwise facilitate visitor activity at destinations. Some of these business operations are destination based, for example hotels and attractions; others are not, for example much of transport and tour operation. Part Three is introduced by our view of the well-known *Three Rs* of sustainability, developed into *Ten Rs* relevant to all sectors. The chapters include current industry examples of leading-edge practice from around the world.

Part Four

There are five specific cases in Part Four indicating how destinations and businesses around the world are addressing the issues of sustainability covered in this book. Each case has been contributed by a senior person directly concerned and they serve to illustrate in practice the themes developed in Parts Two and Three of the book.

Epilogue

In contrast to the doom-laden future scenarios portrayed in most books on the issues of sustainable tourism, this contribution, based on the intentions of AGENDA 21, offers seven positive visions for the future. It reflects the real opportunities to harness and target the global energy of marketing management in proactive partnerships at the leading edge of change for a more sustainable future.

Acknowledgements

Although much of the writing and the editing of this book is the work of Victor Middleton, the inspiration for the book and the thinking that has gone into it has been a joint enterprise throughout with Rebecca Hawkins. Thanks to an initiative by Geoffrey Lipman, President of the World Travel & Tourism Council (WTTC), it was agreed to establish the World Travel & Tourism Environment Research Centre (WTTERC) at Oxford Brookes University in 1991. Victor Middleton was the first Director of WTTERC and Rebecca Hawkins joined the Centre in 1992, subsequently becoming Deputy Director. We were proud to be associated with the Centre and the work it did, and our first debt of gratitude is to Geoffrey Lipman for the breadth of his vision and his active encouragement of many of the ideas that find expression in this book. Thanks also to colleagues at Oxford Brookes University which provided facilities and support for the Centre. Professor John Glasson in particular was most helpful and supportive. Although WTTERC ceased to exist in its original form in 1995, its work and databases were absorbed in *Green Globe*, the WTTC global scheme for promoting and recognizing environmental good practice in the private and public sector, for which Rebecca designed and wrote the first set of industry guidelines for sustainability.

For particular contributions to chapters and case studies, we wish to acknowledge Professor Alfred Bennett of Rand Afrikaans University, who contributed the case of Kruger National Park; Max Shepherd, Operations Director of Quicksilver Connections Ltd; Robert Downie, Tourism Manager of Lothian and Edinburgh Enterprise Ltd; David Moore, Recreation Manager for Anglian Water Ltd (for Rutland Water), and Glen Lawes, Chief Executive of the Ironbridge Gorge Museum Trust. For permission to include a synopsis of their environmental good practice, we are grateful to Dr Hugh Somerville, Head of Environment at British Airways, Marie Daskalantonakis, Executive Director of Grecotel, Dagmar Woodward, General Manager of The May Fair Inter-Continental Hotel, London, and Chairman of the Inter-Continental Hotels and Resorts Environmental Programmes worldwide, Martin Brackenbury, President of International Federation of Tour Operators (IFTO), Dr Mike Monaghan, director for Environment of P&O Ltd, and Dr Wolf Michael Iwand of Touristik Union International (TUI). For agreement to use the survey information reproduced in Chapter 1, thanks are due to Peter Aderhold of the Institute for Tourism Research and Planning, Denmark, and for agreement to use data shown in Figure 6.3, to the European Travel Intelligence Centre (European Travel Monitor), Luxembourg.

Our thanks go to Professor Rik Medlik, who read the initial proposals for this book and saw it in manuscript, making many valuable suggestions for improvements, and to Kathryn Grant and Diane Scarlett at Butterworth-Heinemann who patiently listened to the usual excuses for delays in meeting deadlines. Sue Kitching stepped in from time to time to rescue the authors' typing problems, treating each minor crisis with her much-apperciated cheerfulness and goodwill.

All errors and omissions are the authors' responsibility.

Figures

Tables

Part One

The Context; the Issues;
a Global Overview

1

Environment; tourism; a marketing perspective

... Probably the single greatest concern for every country is the impact tourism will have on its environment (Naisbitt, 1994: p. 140).

So far, the travel and tourism industry has taken little active part in framing the environmental policies so vital to its own interests (Economist Intelligence Unit, 1992).

This book records extensive activity and many examples of international *good practice* in various sectors of travel and tourism since 1992. The judgement expressed in the Economist Intelligence Unit (EIU) Review nevertheless remains fair comment for the bulk of the world-wide international and domestic tourism industry in the late 1990s. Stimulated by the Earth Summit at Rio (1992) and the associated publication of AGENDA 21, there has been a remarkable outpouring of academic contributions and conferences on the issues of sustainability and many exhortations from governments, NGOs, business leaders and from trade associations. At some destinations, among both large and small commercial businesses, there is now real progress to cite. But to turn around the EIU view will require a much greater level of energy and activity within the industry than is evident in 1997/8. As this book goes to print, there is no consensus on where that energy and activity will come from and it is our object to outline practical ways and means to make progress.

To some extent the environmental inertia in the tourism industry noted in the EIU report reflects a traditional view common in many businesses that tourism is not a smokestack industry of the heavy industrial era, and therefore does not create pollution in the same way as manufacturing and other industries. More importantly it also reflects the structure and business economics of a highly diverse and complex industry comprising many different sectors that typically recognize no community of interest with each other. From airlines to zoos, the sectors of travel and tourism are mutually competitive rather than cooperative (see Chapter 5) and they are only an 'industry' in the collective sense that the population of a multi-ethnic town or city can be termed a 'community'. The component sectors typically recognize no common strategy for environmental or any other purposes, either nationally or locally.

This chapter introduces the three themes that are woven into every chapter of this book. It deals first with global environment issues and the concepts of sustainability which are developed with specific examples in Chapter 2–4. It deals, second, with travel and tourism as a global industry, establishing an overview developed in more detail in Chapters 5 and 6. Third, this chapter introduces the role of marketing as a management attitude and process which the authors believe provides the essential management insight and a practical way forward for achieving sustainability in travel and tourism. The marketing approach is further developed in Chapters 9 and 10 and Part Three of the book.

Global environmental issues

The first point to make is that recognition of particular environmental damage resulting from human economic activity is not new. Most people behave now, as they always have, to maximize their personal position by whatever means are most easily to hand and are permissible within social and legal constraints. Small businesses behave in exactly the same way. For example, 2400 years ago, Plato wrote of soil erosion and deforestation caused by overgrazing and tree felling for fuel in the hills of Attica (Chapter 2). The reasons would have been identical to those now driving developing countries to cut down rain forests; those which created the dust bowls in America in the 1930s; and those currently destroying ocean life through overfishing. The difference in the late twentieth century is the environmentally lethal combination of growing population size, universal demand for economic development, and global access to rapid developments in science and technology. For the first time in history economic activity in one part of the world can have an immediate and massive impact on other parts. Acid rain across Europe and overfishing off the coasts of Europe are examples. The fallout and future implications from the Chernobyl nuclear reactor disaster in Russia in 1986 starkly illustrates modern forms of international pollution.

Travel and tourism has developed into a major international 'industry' only over the last twenty-five years or so. It has many critics who believe that tourism is a primary cause of environmental pollution and degradation. Such critics, promoted internationally by the British Broadcasting Corporation, for example (*The Tourist* 1996: p. 13), would have students of

tourism and the public believe that 'tourism packages entire cultures and environments ... producing an emergent culture of tourism made from the fragments of the local cultures which tourism destroyed ... 'Tourism has ended up representing the final stages of colonialism and Empire.'

Away from the heady world of sociological myths, however, practical progress toward sustainability depends on world travel and tourism being understood as just one aspect of the total impact of world-wide human economic activity on the environment. We believe it to be an economic activity which is potentially not only more beneficial to the environment than any other major global industry but also more amenable to management action.

Using the estimates calculated for the World Travel & Tourism Council (WTTC), which include allowance for day and staying visits for all purposes as well as investment in tourism infrastructure, tourism already accounts for over 10 per cent of World GDP (see below). It is nevertheless only one of many players in the global issues of economic development and the associated environmental impact. The principal causes of global environmental pollution and degradation, reviewed in Chapter 2, can be briefly summarized as:

- Exponential population growth (2.5 billion in 1950, 5 billion in 1990 to a projected 10–12 billion by 2030).
- Subsidized/mechanized/chemical assisted agriculture, or 'slash and burn' survival tactics in many of the economically developing countries.
- Waste discharges including outflow of toxic wastes and human effluent into rivers and seas.
- Overfishing; mineral extraction industries; industrial production processes and waste.
- Destruction of species consequent on these economic practices.
- Use of non-renewable energy sources for public and private transport – emission of

carbon dioxide and other gases affecting air quality and global warming.
- Leisure and holiday pursuits, especially by residents of the economically developed countries of the world.

Leisure tourism, a consequence of the free world's achievement of greater affluence, most notably demonstrated at present by tourism trends in the Asia-Pacific Region, is adding to overall pollution in many environmentally fragile areas. As the world's 'largest industry' collectively, and the dominant economic sector in parts of the world such as the Caribbean, South Pacific Islands, and Hawaii, it is essential that environmental impacts are recognized, adequately defined and measured, and tackled urgently.

Travel and tourism – a composite market of global significance

Although travel and tourism is invariably identified as an 'industry' it is best understood as a total market. This market reflects the cumulative demand and consumption patterns of visitors for a very wide range of travel-related products that fall within the internationally adopted definitions of tourism activity (see Chapter 5). In practice, travel and tourism is not one market, however, but literally hundreds of separate international and domestic market segments, mostly with little in common, but usually lumped together for convenience. The total market is serviced by a range of large and small organizations which, depending on definitions used, can now be estimated collectively to represent the world's 'largest industry' (WTTC, 1995).

The main sectors involved in providing services to visitors are noted below for the purpose of introduction and developed in Chapter 5.

Directly involved
Airlines
Airports

Indirectly involved
Cafés
Clubs

Car rental
Coaches and buses
Conference centres
Guest houses/pensions
Heritage sites/buildings
Hotels/motels
Holiday cottages
Holiday villages/
  condominia
Railways
Resorts
Theme parks
Time share
Tour operators
Travel agencies

Discos
Casinos
Exhibition centres
Fast-food outlets
Golf courses
Museums and galleries
Night clubs

Pubs
Restaurants
Retail shops
Sports stadia
Theatres
Taxis
University
  accommodation
Tourist offices (national/regional)
Sea ferries
Visitor attractions

Yacht harbours
Zoos

In this context, *directly* involved means provided primarily for the purpose of tourism; *indirectly* means that visitors are welcomed and may be essential to business prosperity and survival, but typically are not the primary reason for provision. The list above is illustrative of the range of sectors covered, but it does not pretend to be comprehensive.

Treating travel and tourism as a global industry, with a prediction that the industry turnover could double in size in little over a decade, the WTTC estimated that tourism in all its forms accounted in 1995 for:

10.9% of world total GDP
10.7% of the global workforce – 212 million jobs (equivalent to 1 in every 9 jobs), and
11.4% of global capital expenditure
11.1% of total corporate and personal taxes paid
12.6% of global export earnings.

(*Source:* WTTC/WEFA, 1995)

Caveat: It needs to be understood that these are not the same figures as those published by the World Tourism Organization, which estimates the direct expenditure of international tourism involving overnight stays. Nor are they comparable with tourism estimates produced by OECD or the European Commission. WTTC estimates are based on satellite accounting procedures and allow for domestic as well as international travel, for day visits, and for capital expenditure on investment in all types of tourism related infrastructure such as airports and aircraft manufacture. With these additional allowances the WTTC percentages are roughly twice the size of traditional estimates based solely on the direct expenditure of visitors.

World-wide economic activity on this massive scale and growth potential has created powerful multinational major business corporations, some with global interests, and there are close similarities in business operations from Acapulco to Zimbabwe. These large businesses are now under increasing pressure to operate in more sustainable ways and many are responding. But uncounted millions of small businesses around the world are also involved and they dominate numerically in all destinations which are not enclosed resorts. It is a major structural problem in tourism that small businesses located at destinations, such as hotels or attractions, and tour operators negotiating down the prices of product components from distant bases in markets of origin, have not needed to accept responsibility individually for what is happening overall to the local environment. There are typically few constraints on them other than appeals to altruism. The owner of a small travel agency in Iowa or of a guesthouse in the Peak District or the Lake District in the UK, struggling to survive, is unlikely to perceive himself as personally responsible for traffic congestion and the erosion of hills and mountains by too many cars and feet. This deep-seated myopia has to be tackled but it is understandable and a major issue in an industry in which small businesses outweigh larger ones, in some countries by up to 1000:1. It is not a tenable position for the twenty-first century, however, and strategies for change are obviously needed. Such strategies are not going to emerge spontaneously from an 'industry' which in practice is just a convenient label or statistical concept used to embrace a highly disparate combination of thousands of small businesses in many sectors, plus local government and numerous public sector agencies. The numerical dominance of small businesses at most destinations is a key issue for sustainability and addressed later in Chapter 5.

The attraction of tourism for governments

Given the size and growth potential noted above, travel and tourism is a logical target for intensive marketing by all the commercial players within it. It is especially attractive to governments in the economically developing world because of the opportunities inherent in the industry; specifically its:

- Massive size, recent growth and widely forecasted potential for future development.
- Ubiquity – there are few areas in the world in which travel and tourism is irrelevant either as a region of origin or destination for visitors – or both.
- Significance for the economic, foreign currency and employment needs of most, if not all countries of the world – especially for many smaller developing countries with otherwise limited resources to sustain the economic demands of their growing populations.
- Conferment of potential economic values to natural, cultural and other heritage resources such as scenery, wilderness, historic structures, biodiversity in flora and fauna and environmental quality, all of which have intrinsic values measured in world environment terms, but typically have no obvious trading value to most resident populations. Environmental values, with important exceptions in certain cultures, are largely irrelevant to subsistence level or starving populations.
- Contribution to the quality of the lives of virtually all residents, especially in economically developed countries.

- Relatively low pollution output of servicing organizations, compared with other major global sectors of the economy, such as intensive agriculture, fisheries, chemical industries, much of manufacturing, and extractive industries.

Two main directions for sustainable tourism

Readers should note that in practice there are two separate dimensions for the sustainability argument applied to travel and tourism. They are reflected in the structure of this book. The first and in the long run the most important dimension lies in improving sustainable practice at the destinations chosen by visitors, where the impact of tourists can have widely recognized negative effects on:

- *The physical environment*
  For example, erosion of coral reefs for construction and leisure activities, or of mountains through walking and skiing, excessive use of fresh water for bathing, swimming, watering gardens and golf courses, pollution of both sea water and freshwater through discharge of untreated sewage, and the creation of carbon dioxide through use of cars for leisure purposes.
- *The social and cultural environment;*
  For example, turning traditional arts and rituals into a form of entertainment and profit for hotels; by disrupting traditional wage patterns which favour males and perhaps causing the abandonment of traditional ways of earning a living; by encouraging prostitution; and by 'force feeding' generally the cultural and behavioural norms of affluent, especially Western, societies into cultures unfamiliar with such ways, through a process often dubbed 'neo-colonialism'.

In contrast with other industries of comparable scale and relevance in all parts of the world, however, travel and tourism also carries the potential to make major positive contributions to the physical, cultural and social environments of visited destinations. It is the opportunity to harness these positive, sustainable contributions that makes travel and tourism so vital a concern for the twenty-first century. (See also Chapter 6.)

The second dimension for improving sustainable practice focuses on the way that businesses within the travel and tourism industry conduct their development and operational decisions. Some business operations take place at the destination – for example those of resort hotels, inns, or holiday villages, attractions and car rental. Others take place away from the destination, for example operations by airlines, ferries and other transport operators and the activities of tour operators and travel agents. Tourism businesses have much the same reasons for controlling pollution and managing waste as any other form of industry. They bear a heightened responsibility, however, recognizing that they are often operating in areas selected for business purposes precisely because they are attractive and environmentally sensitive. The logical focus of business operations is on implementing programmes for saving energy; controlling noise pollution and emissions; reducing demands for fresh water; reducing the use of toxic chemicals, and recycling or re-using materials necessary for the conduct of trade. (See Part Three of the book.)

In addition, tourism businesses have a particular responsibility for the type and scale of development imposed on environmentally sensitive areas. This is an issue for design and construction techniques, for example in the building and landscaping of resort hotel complexes, swimming pools, golf courses, airport runways and terminals. Good design of modern buildings and plant can greatly reduce the level of pollution produced for a given number of visitor days, for example using heat exchange systems and waste water treatments.

A marketing perspective

Developed in Chapters 9 and 10, a marketing perspective is still associated in many minds with commercial enterprises selling the maximum volume of products for short-run profits. This book stresses that a *marketing perspective* means a particular set of corporate attitudes toward the conduct of operations involving the public as targeted customers or users – the way in which an organization is conducted by its owners and managers. Modern marketing is certainly concerned with delivering products that meet customer expectations, securing additional sales, extra revenue yield per sale, and defending and gaining market share in a highly competitive world. But that is too simple a view. A marketing perspective is essentially an overall management orientation reflecting corporate attitudes that, in the case of travel and tourism, must balance the interests of shareholders/owners with the long-run environmental interests of a destination and at the same time meet the demands and expectations of customers.

As Middleton (1994) puts it, 'Above all, marketing reflects a particular set of strongly held attitudes, and a sense of commitment on the part of directors and senior managers – not just marketing managers – which are common to all marketing-led organizations .... There are four key elements as follows:

- A positive, innovative, and highly competitive attitude toward the conduct of exchange transactions (in commercial and non-commercial organizations).
- A continuous recognition that the conduct of an organization's business must revolve around the long-run interests of both customers and stakeholders.
- An outward looking, responsive (and responsible) attitude to events in the external business environment within which a business operates.
- An understanding of the balance to be achieved between the need to earn profits

from existing assets and the equally important need to adapt an organization to secure future profits, recognizing social and environmental constraints.'

As defined above, the corporate attitudes implicit in a marketing perspective are as relevant to many public sector operations as to private sector enterprises, provided that the former operate to defined service quality standards and treat their publics as valued users or customers, whether or not money is charged directly for the services provided. Museums, state-owned heritage attractions and national parks are examples of public sector operations to which a marketing perspective is increasingly relevant. The only real difference is that many public sector operations are actual or quasi-monopolies whereas commercial operations are mostly directly competitive. Achieving marketing excellence and forging relationships for co-operation with other destination stakeholders are increasingly conditions of business survival.

Within an overall appreciation of the need to recognize and protect the value of assets or resources on which business survival depends, including environmental resources, there is ample evidence that success in a competitive world lies in rethinking and adapting the whole of business operations from the customers' standpoint. Because customers' interests, attitudes, and market conditions, are in a state of constant change, the involvement of managers with marketing also has to be continuous. Identifying, responding, and adapting to changes ahead of competitors is the essence of a marketing perspective. Identifying and targeting specific groups or segments of prospective customers or users whom an organization wishes to serve is the practical expression of that perspective.

If businesses in travel and tourism are convinced that powerful global changes are at work on the physical, social and cultural environment of destinations, affecting the buying habits of current and prospective customer segments, those changes will be fully reflected in decisions taken from a marketing perspective. The continuing prosperity of business investments requires such a response. This does not mean always giving customers what they want, however, it could also mean persuading and influencing them to choose products which meet the long-run sustainable interests of the assets and resources on which products and profits are based. It will be argued (see Chapters 9 and 10) that the travel and tourism industry is uniquely positioned globally to use marketing to achieve sustainable goals.

Characteristics of a marketing perspective

Drawing on the sources noted at the end of the chapter one may introduce the characteristics of a marketing perspective as follows:

- Outward-looking to interpret trends among customer segments, competitors and the overall business environment (including the physical, social and cultural environment).
- Customer-responsive based on detailed knowledge of current and prospective customers – especially repeat customers – increasingly held on computerized databases.
- Research and information based as an integral part of modern decision making.
- Focused on product quality and business operations that reflect the growing expectations of targeted customers and their perceptions of value for money, with close monitoring of customer satisfaction.
- Forward-looking and innovative in terms of product development and delivering added value.
- Concerned to balance the long-run requirements of sustaining the asset base with short-run needs to satisfy customers and generate profit. In travel and tourism the quality of the environment at visited destinations is a vital part of the asset base.
- Focused primarily on the perceived needs of customer groups or segments rather than on

the operational convenience of service providers.

On the evidence presented in Chapter 2 there can be no doubt that the environmental concerns that emerged and focused since the Brundtland Report in 1987 will have a major impact over the next decade on the way that all businesses, including travel and tourism, will be conducted. The key question is not *if* business will be affected, but *to what extent*, and *how quickly*. Much will also depend on the activities of environmental lobby groups, and especially on shifts in the attitudes and purchasing behaviour of the travelling public which marketing managers are paid to interpret.

As stated in the Preface for this book, few doubt that the scale of environmental problems is now such that a combination of international, national and local regulations for environmental protection will influence attitude change in travel and tourism, as in all other forms of industry. In particular, the introduction of controls to limit the scale of tourism activity and set quotas for local capacity and development appear inevitable over the next decade. But tourism is an increasingly competitive industry and consumers have many choices in how to allocate time and money to their preferences. The process of understanding and managing voluntary transactions for consumers with choices in a rapidly developing sector such as tourism is not a matter for lawyers and regulators; it is the business primarily of marketing management. Regulation can, at best, establish the ground rules for competition, and penalize individuals and organizations that flout the rules. But is a blunt instrument for persuasion in a free market. Modern marketing, which is as much concerned with communicating the benefits of ideas, people and places as about selling products in the high street, is the only proven set of management skills for influencing customer behaviour, designing and communicating product benefits, and ensuring high quality and value for money in the delivery of products. These skills can be harnessed to achieve environmental goals.

A key element of our approach is that analysing and communicating best practice in private sector business enterprises, and in visitor management techniques developed specifically for destinations, provides the most practical way to shift toward sustainable tourism. In all types of destination, visitor management is always likely to comprise a mix of regulatory and self-regulatory techniques. Our experience and judgement lead us to believe that marketing will be the primary management tool for interpreting, communicating, and achieving sustainability in visitor destinations over the coming decades, as part of the day-to-day business of designing and delivering products of acceptable quality to targeted customers in the world's largest industry. The knowledge developed in that process will also be a primary input to the development and monitoring of workable regulatory procedures.

In summary:

- A marketing, not a regulatory perspective, provides the vital *management insight* for achieving sustainable development in travel and tourism.
- Marketing strategies can provide a coordinating framework in which the interests of destinations and the powerful energy of business operations can be harnessed to pull in the same direction.
- Marketing management holds the most efficient tools for understanding and influencing what visitors buy; and the techniques for designing and delivering product quality also designed to sustain a local environment.
- Marketing management will have to target, involve, and work jointly with regulators and elected representatives of residents' interests.
- Marketing strategies provide a practical agenda both for proactive new forms of partnership between the private and public sector, and for an equally important partnership between large and small businesses.

Evidence of European demand for environmentally sustainable tourism

There is widespread agreement in the industry that tourism businesses will market more environmentally sustainable products as soon as customers demand them and are willing to pay what it costs, and not before. In an industry generally accustomed to sell its leisure products on the lowest available price and to compete on that basis, there is a great deal of cynicism that the majority of customers will in practice pay more than lip service to environmental benefits. We believe this attitude is too simplistic.

A major difficulty in tracing evidence of customer attitudes is that most people do not use words such as *environment* and *sustainable* to describe their product expectations and satisfactions. These are technical labels for a particular set of management decisions, not the language of the general public, and not the language of holiday brochures. Yet we believe the evidence of demand is perfectly clear if businesses are willing to read between the lines of what people do say, and think through the full implications of customer perceptions. It is not easy to discover up-to-date, comparable survey data covering holiday vacation motivations but in 1995/6 a major series of personal interview surveys comprising a total of over 56 000 interviews were carried out in fifteen of the most important tourism-generating countries in Europe. The surveys were a follow-up of earlier work (1994/5) comprising some 30 000 interviews undertaken for eight countries, and were designed and organized for the Danish Tourist Board by Dr Peter Aderhold of the Bureau for Tourism Research and Planning in Copenhagen. These surveys contain detailed and comparable information about holiday vacation motivations measured as relative agreement/disagreement (5-point scale) in responses to twenty-six motivational statements. The surveys cover holidays defined as of at least 5 days duration and this information is clearly most relevant to attitudes

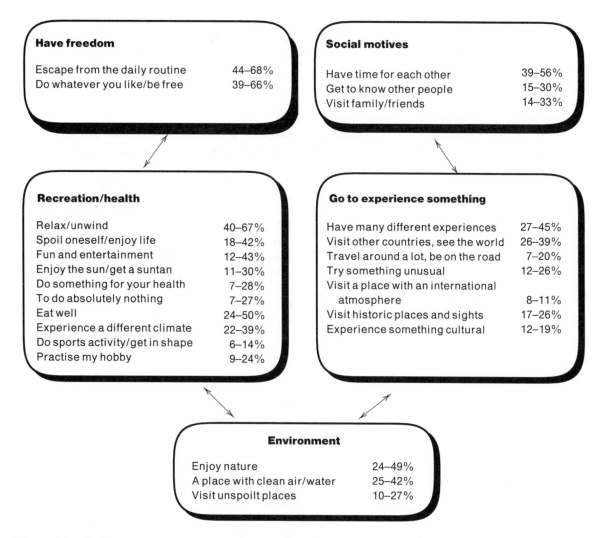

Have freedom

Escape from the daily routine	44–68%
Do whatever you like/be free	39–66%

Social motives

Have time for each other	39–56%
Get to know other people	15–30%
Visit family/friends	14–33%

Recreation/health

Relax/unwind	40–67%
Spoil oneself/enjoy life	18–42%
Fun and entertainment	12–43%
Enjoy the sun/get a suntan	11–30%
Do something for your health	7–28%
To do absolutely nothing	7–27%
Eat well	24–50%
Experience a different climate	22–39%
Do sports activity/get in shape	6–14%
Practise my hobby	9–24%

Go to experience something

Have many different experiences	27–45%
Visit other countries, see the world	26–39%
Travel around a lot, be on the road	7–20%
Try something unusual	12–26%
Visit a place with an international atmosphere	8–11%
Visit historic places and sights	17–26%
Experience something cultural	12–19%

Environment

Enjoy nature	24–49%
A place with clean air/water	25–42%
Visit unspoilt places	10–27%

Figure 1.1   *Holiday motivations of main European countries. Representative survey in eight European countries based on more than 30 000 face-to-face interviews in 1995 (only those completely agreeing with the statements are shown in the figure). © Danmarks Turistrad. Source: Dr Peter Aderhold, Institute for Tourism Research and Planning, Denmark (reproduced with permission)*

to the main holidays of the year. The Bureau's database is capable of comprehensive analysis, including detailed segmentation, but the overall figures shown above clearly demonstrate the importance to European consumers of motivations reflecting quality of the environment, especially among more experienced travellers and those visiting or planning to holiday in develop-

ing countries. The pattern is remarkably consistent over different surveys in the series.

Figure 1.1 indicates the general holiday motivations for residents of eight of the main holiday-generating countries in Europe (the 1994/5 study). The range of percentages indicates respondents in countries at the top and bottom end of those *completely agreeing* with the statements shown. We stress that the word 'environment' does not appear in one of the statements and is only shown in the chart as a researcher's classification. It is obvious, however, that if allowance is made also for personal and socio-cultural dimensions, the environment as outlined in this book is the single dominant underlying motivation. *Environment* to travellers is perceived as quality of experience sought, such as:

- Relax/unwind (40–67 per cent).
- Do something for your health (7–28 per cent).
- Have many different experiences (27–45 per cent).
- Visit historic places and sights (17–26 per cent).
- Experience something cultural (12–19 per cent).

These motivations clearly overlap (some people are likely to agree with all of them), and an unduplicated figure is not available from the published data. But we believe it is realistic to conclude that aspects of the destination environment influence at least half and perhaps up to two thirds of all European holiday visitors in the late 1990s. From the 1995/6 survey (not shown), the motivations of visitors specifically planning to visit developing countries can be judged by the percentages of those agreeing that *places with clean air and water* are 'very important', ranging from 22 per cent to 48 per cent, and *experience an unspoilt area*, ranging from 19 per cent to 43 per cent.

Increasing travel experience and interest in developing countries heightens attitudes

Even more important when looking ahead, although published figures are only available for the German market based on questions asked in 1989 (see Figure 1.2), the influence of travel experience on selected environmental mo-

tivations for those contemplating holidays to long-haul destinations is quite remarkably strong. If equivalent data were available for the UK, Scandinavian, or USA/Canada markets we would expect them to reveal broadly equivalent information.

Massive and growing demand for environmental quality at destinations?

Clearly there is an issue of interpretation and judgement involved in these figures, but we believe there is overwhelming evidence of customer preference for product qualities that are unambiguously concerned with environmental quality at chosen destinations. Even more interesting is the clear evidence of growing preference among experienced travellers, for this is the best indication of trends. The fact that the word *environment* does not appear is just an indication of the vital communication opportunity that marketing managers need to tackle.

Chapter summary

This chapter commences with a quotation from 1992 that businesses in travel and tourism collectively have not done sufficient to frame the environmental polices which are crucial to long-run survival and prosperity. We believe it is partly because the environment has been traditionally viewed as a 'free' resource and something that is mainly the responsibility of central or local government. It is also a consequence of a highly diverse multi-sectoral 'industry' dominated numerically at destinations by small businesses with no common perceptions of environmental issues or any acceptance of their responsibility to respond. The review of sustainability issues developed in the next chapter should make it clear that, however understandable this current position is, it is misguided and will be self-defeating. Fortunately travel and tourism is an industry built intuitively on marketing ideas and it is modern marketing management processes that provide the vital knowledge

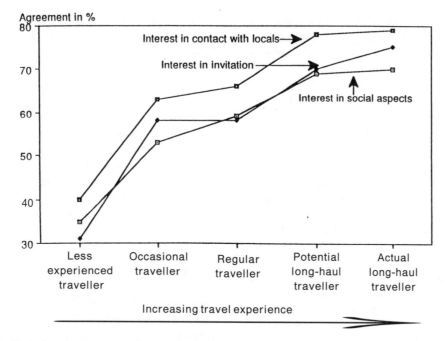

Basis of data: Exclusive question in the German Travel Analysis 1989 which includes more than 6000 personal interviews, representative of the German population

Question:
If I were to travel to far-off countries such as Mexico, Kenya or Indonesia . . .

– I can only learn about the country if I have the possibility to come into contact with the local people (*interest in contact with locals*)
– I would like to be invited by a local family to learn about their living conditions (*interest in invitation*)
– I would like to learn about the living conditions of the local population and the social and political aspects of the country (*interest in social aspects*)

Figure 1.2 *Influence of increasing travel experience on selected attitudes of long-haul tourists (German market 1988). Source: Dr Peter Aderhold, Institute for Tourism Research and Planning, Denmark*

and many of the tools needed for future influence.

It is a guiding principle of this book that a marketing perspective provides the vital insight for achieving sustainability in tourism in both public and private sectors. It leads to the most effective forms of management influence that can be brought rapidly to bear on the characteristics, volume and the behaviour of the multiple, fast-changing segments comprising the global market. Marketing principles are global in their conceptualization and application.

There are five good reasons why the multiple players in the tourism industry must find ways collectively to take a lead in environmental issues. How to do it are the subjects for later chapters.

- *Size and growth potential* – convey growing responsibility for the continuing quality of the environment which can no longer be taken for granted, especially in countries and areas where tourism is identified as a leading economic sector.

- *Prosperity* – the physical environment and the diverse cultures around the world are the core resource for most leisure tourism products. Future commercial prosperity rests directly on the industry's ability collectively to protect and provide stewardship for those resources essentially for their intrinsic values, but in practice treated in the same way as commercial assets needing continuous maintenance, refurbishment, and investment.
- *Global reach* – with modern transport and information communications systems, tourism has now penetrated almost every part of the world. The players in the industry, individually and collectively, have a window of opportunity to put themselves in the vanguard of change and influence and control events, or ignore the process of environmental change for a few years at most while the initiative and control passes to anti-tourism lobbies and to regulators.
- *Market demand* – research and analysis of demand patterns illustrate convincingly that the great majority of leisure visitors expect and want products which offer clean air, clean beaches and bathing water, pristine mountain slopes and uncongested, crime- and pollution-free destinations. When these attributes are not offered, or are lost through an internationally familiar process of overdevelopment, existing customers go elsewhere and only a downward spiral of reductions in price – eventually self-defeating – will hold on temporarily to a less discriminating market.
- *Competitive business advantage* – ample proof now exists that cost savings as well as product quality images flow from good environmental practice by all kinds of travel and tourism businesses

Further reading

Meadows, D.H., *et al.*, *The Limits to Growth*, Universe Books, New York, 1972.

Middleton, V.T.C., *Marketing in Travel and Tourism*, 2nd edn, Butterworth-Heinemann, Oxford, 1994.

The Tourism Industry and the Environment, Special Report No. 2453, Economist Intelligence Unit, London, 1992.

Travel & Tourism's Economic Perspective, World Travel & Tourism Council, London, 1995.

2

Global environmental issues

If the present growth trends in world population, industrialization, pollution, food production, and resource depletion continue unchanged, the limits to growth on our planet will be reached some time in the next 100 years (Meadows, D.H. *et al*, 1972).

Developing from the brief introduction in Chapter 1, this chapter aims to provide a synopsis for people concerned with tourism of six major global environmental issues that influenced and formed the framework for the debate at the Rio Earth Summit meeting of 1992. All of them are now subject to intensive international scientific research and are the main threats to long-run global security, increasingly recognized in all parts of the world. Apart from population growth, there are already some international agreements for coping with key aspects of these issues, or agreements are being considered and are likely to be reached in the foreseeable future. Population growth and what to do about it remains the 'untouchable' subject politically, although it is possible that a combination of medical advances, increases in education, and improvements in the status of women will bring about its own solution over the next two decades by the sort of process that is now emerging. Current global population projections may prove to be exaggerated, but there is considerable evidence that the global environmental implications of increasing poverty may outweigh the advances in medical science.

It is stressed that the issues in this chapter

have reached what many now perceive as crisis proportions only in the last quarter of a century. Individually the problems and their causes are not new. But the cumulative effects of population growth, combined with the universal drive for improved economic conditions and aided by global science and technology, are now pressing against the finite resources and tolerances of the Earth. The atmosphere, fresh water supplies and the capacity of the land and ocean systems to regenerate themselves are threatened in ways which have no historical parallel. The world is entering uncharted territory and the science available to monitor and predict events, and develop possible solutions, is far from exact, notwithstanding the massive international effort and expenditure that is currently being made. We stress that travel and tourism is *not* a primary cause of global environmental threats, but the industry collectively is a significant contributing factor at the margin, and in some cases more centrally where countries and regions rely on the economic contribution of tourism for, say, a fifth or more of their GDP.

Tourism is already an important economic sector for many countries and regions around the world, as we illustrate in Chapters 3 and 4. In resources terms, many states have little more than attractive, currently unpolluted environments to market internationally in order to sustain their growing populations' increasing demands. It is vital that such destinations understand the ways in which modern tourism can be harnessed to serve their needs without damaging the assets upon which prosperity depends.

This chapter identifies some potential implications of the global threats to the future of travel and tourism. It stresses that all concerned with the world's largest industry should not suppose that they are immune from environmental threats because they are not the primary cause of them. There is a powerful case to be made that managers in the tourism industry can and should aim to be at the leading edge of solutions even where they are not the original cause of the problems.

Historical perspective

This time ten centuries ago, the belief emerged in parts of Christian Europe that the earth was in a condition of terminal decline. The belief owed its origins to the conviction that the second coming of Christ would be tidily arranged exactly 1,000 years after the first. Seeking a buttress for their conviction, some adherents persuaded themselves that the earth itself was running down in anticipation of this awesome event. Observational and anecdotal evidence of pestilence, crop failure and disease was invoked in support of that view, and even everyday events such as late harvests and early leaf falls were treated as a signal that time for the planet was almost up.

Another millennium is now at hand and a new environmental eschatology is emerging. In a report published in June 1994, Greenpeace claims to have 'compelling evidence' that global warming is already with us. In the tradition of its tenth century predecessors, this evidence appears to be in the form of several hundred press articles reporting droughts, forest fires, pest outbreaks, tempests and the like. Even the stranding of polar bears on a sub-arctic island which had lost its normal surrounding ice cover was cited as evidence

that the climate time bomb is ticking nicely away (ENDS, No. 233, 1994).

Ever since human beings evolved as a distinct species, we have had a great and unique ability to bring significant change to the ecosystems in which we survive. At the most basic level and in the early years of evolution, these impacts were localized and manifested themselves as soil erosion or salination; localized water pollution, floods, or shortages; and overexploitation of minerals resulting in localized smog and poisoning incidents, shortages of materials, or soil and water pollution. While for the populations involved, the manifestations of these hardships could be disastrous, for the most part they were short term and resolved by the development of new technology, or a shift in settlement patterns to facilitate a new phase of development and exploitation. Mercifully perhaps, communities only a relatively short distance away could remain ignorant of events through poor communication. Historically, as in Africa up to the present century, there has been sufficient space for populations simply to move on to unpolluted areas if they over grazed or otherwise depleted natural resources locally.

Evidence of environmental disaster brought about by human practices was first recorded 3700 years ago when Sumerian cities were being abandoned as poor irrigation practices resulted in salination of the soil, rendering it barren. Hence the system which produced the first food surpluses in the world was toppled. The philosopher Plato wrote 2400 years ago of soil erosion and deforestation caused by overgrazing and tree felling for fuel in the hills of Attica. In Roman times Columella and Pliny warned of the potentially disastrous consequences of overgrazing and intensive farming. Mismanagement of the complex irrigation systems of the Mesopotamian Empire brought about its ruin. In the eighteenth century, logging to construct the fleets of Napoleon and Nelson brought forth a host of comments from as far afield as Italy and England about deforestation and soil erosion. Air pollution from the burning of coal in England brought the first written protest in 1661 by diarist John Evelyn likening the city of London to the 'suburbs of hell'. In 1798 Malthus wrote his treatise on population growth and in the late twentieth century, many authors have noted the *limits to growth* (ENDS, No. 233, 1994).

At the end of the twentieth century it is becoming increasingly evident that human impact has extended to take on a truly global perspective. At the same time the ability for whole populations to shift their settlement patterns and start again in a fresh environment is being reduced. There is now compelling evidence, although not in all cases scientifically proven, that human activities over the centuries have:

- Altered the characteristics of the atmosphere on which we depend for life by changing the delicate temperature balance of the earth, and depleting the Earth's protective sun screen, the ozone layer.
- Changed the delicate ocean ecosystems and depleted their biological content, while also potentially threatening to change the ocean currents which dictate the climate of our continents through direct and indirect pollution, and exploitative fishing activities combined with changes in the Earth's temperature.
- Depleted fresh water resources to a level which may result in a significant increase in desertification and a decrease in productive land available to feed a rapidly growing world population.
- Destroyed and depleted rich biological systems such as rain forests and coral reefs to a level from which they may never fully recover, damaging the potential of the Earth to regenerate the levels of oxygen and diversity of species.

- Consumed and depleted non-renewable mineral resources for short-run economic gain regardless of long-run consequences.

Environmental knowledge today, however, still has much in common with the tenth century. While it is thought that the combination of these issues may threaten the future of the human species, there is little evidence which can prove without a shadow of a doubt that this is the case. The decisions that policy makers in governments, industry, inter-governmental organizations and trade associations need to make is whether, and to what extent, they wish to respond to the clear indications that significant ecological change is occurring and act now to avoid or minimize potential impacts. The alternative is to wait until the impacts occur in the hope that remedial actions will be available and this latter path runs the risk of damage or even destruction of large parts of the world travel and tourism industry and, at least to some observers, impending global catastrophe.

The issues

This chapter deals with the six main environmental issues judged likely to affect the future for travel and tourism:

- Population growth.
- Global warming and the greenhouse effect.
- Ozone layer depletion.
- Acid rain.
- Deforestation, desertification, and degradation of land resources.
- Pollution and depletion of water resources.

Population growth

Population growth and the related struggle for economic development is the issue underlying the whole environmental debate. Politically it is one of the most difficult issues for the inter-

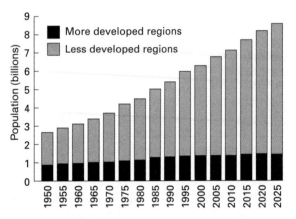

Figure 2.1   *Population growth in developing and developed countries, and in the world, 1950–2025. Source: WRI, GEMS, UNEP (1993) Environmental Data Report, 1993*

national community to address because in introducing measures to control population it is essential to address the complex issues of religion, women's rights and international equity.

Figure 2.1 illustrates population growth since 1950. Scientific advances and improved medical provision have facilitated this population growth and provided economic development opportunities, often by overcoming environmental obstacles. Remote, inhospitable soils, for example, are now cultivated with the help of fertilizers; sea water is turned into fresh water; medical science has extended the average life expectancy; and infant mortality has fallen significantly in the last 50 years.

These triumphs over nature have so far benefited the most developed nations. They have not, however, assisted all of the world's people equally. More than half of the world's population still live in conditions which are considered 'underdeveloped' and it is the populations of the poorest countries which are growing at the fastest rate. Some of the poorest countries, for example sub-Saharan Africa and South Asia, are characterized by rapidly growing populations with average growth rates of 2 to 3 per cent and relatively high total fertility rates (six to seven births per woman). This is coupled with

a slow decline in crude death rates. Recent evidence from these poor regions suggests that fertility could even be growing adding to existing resource and population pressures (WRI, GEMS, UNEP, 1993). People in these developing countries currently use far fewer of the Earth's resources than those in so-called developed countries. It was in recognition of the need to address the imbalance between developed and developing countries that such stress was placed at Rio on fostering the concept of sustainable economic development.

The population in developing countries is demanding development opportunities and the same rights as those in developed countries. These rights include the right to use energy, to eat, to drink fresh water, to own and drive a car, and the right to travel. In exercising these rights in increasing numbers, population growth will place an additional burden onto an already strained global ecosystem and the result could be local and international catastrophe. As the World 3 computer predicted in *The Limits to Growth*, 'If the present growth trends in world population, industrialization, pollution, food production and resource depletion continue unchanged, the limits to growth on the planet will be reached sometime in the next 100 years. The most probable result will be a sudden and uncontrollable decline in both population and industrial capacity.' It is, however, possible for policy makers in all walks of life to change this course and 'establish a condition of ecological and economic stability that is sustainable far into the future. This state of global equilibrium could be designed so that the basic material needs of each person on earth are satisfied and each person has equal opportunity to realize his or her human potential' (Meadows *et al.*, 1992).

Individuals and policy makers in all sectors of the world's economy are responsible for contributing to this global equilibrium. For the travel and tourism industry, management of the increased number of travellers by tourism companies and by those responsible for destination management will be essential to the achievement of sustainability. Such management, in a free and

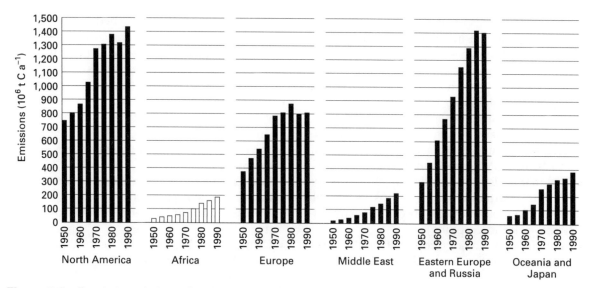

Figure 2.2 *Trends in emissions of carbon dioxide (CO₂) from industrial sources in major world regions, 1950–90. Source: WRI, GEMS, UNEP, Environmental Data Report, 1993*

fiercely competitive market, can only succeed if it develops from a marketing perspective, which is why this book adopts its particular focus.

Global warming and the 'greenhouse effect'

Global warming is a process in which long-wave radiation from the sun enters the Earth's atmosphere, but is prevented from escaping by cloud cover and an accumulation of certain gases around the earth. The effect is entirely natural and facilitated the evolution of the planet as we know it today. Over the last century, however, the natural process of global warming, has been distorted by human activities especially in the developed countries of the world. This means that the Earth is warming up more quickly than it would do naturally. This accelerated warming is caused by emissions of four main gases:

- Carbon dioxide (CO_2), generated by the burning of fossil fuels to generate electricity and for transport purposes.

- Nitrogen oxides (NO_x), also generated by burning fossil fuels for electricity and transport purposes.
- Methane (CH_4) primarily from agricultural and industrial processes, and
- Chlorofluorocarbons (CFCs), chemicals created by humans and used for a wide variety of industrial and household purposes from foam blowing, coolant in air conditioning, and refrigerant systems to component cleaning for computers and TV sets.

Figure 2.2 illustrates how the emission of carbon dioxide has increased in recent years in selected areas of the world. This increased level of emission may bring about increases in Earth's temperature with a number of potential consequences, some of which could have serious implications for travel and tourism. Potential consequences of global warming for the industry include:

- Increased occurrence of algal growths along coastlines (enhanced by the increased nutrient levels of many seas) with potentially disastrous impacts for coastal tourism.

- Changed patterns of precipitation, potentially increasing rainfall in some tropical areas and decreasing snow in some ski resorts.
- Increased frequency of serious storms, such as typhoons or hurricanes, interrupting flights and shipping routes and damaging tourism infrastructure and superstructure.
- Rises in sea level which would threaten low-lying states, such as Bangladesh and the tourist islands of Maldives and Mauritius.
- Potential decline in nutritional value of crops (CO_2 is a fertilizer, which means crops will grow faster, but may not absorb as many nutrients prior to cropping).
- Movement of major crop belts with associated implications for food security.

Ozone layer depletion

The ozone layer is a thin layer of oxygen-related gases in the part of the atmosphere known as the tropopause (the bit between the troposphere and stratosphere), about 25 kilometres above the earth's surface. Only 2 or 3 millimetres thick, the ozone layer acts like a sun screen shielding the earth from harmful ultra-violet (UV-B) radiation while allowing other radiation through. Although the discovery is as recent as 1987, scientific research illustrates that certain gaseous emissions are destroying large quantities of ozone, resulting in 'ozone holes'. (High-level ozone which constitutes the ozone layer should not be confused with low-level ozone which has the same chemical composition but mostly occurs in city centres because of traffic congestion and is directly harmful to human health in urban smog.)

Ozone is created and destroyed by natural processes and some of the chemicals which are responsible for ozone depletion (fluorine, bromine and chlorine) occur naturally. The volumes in which these chemicals are now produced, and the addition of entirely man-made CFCs and halons during the past century, have accelerated the rate at which ozone is destroyed. In the early 1990s, the ozone layer reached a record low, causing widespread concern about the likely effects associated with ozone depletion. These can be summarized for tourism as:

- Increasing incidence of skin cancers with obvious risks to those who expose their bodies through sunbathing.
- Increasing incidence of eye disorders, such as cataracts.
- Less effective functioning of immune systems in humans and animals.
- Increasing occurrence and persistence of skin infections.
- Changes in the climate's heat balance with possible implications for further global warming.
- Shortened life span for plastic products with implications for resources such as oil.
- Potentially reduced rate of photosynthesis slowing plant reproduction and potentially aggravating existing food shortages – posing additional problems for food production to the threat from global warming.
- Some scientists believe that decreases in high-level ozone may also increase low level ozone thus increasing problems for people with breathing difficulties, especially in cities where industrial and traffic pollution reduces air quality.

The issue of ozone depletion has attracted extensive media interest and is relatively high in the public's consciousness. Increased ozone depletion and evidence of its harmful effects on humans in the short term could have more significant implications for the travel and tourism industry than any other single environmental issue. It could result in a consumer shift away from the traditional beach-based holiday in the sun in favour of non-sun destinations and indoor activities which have less potential for harm. Not yet proven, there are indications that emissions from high-flying passenger jet aircraft, the bulk of which are now used for leisure tourism purposes, could be specifically implicated in ozone layer damage.

Acid rain

Caused by air or waterborne transportation of sulphur (SO_x) and nitrogen oxides (NO_x), acid-ification of soils was first noted around iron foundries in the UK in 1660. Some three centuries later the phenomenon put environmental concern on the international political agenda, largely at the demand of the Scandinavian countries. Acid rain is formed when oxides of sulphur and nitrogen mix with water (H_2O) in the atmosphere to form sulphuric acid (H_2SO_4) or nitric acid (H_2NO_3). The SO_x and NO_x responsible for acid rain in the 1990s is largely generated by the burning of fossil fuels in power stations and by transport emissions.

Acid rain observes no national boundaries and has been most severe in Scandinavian countries where critical loads of certain acidic pollutants are now being exceeded. Some scientists estimate that, even if emissions of SO_x and NO_x gases were halted immediately, it would take many decades for the ecosystems in Scandinavian countries to regain their natural level of acidity. The impacts of acid rain vary according to the type of ecosystem affected – impacts are most noticeable on acidic soils and coniferous woodland. The major impacts of acid rain for tourism are:

- Damage to trees and plants leading in some cases to destruction of species within forests leaving soils prone to erosion. The German government, for example, invests heavily in trying to protect the tourist destination of the Black Forest from acid erosion.
- Reduced levels of photosynthesis (photosyntheses is the natural process through which plants use natural sunlight and moisture to grow) thus reducing plant productivity.
- Erosion of building, monuments and other stonework. In some historic towns, in Germany, for example, the costs of fighting decay of historic buildings is estimated at $100 million per year.
- Increased occurrence of urban smog.

- Leaching of essential nutrients (such as calcium and magnesium) from soils, further reducing plant growth.
- Leaching of naturally occurring minerals, including aluminium, from the soil and into watercourses causing poisoning of marine life and, potentially, the human condition known as Alzheimer's disease.

Concern about acid rain has slipped down the political and public agenda as the more pressing issues of climate change and ozone depletion have become evident. It is ironic, therefore, that the steps taken to reduce global warming and ozone depletion (such as fewer coal-burning power stations) have actually done more to reduce acid rain than many of the measures developed specifically to tackle this issue. Acid rain also poses less of an immediate threat to the development of the tourism industry than either ozone depletion or global warming. It will, however, continue to cost destination authorities dearly as they try to protect their natural and cultural heritage from erosion to ensure the continued interest and motivation of visitors.

Deforestation, desertification and degradation of land resources

Earth's natural resources provide us with the basic necessities for life – food, water, fuels, metal ores, and the landscapes and environments which are the core resource for much of the leisure and tourism industries. These resources have been utilized throughout the evolution of humankind, but they are not inexhaustible and many are becoming scarce or degraded as populations make ever more demands for economic development needs.

It is in the area of land resources that the interests of the travel and tourism industry and conservation are most closely aligned. The quest for new sources of fuel is now threatening some of the world's last natural environmental wildernesses such as Antarctica. One-third of the planet's land area is estimated to be threatened by desertification including parts of Europe which are primary tourist destinations. Deforestation is threatening the developing ecotourism potential in the Amazon and African bush. There is massive loss of biodiversity in Europe and the USA as a result of industrial farming practices. Wetlands around the world are estimated to be disappearing at a rate of 35 acres an hour as urban, industrial, and agricultural pressure are brought to bear.

Pollution of land resources from the growing production and disposal of human and industrial waste is also a concern and one which governments have to address in the near future. Landfill sites are becoming scarce in some countries and the dangers from leachate (a highly toxic substance which can pollute watercourses from poorly managed landfill sites) is problematic.

The full potential implications of land degradation are unknown and can only be guessed at by the scientific community, but they include:

- Further desertification as a result of deforestation.
- Increased incidence of landslides as agriculture encroaches onto more unsuitable land as a result of desertification.
- Pollution of watercourses or the water table as a result of leachate from poor waste-disposal practices, ultimately adding to the burden of marine pollution (see next section).
- Disease and illness associated with gaseous emissions from decomposing materials.
- War or famine resulting from lack of food in countries affected by desertification.
- Large-scale disruption of economic systems from shortages of oil or minerals and a possible substantial increase in prices for aviation fuel, for example.
- Loss of potential scientific and medical advances achievable by biotechnology, as a result of destruction of the diverse 'genetic banks' of nature.

- Unsightly environments damaging tourism potential, for example, in parts of Europe and the former Soviet Union.
- Reduction in the number of sites suitable for urban settlements, industrial production, and tourism development.

Pollution and depletion of water resources

Essential to human survival, water covers 79 per cent of the globe. Less than 1 per cent of this water is suitable for drinking purposes, however, and it is very unevenly distributed. With proper management there is more than sufficient water to fulfil current and future needs of the world's population, but water availability does not coincide with population density, and it is estimated that a relatively high percentage of fresh water resources are currently wasted before reaching their intended end use, leaving many regions in a situation of existing or impending shortage.

Water, or rather the lack of it, has become the key environmental issue in many areas and prevents a number of populations from reaching their development potential. Populations threatened by serious or severe water shortages in the next decade include those in parts of Spain, the USA, Australia, Italy, sub-Saharan Africa, large areas of Asia, and parts of Eastern Europe. Many of these countries have resorted quite literally to 'mining water' as a short-term solution. Such 'mining' may in itself affect the level of groundwater, however, and increase salinity of groundwater reserves around boreholes, rendering them useless.

The environmental issues associated with water include poor waste water treatment and the impact of polluted waters on the world's fisheries (the largest single source of human protein). Untreated waste water is estimated to be the most environmentally damaging pollutant in the world, responsible for four out of every five deaths in the developing world. Poor waste water treatment is also responsible for pollution of the prime destination of leisure tourism, the coastal zone. Some 77 per cent of marine pollution comes from land-based sources (waste water, agricultural run-off, industrial effluent deposited into rivers, leachate from landfill, etc) and these pollutants in part contribute to algal blooms, death of marine life and poisoning of other marine life. According to Pearce (1993), for example, 93 per cent of shellfish caught off the Mediterranean coast contain sufficiently high concentrations of pollutants to make them fail WHO standards. The situation is likely to worsen if the world's population living within 60 kilometres of the coast increases, as predicted, to reach two-thirds of the total population by 2010.

Fisheries are a vital food source for the world, providing the essential protein needs for many populations. Pollution of watercourses and especially of coastal waters, combined with overfishing to feed growing populations, has already plunged the world's fish stocks into a major crisis. In 1990, the total commercial world fish catch monitored by the UN Food and Agricultural Organization (FAO) declined by over 4 million tons. It was the first significant fall in the fish harvest since 1972 and appears to have been a turning point, reflecting the overfishing of prime areas. There is ample evidence of overfishing and of fisheries collapsing in some areas, notably off Newfoundland and in the Baltic and parts of the Mediterranean and North Sea, for example. By the end of the 1980s nine of the ten fishing zones monitored by the FAO were being fished above the lower limits of estimated sustainable yield and several fish species are threatened with extinction in various parts of the world.

New technology, including refrigerated boats, radar, sonar and satellite spotting devices, drift nets and deep trawling, have allowed fishing to become ever more industrialized and efficient while depleting stocks and reducing the level of natural reproduction.

In Europe the fisheries situation had reached such a crisis in the late 1990s that the imposition of quotas has become one of the most serious wrangles for countries within the EU. Meanwhile, fine nets were literally scooping up the life from the ocean bed around Europe and, in the case of unregulated sea-bed dredging off the north coast of England in 1996, destroying a vital aspect of marine ecosystems on which other forms of sea life depend. Interestingly one solution to this unsustainable practice comes not from the EU or UN but from a major trade association in cooperation with the World Wide Fund for Nature (WWF). The Marine Stewardship Council, in collaboration with commercial giant Unilever and major retailers such as Sainsbury's, has proposed to use only produce from boats using sustainable practices. The reason is not philanthropy, simply an interest in the long-run business prospects.

The most likely impacts of global water shortages and pollution over the next decade are:

- Dire shortage of drinking water in some countries. In popular tourism destinations the industry is bound to become a focus of conflict because of its conspicuous consumption patterns (a tourist may use eight times more water per day than a resident on the island of Mallorca in Spain, for example). Irregular and inadequate water supply can also be a cause of significant dissatisfaction among tourists.
- Increased mortality from cholera, malaria, bilharzia and other waterborne diseases.
- Increased incidence of poisoning related to seafood. The incidence of paralytic shellfish poisoning, for example, is expected to increase in the next decade. For tourism companies, this could have serious implications for the profitability of some destinations and be a cause of litigation proceedings.

- Reduction in sea life, such as coral reefs, striped dolphins, and giant turtles, as a result of sea pollution and human interference.
- Reduction of available agricultural land as a result of salination and other water-related damage.
- Reduction of nutrition for the high proportion of the global population that relies on fish as a staple part of their diet. Such shortages have considerable implications for food famine and as a cause of other environmental damage by hungry people.
- Decrease in the number of sites suitable for human or tourism development because of the incidence of disease.
- Increased incidence of algal blooms (see above).
- Decreased attraction of coastal zones for holiday taking, with implications for the travel and tourism industry.

These issues have strong world regional implications expected to affect the development and structure of the tourism industry over the next decade. Chapters 3 and 4 provide an overview of the developments influencing regional growth and, in some cases, the possible decline of the tourism industry.

Chapter summary

This chapter identifies the six principal global environmental threats facing the world, looking ahead to the implications identified by scientists and environment pressure groups as likely to reach crisis proportions over the next ten to fifty years. All six threats are already influencing consumer and business behaviour generally, but not yet on the scale that many anticipate. It is not certain when and where these threats will have serious impacts on travel and tourism and damage the associated businesses. Some current expectations may not occur within the predicted period. Others could be averted by the introduc-

---

Threats of loss or erosion to places and natural and built resources

- Scenically attractive areas such as beaches, forests, lakes and mountains.
- Wilderness areas such as Antarctica still relatively untouched by human development.
- Areas currently sustaining wildlife and bio-diversity such as safari parks, rain-forests and coral reef systems.
- Heritage monuments, sites and cities suffering acid rain, other air pollution and traffic congestion.
- Destinations declining through overcongestion of visitors/overdevelopment/loss of quality.

Threats to health and safety

- Skin cancers and possible damage to eyes.
- Inadequate clean fresh water supplies.
- Pollution of water supplies and bathing water.
- Food contamination and poisoning.
- Air quality in urban areas.
- Violence and wars triggered by environmental causes such as famine.

Figure 2.3 *Threats to the environmental quality of resources and to visitors' health and safety in the twenty-first century*

---

tion of new technology and by better visitor management techniques not yet in common use.

Growing international awareness of the sheer scope of the issues and the certainty of future impact, provided the rationale for AGENDA 21 and the international agreements signed at the Rio Earth Summit in 1992. There is more than enough in these issues to focus tourism industry minds on the nature of the threats and how best to position the different sectors of the industry to cope. On current evidence the bulk of the travel and tourism industry takes too much for granted. In our view the time for thinking, analysis and innovative responses is now. The alternative is likely to be punitive legislation based on inadequate knowledge, which will damage the industry, be burdensome to monitor, and anyway fail to change the attitudes and industry behaviour which causes the problems. Subsequent chapters suggest how this can be tackled.

In Figure 2.3 in summary format, we list the main threats to visitors' health and safety and to the quality of tourism resources implicit in this chapter. It will not be tenable over the next decade for travel and tourism to claim its position as the world's largest industry while collectively and individually ducking the en-

vironmental responsibilities which such size and impact inevitably imposes.

Further reading

Environmental Data Services Ltd, No. 233, London, 1994.

Meadows, D.H. *et al.*, *Beyond the Limits: Global Collapse or a Sustainable Future*, Earthscan, London, 1992.

WRI, GEMS, UNEP, *Environmental Data Report*, 1993.

3

International summary of tourism and the environment: north Europe, the Mediterranean region and North America

Travel and tourism with telecommunications and information technology will be one of the main driving forces of the 21st Century global economy (Naisbitt, 1994).

It is the current size and growth potential of the travel and tourism industry that justifies the level of concern about its environmental impact. In the Preface and elsewhere, we stress our view that the environmental issues facing travel and tourism around the world are, in principle, remarkably similar. This similarity is one of the most encouraging aspects of the world's largest industry because it means common solutions can be developed to deal with common threats and problems. There is nothing unique about Britain, the USA, or anywhere else in this context although the severity of problems and their perceived importance will vary greatly between destinations. In Chapter 2, we set our appreciation of the common global threats, some of which are widely judged to be reaching crisis proportions in the final decade of the twentieth century. In this chapter and the next, we attempt

to do the impossible in reviewing tourism developments and environmental implications in the major regions of the world on a broadly comparable basis. This review sets the scene for developing in subsequent chapters our view of the marketing perspective that we consider essential to lead and orchestrate international responses in the coming decade.

We fully understand the difficulty of providing such a wide-ranging world view in just two short chapters. The many nuances of travel and tourism in each country are inevitably lost in a global overview and some sweeping generalizations are made. Yet we believe a coherent pattern emerges that will be helpful to many readers who are knowledgeable about their own sector of the tourism industry, and their own country's position, but unfamiliar with the global pattern. Common global threats require globally relevant solutions and the international relevance must be made transparent for effective action to be taken.

In this chapter, we look at three world regions: north Europe and North America comprising countries that are among the most highly developed nations within the OECD, and also the traditional main sources of both origin and reception of domestic and international tourism. We look also at the Mediterranean region as the major destination of world tourism since the 1960s, especially tourism originating in north Europe. In 1960 the World Tourism Organization estimated that the three regions accounted for some 95 per cent of international tourism and their global dominance remains, even though the share had fallen to just over 80 per cent in 1993 as international tourism grew faster in newer areas, especially Asia and the Pacific (see Chapter 4). Countries in Europe and North America, having experienced the full range of positive and negative impacts of tourism over the last three decades, are among those best equipped to understand and deal with sustainability and pursue effective environmental responses. They also have the destinations best equipped to manage tourism through controls and regulations available to local authorities. Finally, many of these countries have a great deal to gain or lose in the approaches they take to travel and tourism as a vital and growing sector of their post-industrial economies.

This overview is intended to provide broadly comparable information for each region, looking briefly at:

- Stage of tourism development – the current tourism situation.
- Pressures for environmental change from consumers, local government, and through regulation.
- Some future implications for the more sustainable development of the travel and tourism industry.

North Europe

Tourism development – the current situation

This region includes the British Isles, central European and Scandinavian countries, and Aus-

tria. The area has been the dominant generator and most important recipient of international tourism over the past century. In many ways north European companies and travellers have shaped the world travel market as we know it today and are likely to continue to have a major influence for the foreseeable future. There is a general consensus that most north European markets are mature in the sense that most of the people who wish to travel domestically and internationally already do so, and markets can only grow by greater travel frequency – more visits per person in any year.

The propensity for north Europeans to travel away from home for leisure purposes has had a significant impact upon the development of tourism products both within and outside the region. So-called 'traditional' seaside resorts in northern countries, which had expanded in the 1950s and 1960s to accommodate the increasing number of working-class people able to afford holidays, experienced a marked decline in visitor numbers throughout the 1970s and 1980s (although some experienced a minor revival in the early 1990s). This decline brought about localized unemployment in the tourism sector, affecting also the agricultural, fishing and craft sectors that support a tourism economy; redundancy in significant buildings such as hotels and theatres; and neglect and deterioration in infrastructure amounting to a major erosion of the quality of the environment offered to visitors – always their principal attraction. In recent years, many 'traditional' resorts have implemented refurbishment programmes and devised new advertising campaigns designed to attract the conference and short-break market. Often these campaigns rely on promoting the natural attributes of the area and developing cultural festivals to generate interest but always at a reduced volume from their heydays in the 1960s.

Between the 1960s and the 1990s, although domestic holiday tourism in most north European countries has generally declined in volume in favour of visits to sunshine destinations abroad, there has been a remarkable growth of interest in domestic tourism to rural destinations and national parks, and to historic towns and cities, demonstrating a growing consumer interest in outdoor activities and in the quality of natural, cultural and heritage environments. There has also been strong growth in same-day visits from home for all purposes included within the definition of tourism, facilitated by increasing access in all countries to private motor cars.

As domestic tourism to traditional resorts declined in north Europe, the technology of air transport and sea ferries reduced the cost of international visits and all northern countries have benefited massively from inbound tourism in the last two decades, especially from other countries in the same region. Growing visitor interest in culture, heritage, and the arts led the European Commission to designate cultural tourism as a key area of development in Europe in 1990.

The combination of growth in car-borne domestic tourism and day visits and the increase in inbound tourism from other countries has produced conditions of increasing congestion and concern for the integrity of popular destinations in all countries that seems certain to fuel the tourism and environment debate well into the next century.

North European cities in particular have benefited from rapid growth in both domestic and international travel, and for many tourism is now a significant element in their local economy. Traditionally attractive cities such as Amsterdam, Bath, London, Paris, Vienna, and Salzburg have all attracted increasing numbers of tourists over the past few decades. Industrial cities such as Leeds, Manchester, Cardiff and Glasgow, having suffered massive decline in their manufacturing base, are increasingly focusing on tourism as a primary means of urban renewal and regeneration and a leading economic sector to take them into the post-industrial era of the twenty-first century.

For the cities and rural areas which have attracted visitors, success can be a two-edged sword. On the one hand, tourism generates employment, funds for regeneration, support for cultural diversity, pride of place, infrastructure improvements and increased ability to attract investment from other industry sectors. It is also identified as a key contributor to the quality of life for residents, especially in its support for the arts, heritage and culture. On the other hand, for some cities and national parks, tourism has aggravated existing problems of congestion, pollution, heritage degradation, housing shortage, litter, crime, and, in some cases, generated conflict with residents. These environmental problems – and especially traffic congestion and associated air pollution - are now the biggest threat to the continued growth of tourism in many of Europe's cities. We discuss solutions to these problems in later chapters.

The pressures for change

(a) Consumer choices

The key pressures for change within the European market are being brought to bear by the visitors themselves. The evidence indicates that tourists are not specifically demanding so-called 'green' or 'ecolabels' on the products that they select, but they will not return to destinations which fail to offer environmental quality as a part of the tourism experience. This trend became evident as early as 1985, when one out of three German holidaymakers recognized and reacted to water or air pollution, damaged forests, waste or blighted landscapes. In 1989, this has risen to two out of three and the most serious problems were experienced in Britain, followed by Italy, Greece, Denmark, and France. In 1985, research indicated that 20 per cent of tourists found their experiences so bad that it would deter them from returning to the destination (Boers and Bosch, 1994, pp. 39–40). See also the research evidence in Figures 1.1 and 1.2 in Chapter 1.

The next generation of travellers will be even more aware as almost every child educated in north Europe has received some form of environmental education since the early 1990s. Some operators are already responding to these demands. The largest German outbound tour operator, Touristik Union International (TUI), for example, makes environmental commitments to all clients in brochures as a part of its drive to ensure that it provides good-quality holiday products (see case study in Chapter 15).

Environmental degradation has already affected the fortunes of some destinations. Consumers have boycotted beaches which gained a reputation for being polluted (for example, Rimini in 1989), avoided resorts which have a reputation for being overdeveloped (for example, the Costa del Sol in the late 1980s), and moved from areas where there is evident cultural conflict (such as the Basque country).

(b) The role of local authorities

Local authorities are relatively powerful in north European states. Some are beginning to develop and enforce strategies designed to reward companies which have good environmental credentials with competitive benefits, and to penalize or preclude certain activities. Local authorities have focused specifically on the road-congestion issue and operators (especially coach tour operators in Europe's top cities) have found access rights more and more difficult to negotiate as illustrated by the case of Salzburg, Austria.

Salzburg is an example of a destination that has faced severe tourism-related congestion problems. It is a medium-sized town drawing millions of visitors annually to its attractions and cultural events. The town has been seeking a solution to its congestion problems for some years and in 1990 the town council sought to introduce a traffic-management system. The scheme was introduced with little consultation of operators and management measures included the use of obligatory passes on coaches to enable them to enter Salzburg, and an obligatory shuttle bus system operating from a parking place for all coach clients who did not have reservations in the town.

The scheme was very unpopular with opera-

tors since it required them to change their itineraries entirely and they lost control of the quality of the guest experience. Dissatisfaction was such that Salzburg experienced a virtual boycott by tour and coach operators, resulting in a reduction in the total number of visitors to the town and a corresponding fall in the profitability of restaurants, tour guides, and other facilities. This had a knock-on effect on the income of hoteliers, tour guides, and restaurateurs who became discontented with the scheme. The situation has now been remedied by the introduction of a more user-friendly and inexpensive access permit scheme which has been agreed between the operators, tourism facilities, and town authorities.

Source: Director of Salzburg Tourism Office in conversation with European Tour Operators Association

(c) The burden of clean-up costs

The health and economic costs of tackling the acid rain problem have led some Scandinavian countries to demand change in countries from which the pollution originates. For some countries, the costs of restoration from acidification runs into millions of dollars and prevention is identified as more beneficial than cure. The German government, for example, spends US$ 100 million per year in maintaining its historic buildings against acid-related erosion (WTTERC, 1993, p. 23). The countries which are most severely affected are demanding change in standards, for example for vehicle emissions, and new international regulations for polluting industries.

The authorities of Venice, for example, are likely to enforce some form of waste water treatment for agricultural, industrial, and urban waste water treatment facilities operating along the river Po in an attempt to reduce the 1 million tonnes of algae which it has to remove to prevent it putrefying just as peak season visitors arrive in July. And the costs of discharging effluent in Germany will have more than doubled between 1986 and 1999, providing a market incentive for companies to reduce the level and content of their waste water emissions (*Journal of Institute of Water and Environmental Management*, 6 March 1992, p. 28).

(c) The development of environmental regulation

The European Union has taken one of the more stringent of world region attitudes to the environment, introducing more than 200 pieces of legislation covering pollution of the atmosphere, water and soil, waste management, safeguards in relation to chemicals and biotechnology, product standards, environmental impact assessments and protection of nature. These regulations are developed within the framework of action programmes which set broad policy goals, and further strategies are also produced to guide developments. In 1992, the EU responded to the sustainable debate at Rio by producing 'Towards Sustainability: A European Community Programme of Policy and Action in Relation to Environment and Sustainable Development'.

Regulations or Directives agreed by the Community are implemented via national laws and throughout the 1980s and 1990s the travel and tourism industry has been directly affected by an increasing number of these regulations, for example:

- The requirement for all member states to introduce environmental impact assessments (EIAs) prior to the development of large-scale projects (major hotel and airport developments are included under section II of this regulation).
- Phasing out the manufacture of CFCs and halons by the end of 1996 under the requirements of the Montreal Protocol on Ozone Depleting Substances and its London and Copenhagen amendments. Such chemicals were widely used in the tourism industry.
- Bathing-water quality directives to improve water quality standards at beaches.

Some development implications for the travel and tourism industry

The demands of increasingly experienced and sophisticated travellers seeking enriching holiday experiences are likely to push environmental improvements up the agenda for many travel and tourism companies in the next decade. In many cases the environment will be dealt with not in isolation but as a part of a total quality approach to tourism management. This commitment will be communicated to the public through the publication of statements about the companies' environmental performance; by developing environmental codes of conduct or standards for suppliers (German-based Touristik Union International have already taken steps to this end); by developing integrated resorts whereby a company owns and manages all the product components at a location; or by selecting destinations which have put effective and enforceable environmental standards into place.

The threat of increased regulation and economic penalties is likely to push leading companies in all sectors to take some form of 'voluntary' pre-emptive action. Energy taxes are a particular threat for European companies and especially threaten the development of the transport sector. Travel and tourism companies may follow the lead set by some of the heavy industry sectors in Germany and the Netherlands of devising and imposing their own reductions in carbon dioxide emissions to alleviate the threat of increased energy taxation.

Congestion at specific destinations through too many people and too many cars is likely to be the key challenge in many north European destinations. It is already threatening further expansion of tourism in many places. Congestion is likely to be tackled on an *ad hoc* basis by individual authorities but, as experience of tourism management increases and appropriate solutions become more evident, it is likely that accommodation interests and tour operators will cooperate with destination authorities to ensure that they are able to continue their trade. Car-hire companies are also likely to come under fire by some authorities which are examining the imposition of tariffs or car ownership/entrance quotas. National parks in the UK are currently grappling with complex traffic management initiatives.

It is unlikely that travel and tourism will escape the notice of mainstream environmental pressure groups in north Europe in the next decade. Some of the mistakes of the past and the environmental issues now associated with the industry (especially its transport demands) are likely to be tackled by these groups and this will certainly raise the profile of tourism impacts on both the political and public agenda generating a greater impetus for change. In 1996, for example, Friends of the Earth launched their first tourism campaign. Representing the interests and views of thousands of consumers in north Europe alone, the effectiveness of this campaign could be influential in shaping business attitudes to the environment over the coming years.

The Mediterranean region

Tourism development – the current situation

The Mediterranean region includes the southern coastline of the states of Portugal, mainland Spain, France, Italy, Greece, Turkey, the islands of Malta and Cyprus, the Balearics, plus the northern coastline of Egypt, Tunisia, Algeria, Israel, and Morocco. This region is the world's favourite holiday destination area receiving more than 100 million visitors a year, around a fifth of global international tourist activity. Despite a recent decline in the area's share of world tourism, the absolute number of international tourists in the region has been predicted to increase to reach 160 million tourists with 150 million cars by the year 2000 (MEDPLAN, 1988; Gajraj, 1988, p. 8). By 2025 the total number of tourists may have grown to reach 260 million (MEDPLAN, UNEP). Around 95 per cent of this tourism takes place within the EU states of France, Italy, Greece, Portugal, and Spain, with much of the remainder going to Turkey, Cyprus, Malta and the north African states.

Tourism growth, like urban and industrial development in the area, has occurred at a remarkably rapid pace, and the travel and tourism industry competes with industrial, recreational, military and residential uses for space and resources. Infrastructure development has typically not kept pace with the rapid development and this has caused some localized pollution and congestion problems.

The area has developed a distinctive regional style of tourism which is dominated by the inbound travel market with a high proportion of intra-regional trade. Despite the growth of 'winter-sun' tourism, the industry is highly seasonal in nature with the majority of visitors arriving between the months of May and September. Tourism to the area is heavily dependent on the north European markets and the tourism industry has been very successful in serving the needs of holidaymakers with package tours, often dubbed 'mass-tourism'. Although there has been recent diversification into cultural tourism, the characteristics of the tourism product in the Mediterranean region is still based primarily on beaches and climatic attributes that are similar between cultures, and this has led some tour operators into a high degree of product similarity and competition on lowest prices to achieve business.

Measured in visitor numbers and growth, the area is without a doubt the most successful tourist region in the world. It is also facing potential disaster resulting from pollution and overdevelopment of its greatest and unique asset, the Mediterranean Sea. Tourism is rarely the sole or even a major cause of this pollution, but in a mainly tideless sea any additional waste discharge has a powerful marginal impact in many favoured visitor locations and further marine pollution has potential to damage the fortunes of the industry in the region.

Already carrying the dubious honour of being among the dirtiest seas in the world (Pearce, 1995), the Mediterranean receives 10 billion tonnes of industrial and urban waste annually of which only a tiny proportion has received even primary treatment. Many French beaches fail cleanliness standards laid down in the European Union's Bathing Waters Directive and the UN estimate that swimming in its waters can cause infections of the ear, nose and throat, hepatitis, enteritis, dysentery, and occasional cases of cholera (Pearce, 1995). Over seventy rivers drain into the Mediterranean's waters and many of these are virtually open pipelines for industrial, agricultural, and human effluent, especially the Rhone, Nile, Ebro and Po. Also, 120 000 tonnes of oil reach the sea from drilling and up to 1 million tonnes of crude oil are dumped by all activities (that's more than seventeen times the amount spilled by the *Exxon Valdez* disaster); 60 000 tonnes of detergents; 100 tonnes of mercury; and 3600 tonnes of phosphates are also discarded into the waters each year.

Environmental problems are not confined to the coastline. Vehicle pollution generally and pressure from tourists in particular is pushing many heritage towns and attractions, such as Venice, up the league of the most polluted cities as the city authorities seek solutions to the problems posed by housing and feeding thousands of tourists as well as their growing urban and industrial populations (Pearce, 1995).

The region's remaining wildlife is under siege from this wide range of pressures and many species are already on the verge of extinction. The loggerhead turtle, for example, is evident in only a handful of locations; the monk seal has become a fugitive, making its home in the few protected marine areas and avoiding human contact; several thousand striped dolphins died between 1990 and 1992 from a mysterious disease; red tides and algal blooms disrupt the ecosystems of the area by their frequency (not to mention tourist dissatisfaction should they catch a whiff of the foul-smelling hydrogen sulphide or ammonia from such 'blooms'). Attempts were in progress in the late 1990s to save the remaining Mediterranean forest, France's Camargue, Portugal's western Peninsula and Spain's Coto de Donana.

Conflict between the tourism-related environment and development lobbies are perhaps among the fiercest in the world in the Mediterranean region and it is often tourism developments which are the trigger for dispute. Environmental concerns hardly top the regions'

political agendas, however, and it is development which has been the greatest political motivator. The search for new destinations to serve the needs of an increasingly sophisticated clientele has made some tour operators examine their practices in the 1990s, and those of host destinations, in an attempt to improve and preserve their product resource base. The bulk of north European holiday business is expected to stay in the Mediterranean for reasons of location, cost, and available infrastructure (WTTERC, *Environment and Development*, No. 2, 1994). As noted, this is a very large market with a great deal at stake, and there are at least encouraging signs that tour operators are considering their options for cleaning up and preserving the Mediterranean coastline with the support and often the initiative of local government.

The pressures for change

(a) Consumer choices

The forces which are driving consumer demand in the Mediterranean region are much the same as those in the north European area, because north Europeans are its key international customers. Sophisticated, travel-experienced consumers are demanding better products offering cultural and environmental quality and diversity, as well as the more traditional sun, sea and sand elements of the product. Price remains an important consideration, but is less important to many visitors than the environmental qualities of peace and quiet, views and scenery, and an attractive relaxing ambience and sense of place.

There is some evidence that consumers are boycotting areas perceived to have sea pollution or congestion, or that are overdeveloped, and have moved on to areas which are able to offer the qualities noted above. Tour operators have already found themselves taken to court over illnesses caused by sea pollution and poor food hygiene as travellers have become more aware of problems and their rights to compensation. A rise in such cases or incidence of algal blooms could change consumer demand rapidly, possibly triggering bankruptcies for the operators involved.

Dissatisfied with their recent experiences in the Mediterranean, some customers are shifting to alternative long-haul destinations, notably in the Caribbean. If this becomes a major trend, it could have serious implications for the economy of the region, as many local authorities are increasingly aware.

(b) The role of local authorities

Local governments in the more developed areas of the Mediterranean region have become more discriminating about the type of tourism they encourage, and many have taken initiatives to diversify the nature and type of tourism they promote. Many authorities are beginning to apply stricter planning and management criteria as a condition for the development of tourism facilities. There have also been a significant number of initiatives to 'clean-up' and change the image that tourists have of the destination. The Spanish government has led the field in this area and Italy and Greece are following suit. For Spain at least the effort seems to be paying off in the late 1990s as tourist numbers increased consistently.

The long-run fortunes of the south Mediterranean countries with rapidly developing tourism potential such as Turkey, Morocco and Tunisia have yet to be determined, but it appears that they continue to make many of the mistakes of overdevelopment made by their northern counterparts some twenty years earlier. Many of these countries have the benefit of smaller coastal populations, making development space available at a lower premium. In the late 1990s, however, it seems that overcapacity and development on the north African coast is imminent in an attempt to boost tourism incomes in Tunisia, Morocco, and Egypt.

(c) Initiatives by the travel and tourism industry

In its prime destinations the travel and tourism industry in recent years has become more involved in shaping its own future. Some large operators have bought large tracts of land and developed planned, often enclosed and fully managed integrated resorts, typically providing for specialist pursuits such as golf and controlling directly all aspects of quality. Other operators have formed innovative partnerships with local authorities to improve product quality. TUI, for example, has worked with Grecotel (Greece's largest hotel chain) to bring about significant environmental improvements, and the International Federation of Tour Operators has worked with the authorities of Mallorca (Spain) and Rhodes (Greece) to devise ways in which the tourism industry could be made more sustainable through a collaborative research project funded by the European Commission. Such initiatives were not even contemplated a decade ago and are motivated by a growing recognition of long run vested interests by both operators and tourist destinations.

(d) National/international regulation

Environmental regulation has not thus far played a major role in the region as a whole and has, for example, been unable to ensure the quality of the sea. Development and enforcement of regulation has been particularly difficult between the diverse states in the region, and the Maltese government has been trying to promote an agreement on protection of the Mediterranean sea for some years (largely because of its own vulnerability to sea pollution). An action plan has been developed for cleaning up the region and, under the aegis of the United Nations Regional Seas Programme, the Mediterranean Action Programme was established in 1985 setting ten practical objectives for achievement by all consenting states by 1995. These were:

- Measures to reduce the amount of contaminated water discharged by ships into the sea.
- Installation of sewage-treatment works for all cities of populations in excess of 100 000 people, plus appropriate sewage outfall pipes

into the sea or treatment plants for towns with over 10 000 people.

- Environmental impact assessment requirements for new ports, marinas and holiday resorts.
- Improved navigation safety for shipping.
- Statutory protection for endangered marine species, such as sea turtles.
- Reduced industrial pollution.
- Identification and protection of 100 historic coastal sites.
- Identification and protection of fifty marine and coastal conservation sites.
- More protection against forest fires and soil loss to minimize erosion into rivers.
- Reduction of acid rain.

Region-wide few, if any, of these objectives had been met by the participating states in 1995 and the failure of many of them even to pay their dues to the Programme makes achievement of objectives seem unlikely. Progress has been made in some areas by some European Union states and in many of the island states, but there remains much to be done if the quality of the environment is to be restored and then maintained. The European Union seems less likely to give Mediterranean member countries the long periods of grace to implement environmental regulation which were initially granted. It should now back up its determination by ensuring that controversial programmes which ignore the reality of environmental impacts do not receive EU funding, even where economic and employment benefits are promised.

Some development implications for the travel and tourism industry

North European tour operators dealing with ever more demanding customers and seeking to assure customers of product quality are increasingly pressurizing hotels and other contracted organizations to adopt environmental criteria, building partnerships with local or regional authorities, or selecting to operate into integrated and carefully controlled resort devel-opments. Negotiations with planners to prevent the classic cycle of decline are becoming more common and a few enterprising companies are undertaking local area- or company-wide environmental audits for the first time.

As competition intensifies in the region, which already has extensive surplus tourism capacity, the ability to offer holidays in a pollution-free environment is increasingly attractive. Fresh water supply is becoming a particularly important issue as demand outstrips supply and desertification poses a threat to Spain, Greece and Cyprus. Fresh water management is, therefore, likely to become more important, especially for tourist facilities which are conspicuous consumers. To give some indication of the relative rates of consumption, it has been estimated that a rural Mallorcan traditionally uses some 140 litres a day; a city dweller in Spain uses some 250 litres; but the average tourist uses 440 litres per day. With allowance for watering gardens, golf courses and filling swimming pools, this can rise to the equivalent of some 880 litres per day for visitors in luxury accommodation. (Boers and Bosch, 1994, p. 59). Fresh water management systems can bring immediate reductions in the volume of waste water produced and this in turn reduces the additional pollution load discharged to the sea.

Forms of partnership between large commercial companies and destination authorities of the ECOMOST type (see Chapter 15) are likely to become more common as the mutual benefits become evident, and smaller companies can be persuaded to participate in agreed programmes for environmental improvement. See also Chapter 10.

Many watching the region's development predict that the next decade will be critical for the Mediterranean region and, while tourism is responsible for only a relatively small percentage of the total pollution and development pressure, the industry has the most to lose from an environmental disaster in the Mediterranean sea. The only way the industry can protect itself from such a disaster is to act now – and act in a concerted way through effective commercial sector and public sector partnerships of the kind noted in Chapter 15.

North America

Tourism development – the current situation

This region comprises the USA and Canada whose affluent populations, like those in north Europe, provide a relatively mature market for travel and tourism. The area has an advanced market economy and offers a very wide range of tourism experiences from the great natural open wilderness areas of the Arctic circle and northern Canada, through the national parks and the cultural and sporting facilities of the big cities, to the built visitor attractions of Disneyworld and other major themed attractions in the southern States, especially Florida. North America can cater for every type of visitor activity in almost every type of tourism destination.

Throughout the 1980s domestic and inbound tourism in North America has grown, consolidating a position established in the 1950s. In 1950, 1970 and 1990 the USA was the world's top spender on international tourism, with Canada in the top seven. More interestingly, the USA was also the world's top earner from international tourism over the last forty years, with receipts from tourism expanding at a more rapid rate than arrivals. Canada and the USA between them account for nearly 80 per cent of all tourism in the Americas Region (WTO, 1993, p. 10). These figures do not include estimates for domestic tourists but the North American market is probably the largest domestic holiday market in the world so the data above are a significant underestimate of the total tourism market and receipts. Most international tourists to the region still originate from European countries, traditionally the largest market area, although Japan was the largest single country of origin in the late 1990s and the East Asia-Pacific Region is of growing importance.

Tourism is an important sector of the North American post-industrial economy, estimated to account for nearly 11 per cent of GDP and 12 per cent of all jobs (WTTC, 1995, p. 8). This contribution to employment and income in the region is predicted to increase significantly in the decade to 2005.

Pressures for change

The environmental problems associated with tourism in North America are specific to popular destinations and mostly dwarfed by pressures from agriculture, industry and urbanization. The pressures driving change vary greatly between the region and include the following.

(a) Consumer choices

Consumer pressures are similar in essence to those in Europe. Consumers are demanding ever more fulfilling and meaningful experiences from higher-quality products in the destinations they select. As travellers become more experienced, they are becoming more discerning in the products they choose and in some cases this has changed the structure of the tourism industry. It is probably American consumers more than those in any other world region who are driving the growth in the ecotourism market and the demand for 'green' consumer labels on tourism products. Time will tell how powerful the relatively small but articulate group of consumers leading these developments is in causing real change in industry attitudes and practices.

Consumers in the North American markets generally have also become used to a system of disclosure, whereby companies have to make information about their environmental practices freely available. Although tourism businesses (with the possible exception of airlines) have not yet been greatly affected by disclosure laws, the general expectation of being informed about potentially damaging activities is expected to affect their practices in the next decade or so and this could have the huge implications for the way in which the industry approaches environmental issues and insures against risks and compensation claims. Traveller safety has become a major issue in some destinations and tourist numbers have suffered in areas, such as parts of Florida, where acts of violence have had widespread publicity.

(b) National/international regulation

Environmental regulations in this region are among the most stringent in the world and were led by the creation of the Environmental Protection Agency in the USA in 1970. The proactive regulatory stance of the US government has led some companies to adopt particularly environmentally responsible practices. The directors of companies which fail to comply with some standards may find themselves personally liable for fines or imprisonment and many are not prepared to take this risk. The American states also have a sophisticated range of permit and licensing systems in place for pollution and this has set the pace for many companies, encouraging the adoption of energy- and water-saving technologies.

Visitors to some popular tourist destinations, such as national parks, are now heavily regulated and tour guides in those areas must follow strict standards and criteria or risk losing their permit to operate.

(c) Pressure from investors and insurers

More than in any other market, investors and insurers in North America are examining the record of companies prior to committing their own resources. Large liability claims against insurers and subsequent losses by investors have pushed many companies to question the environmental record of the companies with whom they do business and this may provide a growing incentive for self-regulation by travel and tourism companies over the next decade.

Some development implications for the tourist industry

In the future North America will continue to play a major role as both a generator and receiver of tourists, especially as further liberalization of the airline market reduces fares. The appeal of the North American market is likely to continue to grow and the diverse range of tourism experiences available within this continent will continue to serve the needs of a broad base of domestic and international consumers.

The combination of sophisticated consumers for tourism, concern for health and safety and a culture which promotes law suits against companies that fail to deliver quality products, is likely to keep the North American travel and tourism industry in the vanguard of positive environmental developments.

Chapter summary

The chapter provides a broad overview of the stage of tourism development and the main pressures for environmental changes influencing tourism in three regions of the world comprising mainly developed OECD member nations. Many of these countries are moving into the post-industrial era in which quality of life, meaning a combination of environment, culture, heritage and the arts as well as economic development, is increasingly identified with the development of domestic and inbound international tourism. These are also countries with the most experienced and demanding consumers of travel and tourism in the world and the affluence to indulge in their already high propensity to travel.

In Europe and North America, the leisure markets for travel and tourism are by no means saturated, but they are mature in the sense that future growth depends not so much on persuading more people to take holidays and day visits but more on increasing the frequency and variety of travel. The inevitable consequence of market maturity and growing travel frequency is congestion in popular destinations by people in their cars. This already approaches crisis proportions in parts of Europe, where the Alpine regions of Austria, France, and Italy, the national parks of the UK, and cities such as Amsterdam, Bath, Florence, and Venice are all examples. The fragile natural landscapes and settlements of many coastal areas and national parks in Europe and North America are equally under growing pressure.

The tourism industry in Europe and North America has, therefore, the strongest possible incentive to make progress towards more sustainable forms of tourism, and later chapters deal with some of the initiatives now taking place. Although there is growing awareness of environmental issues, evidenced in the number of conferences, books and guidelines, there is little evidence of real progress being made in the late 1990s despite the fact that the environmental resources upon which the tourism industry is based are deteriorating. Only a few companies, local authorities and governments have yet devised *practical* management solutions to the problems posed by pollution, congestion, crowding, and building which threaten the future of the industry (whether the impacts arise from the tourism sector or other industrial activities). We believe the challenge for the next decade lies especially with involving more companies in partnerships with local authorities to devise and implement solutions to acknowledged environmental problems.

Recommended Reading

Boniface, B.G. and Cooper, C.P., *The Geography of Travel and Tourism*, 2nd edn, Butterworth-Heinemann, Oxford, 1994.

Gajraj, A.M., 'A Regional Approach to Environmentally Sound Tourism Development', *Recreation Research*, Vol. 14(2), 1988.

MEDPLAN, *Report of the Seminar on the Development of Mediterranean Tourism Harmonized with the Environment*, MedPlan, Greece, 1988.

Travel and Tourism Analyst, Economist Intelligence Unit, London, UK.

World Tourism Organization, *Tourism Trends World-wide Series – The Americas*, Madrid, 1993.

World Tourism Organization, *Tourism Trends to the Year 2000 and Beyond*, Madrid, Spain, 1995.

4

International summary of tourism and the environment: East Asia and the Pacific; the Caribbean; Eastern Europe and states of the former USSR, and rest of the world

Tourists will be courted by developed and Third World countries alike for the enormous infusion of capital that comes with tourism ... Tourism is the force that will make the global village truly one world (Naisbitt, 1994, p. 141).

This chapter reviews some of the key issues facing travel and tourism in three regions of the world in which tourism has been growing very rapidly in the last decade and is predicted to grow most strongly into the twenty-first century. In 1960 the WTO estimated that East Asia and the Pacific region had just a one per cent share of world international tourism arrivals. Thanks to an average annual growth rate of no less than 15 per cent between 1960 and 1993,

the same region had a share of around 15 per cent by the mid-1990s which is predicted to grow to around 23 per cent by 2010 (see Tables 5.1 and 5.3 in the next chapter).

East Asia and the Pacific is in many ways the most interesting world region. It is interesting because of population size and the diversity of its economic base; the range of its players, from the already highly developed Japan, Singapore and Hong Kong through Australia and New Zealand to the northern regions of China; and the breathtaking speed and scope of its recent economic performance and growth potential. For the next five years at least, travel and tourism domestically and intra-regionally appears likely to borrow heavily from Western models and in all the countries reviewed in this chapter there is clear evidence of heavy investment by Western airlines, hotel groups, car rental operators, and so on. Once again the global nature of the tourism industry is confirmed.

From the environmental perspective there is a particularly important contrast to draw with North America and Europe. With the obvious exception of Australia and New Zealand there is generally no established tradition in most parts of the Pacific Rim, Caribbean, or Eastern Europe for destination management influences and controls of the type developed over a century and practised, for example, in the UK and USA or in Germany or France. Local government is far from perfect in any country, of course, but we believe the world's best hope for securing sustainability in travel and tourism lies not so much with the national authorities but with the cŏmpetence and authority vested in local government responsible for specific tourism destinations, working in partnership with private sector businesses. There has to be concern for massive uncontrolled growth in tourism in the context of relatively weak local governments at destinations.

With the exceptions already noted, most of the countries ranged over in this chapter are not among the leading OECD economies. On current evidence, many of them are very vulnerable to exactly the same mistakes in tourism development as those committed in Europe and North America since the 1960s – and many lack the established tradition of local democratic safeguards to control the worst excesses. Simon Jenkins, for example, claims that 'most of Asia is fast becoming a historical desert. From Bangkok to Singapore, from Hong Kong to Tokyo [central] governments have permitted the despoliation of their past' (*The Times*, 23 December 1995). This may be an exaggeration, but it expresses bluntly a widely held view about the failure in many developing countries to provide the infrastructure and local government systems on which much progress towards more sustainable development for tourism depends.

As in Chapter 3, this overview looks at the stage of tourism development, the regional pressures for environmental change, and some implications for the sustainable development of travel and tourism.

East Asia and the Pacific

Tourism development – the current situation

This region includes the Pacific Rim countries, Melonesia, Micronesia and Polynesia, and Australia and New Zealand. As an area it has exhibited the strongest recorded growth in tourist arrivals and income in the world over the last decade or so. International tourist arrivals more than doubled between 1980 and 1992 from 21 to 58 million, a growth rate more than double the world average (WTO, *Regional Analysis, East Asia and Pacific*, 1994, p. 12). Growth is primarily a direct result of the remarkable pace of economic development in the region, but also reflects intensive and successful marketing activities by national tourism administrations; the lifting of barriers to travel in, for example, China; the rapid growth in disposable incomes in the newly industrializing economies; and rapid growth and modernization of tourism transport and accommodation facilitated by massive inputs of private capital investment.

Tourism development in the region is driven both by the rapid rate of economic growth generating intra-regional travel, and by the growth in long-haul travel. Tables 5.2 and 5.3 (Chapter 5) show the region has grown much faster and thus gained world market share from the more mature European market. As a newly developing destination, it has much to offer to both business and leisure travellers. Some destinations in the area, such as Thailand, Indonesia and Malaysia, trade on their exotic image, their cultural diversity and their 'unspoilt' beaches. Others such as Australia and New Zealand have found themselves well placed to profit from the growth in interest for adventure, eco, activity or 'sun-plus' tourism. For North American and European visitors, the East Asia/Pacific image promises an enticing combination of oriental mystery, culture, environmental attractions and winter sun, which clearly has great appeal.

Many destinations in the region have the advantage of building new accommodation and resorts, and a major opportunity to avoid the often tarnished image of some of the more traditional Mediterranean or Hawaii-style destinations, learning from their mistakes. It has to be acknowledged, of course, that the developed tourism markets of Australia also have the more 'traditional' resort areas of Bondi Beach and the Gold Coast, and many would argue that Phuket in Thailand displays some of the traditional mistakes of Mediterranean tourism destinations. Yet over the last decade or so many of the Pacific/Asia countries have developed promotional materials focusing on the culture and environment of the region, and increasingly they make reference to sustainable development in their tourism development and management plans. As they look to future growth, many of these countries are further along the road to sustainable development than most of north Europe and there are lessons for Europe in this region. Australia, for example, has evolved a comprehensive sustainable development strategy, examining the implications of each of its eleven key industrial sectors, of which tourism is one; New Zealand has one of the best respected tourism management regimes; Thailand's Hotel Association recently (1995) acknowledged the importance of environmental issues for long-run development; the Philippines government has played a major role in the establishment of pilot projects which seek to use sustainable tourism as a tool to protect the considerable coral reef resources of that country; and Malaysia published a comprehensive national ecotourism strategy in 1995. These are just some of the recent initiatives and many more are in the pipeline.

Some mistakes have inevitably been made in the region and the high-profile promises of the environment in publicity materials are often not delivered in practice, which may prove costly in terms of repeat tourism business. Environmental degradation in Phuket in Thailand, child prostitution for tourism in the Philippines, and environmental degradation along the Gold Coast of Australia have all received some criticism, but this is mostly not yet on the scale applied to tourism developments in other regions of the world. As a whole, the region has so far been remarkably successful at marketing itself, largely on culture and environmental credentials. Only time will tell whether current marketing initiatives are coupled with adequate safeguards to protect the resource upon which success so clearly depends, as the number of travellers to the area grows and urban development pressures increase the need for adequate infrastructure provision. In particular, the traffic congestion of many East Asian cities and the poor state of sanitation, drainage, public transport and other city infrastructure will be a major deterrent to continuing tourism growth.

Many countries in this region have huge tourism potential, They must, however, resolve many of their infrastructure problems to develop this potential and sustain the environmental quality on which it is firmly based:

- Indonesia, for example, already has a problem with water quality; over half of Java's rivers are polluted; less than one per cent of the urban population has access to sewage treatment facilities.
- Taiwan has some of the worst pollution in the region.
- Thailand has a growing municipal waste problem and some 20 000 factories registered as water polluters.
- Delhi, Calcutta, and Bombay in India have some of the world's highest levels of suspended particulates and 70 per cent of the water supply is already polluted; industrial pollution is seriously eroding the Taj Mahal and other monuments.

All of these problems could compromise the future scale and nature of tourism development attracted to these regions.

Source: Tomorrow Magazine, Vol. 5, No. 3, 1995

The pressure for change

The pressures for maintaining high environmental standards in the region include the following:

(a) Consumer choices

Consumers from within and outside the region are a powerful force, especially when combined with the strong environmental and cultural focus of much of the tourism marketing of the area. Almost without exception these countries are targeting high-profile and high-expenditure business and leisure travel segments, and incentive travel. High expenditure in tourism is invariably accompanied by high environmental quality expectations, and the region's aspirations can only be met through a commitment to such quality, underpinned by adequate measures for protection.

In countries such as Australia and New Zealand, there is already a strong and growing environmental movement among the resident population and many of the developing island states of the Pacific also have a strong environmental commitment (not least because any increase in sea level resulting from global warming could threaten their continuing viability as states).

(b) Pressure from resident populations

Some of the populations in these areas are perhaps among the more environmentally aware, with strong traditional cultural links to the earth and sea. While in some areas the need for income and employment has provided tourism companies with strong arguments for development, others have found development in the region less easy to secure. Rigorous planning procedures are now undertaken by many companies who, in response to the demand from international consumers for traditional and exotic experiences, and demand from governments for sustainable products, develop facilities which blend into their chosen locations areas and cause minimal disturbance. Companies which fail to take account of consumer pressures have come unstuck even in the early stages of proposals.

(c) National and international regulation

Certainly in Australia, New Zealand and Japan, the regulatory authorities have taken a strong stance on environmental performance and are making growing use of the mechanisms of the market to ensure compliance. In these countries at least, there appears to be both the political will and financial resources to improve environmental performance rapidly. Many of the regulations in these countries flow from precedents established in the USA and it may give tourism businesses a market advantage if they are familiar with the US approach to environmental issues.

The regulatory framework in Taiwan, Hong Kong, Singapore and South Korea is also developing rapidly. Early indications are that these governments have the financial wherewithal to back up environmental regulations, making entry to the market easier for companies who take initiatives to tackle pollution and resource over-use. Many regulations, however, have been developed for large manufacturing and extractive industries and may miss the problems caused by urban populations and tourism at particular destinations. While protecting the natural and built resources on which tourism depends, many of these regulations have only limited direct implications for tourism businesses.

New Zealand has taken an innovative approach to managing the impacts of the tourism industry by using the mechanisms of the marketplace to provide incentives to tourism companies to protect environmental resources. In national parks and related areas, price differentials have been introduced for hiking tracks. As well as reflecting the different standards of huts and facilities, these encourage a better regional dispersal of visitors by the higher pricing of popular tracks and a better seasonal spread of visitors by heavy discounting of fees during low season.

Source: WTTERC, 1995, p. 3

Air pollution and water pollution control are key issues for regulatory authorities in many countries, alongside conservation of water resources. Desertification and increased levels of algal growth threaten future tourism developments in some areas, while in others, such as the Philippines and Thailand, tourism is seen as one of the few viable alternatives to destructive fishing practices, thus offering the means for securing reef preservation.

Following the lead of Japan, it seems that many of the countries in the region may tackle environmental pollution by expressing a willingness to build partnerships with industry. Local companies that want to benefit will need to seek out local partners which have innovative products and appropriate environmental safeguards. See also Chapter 10.

(d) Initiatives by the travel and tourism industry

In this region the industry itself has also made some progress in environmental protection, especially within the ecotourism sector. A desire to ensure business success has inspired some companies to develop their own stringent standards for environmental performance. This is especially true for some of the large international companies which have developed in the region. The Taj Hotel Group have implemented a number of measures within their hotel chains to conserve water resources and others, such as Mandarin Oriental have joined the Green Globe environmental management initiative. Some of these groups are directly protecting the environment by developing integrated resorts, thus guaranteeing environmental control. The typical exclusion of local people from such resorts in the area, however, may result in conflict and ultimately make partnerships a more appropriate way to guarantee product quality.

Some development implications for the tourist industry

The outlook for tourism growth in the region is currently good and the number of international arrivals alone is projected by WTO to more than triple between the early 1990s and 2010. Even with this level of growth. the region still has sufficient development space to fulfil the requirements of its resident populations and industry developments. The predicted large population growth within the region, combined with rapid growth in income levels, means that domestic and intra-regional travel will also continue to grow and this will more than compensate for any levelling off in the number of long-haul travellers from North European and American markets as they reach their ceiling growth levels.

Travel and tourism companies in the area are particularly well placed to benefit from both the small but growing ecotourism market and the 'sun-plus' market, and many marketing initiatives already target these market niches. In developing these products, the region will need to influence marketing decisions to ensure that rapid growth prospects and the promise of economic gains do not overtake development planning and tourism strategies within the region. Future success is geared to the quality of the environment and culture at favoured destinations and this means implementing planning mechanisms, raising awareness within all industry sectors, ensuring that infrastructure is put in place prior to development and stemming the tide of integrated resort developments which exclude local people. Only time will tell how well the region will live up to the promises made in the many sustainable development strategies which it has produced. In the mid-1990s it appears likely that Pacific Rim countries will provide models of destination tourism management over the next decade, from which Europeans and North Americans can learn.

The wider Caribbean region

Tourism development – the current situation

There are three main parts of the wider Caribbean region; the islands (including Cuba and the Bahamas but not Bermuda); the mainland of

Central America including Costa Rica, Belize and Nicaragua; and the north coast of Venezuela. The region, with its powerful natural advantages and good access to the North American market, has a long and diverse history of tourism development. It includes seven of the sixty most-visited destinations in the world as well as fifteen out of the top twenty most-visited destinations in the Americas as a whole. The area receives just under 3 per cent of international tourism and just under 4 per cent of its receipts (Hawkins, 1995). Tourism is essential to the economy of the region accounting for 24 per cent of the region's GDP and generating one in six jobs (WTTC, 1995).

The policies developed by the governments of the region towards tourism are diverse, resulting in a rich patchwork of different types of tourism development. Regional products range from cruise tourism around the island states, dive tourism, sailing, adventure tourism, ecotourism on the mainland (especially Costa Rica and Belize), incentive tourism, all inclusive resort tourism, and the more traditional so-called mass market packages that are also common to the Mediterranean region.

International tourism in the region is dominated by the North American market which accounts for over 90 per cent of all visitors to Mexico and 80 per cent of visitors to the Central American Common Market countries (WTO, 1994). The relative plateau in the region's tourism fortunes in the early 1990s was linked by some commentators to the relatively slow rate of recovery in the US economy. In addition, political problems, for example in Dominica, did little to enhance the image of some parts of the region, potentially further damaging market share.

Despite the wide range of products available across the region, the superficially similar characteristics of these products have sometimes led to competition between destinations for visitors, resulting in promotion based on low prices and high volumes, rather than level of receipt per tourist. A reduction in air fares brought about an upturn in the region's tourism fortunes in the mid-1990s and there is some evidence that the region is gaining a share of European markets disenchanted with the quality of the environment and products available in the Mediterranean, and switching to long-haul destinations.

Pressures for change

The pressures for change within the Caribbean result from growing recognition of cultural, environmental, and economic dependency on tourism. The pressures are perhaps lower than in other tourist-dominant economies and are often driven more by a negative fear of losing market share than a positive desire to reduce the impact of tourism and enhance its environmental contribution. Pressures include the following.

(a) Consumer choices

Consumer pressures are similar to those experienced in Europe and North America. Consumers are demanding ever more fulfilling and meaningful experiences from the destinations that they select. As travellers become more experienced, they are becoming more discerning in the environmental quality of the products they choose and in some cases this has changed the structure of the tourism industry. Certain destinations in the Caribbean, for example, are losing market share as they are unable to provide the product quality or diversity that is required by the changing market.

The Latin American and Caribbean markets are both heavily dependent on North American markets for their tourist trade. The sensitivity of North Americans to potential environmental risk, especially if there are negative health implications, makes the area very vulnerable to environmental issues. One of the major concerns for the wider Caribbean is sea pollution, and there is great concern about an accident with one of the numerous tankers carrying effluent or toxic substances in the busy waters close to the islands.

(b) National and international regulation

Some Caribbean states have adopted stringent regulations but competition between the states for tourism trade has made enforcement in some areas difficult. Areas which could become the focus of stricter regulations include the cruise-ship sector, waste water disposal, land-use planning and management, and especially for some island states, waste disposal.

Some of the island Caribbean states have taken measures to reduce the day-visit impact of cruise shipping, which is often perceived as providing only limited economic benefits and adding to visitor management problems. The Cayman Islands took steps to impose heavy fines for cruise ships which fail to comply with regulations at the potential cost of loosing the cruise trade to neighbouring islands.

(c) Increased competition

For many Caribbean states, increased competition from other destinations is driving changes. The sun, sea, sand product offers in exotic tropical climate and scenery no longer have the same appeal in the light of the rapidly developing Asia-Pacific destinations. The islands in particular are, therefore seeking a new marketing profile and the environment, culture, and niche markets are particularly important in this respect. For the mainland Caribbean countries, such niches are proving relatively easy to exploit in the initial stages as visitor interest develops in their vast resources of nature, heritage and culture. New products, such as La Ruta Maya, are already proving popular and are practically unrivalled.

(d) Resource shortages

For the Caribbean, resource shortages will inevitably lead to a change in operating practices by travel and tourism companies. One of the pressing issues for the region is the shortage of fresh water which is essential to the continuation of the tourism industry. Fuels to generate power and cars are mostly imported; agricultural products are imported from far away; and destructive practices coupled with poorly enforced regulations have damaged reefs and other natural tourist attractions. Governments are acutely aware of these issues and the fact that they will limit the level of tourism development which the islands can ultimately sustain. Management decisions taken in the next five years to conserve resources and control their use for long-run benefit will determine the future prosperity for many of the area's island economies.

In April 1997 the Caribbean Hotel Association and the Caribbean Tourism Organization (CTO) held their first international hotel and tourism investment conference in which environmental criteria for tourism investment were a key issue. The CTO has been influential in promoting environmental sustainability among its member states and a current EU-funded tourism development initiative in the region also has a strong environmental focus.

Some development implications for the tourist industry

With its obvious geographical advantages, the Caribbean will continue to be a major tourism destination. The level of income that is generated by tourism and the economic fortunes of the region will be largely determined by the ability to improve and sustain the environment of destinations, and differentiate the products on offer for the client-base away from pure sun, sea and sand holidays. To some extent, the success of the Caribbean region will also depend on developments and the price of tourism products in the Mediterranean Basin as well as the ease of access to European markets through the major gateway ports of Miami and Dallas. The mainland states are likely to continue to prosper, but there are already some signs that the national parks of Costa Rica are becoming degraded and protection will be essential to long-term success.

Protection of the Caribbean sea is vital to the

whole region and this will require concerted action by all states. As for the Mediterranean, the evidence to date illustrates that such cooperation will be difficult to secure. Other issues which will require action in the near future include land-use planning, the operation and environmental practices of the cruise ships, the heavy dependence on the North American market, and waste water management.

Eastern Europe, Russian Federation and the CIS

Tourism development – the current situation

This huge region consists of the Russian Federation and the other eleven republics in the Commonwealth of Independent States (CIS), three Baltic states, five former satellite states in Eastern Europe and the former Yugoslavia. All were part of the former Soviet Union until the political changes commenced in 1989. During the great growth phase of West European tourism, the Eastern European and Soviet travel markets developed almost in isolation from the rest of the world's travel and tourism industry. Travel restrictions and visa requirements imposed by the former USSR until 1989 meant that, with the important exception of isolated pockets such as the former Yugoslavia, the industry was centrally planned and regulated and developed as an isolated social and pleasure periphery mostly dependent on domestic tourism and the other states of the region to provide clients. The nature of the Communist regimes meant that this client-base was effectively guaranteed and, for most of the tourism industry (with the notable exception of Yugoslavia), competition with other countries and with the outside world was unnecessary. The international companies which played such a major role in shaping travel and tourism in the Western world were almost completely absent from Eastern Europe until the end of the 1980s and from Russia until the mid-1990s. This has resulted in very different tourism products from those in Western Europe. The centralized nature

of the planning and management regime in many of these states combined with lack of market competition, meant that the normal rules of demand and supply did not apply. The result was a very structured industry, especially in coastal zones and rural areas, largely dependent on purpose-built resorts and hotels of a quality inferior to that in other parts of the world.

With the collapse of traditional Communist regimes and the lifting of travel restrictions on residents of the region from the end of the 1980s (1991 for Russia) the established tourism industry structures and its social orientation were no longer relevant to current conditions. These changes faced the industry with major challenges as the level of outbound tourism generally has risen at a far faster rate than inbound tourism, especially in the Russian Federation. The statistics of tourism are notoriously unreliable throughout the region and present a huge problem for decision makers concerned with restructuring. The new freedom to travel has been responsible for much of the growth in outbound tourism, while low incomes, combined with environmental problems and civil unrest, have deterred both inbound and domestic tourism in large parts of this region.

The region is one of immense contrast in cultures, environments, and levels of development. It has some of the most pristine environments in the world which offer huge potential for tourism development – the Polar regions, the mountain zones, the tundra lands, the coastal zones, and the massive architectural and cultural treasures of the main cities such as those in the Russian Federation, the Czech Republic, Poland and Hungary, etc. The region also carries some of the deepest pollution scars ever wrought by industrial development on the landscape in the developed world. Among the more notable problems are nuclear fallout; massive air pollution; acid rain; contamination of millions of acres of land from inadequate waste disposal; large-scale pollution of most major rivers by chemical and toxic effluents and nuclear waste; and pollution of the enclosed Black Sea. The drying up of the Aral Sea is a particularly powerful demonstration of the effects of careless industrialization carried out in some of the most tightly State-regulated societies in history. Those who believe that state regulation is the primary requirement for sustainable development should visit some of the industrial wastelands behind the former Iron Curtain.

Travel and tourism has become a logical focus for economic development in some countries in Eastern Europe and parts of the CIS states as they seek to generate hard currency, sustain populations in the remaining pristine environments, provide an incentive to fund part of the clean-up of pollution resulting from industrialization, and fund urban renewal and regeneration. The Bulgarian government, for example, is focusing on tourism as a major potential development option; Rumania is examining the potential for tourism to provide the incentive to clean up the pollution of the Danube Delta; WTTC have recently undertaken a study of tourism potential in Hungary; and a study of tourism development in Kyrgyz Republic has recently been completed. Through its PHARE and other development programmes, the European Union is directing significant aid funding to the states having borders with EU countries and to the Russian Federation. This aid will only be effective, however, if the newly emerging private sector can be encouraged to change its traditional attitudes to business rapidly enough and to invest the resources required in the area.

Pressures for change

This region divides fairly naturally into the states bordering Germany, Austria and the Baltic; the Russian Federation; and the republics now linked in the CIS formed in 1989. The first group have deeply rooted cultural and political traditions associated more with the Germanic and Austro-Hungarian spheres of interest and trading partnerships, of which they were historically a part. To these countries, the development of heritage and cultural tourism of a style that appeals to West European markets comes naturally. They are catching up on lost time. Russia and the CIS republics, especially the Muslim states of the south, have very different traditions and little experience of a market economy for travel and tourism. While the intention to participate in international tourism is already evident, the development process is likely to take much longer than for the East European countries and the Baltic group of former USSR states.

(a) Pressures from the international community

The primary generator of change in the area of the environment is the international community. Condemnation of pollution and fear of future incidents, the apparent willingness of the international community to fund projects which have an environmental element, and the desire of many former USSR states to join the EU which has a stringent policy stance on the environment have all brought environmental initiatives higher up the political agenda. Tourism is also seen by most of the former satellite states at least, as a means of integration with the international community. For most countries, however, the environment is still a low priority, way below the overriding need to earn foreign currency, generate income and alleviate unemployment. For some the environment has become an effective bargaining tool with funding agencies.

There can be little doubt that the clean-up costs which governments must face are huge – the Ukraine alone 'guesstimates' that it spends 20 per cent of its GDP on environmental clean-up projects (*Tomorrow Magazine*, Vol. 4, No. 4). The international community has yet to grapple with the true enormity of the task ahead and the need to provide technical support as well as funding. The current policy of many donor governments favours the establishment of environmental criteria for new projects rather than tackling the costs of rectifying past mistakes. Some of the donor programmes have been particularly effective and very innovative (for example, the World Bank's *Debt for Green* Investment programme). Sooner or later, however, someone will have to pay for past mistakes, and the way in which this is done will shape tourism development in the region (making it a possible harbinger of positive improvement or another casualty of pollution).

(b) National and international regulation

Governments involved in funding and political aid in the region are demanding change and a shift to compliance with existing international agreements on the environment, both from individuals and business corporations. Ironically, for a region which is a relative newcomer to the market economy, although no stranger to the enforcing of government regulations, some countries have already made significant strides in implementing taxes (primarily for SO_x and car emissions) on polluters. Poland is estimated to lead the world in this respect (*Tomorrow Magazine*, Vol. 4, No. 4).

While taxation is proving an effective tool, other governments are experimenting with permits, and regulation. Environmental monitoring for all sectors is, however, proving a complex, expensive and ineffective task, especially when dealing with nations that have treated the environment as a free resource and waste ground for the last fifty years or more.

(c) Pressure from resident populations

The environmental movement in the region is in its infancy and environmental issues are a long way down the priority list for most voters. Slowly, however, pressure for change is growing from the resident communities affected by pollution. This is evidenced by the increase in the number of environmental pressure groups which have become active in the region, usually in response to threats to human health.

As the populations in these regions have democratic voting rights, many of them for the first time, it is likely that environmental improvement will move up the political agenda in the worst-affected areas. This will not come about from a deep-seated commitment to environmental improvement but from a desire to protect the next generation from the evident health effects of air pollution, nuclear fallout, excessive use of pesticides and fertilizer, toxic poisoning from industrial processes and so on.

(d) Pressure from investors

Most countries in the region are desperate to attract foreign investment to provide income for the rapid transition in their economies. Many areas have focused on tourism as one sector which can rapidly provide investment and employment opportunities. For some countries, tourism is also the focus of drives to improve environmental quality, and for them improvement is essential because tourism is by its very nature environmentally sensitive.

Driven by developments in the USA, insurers are increasingly conscious of the cost liabilities and financial penalties associated with environmental damage and its effect on health. High-risk assessments resulting from environmental damage will render companies unable to invest in certain countries unless environmental standards are established and upheld. In the scramble for development, the demands of external investors for better environmental control may have more force than any of the other pressures for change identified within this section.

For countries with rich and well-protected natural or cultural resources, such as Bulgaria, Slovakia, the Czech Republic, Poland, Slovenia and the Ukraine, the foundations and infrastructure of a modern tourism industry are already in place. The challenge in these countries is to assess the extent and rate of progress with which the industry shifts to operate in more sustainable ways or simply utilizes the resources and funding available for short-run profit.

Some development implications for the tourist industry

With the exception of the internationally known heritage cities and towns, some rural locations, and beach resorts, international tourism has been relatively slow to move into Eastern Europe and the CIS, despite the very favourable conditions offered by many host governments. Where tourism has developed it has often done so at a rapid pace and with few checks on growth. Some commentators, for example, already describe cities such as Prague as over-commercialized and loosing character and charm. Management responses will need to be speedy to ensure that damage to such natural and heritage attractions does not compromise future tourism growth prospects.

The scramble by governments to exploit the region's remaining forest and mineral reserves in inaccessible environments for much-needed hard currency threatens further degradation of the resource base and the potential for tourism development. The Siberian forest, the oils and minerals of the desert, tundra and wilderness areas are all threatened by rapid industrial or agricultural exploitation with few environmental controls which are actively enforced.

Uncertainties over environmental protection, the current state of development of domestic tourism markets (although with a rise in incomes these markets have huge growth potential), and a combination of bureaucracy which still characterizes the government of many of these countries with the lack of enforcement of environmental regulation are doing little to encourage mainstream tourism investors in the short term. The important exceptions of heritage city tourism and niche markets are noted above. This is especially true in the face of competition for international tourism from the growth destinations of East Asia and the Pacific, which can offer a guaranteed climate, unique culture, 'exotic' image, relatively unpolluted environment, high product quality, market orientation ingrained into the culture, and welcoming attitudes to the industry.

The rest of the world

Consisting of the relatively small international tourism markets of the African continent, South America, South Asia, and the Middle East, the rest of the world is still relatively underdeveloped in tourism terms accounting for less than 6 per cent of all international tourist arrivals in the mid-1990s. While some continents such as South America and parts of Africa are sometimes said to be the sleeping giants of the tourism world, a combination of underdevelopment, political instability, crime, and poverty hold back their overall tourism development prospects for the foreseeable future. In other countries, religious fundamentalism, as in some countries in the Middle East, sometimes portrays modern tourism as one of the worst excesses of the Western world, definitely not to be encouraged.

As always when dealing with such vast areas, there are exceptions. Notable ones are South Africa, Botswana, Kenya, Tanzania and Jordan, all of them developing their appeal to specific international market segments and marketing various forms of ecotourism based on their natural resources. The Kruger National Park is an interesting example of good international practice included in Part Four of this book. Other countries such as Namibia and Zimbabwe are also targeting international tourism growth. The Serena Hotel Chain in Tanzania, owned and operated by the Aga Khan Fund for Economic Development, operates to environmental standards which are among the world's best. Four new hotels in the chain underwent no less than four separate Environmental Impact Assessments in obtaining permission to build in sensitive areas such as the Serengeti Park World Heritage Site.

Most countries in these regions are economically underdeveloped and currently lack the level of infrastructure development and the economic growth from which domestic tourism can develop to support their growth opportunities in international markets. In the longer term, large parts of these regions have vast environmental assets and great tourism development potential from a resource standpoint. They mostly also have large and growing population problems and are unlikely to play a major role in world tourism development for the foreseeable future.

Chapter summary

This chapter looks at the stage of tourism development and the main pressures for environmental change in regions of the world comprising a mix of developed and developing countries. The latter, being the majority, are politically dominated by the need for foreign currency, foreign investment, and employment opportunities in internationally competitive industries. Hong Kong, Japan, Australia, New Zealand, and Singapore do not fall into this category, of course, nor do some of the East European countries, and they provide role models for their developing neighbours, not least in their progress in environmental matters. Heritage, exotic culture, de-luxe hotels, ancient cities and pristine beaches dominate the region's holiday tourism offering. For most of them the priority for the next two decades will be international rather than domestic tourism, and the quality expectations of international visitors will tend to set the environmental standard to be provided.

Economic growth, rapid by OECD country standards, is achievable by many of the developing countries in the regions covered in this chapter although the down-side of this is the short cuts that tend to be taken in environmental matters. The duration and density of air pollution in parts of Asia provoked by extensive forest fires in Indonesia in 1997, demonstrates the risks. Market maturity is not generally an issue and ceilings to the growth of the tourism industry are significantly higher than in the more mature Western markets. The major threat to many of these destinations is degradation and pollution of the resource base – cultural and environmental. For the most part, tourism growth in the successful areas is being driven by strongly rising demand, especially from distant mature tourism markets, and it tends to be heavily influenced by the decisions of companies and consumers in the markets of origin where customer decisions are made.

In Chapter 3 we concluded that in mature tourism markets, where most international companies are based, corporate business attitudes and interests can be influenced and they must be the main agents of change. In this chapter, the challenge for the next decade lies especially with national and local governments which have to decide the type and value of tourism that they wish to develop. Australia and New Zealand in particular in the mid-1990s are making significant progress in this direction.

Further reading

Boniface, B.G. and Cooper, C.P., *The Geography of Travel and Tourism*, 2nd edn, Butterworth-Heinemann, Oxford, 1994.

WTO, *Tourism Trends World-wide Series*, Madrid, 1994.

WTO, *Travel and Tourism Forecasts to the Year 2000 and Beyond*, Madrid, 1994.

WTTERC, *Environment and Development*, No. 4, 1995.

WTTC, *Travel and Tourism in the Caribbean*, Brussels, 1995.

5

Travel and tourism: the world's largest industry

Tourism comprises the activities of persons travelling to and staying in places outside their usual environment for not more than one consecutive year for leisure, business and other purposes (WTO, 1993).

Developing from the introduction in Chapter 1, this chapter defines the terms *tourism* and *travel & tourism* drawing on internationally ratified agreements and practice going back at least a quarter of a century. Without a common understanding of what it comprises, we stress that no sense can be made of the world's 'largest industry' and there can be no progress in sustainable development.

Regrettably, what is clear beyond doubt on the basis of internationally accepted definitions and practice continues to be muddied endlessly in practice as journalists, politicians, and many academics new to the subject unthinkingly adopt whatever definitions suit their particular points of view. This is probably no more than a reflection of the comparative newness of the concepts of tourism, but it is surely remarkable that it should take more than fifty years to reach agreement even on the basic characteristics of the *world's largest industry*. Lack of agreement seriously inhibits the understanding of tourism in most parts of the world and impedes the development of sustainable strategies. There is a particularly widespread misconception that tourism is primarily about travel for holiday or vacation purposes, the so-called 'pleasure periphery.' When even a reputable international journal such as *The Economist*, with its frequent and perceptive analyses of different aspects of the travel industry, subtitles a major survey of world tourism 'The pleasure principle' (*The Economist*, March 1991), and informs its readers that 'travel for pleasure ... is otherwise known as tourism', the industry should be seriously concerned.

This chapter provides the international standard definition of tourism and outlines the main dimensions of demand and supply. From a demand perspective it identifies the wide range of purposes of travel within the definition and introduces the two main guiding principles for any approach to sustainability. The first is the identification of market segments and their differential impact on the environment at any given destination; the second is the design of visitor management techniques tailored to the characteristics of the identified segments. From a supply-side perspective the chapter introduces the main sectors in the tourism industry, noting the particular significance of small businesses for achieving sustainability. Chapter 6 deals with holiday tourism in more detail.

A working definition of travel and tourism

There is often confusion about what, if any, are the differences between the words *travel* and *tourism* used separately, and *travel & tourism* used as a combined term. *Travel industry, travel trade, tourism industry* and sometimes *hospitality industry* are other terms, often used to mean the same thing. We wish to stress that the agreed international definition of tourism (see the quote that introduces this chapter) covers all relevant aspects of travel and hospitality. Ratified by the UN Statistical Commission, the definition reflects a global process of consultation culminating in the Ottawa Conference on travel and tourism statistics in 1991. Since then the WTO, in collaboration with the European Commission (EC) and other organizations, has been working to develop an agreed framework for measurement. The EC, for example, produced its first draft Council Recommendations on Community Methodology for tourism statistics in 1996.

Among academics it may be true to state that 'there is still no agreement over definitions of tourism or just what comprises the tourism industry ...' (Cooper *et al.*, 1993, p. 2). But for all those working or aspiring to work in the industry, the international definition of tourism quoted at the head of this chapter is now the official rock on which all interpretations should be examined. For practitioners *travel & tourism* tends to be the term used most often by managers, especially in North America, because it is comprehensive and widely understood. Travel is not synonymous with tourism, however, because it includes commuter and other forms of travel outside the agreed definition. Nevertheless both *tourism* and *travel & tourism* are terms used to describe the same market and industry and they are used interchangeably in practice and throughout this book. It is significant that the WTTC always uses the *&* as a formal acknowledgement of the links underlying the globally agreed definition. Where for the sake of convenience in this book, the term 'tourism' is used alone, it also means travel and tourism, and vice versa; students should be aware that no conceptual difference is implied between the two expressions. We avoid the term *travel industry* because it is associated primarily with tour operation and retail travel distribution, and these are important but minor parts of the total market for travel and tourism.

The WTO definition pulls together the three fundamentals that:

- Visitor activity is concerned only with aspects of life outside normal routines of work, education, subsistence and social commitments, and outside the location of those routines for periods of less than a year.
- All visits necessitate travel and, in nearly every case, some form of transport to a destination.
- Destinations (places) are the focus for a range of activities, and a range of facilities required to support such activities.

Readers should note that the WTO definition is based on demand rather than supply, and in practice demand for tourism is easier to measure than supply. Understanding demand underlies all forms of consumer marketing, of course, and provides a logical link between the definition and a marketing perspective. Six important points related to demand are:

1 There is nothing that restricts tourism demand to overnight stays; it includes day visits.
2 There is nothing that restricts tourism demand to travel for leisure or pleasure; it includes travel for business, social, religious, watching and playing sports, and most other purposes, provided always that the destination of travel is outside the usual routines and place of residence or work.
3 All tourism includes an element of travel but all travel is not tourism. The definition excludes routine commuter and educational travel and purely local travel, such as to neighbourhood shops, schools or hospitals.
4 Much of travel and tourism takes place in leisure time and gives expression to many recreational activities, but it is not synonymous with either of them because the bulk of all leisure and recreation takes place in or around the home.

5 All travel and tourism is temporary move-ment; conceptually up to twelve months, but in practice nine tenths of the total market comprises visits of between a few hours to around 14 nights' duration.

6 All visitors go somewhere to do something. Tourism management issues generally, and sustainability in particular, always focus on specific activities at particular places.

An overview of travel and tourism demand

For the purposes of this book it is useful to follow the basic tourism classification system adopted in nearly all countries where measure-ment exists. This system is discussed in detail in most introductory texts; see, for example, Bur-kart and Medlik (1981, p. 14), Cooper *et al.* (1993, Part 1) and *Dictionary of Travel, Tourism and Hospitality* (Medlik, 1996). It is based on the three categories of visitor demand that any country is concerned with:

- International visitors, travelling to a country, who are residents of other countries (inbound tourism).
- Residents of a country, travelling internation-ally as visitors to other countries (outbound tourism).
- Residents visiting destinations within their own country's boundaries (domestic tourism).
- Within the three categories of visitor demand, the following key terms were adopted by the WTO following the conference in Ottawa in 1991.
- *Visitors*, to describe all travellers who fall within agreed definitions of tourism (day and stay).
- *Tourists* or staying visitors, to describe visitors who stay overnight at a destination.
- *Same-day visitors* (formerly excursionists), to describe visitors who arrive at a destination and depart on the same day. These are mostly people who leave home and return

there but may include tourists who make day visits to destinations away from the places where they are staying overnight. They may be domestic or international visitors.

As outlined above, these three terms are easy to understand. In practice the technicalities of achieving statistical precision in measuring visit-ors are extremely complex. Although various international guidelines now exist, and there are continuing efforts by the WTO and the EC, for example, no uniformity yet exists in the methods for measurement used around the world. Lack of adequate information, especially at destinations, seriously undermines progress toward sustainability in travel and tourism and this issue is developed later.

International tourism

International tourists are visitors who travel to and stay overnight in countries other than their country of residence for less than 1 year. They are usually treated as the most important market sector of tourism because, compared with domestic tourists, they typically spend more, stay longer at the destination, use more expen-sive transport and accommodation, and bring in foreign currency which is often vital for the economies of developing countries.

Around the world, measured as arrivals or visits, the number of international tourists and their expenditure has grown strongly since the 1950s from an estimated 25 million arrivals in 1950 to over 500 million in the late 1990s. This growth has been achieved notwithstanding tem-porary fluctuations caused by the international energy and economic crisis of the early 1970s, 1980s, and 1990s. The overall growth pattern is revealed in Tables 5.1–5.3. For the purpose of this chapter, it is sufficient to note the recent growth and current dimensions of the international market, and to be aware of consistently confi-dent projections in the early 1990s that inter-national tourism will continue to grow well into the twenty-first century. Although annual fluc-

Table 5.1 *Recorded and projected growth in worldwide international tourist arrivals, 1950–2010*

Years	International arrivals (millions)	Index of growth for each decade
1950	25.3	–
1960	69.3	274
1970	165.8	239
1980	286.3	173
1990	459.2	160
2000 (e)	661.0	144
2010 (e)	937.0	141

Notes
These are arrivals as supplied over the years to WTO (and projected); although they may be treated as indicators, their accuracy and comparability cannot be established.
(e) is a projection.

Source: World Tourism Organization, *Compendium of Tourism Statistics.*

Table 5.2 *Growth and destination of international tourism arrivals since 1950 (average percentage increases per annum over each period to each area)*

Years	Europe	Americas	East Asia/Pacific
1950–60	11.6	8.4	14.0
1960–70	8.4	9.7	22.4
1970–80	5.2	3.8	14.7
1980–90	4.3	4.3	9.7
1990–95	3.3	3.7	9.6
1995–2000 (p)	3.2	5.1	7.5
2000–2010 (p)	2.5	3.5	6.5

Notes
(p) projected at mid-1996.

Source: WTO data and projections.

Table 5.3 *Change in world regional shares of international tourism arrivals, 1950–2010*

Years	Europe	Americas	East Asia/Pacific
	Shares at end of each period shown		
	%	%	%
1950	66	30	0.8
1960	73	24	1.0
1970	71	23	3.0
1980	66	21	7.0
1990	62	21	11
1995	59	20	15
2010 (p)	50	20	23

Notes
(p) projected at mid-1996.

Source: WTO data and projections.

have made one or more international tourism visits during the previous five years, mostly on vacation. Experience of international travel is very much lower for Americans, reflecting the size of the USA and the distances most of them have to travel to make international visits. US inter-state tourism, for example between the North East and Florida, should perhaps be viewed as conceptually similar in kind to tourism between European countries over similar distances.

Although not included in Tables 5.1–5.3, international same-day visits are an important market sector in countries with common land frontiers, such as the USA and Canada, the Netherlands and Germany, or Malaysia and Singapore. Because of the speed and efficiency of cross-Channel ferries and the Channel Tunnel, same-day visits between Britain, France and Belgium are also an important market.

Domestic tourism

Domestic tourists are visitors who travel and stay overnight within the boundaries of their own country. Estimates of the size of this sector of the market vary because in many countries domestic tourism is not adequately measured at present.

tuations in volume caused by economic and political events will certainly occur, current expectations are for annual global growth of the order of some 3–4 per cent per annum over the period 1995–2010 as a whole.

In north Europe, it is now normal for between half and three quarters of the adult population to

The WTO acknowledges the size of this demand and, commenting on international arrivals, Paci noted 'If we consider total travel demand including domestic travel, the figure would be at least ten-fold higher – to almost 5 billion tourism visits world-wide' (WTO, 1994). In the USA, where good measurement does exist, Americans make only one visit abroad for every 100 domestic visits defined as travel to places more than 100 miles distance from home. Even for longer visits of over 10 night's duration, international visits are not more than 3 per cent of the total. For the British, where adequate statistics are also available, and reflecting the shorter distances to travel abroad, there were some four domestic tourism visits (involving overnight stays) for every visit abroad in the mid-1990s. The comparative growth figures over the last 20 years are shown in Table 5.3.

Evidence from surveys of the vacation markets in Europe and North America in the early 1990s indicate that between around two-thirds and three-quarters of the adult population took at least one holiday away from home in most countries, over a 12-month period. Increasing numbers of people take more than one vacation trip a year. This includes international and domestic holidays with the latter being the largest category in most countries. A recent analysis (ETC, 1993), covering evidence drawn from eighteen European countries, estimated that 295 million adults (aged 15+) made 750 million domestic tourism visits and 205 million international visits in the early 1990s. This means an average of 3.2 visits per capita in a year, with domestic visits outweighing international visits by just over 3.5 : 1.

Market research data analysing the complete tourism experience of the same individuals over periods of a year or more are rarely available. But excluding the very old, the sick, the severely disabled and those facing particular financial hardship it is clear that *recent and frequent* experience of some form of staying and same-day tourism now extends to over nine out of ten people in most economically developed countries.

Same-day visits from home

Same-day visits are the most difficult tourism market segment to quantify. In developed countries the frequency of day visits is already so great that it is not easily measured by traditional survey techniques because many people find it hard or impossible to remember the number of visits they have made over a period of months or even weeks. In the early 1990s there is, however, a rough but useful estimate for developed countries that there are at least as many domestic day visits from home for leisure purposes within a country as there are tourist days or nights spent away from home for all purposes. Thus, for example, in the UK in 1994, an estimated 110 million domestic tourism visits for all purposes generated 416 million nights away from home. Around 600 million same-day visits for leisure purposes were made by the British population in the same year with a duration of at least 3 hours and a travel distance of at least 20 miles. With a population of some 55 million in Britain, this is equivalent to over ten awaydays per person for leisure purposes, over a year. UK estimates of day visits for non-routine business purposes do not exist, although such visits are obviously a very large market, for transport operators in particular.

To summarize, the total market for tourism comprises three main elements: international visits inbound, visits made to foreign destinations by a country's residents; and domestic visits. The total market has grown rapidly in recent years and it generates the equivalent of 10 per cent or more of GDP in developed countries of the world (WTTC data). Either as visitors elsewhere or as residents of visited destinations, tourism directly affects the lives of around 90 per cent of the population in developed countries. In other words, *frequent, repeat purchase of travel and tourism products in any period of 12 months is already a normal experience for most people, for one or more of the reasons noted later in this chapter. In developed countries tourism has become a structural element in the conduct and quality of most people's lives and strategies for sustainable development must commence from that fact. The obsession with 'pleasure peripheries' is counterproductive to the cause of understanding sustainable issues in tourism.*

Two guiding principles for sustainability – segmentation and visitor management

Chapter 1, introducing travel and tourism as an 'industry,' stressed that it comprises a wide range of sub-markets or *market segments.* For marketing and visitor management purposes, especially in mature market conditions, the first fundamental principle is that segments must be identified and measured in terms of the key variables which define them and their patterns of behaviour. For example, behaviour reflects visitors' ages, socio-economic status, psychographic make-up, chosen activities at the destination, length of time away from home, seasonality and distance travelled internationally or within a country of residence. The essential point is that all destinations, even enclosed resorts such as Disneyland Paris and Center Parcs, derive their customers from a spectrum of customer types. Enclosed resorts can specify the segments they target with precision and such resorts are effectively purpose-built for specified customers. Non-enclosed destinations, such as heritage towns and cities in Europe and most national parks, have to deal with a much wider spectrum of segments. Even so, they can select some segments for active promotion, some to be discouraged and possibly controlled, and there are some which have to be planned for because they will arrive anyway. Examples of the last category are visitors to friends and relatives, business visitors, and visitors for a range of other non-leisure purposes that will be part of the economic, social and cultural life of any developed tourism destination in the twenty-first century.

The second guiding principle is that understanding the impact of tourism on the environment, and making progress toward sustainability, are matters to be tackled by visitor management techniques at any given destina-tion. Such techniques, especially product development (see Chapter 6), must respond to the known behaviour patterns of the particular groups or segments of people who visit specific destinations for particular purposes, at specific times. Purpose or reason for visit, discussed below, is by far the most important single variable determining visitor behaviour and seasonality patterns. In the late twentieth century it is remarkable that governments, tourist boards and even many destination authorities in all parts of the world still attempt to approach the issues of sustainability from the standpoint of 'tourism' in the aggregate. We can be certain that attempts to manage tourism as a broadly homogeneous total market will fail.

We wish to stress that tourism at the end of the twentieth century is never homogeneous, and with a few exceptions in the early stages of tourism development in leisure resorts, it never has been. We believe that sustainability is achievable only through the application of the two guiding principles based on the marketing perspective underlying this book. In summary:

- First understand (research) the characteristics and nature of the sub-sectors or segments at any given destination and target those that maximize environmental benefits and minimize environmental damage.
- Develop specific visitor management techniques to achieve the optimum sustainable balance of segments at the destination.

Most strategies in the 1990s aimed at sustainability are typically reactive in approach, attempting to respond to rather simplistic notions of 'limiting the number of tourists destroying what they come to see'. Over the next decade, setting volume limits to tourism on specific days at specific places is likely to become an essential tool of visitor management but limits will never work in the context of tourism as a whole. To make the point, 5000 nuns using public transport to attend a religious convention for five days (say 25 000 nights) are likely to cause much less environmental impact at a destination as a group than, say, 100 teenagers in cars or on motorbikes, high on alcohol or drugs, driving into the same place to spend a few hours in bars and amusement arcades. In this context, a **targeted** *increase* of volume (more nuns) would be a very much more sustainable strategy than a superficially attractive but foolish attempt to *reduce total tourism* volume by, say, 10 per cent. (i.e. 10 fewer teenage bikers and 2500 fewer nun nights).

An international framework for understanding segments in travel and tourism by purpose

Drawing on detailed discussions and broad agreement with officials responsible for tourism statistics in eighteen European countries in 1992, as part of the consultancy process that led to the EC Tourism Statistics Directive of 1994, the wide range of segments or sub-markets within the total demand for travel & tourism are noted in Table 5.4. The segments are organized broadly according to the categories identified by the WTO and, although not in this precise format, were subsequently endorsed by EUROSTAT in their development in 1996 of methodological guidelines to be adopted in EU member states.

Notwithstanding widespread international recognition of these very basic segments by purpose, very few countries could measure more than three or four of them on a national basis in the late 1990s. Even fewer measure international and domestic tourism on the same basis, while the number of specific destinations, such as cities and resorts, which can measure *any* of these categories on a systematic, continuous (say, annual) basis is very low indeed. Yet measurement is the basis for effective targeting, and targeting is the guiding principle for effective visitor management leading to sustainable tourism. We return to this important issue in subsequent chapters.

Understanding the environmental contribution and impact of segments in tourism at a regional destination

Based on published data for the county of Cumbria in the UK, Table 5.5 outlines a simple segmentation framework for targeting the more sustainable groups of visitors. Provided it is possible broadly to estimate staying and day visitors by type and purpose of visit, such a model could be developed for any destination in the world.

Located in the north-west of England, Cumbria includes the area generally known as the 'English Lake District'. The county has a population of around half a million and covers an area some 120 km north to south and 100 km west to east. Cumbria is not one but several visitor destinations, each with different segments, characteristics and behaviour patterns, and different needs for locally organized visitor management techniques. Tourism, or rather a widespread concern for the visible effects of visitor pressure and cars, is popularly considered to be a major problem in the county and there is strong local resident opposition to proposals for its further development on the grounds that there are too many tourists now. Cumbria is historically of interest in that so-called destructive visitor volume pressures were identified by different authors at least 150 years ago even in the pre-railway era of horses and coaches. The county witnessed the birth of the National Trust movement in the 1890s, a forerunner in the UK of the world-wide conservation and sustainability movement of the 1990s. Cumbria has its own tourist board and as sophisticated a local government system for planning and managing tourism pressures as can be found in England.

Table 5.5 broadly quantifies the main segments of tourism in the 1990s. The 'volume indicator' column estimates volume by main purpose of staying visitors (nights) and of day visits from home (visitor days). The staying and day visitor totals are fairly equal, being estimated at 15 million and 18 million, respectively. Based on

Table 5.4 *Principal market segments in travel and tourism by main purpose or reason for visit*

Main purpose of travel away from home	Types of visit included as travel and tourism
Leisure, recreation, holidays	*Comprises:* day visits and staying visits for which the activity and destinations are typically selected from a range of choices *Includes:* visits for sport, recreation, hobbies, cultural activities, leisure shopping and entertainment as well as main and additional holidays, short breaks, and visits to second homes *Excludes:* all forms of in-house leisure and local recreation pursuits such as golf
Business/professional meeting, Conference/exhibition Incentive visits	*Comprises:* day and staying visits for which the activity and destinations are determined by work-related criteria *Excludes:* commuting and other travel to normal/regular routine places of employment; all forms of temporary employment remunerated at the visited destination; members of armed forces and diplomatic representatives
Visiting relatives and friends	*Comprises:* day and staying visits for which the *primary* purpose is to visit friends and relatives and activity and destinations are determined by the nature of the visit *Excludes:* regular (at least once a week) visits to sick relations or to parents, i.e. part of a normal routine
Education training or study	*Comprises:* day and staying visits for education/training courses of less than 12 months' duration outside the normal routines of full-time education. The activity and destinations are determined by the location of courses and work/career-related criteria *Excludes:* attending schools and other educational establishments involving regular travel to places of education within the normal routines of full-time education
Health resorts/spas and recuperation (voluntary reasons)	*Comprises:* day and staying visits for which the activity and destination is typically selected from a range of choices *Excludes:* non-voluntary stays in hospitals and other medical institutions providing residential clinical/medical treatment, which are prescribed by doctors and mostly paid for by the state or by recognized health insurance schemes
Religion or pilgrimage/religious conferences/retreats	*Comprises:* day and staying visits for which the destinations are determined by the chosen activity outside a normal routine *Excludes:* regular, local acts of worship
Transit purposes	*Comprises:* international visits involving day travel and overnight stay for which the main purpose is 'en route' to destinations in other countries *Excludes:* cross-border workers, nomads and refugees
Other purposes	*Comprises:* day and staying visits for purposes such as organized school trips

Source: Adapted from VTCM, 'The Measurement of Tourism Demand', unpublished paper to EUROSTAT, 1992.

Table 5.5   *Tourism in Cumbria, mid-1990s – five impact indicators by visitor segments*

	Volume indicator ↓	← Impact Indicator →				
		Economic benefit	Fragile environment impact	Traffic congestion impact	Seasonal impact	Social/Culture impact
		For each indicator, 5 indicates high impact; 1 indicates low impact				
STAYING VISITORS						
(approx. 15 million nights)	%					
On business trips	10	5	0.5	1	1	0.5
Short breaks – commercial	15	4	3	3	2	2
Main holidays – commercial	25	3	4	5	5	4
Additional holidays - commercial	20	4	4	4	3	3
Visitors to friends/relatives	20	1	2	3	3	1
Use of holiday homes	10	1	3	3	3	5
DAY VISITORS						
(approx. 18 million days)	%					
On business trips	10	4	0.5	1	1	0.5
VFR	20	1	1	3	3	1
Distant recreation trips	35	2	5	5	5	5
Country resident recreation	35	1	3	4	4	4

Notes
Volume estimates are based broadly on published Cumbrian Tourism Board estimates for 1992 (day) and 1994 (stay).
Economic benefits (employment and support for local economy) are positive: 5 is high; 1 is low.
All other impacts are negative (e.g. impact on fragile environment): 5 is most negative; 1 is least negative.
VTCM – Author's estimates: 1996: Conference on Sustainable Tourism held at Newton Rigg College, Cumbria.

judgement, the other five columns indicate the relative influence of each of the segments on dimensions covering positive economic contributions and negative environmental impacts. Each segment is scored on each dimension out of five. To take two examples, business visitors contribute highly on economic benefit because they typically use hotels and many use restaurants, public transport and taxis. They make relatively low impact on the physical and social environment because they are typically involved in meetings within urban areas.

Owners and users of holiday homes/second homes generate low economic benefit because many bring food and drink and other supplies with them. They have moderate impact on the physical environment, largely because they are dispersed and not located in main pressure points, but they have the highest negative social/cultural impact as their dress, speech and behaviour patterns distinguishes them from most local residents. In Cumbria many holiday or vacation homes are located in villages, are empty for many weeks of the year, and have owners whose relative wealth pushes property prices beyond the reach of many local people. From Table 5.5 it emerges clearly that, putting day and staying visits together, more than 50 per cent of what is popularly perceived as Cumbria's 'tourism' is actually accounted for by a combination of visits to friends and relatives, business, residents' recreation and second-home owners and their friends. Not shown in the table, other evidence indicates that it is the non-commercial holiday sector and residents' recreation usage and car ownership which has shown the fastest rate of volume growth over the last decade and constitutes the larger future environmental threat. A successful approach to sustainability in an area must surely recognize these facts.

Clearly, for this type of model framework to be used successfully for planning and monitoring purposes, it is necessary to update the statistics at regular intervals. The model meets the basic requirements for segmentation, targeting according to environmental impact, and implementation of targeted visitor management techniques, that underlie the principles for achieving sustainability stressed in this chapter.

The tourism 'industry': systematic links between demand and supply

In Chapter 1 we used inverted commas for the term 'tourism industry' to make the point that travel and tourism is quite different from other industries defined by their output or products in Standard Industry Classifications (SICs), now found in all developed countries. As defined by Medlik the tourism industry comprises 'firms and establishments providing attractions, facilities and services for tourists. Economic activities are normally grouped into industries according to their products. As tourists use a range of attractions, facilities and services, they are customers of a number of industries as conventionally defined ... To the extent to which they supply tourist rather than local or neighbourhood demand, they make up a tourism industry, that part of the economy which has a common function of meeting tourist needs' (Medlik, 1996, p. 252). It should be noted that some of the firms and establishments in tourism are fully commercial and operated for profit, for example hotels and many airlines. Some are operated according to commercial principles and practice but for objectives other than profit, for example safari parks and many heritage sites. Some of the establishments are in the public sector and do not operate on commercial lines, for example many tourist organizations, national museums

and some transport systems. A marketing perspective is relevant to all of them, however, if they offer targeted services to the public and recognize the need to provide products or experiences that satisfy customer demand.

It is important to understand the extent to which many businesses in the 'industry' see tourism markets as only a part of their total business operations. The hospitality industry, for example, covers not just hotels but accommodation and or meals in hospitals, schools, prisons, armed services and contract catering. Airlines, trains, buses, restaurants and hotels all deal with a wide variety of market segments, many of which do not fall within the definition of travel and tourism. Hotels have local trade for bars and meals, transport operators carry commuters, and restaurants serve local markets for business and non-business purposes. Many visitor and cultural attractions, such as museums, cinemas and theatres and most visitor information bureaux, also provides services to local residents. There are no precise ways to measure the proportion of each sector's total demand that is derived from travel and tourism, although recent work by the WTTC to assess the size of the tourism industry around the world, uses a promising new statistical methodology known as *satellite accounting*, based on national accounts (WTTC, 1995).

Figure 5.1 provides an overview of the systematic links between the four main component sectors of the travel & tourism industry, focusing on the influence of a marketing perspective. The four sectors, with chapter references explaining what the sectors comprise and the implications for sustainable development, are as follows:

Business operations taking place at the destination and dependent on it

- Accommodation (Chapter 12).
- Attractions (Chapter 13).

Business operations taking place mainly away from the destination and independent of it

- Transport (Chapter 14).

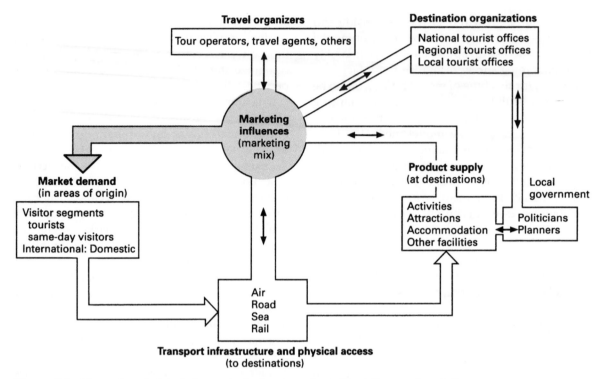

Figure 5.1 *The systematic links between demand and supply, and the influence of marketing*

• Travel organisers such as tour operators, retailers and conference brokers (Chapter 15).

Figure 5.1 does not identify all providers of facilities such as transport within the destination, restaurants, clubs, festival organizers and so on, but it serves to highlight the four main sectors on which the future of sustainability in travel and tourism depends. If sustainable practice is developed within these sectors, all the ancillary providers of facilities will follow suit. The planning and regulatory influence of local government is shown on the right-hand side of the figure where its influence is strongest, in relation to product supply. Linkage is also shown with tourist organizations which typically play an important role in destination marketing. The vital role of local government and planning, and the growing level of partnership activity with commercial businesses in the tourism industry, are dealt with in Chapters 7 and 8.

Tourism businesses large and small

Developments in the travel and tourism industry tend to be dominated by the activities of large, multinational corporations. The media generally, and the travel trade press in particular, trace and analyse the personalities and activities of airline manufacturers, global airlines and their reservation systems, leading hotel corporations, resort operators such as Club Méditerranée and Center Parcs, travel companies such as American Express or Thomas Cook, and the giants in the theme park world such as Walt Disney Corporation, Universal Studios, and Legoland. The significance of the multinationals is perhaps best reflected in the formation in 1989 of the World Travel & Tourism Council (WTTC). WTTC is a global coalition of chief executives from all sectors of the industry, including transportation, accommodation, catering, recreational/cultural and travel service activities. There are less than

100 members but between them they are responsible for the travel and accommodation of several hundred million customers a year, to and within over 100 countries around the world.

These corporations are important. They drive the process of change in product developments, technology and prices, and they are leaders in marketing. But for every large organization that warrants headline attention, there may be at least a thousand or more small and very small businesses in travel and tourism. Apart from airlines that dominate much of international travel, all the other multinationals serve only a small proportion of the total market for international and domestic travel and tourism, especially in developed countries. Collectively, although seldom in any coordinated way, it is small businesses that determine what visitors appreciate of the attractions of a destination, the quality of the experience provided, and the value for money provided. Even more important looking ahead to the next century, it is small businesses owned by residents of visited destinations that will collectively influence the extent to which any specific visitor destination makes progress toward sustainability as it is defined in this book. In terms of tourism in Cumbria, for example, (Table 5.5) it is unlikely that more than 15 per cent by volume of all the tourism nights and days are influenced or serviced by national let alone international businesses. Cumbria, in common with most destinations, prospers or falls by the management decisions (collectively) of its small businesses.

An interesting prediction in *The Global Paradox* states the bigger the world economy, the more powerful its smallest players (Naisbitt, 1994). If not quite in the way anticipated by Naisbitt, it is increasingly the case that small businesses with less than five employees, many of them 'micro operators' with no full-time employees at all, have the power to determine (or frustrate) the sustainability of tourism at destinations, for the following reasons:

- *For all destinations* except the enclosed resorts it is small businesses that determine what the

majority of visitors experience of a sense of place – its individuality, character, and charm. Small businesses reflect most of the features and characteristics unique or special to the destinations in which they live, such as dress, food and drink, architecture and ambience of accommodation, and access to local culture. The more professional have a deep knowledge of their own customers, especially repeat visitors, which transcends the need for market research among large companies – a powerful advantage for serving niche markets. They have the flexibility to respond quickly to changing market circumstances and they go out of business if they do not meet customer requirements and expectations. In developed country destinations small local businesses may also have a significant influence over the decisions of local government.

- *For visitors*, small businesses effectively represent the only real personal contact or 'encounter' most people have with the 'host community'. The personality of the owner and any staff are a critical element in the overall product experience for leisure visitors and they determine the quality of the welcome offered. Collectively their operations deliver much of the attractions, activities and facilities which comprise the primary motivation for a visit. (See also Chapter 6.) From taxis, through museums, ski lifts, ice cream vendors and most restaurants and retailers, the *tourist experience* is primarily supplied by small businesses. If the quality of a destination's environment (physical, social and cultural) is attractive, small businesses reflect it and prosper. If it is at risk, small businesses in pursuit of their livelihood may push it over the edge into significant erosion. Coordinated with larger businesses and through trade associations, they could in future provide the principal means of achieving sustainable goals. (See Epilogue.)

- *For large international corporations* small businesses are important because, although they are not directly competitive, they have a major influence collectively over customer decisions to visit a destination, especially over repeat visits. Collectively they dominate the quality of the environment as it is perceived by visitors. For most of the last thirty years multinational businesses could express regret if destinations were overdeveloped and destroyed their own environmental attractions, and they could go elsewhere. As we approach the twenty-first century the option to go elsewhere is becoming more limited and the importance of small businesses for the environment is increased. Large businesses will have to find ways to work with, and to some extent support, small businesses in order to secure their own long-term interests at a destination.

To summarize, multinational corporations, often in association with national governments and national tourist boards, increasingly have the capability of motivating, moving, and accommodating customers, and marketing themselves around the world with ever greater efficiency. But it is small businesses that collectively determine the quality of the welcome that the majority of visitors receive, and most of the ambience. quality, and sustainability of the environment at specific destinations on which so much of the motivation of future leisure travel depends.

In the stereotypes used by the popular press it is a combination of 'hordes of visitors' and cynical 'mass tour operators' that 'destroy the things they go to see ... killing the environmental geese that lay the golden eggs, etc.'. In reality it is more likely to be individual small businesses, scenting a commercial opportunity and having minimal barriers to entry into the tourism industry, who massively hike the capacity of facilities for visitors, motivated solely by short-term gain. Such was the experience of Cyprus and parts of Greece in the 1980s, such is the experience in parts of Thailand, and such may be the experience in much of Eastern Europe. Many large operators and developers in tourism are clearly responsible for causing

environmental damage at destinations, but at least they can be identified and pilloried in the media if their culpability can be demonstrated. Most small businesses operate, in effect, outside the modern climate of apportioning blame and can often slip through the regulations designed for larger businesses.

Chapter summary

The definitions of travel and tourism outlined in this chapter will be adequate for most working purposes and it is not the intention to debate all the niceties and nuances of tourism concepts. Readers seeking further elaboration are referred to the reading suggestions noted at the end of the chapter. The key point is that travel and tourism, far from being the leisure periphery so unthinkingly identified in the media and elsewhere, is a structural component of the modern mobile way of life in all developed countries. It is for this reason that achieving sustainability in tourism is such a vital issue for post-industrial societies. A pleasure periphery might be controlled or even regulated out of existence; a core element of modern life requires a proactive strategic response.

The two internationally relevant principles of segmentation and developing visitor management techniques around targeted segments and products are stressed as the basis for sustainable tourism development. Such principles are information based and lack of research emerges as a major factor inhibiting environmental progress in tourism destinations in all parts of the world.

Marketing managers of larger tourism businesses compete using detailed research covering visitor profile characteristics, purpose of visit, length of stay, type of expenditure and so on. Those responsible for visitor management at destinations will increasingly need the same data to target the forms of tourism best calculated to lead to sustainable futures and establish effective influence and control over them. (See also Chapters 8, 9 and 10.) The chapter provides a simple destination segmentation model based on a particular area of the UK.

Finally the chapter reviews the massive significance for the environment of smaller businesses, stressing that the long-term prosperity of destinations and of big business is uncomfortably in the hands of thousands of small businesses and self-employed individuals. New forms of effective collaboration and coordination will be essential for achieving sustainability at destinations and the issues are dealt with in the next three chapters.

Further reading

Burkart, A.J. and Medlik, S., *Tourism: Past, Present and Future*, 2nd edn, Heinemann, Oxford, 1981.

Cooper, C. *et al.*, *Tourist Principles and Practice*, Pitman, London, 1993.

Medlik, S., *Dictionary of Travel, Tourism and Hospitality*, 2nd edn, Butterworth-Heinemann, Oxford, 1996.

Paci, E., *Global Tourism Forecasts to the Year 2000 and Beyond*, WTO, 1994.

WTO, *Recommendations on Tourism Statistics*, 1993.

6

The environmental significance of holiday and leisure tourism

The *Oxford English Dictionary* (*OED*) defines tourism and tourist respectively as:

The theory and practice of touring; travelling for pleasure ... the business of operating tours.

One who travels for pleasure or culture, visiting a number of places for their objects of interest, scenery, or the like (*OED*, 1989, vol xviii, p. 306).

Developing from Chapter 5, this chapter puts holidays and leisure travel within the context of the overall travel and tourism market, noting the damage to understanding tourism that stems from standard dictionary definitions. It notes seven books on tourism in the last two decades that have had a particular influence internationally on the sustainability debate. Stressing that holidays and leisure are less than half of all travel and tourism in many developed countries, the chapter outlines the concept of holiday product formulation which, with segmentation, is one of the two principal management techniques that can be used to influence destination volume and capacity and, therefore, sustainability. Finally it summarizes the positive and negative impacts of holiday travel as perceived in the late 1990s. As the principal management influence over product formulation and the number and types of visitors targeted, marketing techniques are iden-

tified as the most important means of achieving sustainability in holiday tourism.

Dictionary distortion

It is useful to start with the unequivocal identification of tourism with pleasure and leisure to be found in the latest *OED*. In common with other leading dictionaries, the *OED* definition helps to explain why the world's largest industry is so often misunderstood and misrepresented. Inevitably it takes decades for standard dictionaries to bring themselves up to date with changing circumstances and students of the history of tourism may detect a lingering echo in the *OED* of the eighteenthth and early nineteenth century practice of the 'Grand Tour', undertaken by a small proportion of the affluent leisured English elite. As recently as 1973 the addenda to the *Shorter OED* designed to reflect new usage noted that tourism as an adjective means 'the inferior or lowest class of accommodation on a liner, train, etc.'. Airlines were not mentioned.

When reaching for their dictionaries to reassure themselves about an unfamiliar concept, small wonder if politicians, policy makers and the media – and thus the general public – typically equate tourists with holiday makers, especially those who travel abroad for sightseeing purposes. No surprise then, if the word *tourism* is so often associated with the cheap end of non-essential travel and seen as a peripheral form of activity. In this context the adjective 'mass' appears to fit naturally with tourism to denote a passive form of lowest common denominator leisure travel in which millions of people are shifted around the globe by tour operators motivated solely by profit.

An excusable misunderstanding on the part of the general public should not, however, extend to academics, authors of tourism texts, and students. As Medlik puts it, 'the final test of any definition cannot be its apparent harmony with its usage in everyday speech ...' (Medlik, 1996, p. vii). To discuss holiday tourism sensibly, and to plan for it effectively in environmental terms, it is essential always to put it into the broader spectrum of travel and tourism explained in Chapter 5. Holidays and leisure are obviously significant, partly because they are often the largest and always the most visible sectors of tourism in popular destinations, but more so because the various segments they comprise are the principal source of negative environmental impact. Damage recorded at natural and built heritage resources, to the way of life of residents of visited destinations and to their local culture, is especially attributed to so-called 'mass tourism' package foreign holidays by air, taken by the population of developed countries. Commonly cited examples are vacation travel to developing countries, such as the impact of North American tourists in the Caribbean and Asia-Pacific, or of Australian tourists in the South Pacific.

Mass holiday tourism concepts associated with environmental damage

The propensity of academics since the 1980s and 1990s to write books and articles about the environmental impact of 'tourism' has com-pounded the popular confusion of travel and tourism with holidays. Too many authors fall into the trap unintentionally laid by the major dictionaries, treating tourism conceptually as if it were all so-called 'mass tourism', especially international packaged tours by air. Some economists, geographers and sociologists in particular find it convenient to represent tourism as a homogenous mass, because it makes their preconceived theories easier to explain. All leisure-based conceptions of tourism are partial and selective, ignoring the world definitions evolved over several decades. At worst they are spurious academic theories in search of an 'industry' which can be bent to fit them. Students and practitioners should beware.

Although its antecedents may be traced back for over a century, the idea of environmentally responsible tourism, or sustainable development through tourism as it is now recognized and used globally, dates back only about a decade to 1987 and the Brundtland Report. In terms of tourism industry responses to sustainable issues, practice on any significant scale dates back less than a decade to the early 1990s. In appreciating the particular impact of holiday tourism on the environment one may identify seven influential books published in the 1970s, 1980s and 1990s by authors approaching the subject from backgrounds in economics, sociology, anthropology, geography, psychology, and information technology. These books draw on the mainstream of sustainable thinking, influenced, for example, by international contributions not related to tourism directly, such as Meadows *et al.*, *The Limits to Growth* (1972) and Richard Lovelock's *Gaia* (1979). They provide clear evidence and warnings that much of the international leisure and holiday tourism growing so rapidly around the world in the quarter century since the introduction of cheap air travel in the 1960s was economically less beneficial than many of its protagonists claimed, and much of it is inherently destructive of the environment. In other words, 'not sustainable'.

The seven, in order of publication, are George Young's *Tourism: Blessing or Blight?* (1973); Louis

Turner and John Ash, *The Golden Hordes* (1975); Valene Smith, *Hosts and Guests: The Anthropology of Tourism* (1977); Emanuel de Kadt (ed.), *Tourism, Passport to Development* (1979); Jost Krippendorf, *The Holidaymakers* (1984); Peter Murphy, *Tourism: A Community Approach* (1985), and Auliana Poon, *Tourism, Technology and Competitive Strategies* (1994). From these books one may trace the underlying issues of what is now invariably termed sustainability, approached from the standpoint of overdevelopment of destinations (Young and Turner and Ash), inefficient use of economic resources (de Kadt), exploitation of host communities and their cultures (Smith and Turner and Ash), exploitation of visitors themselves (Krippendorf), planning and development from a destination focus (Murphy) and the future implications for tourism businesses of information technology (Poon).

These seven authors have undoubtedly contributed significantly to highlighting the dimensions of tourism impact and many of the principles of sustainability for holiday tourism. But in different ways, using the only market information available, all of them deal with 'tourism' in aggregate and primarily with holiday tourism. Most are doubtless aware of the wider definition of tourism but only Krippendorf specifically clarifies that his contribution relates to holidays. None of these influential books treat tourism in the broad context in which it is actually practised in the world-wide travel and tourism industry. Yet in volume and revenue terms, as we illustrate in this chapter, the bulk of the world's tourism remains primarily a business of domestic travel for all purposes, generated by and received in developed countries. Because of their primary concern with leisure and the social, cultural and economic impacts of holidays, none of the authors developed the specific practical implications of a marketing perspective for sustainability, although Poon comes closest to it. There are by now several dozen other books developing the same core themes as the seven noted here.

Most importantly the characteristics of global tourism have been changing rapidly and irreversibly in the last twenty-five years as summarized in Table 6.1. The academic concepts of mass holiday tourism developed for the specific market circumstances of the 1970s and 1980s look increasingly irrelevant to realistic planning for a more sustainable future and they are now overtaken by the much broader concepts of tourism endorsed internationally by the World Tourism Organization and most governments in the 1990s.

Holidays and leisure in the context of tourism for all purposes

In the 1990s most countries still have little reliable information about the principal component sectors of travel and tourism because governments do not yet accept the need to measure demand. The 'tourism' data presented in reports by WTO, WTTC, OECD, and EC, for example, are commonly presented as aggregate totals of tourism for all purposes. Most of the data are rough estimates compiled by different methods. They are not audited and they are not strictly comparable.

Figures 6.1 and 6.2 indicate the composition of international (inward) and domestic tourism in the UK. The data are presented as percentages of nights since these are a more useful indicator of environmental impact than the number of visitors. Holiday visitors typically stay longer than other types of visitor and nights reflects this important weighting. For example, 10 000 long stay visitors spending 100 000 nights in a fragile environment are likely to have a much greater impact than, say, 50 000 short-break visitors spending 100 000 nights in a purpose-built seaside resort. Environmental impact is determined by the characteristics of visitor segments.

It can be seen that for overseas visitors to the UK, holidays and inclusive tours combined account for 35 per cent of all nights spent in the UK by overseas residents. As some of these holiday nights are undoubtedly spent with friends and relatives (even if the primary reason for visit is

Table 6.1 *Fundamental trends in the business environment for leisure-related international tourism.*
Source: Compilation drawing on multiple sources, specifically Middleton (1988) and Poon (1993).

	1960s, 1970s, 1980s	1990s, 2000s
Government attitudes to tourism	• National economic growth focus – employment, balance of payments • Subsidies for development – grants, loans, fiscal reliefs • Master plans/development plans • NTO promotional focus	• Destination focus for economic contribution; balance of payments: use of tourism to regenerate economy in rural and urban areas • Concerns for sustainability as capacity limits emerge • Fewer subsidies and some state withdrawal from NTO support • Visitor management within overall strategies • NTO marketing and partnership collaboration
Attitudes towards the environment	With limited exceptions in national parks, the environment perceived as a free resource to be developed and exploited for economic/commercial gain	Physical, social and cultural environment increasingly perceived as a fragile set of resources endangered by over-exploitation with consequences of seriously damaging the core resources for leisure tourism
Competition	Often relatively weak because demand growth exceeded supply of capacity. In many places what could be built could be sold. Regulated air transport limits competition.	Increasingly fierce competition where growing capacity of supply exceeds growth in demand. Where consumers have choices of high quality and value for money prices, low quality and cheap price providers are put out of business. Deregulation promotes competition
Information technology shifts	Limited primarily to computerization of producer-owned reservation systems – especially airlines, tour operators and hotels. Initially restricted mainly to business travel and inclusive tour packages. Telephone links to computers predominate.	Global IT development increasingly link producers, intermediaries and customers on an on-line basis. PC technology, INTERNET and Web sites open up potentially limitless access on a global basis. Destination information systems bring smaller business into information networks
Consumers	Many first-time international holiday travellers; 18–50-year-olds the bulk of the international market; many taking one holiday a year, booked months in advance of departure. Sunshine and beach resorts dominate: *'chicken and chips in a plastic bucket – with lager and cheap wine'*	Increasing numbers of sophisticated, travel-experienced, international customers; over-50s have growing influence; many taking two, three or more holidays a year. Focus shifting to rural and city destinations and active recreation pursuits on holiday. Short booking periods: *'smorgasbrod and local schnapps – with quality wines'*
Products and positioning	Inclusive tour packages of a relatively standardized undifferentiated formula predominate international markets – competing on price rather than destination qualities. Sunshine and beaches plus short-break packages predominate – charter flights dominate air travel	Inclusive arrangements still important but – aided by IT – are presented as bespoke, customized arrangements often using scheduled transport and not involving group movements. Product differentiation matches customer segmentation. Product quality and the relevance of place are increasingly main aspects of positioning

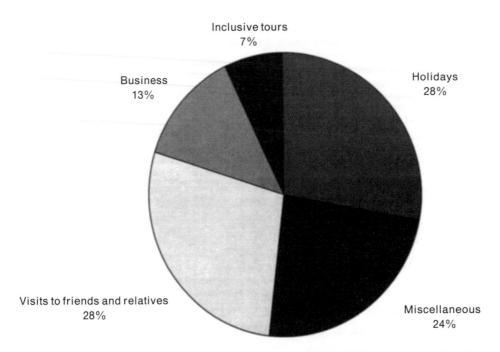

Figure 6.1   *Overseas tourists to the UK – nights by purpose of visit, 1995. Source: Travel Trends: Report on the 1995 International Passenger Survey, Office for National Statistics, London, HMSO, 1966*

stated as holiday), the true figure for holiday impact is unlikely to be more than one third of the total nights. Holiday nights are likely to have a greater impact on the environment but visitor management policies targeted primarily at leisure tourism will deal with only one in three visitors. Package tourism, so often identified as 'mass tourism', accounted for just 7 per cent of inbound international visitor nights to the UK.

For domestic tourism in the UK the proportion of commercial holiday nights is similar at 32 per cent but it is still only a third of all tourism nights. Packages in the domestic market are estimated at only 4–5 per cent. As in other developed countries, substantial proportions of domestic holidays are taken in second homes such as caravans, cottages and boats, and staying with friends and relatives. Reliable figures for same-day visits from home are not available but it is probable that two-thirds or more of such visits are mostly outside the direct influence of the private sector. More than 50 per cent of

tourism to Cumbria, for example (days and nights combined) arises from same-day visits, the bulk of which follow routines and habits not influenced by commercial holiday tourism interests. (See Table 5.5.)

For outbound international tourism originating in twenty-four European countries we have obtained permission to draw on comparable survey data provided by European Travel Intelligence Center, Luxembourg, from the European Travel Monitor for 1993. (See Figure 6.3.) Bearing in mind that European tourism to all the major summer sunshine packaged tour destinations such as Spain, Greece, Portugal, France and Italy is covered in this figure, it can be seen that the total for nights on all types of inclusive tour is just 23.6 per cent. Data for package tours by charter airlines, the sector typically dubbed 'mass tourism', were not available for publication, but we can safely speculate that charters comprise less than a fifth of all outbound tourism from European countries. If allowance is made for

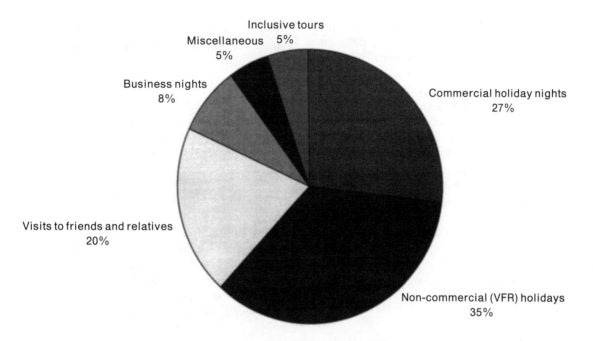

Figure 6.2   *UK domestic tourists in the UK – nights by purpose of visit, 1995. (Note: Inclusive tours authors' estimate of 5 per cent and are an additional part of commercial holiday nights (32 per cent in total))*

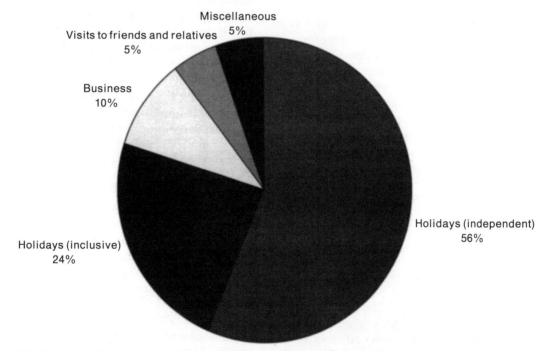

Figure 6.3   *International tourism generated in eighteen countries of Western Europe and six countries in Eastern Europe – nights by purpose of visit. Source: European Travel Intelligence Center, Luxembourg, European Travel Monitor, 1993 (reproduced with permission)*

domestic tourism in the same countries and same-day visits, for which comparable data do not exist, the 'mass tourism' element and the holiday element are clearly revealed to be small sectors of the total tourism market in Europe.

Comparable data for most countries outside Europe do not exist either but we have no hesitation in stating that for developed countries in north Europe, North America, and the Pacific Rim (i.e. the countries which generate and receive the bulk of the world's international and domestic tourism), holidays generally and packages in particular are important but a minority sector within the total market for travel and tourism. Effective long-run strategies for sustainable development through tourism may commence with holidays but must also reflect the wider perspective.

Identifying the promotable margin of tourism accessible to tourist boards

Common sense indicates that in any given year tourist boards, often seen as the instigators of sustainable practices, will not be able to influence the bulk of a destination's tourism. They will have next to no influence on visits to friends and relatives or on most tourism for business purposes. In the UK, where the British Tourist Authority has earned many awards for the quality of its international marketing, the chief executive noted 'Independent research shows that our activities in 1994/5 were responsible for some 7.5 per cent of the total inbound tourism spend' (BTA, Annual Report, 1995, p. 4).

The promotable margin of nights in the UK

Working on the data shown in Figures 6.1 and 6.2:

1 If 25 per cent of the holiday nights by overseas visitors to the UK are directly influenceable by the national tourist board (BTA).

25 per cent × 35 per cent = 8.75 per cent of all

overseas nights spent within the UK (close to the BTA estimate of 7.5 per cent noted above which refers to all tourism).

2 If 25 per cent of the commercial holiday nights by UK domestic visitors are directly influenceable by national, regional and local tourist boards as to choice of product type and destination.

25 per cent × 32.0 per cent = 8 per cent of all domestic nights spent within the UK.

From this simple calculation we can safely conclude that a maximum of just one in ten of all visitor nights spent within the UK in the early 1990s are directly influenceable by tourist boards in their choice of product type and destination. The key word here is 'directly' since there is a considerable influence indirectly that tourist boards are able to exercise, for example through the provision of visitor information and accommodation grading schemes. We believe that the relative proportions of directly promotable tourism justified in a British context would broadly hold good for other developed countries. For developing countries the proportions of tourism directly influenced would undoubtedly be higher, reflecting the stage of tourism development, the greater importance of holiday tourism, and the relatively higher proportion of total budgets (in relation to visitor numbers) which their tourist boards control directly. Even so, one may reasonably conclude that the direct influence for countries other than those in the initial tourism development stage, is unlikely to be higher than 25–33 per cent of all tourism.

We estimate, without in any sense denigrating the value of tourist board marketing and their leadership role, that their direct role in promoting sustainable tourism in developed countries is limited to a working maximum of around 10 per cent of all visitors. Sustainable development policies cannot be effective, therefore, without the involvement of the commercial sectors of the tourism industry in targeting, reaching and influencing the majority of all visitors.

Nature of the product in holiday tourism – a components view

Chapter 5 introduced product formulation as a key element in the second of the two guiding principles for sustainable development (segmentation and visitor management techniques). In particular, the concept of the *overall tourism product* is central to understanding the potential role of marketing and visitor management in all sectors of travel and tourism and a logical corollary of market segmentation. It has important implications for marketing in commercial organizations and national and regional tourist offices; it is also highly relevant for planning and development, both in its community aspects and as a focus of feasibility studies for commercial organizations. In particular, it is a core issue for managing all forms of holiday tourism.

From a general marketing standpoint products are defined by the leading American marketing author, Kotler, as 'anything that can be offered to a market for attention, acquisition, use or consumption that might satisfy a want or need. It includes physical objects, services, persons, places, organizations and ideas' (Kotler, 1994, p. 463). As such, product decisions in any industry are the focal point of all marketing activity around which the other aspects of the marketing mix (people, pricing, promotion and distribution) are organized. In the long run, marketing strategy is concerned with product positioning, development and enhancement around the identified needs of target segments. In the short run, however, marketing tactics for tourism products often have to be concerned with managing and moulding demand around available product capacity. The latter requirement is especially relevant where capacity is relatively fixed at any point in time, while demand is relatively volatile, as it normally is for most forms of promotable holiday tourism.

In travel and tourism products have to be understood on two levels:

- *The overall tourism product*, which comprises a combination of all the service elements a visitor consumes from the time he or she leaves home to the time of return. This product is an idea, an expectation, or a mental construct in the customer's mind, at the point of sale. It is an amalgam of elements usually provided by a range of different private and public sector businesses.
- *The specific, mainly commercial products*, which are always components of the overall tourism product, such as the particular product offers of attractions, accommodation, transport, and other facilities and services for visitors, such as car rental and ski hire.

Drawing on concepts first published by Middleton in the early 1970s this chapter is concerned only with overall tourism products. It deals with products as they are perceived on the demand side by visitors (especially for leisure/vacation purposes); and as they are conceived on the supply side by national tourist offices (NTOs) and regional and local tourist offices (RTOs and LTOs). From a supply-side perspective, the overall tourism product view is also that adopted by tour operators who, acting on behalf of customers, put together or 'package' the individual components of travel, and market them as entities. Specific products marketed by the component sectors of the travel and tourism are dealt with later, in Part Three.

The overall tourism product is defined as 'a bundle or package of tangible and intangible components, based on activity at a destination. The package is perceived by the tourist as an experience, available at a price' (Middleton, 1988). It is central to the definition that the components within the 'bundle' can, and should, be designed and fitted together in a variety of ways calculated to match consumer needs. It is just a logical extension of the definition to stress that the components must also be designed and fitted together in ways that reflect the capacity, quality and 'needs' of the resources available at the destination. There are five main components in the overall tourism product, discussed separately below.

1 Destination attractions – international quality standards

Attractions are the elements within a destination's environment which, individually and combined, serve as the primary motivation for holiday tourism visits. They comprise:

- *Natural attractions*, such as landscape, seascape, beaches, wildlife, and climate.
- *Built attractions*, such as historic townscape (e.g., Amsterdam, Boston – USA, Venice or Bangkok) or new townscape as in newly built resorts (e.g. Disneyland Paris or ski resorts in the Alpine regions of France).
- The wide range of purpose-built, *managed visitor attractions*, such as theme parks, industrial heritage sites in the United Kingdom or urban regeneration projects, such as Darling Harbour in Australia.
- *Cultural attractions*, such as theatres, museums, and presentations of history and folklore, many of which are organized as festivals and pageants with heritage themes.
- *Social attractions*, defined as opportunities to meet with, or 'encounter' the residents of destinations and to some extent experience their way of life.

In the 1990s, it is clear that destination attractions judged to be environmentally attractive and of high relative quality – in natural, cultural and social terms – are in growing demand by visitors. In a global industry many customers can literally choose products from anywhere in the world, and obtain relevant information about them including pictures, at the touch of a button. As a result, the perceived quality of a destination's attractions, *evaluated in competition with other equivalent destinations*, will be increasingly a matter of internationally recognized standards. The environment, broadly defined, will be the basis for competition on a value-added basis,

and, therefore, a logical focus for marketing management.

2 Destination facilities

Destination facilities (sometimes also referred to as 'amenities') are defined as the elements within the destination, or linked to it, which make it possible for visitors to stay at a destination and to enjoy and participate in the attractions it offers. They include accommodation of all types, restaurants, cafés and bars, transport at the destination including car rental and taxis, and other services such as sports and recreation equipment rental, retailing, craft markets, hairdressing, and visitor information. There is inevitably some overlap between attractions and facilities, for example where a famous hotel is not just a facility but an attraction in its own right, and the primary motivation for a visit. As with attractions, internationally recognized quality standards increasingly apply.

3 Accessibility

This is defined in terms of speed (time taken), comfort and the relative ease or difficulty with which visitors can reach the destination of their choice, as well as cost. Access is a matter of transport services and infrastructure, such as airports, harbours, motorways and rail networks. It is also a matter of transport technology which alters the cost of travel and the time it takes to reach destinations. For example, the development and rapid expansion of tourism in the Asia-Pacific area in the 1980s was made possible primarily by the technology of wide-bodied, long-haul, jumbo jets, which radically improved the timing and reduced the cost of transpacific travel. Internationally recognized quality standards also apply here, especially to transport operations.

4 Images

Images, meaning the ideas and beliefs which people hold about the products they purchase or contemplate, become attached to all forms of tourism product. Destination images are not necessarily based on experience or fact but they are usually very powerful motivators in leisure travel decisions. For example, of the millions of Americans and Europeans who have never visited Las Vegas in Nevada, USA, there can be very few who do not carry in their minds some images and expectations of the experiences such a destination offers. Images are the logical focus for much of promotion and it is always an objective of destination marketing to identify, sustain, alter or develop images, in order to influence prospective buyer's expectations. As internationally recognized environmental quality standards become more significant in destination images in the 1990s, growing numbers of customers will avoid destinations perceived to be associated with negative environmental images.

5 Price

This is the total of what it costs for a visitor's choice of the components of travel, accommodation and participation in a range of selected activities and services at a destination. The price of holiday products varies according to choice of accommodation, such as de luxe or economy, season of the year, the types of activity chosen and the distance travelled to a destination. It also a function of the deals which can be struck individually, or more commonly by the specialist contractors employed by tour operators. Once again, in a global industry, international price comparisons are made and internationally recognized value for money applies. Throughout the thirty years prior to the 1990s, the cost of environmental protection was very seldom factored into holiday products because it was not seen as necessary. As a result, competition between the major suppliers of package holidays focused almost exclusively on lowest price for the transport, accommodation and local tour components. Looking ahead, we have no doubt that the true cost of providing access to high-quality environmental resources, and conserving them for the benefit of future generations of residents and visitors, will have to

be built into product prices over the next decade. This will shift the nature of competition from its existing focus on price to greater emphasis on environmental value-added.

An illustration

The practical relevance of a components view of the overall tourism product can most easily be recognized in the context of planning a new leisure destination, such as a winter ski resort. The attraction is based on the range, sporting quality and capacity of the ski slopes available, the scenic appeal and environmental quality of potential sites, and the architectural appeal of the built environment of the resort's structures (new or preserved). When planning any new destination it is relatively straightforward to calculate the number of visitors or capacity which the environmentally most fragile link in the chain can handle on the busiest days. For a new ski resort the key capacity is likely to reflect the number of visitors who can ski without eroding the slopes, leaving scars visible in summer, and without structurally altering the balance of the established ecosystems. Accommodation and other facilities can then be purpose-built around the needs and wants of targeted prospective visitors in quantities/capacity identified by market feasibility studies and judged acceptable in environmental impact terms. Since the early 1990s, the conduct of Environmental Impact Studies has been a legal requirement in many countries for all major new developments such as resorts (see Chapter 11).

Other facilities include the hourly capacity of ski-lifts, restaurants, bars, ski-hire and so on, and these can be designed with some precision to meet the needs of a targeted volume of customer segments at the planned busiest times. Access for the planned maximum number of staying and day visitors is a matter of access roads to the resort, provision of sufficient car parking and coach parking, and transport access to the nearest airport. A new resort will have to develop an image for the purpose of promotion, and a style which projects its attractions and individuality.

Such an image, for a new resort, will typically reflect the intrinsic qualities of the destination region and the design, quality and style of its attractions and especially the quality of its built and social environment. Price will be directly related to the cost of building and operating the attractions and facilities provided, with a range of prices according to the needs of target visitor segments.

Thus, in a new resort, it is possible for every single component of the overall tourism product to be precisely planned, managed and orchestrated around a systematic evaluation of customer segments and volume, and the calculated sustainable capacity of resources. Capacity of resources in this context equates to the volume of products to be offered for sale. The process is equivalent to a form of product engineering such as that practised in modern customer-orientated car manufacture, which nowadays is far removed from the mass-production methods pioneered and appropriate for the needs of the 1920s to 1960s. Of course, product planning is not so easy for an established destination, especially if it is a large town or city and the promotable holiday tourism segments are a small minority of the total visitors. The principles of product engineering remain the same, however. They are marketing led and developed in Part Three of the book.

Practical marketing implications of the overall tourism product

Four main practical implications for sustainability can be drawn from the understanding of overall holiday tourism products. All are reflected in the examples provided in Part Three of the book.

1 First, unless it is achieved by management decisions, as in the packaging arrangements made by tour operators or in planning for a new resort, there is no automatic harmony between the different owners of the various components of the overall tourism product at a destination. Unless managed around an agreed set of destination goals, there is unlikely to be any consensus between owners on appropriate levels of environmentally sustainable capacity. Even within the same sector such as accommodation, there will usually be many different businesses often with conflicting objectives and interests. It is the dispersion or fragmentation of control and ownership within the tourism industry, and the relative freedom of individual organizations to act according to their own perceived self-interests at destinations, which has traditionally made it difficult for national and regional tourist offices (NTOs and RTOs) to exert much coordinating influence either in marketing or planning. But sustainable development is only achievable through coordination and recognition of mutual long-run interests between the main components of the overall tourism products.

2 Fortunately, reflecting the marketing dynamics inherent in this view of overall products, there is considerable evidence now of effective marketing partnerships between businesses in different sectors, and much greater potential looking ahead. Such collaboration may be formally designed into new resorts, as in the ski resort example noted above, where it includes mutual goals, and product engineering incorporating environmental quality decisions. At national, regional and local level, there has for years been participation by businesses in joint advertising, print and public relations initiatives sponsored by NTOs, RTOs and local tourist boards. Participants seek logical synergy in spending budgets which are mostly far too small individually to have any significant impact on prospective customers. Such participation is a proven foundation for future partnerships developed to achieve environmental quality and sustainable goals, in which most tourism businesses are too small individually to achieve results.

3 The fact that most changes in the demand for and supply of holiday destinations are not planned but happen naturally through the effects of market changes and transport technology and access, adds to the need continuously to monitor customer perceptions of the overall products, for development and promotional purposes. For European travellers in the 1990s, the shift of demand away from short-haul tourism destinations around the Mediterranean toward long-haul destinations in the USA and Asia Pacific, is an example of a structural market shift. Such a shift requires reappraising customers' overall destination needs and wants in the light of modern competition, followed by systematic planning for achievable tourism futures. Improved marketing intelligence and planning in the 1990s may reduce the impact of such major market shifts by better anticipation, but in a volatile industry with many choices open to international markets, unexpected fluctuations will always occur. Marketing will be the major factor in the necessary management response.

4 Related to targeting decisions and monitoring customer trends is the need for continuing market research. There are few 'facts' and 'truths' in the marketing of tourist products, and customers' perceptions and images of a destination's attractions are in a constant state of change. Research is the basis for effective tourism promotion as well as for product development, yet for most visitor destinations it has been totally inadequate in the last twenty years. Very few destinations have anything but guesses as to the volume and value of tourism they handle in the 1990s, and even fewer have established systems for the regular assessment of trends by visitor segments and their product needs and interests. Visitor management techniques in this context can never be anything other than a fairly haphazard process of guesswork and it is not a matter for surprise that environmental problems arise. Improved research and data sharing are a key part of future partnerships.

The positive and negative environmental impacts of holiday tourism

Most modern books and articles on sustainability in tourism dwell at length on the negative impacts on the environment, typically drawing evidence from the more extreme examples stemming from *mass tourism* holiday packages. For students in particular, and for all practitioners that keep up to date with the general media, it is unnecessary simply to repeat what is already well known in every part of the world. There are endless lists of negative impacts attributed to 'tourism' ranging from Aids to the abuse of children as prostitutes and the exploitation of animals displayed in urban zoos. For the purposes of this book we have developed two charts (Figures 6.4 and 6.5) in which we summarize the main issues. Most of these were outlined and illustrated in the seven books briefly reviewed earlier in the chapter. Figure 6.4 summarizes negative impacts at destinations under the broad headings of physical, social/economic, and cultural/ educational impacts. Figure 6.5 summarizes the less well-known positive effects and potential benefits, using the same three headings.

In reviewing the negative impacts some caution should be exercised. It is tempting, but wholly unrealistic to suppose that there exist communities around the world with an Arcadian way of life, in which local populations have learned to live in fundamentally sustainable ways, at peace with themselves and their neighbours and with nature. One may imagine these happy communities respecting their cultural traditions and moral values, untroubled by population growth, pressure on available resources, and immune to the impact of international political chaos and disaster purveyed by modern radio and television. Into these idyllic sustainable communities, imposed by western capitalists aided and abetted by complaisant governments, is injected a ruthless alien economic force called 'tourism.' Multi-

Physical

- Erodes natural spaces through construction of airports, marinas, resort complexes and so on.
- Pressure of overdevelopment and too many visitors erodes and damages fragile natural and built environments – from Alpine ski resorts, coral reefs, to cathedrals and heritage cities such as Venice.
- Produces congestion and overcrowding leading to loss of wildlife habitats and damage to ecosystems.
- Generates litter, sewage, noise, emissions and use of chemicals and pollutants for maintaining landscapes, golf courses, laundries and visitor transportation.
- Leads to ugly uniformity of buildings and townscape with no respect for architectural integrity or for such traditional styles as may exist.
- Diverts local resources and amenities such as water and land for tourism developments which disadvantage residents.

Social/economic

- Commercializes the environment for profits which are diverted from the destination and do not accrue to local residents.
- Employment at management level often goes to non-residents leaving only low-paid menial jobs. Tourism employment disrupts traditional employment patterns and the community structures they created.
- Economic benefit leaks away from destinations through imports of materials and food and beverage, exacerbated by imposition of Western business methods alien to many local communities in the developing world.
- Tourism provides a market for prostitution and is associated with drugs and crime.
- Introduces developed country moral standards into local communities, generating greed, indolence, violence and crime.
- Effectively lowers traditional qualities of life by introducing an alien, dominant, all-pervasive industry imposed upon and controlled from outside the community.
- Generates tension and animosity between visitors and residents.

Cultural/educational

- Undermines local arts and cultural traditions of local residents by removing their original rationale and turning them into artificial staged events, for profit.
- Undermines and eventually destroys original local identities and traditions of place.
- Communicates messages of environmental destruction, by examples of bad practice.

Figure 6.4 *Negative environmental impacts of tourism – especially holiday tourism*

Physical

- Provides a long-run justification for the protection, preservation and enhancement of natural and built resources, including the protection of biodiversity.
- Provides access to internationally recognized quality standards for environmental resources.
- Stimulates improvements to the quality of the physical environment available to residents.
- Provides an economic justification and means for the regeneration of degraded/disused heritage environments based, for example, on nineteenth-century harbours, railways, warehouses and manufacturing sites for which the original economic rationale has disappeared.

Social/economic

- Creates economic value/generates markets for natural or built environments that otherwise may have no direct economic contribution to resident populations.
- Generates revenue which may be used for conservation goals.
- Provides employment and opportunities for small businesses. Stimulates compatible new economic activity to supply tourism businesses.
- Raises the standard of living for resident populations, especially if tourism generates otherwise unobtainable foreign currency and tax revenues.
- Underpins the provision of restaurants, sports recreation facilities, local transport and generally improves the quality of life for residents.

Cultural/educational

- Supports and helps to fund local music, theatre, the arts, folk traditions, festivals and events. Provides a market for local crafts and manufacturing.
- Reinforces and focuses local identities and the traditions of particular places. Helps to sustain and focus pride of place.
- Provides a medium for demonstrating and communicating environmental appreciation and values to both visitors and residents.

Figure 6.5 *Positive environmental impacts of tourism – especially holiday tourism*

national corporations motivated solely by short-run profit proceed to destroy community values and cultures and undermine the physical environment. . . . In reality, as Inskeep puts it, 'tourism is only one source of change in society' (Inskeep, 1994, p. 35).

That *laissez-faire* development of tourism is capable of excesses and environmental damage is not in question. The evidence is everywhere to hand and, as with logging and mining, it would be foolish to deny it. But it is also the case that developing countries in the real world have growing populations desperate for food, shelter, health care and education. Many have no choice but to find means of generating income other than from subsistence agriculture and fishing, already increasingly exploited beyond the limits of sustainability by population pressure. For populations locked into a bitter struggle to survive, the alternative to tourism development may be starvation and disease and, for many, a permanently damaged environment incapable of sustaining the existing communities. Environmental resources such as wild-life habitat and even cultural traditions do not have 'intrinsic' values for starving people. The real motivation for people in developing countries is better gauged by the following two examples, which have nothing to do with tourism.

An Albanian fisherman who sought a bumper catch by dropping a Second World War bomb into the sea was killed when it blew up while he was handling it in the port of Vlore.

The Times, 24 July 1996

60 000 coca-leaf growers in Columbia this week staged violent protests against a government plan to destroy vast plantations of the crop used to make cocaine (to supply the world narcotics industry)

The Times 3 August 1996

More than most simple stories these two reveal the opportunism and unconcern for environmental issues common to impoverished people everywhere. Survival takes precedence over altruistic concerns for the environmental capacity of a destination, or increases in costs for the sake of sustainability. Realistic sustainable programmes need to start from that fairly brutal understanding, not from wistful dreams of community participation in imaginary Arcadias.

In the list of positive environmental contributions achievable at destinations through holiday tourism we identify in particular an education or communication impact which does not yet appear to be widely understood. It reflects the fact that some nine out of ten of the population in developed countries now take holidays or day-visits for leisure every year. In this process prospective visitors may browse though some form of tourist board or commercial organization literature before taking a trip, or may be influenced en route to the destination, or at it, for example in air transport or at hotels, museums, theme parks and activity centres. Most visitors are in as relaxed a frame a mind at the destination as they are likely to achieve during a year. Increasing numbers of them are aware of and interested in the environment – identified by them as a key aspect of perceived product quality. Apart from the communications media there is no other global 'industry' of equivalent scale and ubiquity which can reach so many people at the time and in the places where they are most likely to be susceptible, and able to recognize messages about environmental quality. This fact creates an immense communication opportunity for the tourism industry which is only just beginning to be tackled. The communications industry is a logical partner in the process.

Chapter summary

Making the vital caveat that holidays and leisure are only a minor part of all travel and tourism in many countries, this chapter stresses that the environmental impact of leisure tourism constitutes the principal immediate challenge for sustainable development. If the practice of sustainability is relatively new, understanding the negative economic, social and cultural impact of tourism is not. The chapter notes the contribution of seven books since the 1970s but places greater emphasis on the positive environmental contributions achievable and the links with proven marketing techniques.

Because the promotional influence of tourist boards reaches only a minority of holiday visitors, effective sustainable tourism strategies have to be based on a wider focus of the public and private sector businesses that deal with tourism at a destination. For holiday tourism the concept of product formulation – the 'engineering' of product components to achieve agreed goals – is presented as the primary visitor management tool available for implementing sustainable strategies. The scope for planned product formulation is most obvious for new resorts but is capable of implementation at established destinations too. It is stressed that the principal obstacle to effective product engineering is the lack of systematic research to identify destination goals, customer segments and their needs and satisfactions related to environmental qualities.

Finally, it is implicit throughout the chapter that in implementing effective segmentation and product formulation, and devising and communicating effective targeted messages to influence individuals and businesses, marketing is the principal management tool available. Marketing is, of course, a means and not an end in itself. The process for formulating ends or goals is dealt with in Chapters 7–9.

Further reading

Inskeep, E., *Tourism Planning: An Integrated and Sustainable Development Approach*, Van Nostrand Reinhold, New York, 1991.

Middleton, V.T.C., *Marketing in Travel and Tourism*, Butterworth-Heinemann, Oxford, 1988.

Poon, A., *Tourism, Technology and Competitive Strategies*, CAB International, Wallingford, 1993.

Part Two

Managing Tourism for Sustainability at Specific Destinations

7

Managing tourism – the local destination focus

All visitors arrive somewhere to do something (Medlik & Middleton, 1973).

The 'somewhere' in the above quote is always a local tourism destination; the logical focus for practical techniques for tourism management and for developing the necessary tools for achieving sustainable goals. Traditionally, the focus of tourism policy has been national and international, but to make sense of sustainable development, it is local destinations that are increasingly recognized in the 1990s as the centres of energy and direction for tourism strategies and programmes. This chapter explains what is meant by managing visitors and tourism businesses at specific destinations. It introduces the principal 'players' involved in any destination and highlights the *principle of selective influence and control* underlying effective management at local level. It serves as an introduction to Chapters 8 and 9, which develop the explanation of tourism management from the standpoint of the public sector and the private sector, respectively, stressing the vital role for proactive partnership between the sectors.

Fortunately, because tourism is a global industry, good practice in tourism management at destinations tends to be applicable internationally. It is possible for all parts of the world to learn from the experience and developments in management taking place in any particular country, although techniques developed in one culture have to be adapted for application in another. For example, techniques of visitor management pioneered in US national parks or in South Africa's game parks could be adapted for use in China or the UK, and vice versa. Part Three of the book provides examples of good practice in tourism management contributed by practitioners.

The growing importance of the local destination focus for visitor management

Around the world much of the discussion of tourism policy, its impacts and its implications, still takes place at the macro or national level for the simplest of reasons – most governments do not have adequate measures of tourism demand and supply to tackle the issues on any other basis. Where data are available they are typically provided for overall national (domestic) and international (inbound and outbound) tourism but not for tourism at local level. Although it is sometimes possible to disaggregate national survey data to identify trends and impacts at regional level, the sample sizes of such surveys are seldom adequate in practice to yield data accurate enough for local tourism management purposes.

Top-down approach to sustainability – the current approach

To date, where sustainable tourism has been identified as an important issue by national governments it tends to be treated primarily as a matter for policies and planning at national level, usually involving national tourist boards. (See, for example, the top-down planning concepts offered by WTO, 1995.) Promotion, planning, and development policies are normally handled from a macro analysis of economic, social and cultural impacts. The assumption underpinning most tourism policies is, therefore, that it is possible to work downwards from an understanding of the aggregate or macro level of tourism to derive sustainable policies for the component destinations.

Bottom-up approach to sustainability – the emerging approach

For the purposes of sustainable tourism, however, the traditional macro level approach is too generalized and becoming out-dated as we approach the twenty-first century. There is a growing recognition that the local *destination* is the only logical basis for understanding the specific impact of tourism and for developing the tools of visitor management needed for sustainability. In the long run, a bottom-up approach opens up the attractive possibility for evaluating and coordinating nationally 'grassroots' policies that are derived from detailed knowledge at destinations.

Defining tourism destinations

It is not possible to provide one simple watertight definition of a local destination although such areas are easily recognized and understood in practice by those who have to make tourism decisions. Destinations include, for example, coastal, lake or mountain resorts, and cities, historic towns or geographical areas such as national parks. Some destinations are enclosed resorts, such as Disneyland Paris, but the great majority combine residents and a range of economic activities within their boundaries as well as tourism businesses and visitors. An important common feature of many destinations is that they can be marketed and planned as an identified place and most have established systems

and procedures for local government purposes, such as District Councils in the U.K. Exceptionally, for example in the case of small island states in the Caribbean and South Pacific, national and destination interests may coincide. But in most countries the national level typically comprises many separate destinations. A destination may be defined also through the perceptions of visitors making choices where to visit and what to do. They will be influenced variously by the particular marketing images of the place, by the promotional activities of the local tourism industry, by their perceptions of the quality of the local environment, and the welcome of local people. In the rest of this chapter, destination always means local destination and should not be confused with the national level.

Because most countries cannot measure tourism demand and supply adequately at local destinations, and also lack the means of systematically researching environmental impacts and indicators, local authority and local business policies for the promotion and development of tourism typically operate on wholly inadequate management information. Attempting to develop sustainable strategies for tourism without adequate management information reduces the process to political aspiration and guesswork. Notwithstanding the pioneering contributions of authors such as Murphy (1985) and Pearce (1989) in developing logical concepts of community planning for tourism, such ideas will remain in the realm of academia unless tourism and its specific impacts can be measured consistently and systematically at the local level. Sophisticated concepts such as tourism-carrying capacity, impeccable in theory, are immensely complex in practice and they cannot be applied in planning practice until the various measures of capacity can be routinely monitored and measured against different types of visitor demand. At the time of writing, although countries such as Australia, New Zealand and Switzerland are moving in this direction, there is no known major tourism destination country which has adequate measurement for tourism and its impacts at local level, or proven techniques for the simple collection and communication of such data for local visitor management purposes.

Looking ahead to the next century we identify several internationally relevant factors influencing tourism which appear certain to increase the importance of visitor management and marketing at local destination level. These reflect growing awareness internationally of the environmental impact of tourism, the consequent concern for the idea of 'capacity' of resources (however it is defined), notions of limits to growth, and a recognition of the need for better visitor management at destination level (Middleton, 1994c, p. 117). Specifically there is a growing:

- Need to conserve and enhance the special intrinsic qualities and character of 'place' at destinations, both for its own sake and as a core element of its attractiveness to visitors.
- Competition between destinations to achieve shares of more mature tourism markets, with an associated endeavour to ensure consistently higher standards of product delivery at destinations, and to appeal to ever more sophisticated and demanding customers.
- Recognition that for holiday tourism, the quality of the local environment is the key element in the product quality provided by tourism businesses and the basis for effective competition with other destinations.
- Need to plan and control environmentally sustainable development in new resorts to avoid or limit the 'traditional' effects of overdevelopment of tourism – plus the need to refurbish and redevelop existing destinations no longer offering acceptable environmental quality.
- Need for tourism destination management to be more responsive to residents' interests.
- Recognition that research-based market segmentation is an essential first step for achieving effective tourism management at local destinations.
- Need for local authorities to be more accountable for their activities, in accordance with the local implementation of AGENDA 21 policies.

All these factors have an impact at the national level too, but it is at individual destinations where the problems and opportunities occur and the principal energy for change must come. Both marketing and planning strategies will be required to achieve effective visitor management locally, and a much-improved research effort will be needed to provide management information for the local decision processes.

Commitment to a local destination – and factors inhibiting destination management

However committed specific sectors, such as airlines, tour operators and hotels are towards environmental good practice in their investment and operations, it is a fact that most large organizations have no necessary commitment to individual places. At least until the 1990s one could not expect such businesses to take a lead in destination management. Small individual businesses are more obviously committed to the particular places in which they live and operate but they do not necessarily recognize or support sustainable goals. Elected local governments and the public sector managers responsible for planning and regulatory matters in a destination are, at least in theory, the most obvious source of destination management. But experience proves they cannot manage effectively in practice without the active support and participation of tourism businesses.

Readers should be aware that the classic problem in local management for tourism in all parts of the world is that, in theory, the public sector has all the powers needed to manage tourism but in practice lacks the combination of political will, tourism industry expertise and basic research information with which to act effectively. Private-sector businesses possess the practical influence needed to shift key aspects of tourism towards sustainability, especially leisure and holidays, but too few perceive an obvious incentive to do so in the late 1990s.

The meaning of tourism management at destinations

Tourism management must cover demand and supply. It may be summarized as 'Strategies and action programmes using and co-ordinating available techniques to control and influence tourism supply and visitor demand in order to achieve defined policy goals for the local destination' (Middleton, 1994).

In essence, tourism management means persuading visitors and businesses voluntarily to change their naturally occurring behaviour – by selected inducements, or by obliging them to change through the imposition of controls, regulations, taxes and penalties of various kinds. 'Naturally occurring' means what people do when exercising their instincts and choices in a free society. It is normal, for example, for people to wish to visit the countryside in north Europe when the weather is fine and warm; it is normal for them to use their cars and park as close as possible to the places they visit regardless of their cumulative visual and other environmental impact. It is normal for a significant number of visitors to create litter and noise and generally to intrude on places visited, with little regard for the effects of their behaviour on other visitors or residents. It is normal for businesses to set up wherever they perceive profitable streams of potential revenue for whatever activities are permissible within the law including the provision of shops, catering outlets, pubs, clubs, accommodation, gaming, sports facilities and so on. It is normal for many small businesses to evade building, planning and licensing regulations if they can.

Tourism management tends not to be an issue at a destination until naturally occurring behaviour can be seen to cause impacts of a sufficiently negative nature to warrant interference by whatever forms of planning and regulatory mechanisms exist. In practice, of course, there are no easy ways to establish the points at which behaviour requires some form of regulation. The limits vary from time to time and from place to place, and they are interpreted differently by different people as well as being influenced by current local social norms of what is acceptable. In economically developed countries it is often impossible without research to distinguish between the impact of residents' recreation and the pressures of tourism. In all the circumstances it is not so surprising that local tourism management thus far has typically been a reactive rather than a proactive process; usually too little, too late. The need in the 1990s is to be proactive and to address the predictable issues before they reach crisis proportions. In all the complexities surrounding tourism management, students are advised to hold on to the essentially simple concept of reluctant but necessary intervention to change otherwise naturally occurring behaviour.

In practice, tourism management means procedures to influence five primary variables, central to the sustainable debate:

- *Location*   too few or too many people and tourism businesses choosing a particular place.
- *Timing*   too many people or too few at particular places, at certain times of the day, or week, or month.
- *Access*   the relative ease or difficulty and the associated cost of reaching chosen places and moving about within them – including transport infrastructure.
- *Products*   too few or too many 'products,' or too many products of an unsustainable type – including the infrastructure needed to service the products provided (for example sustainable waste-disposal facilities and fresh water supplies).
- *Education and knowledge*   the level of awareness of sustainable issues, and specific knowledge (research) of the cumulative impact of the behaviour of visitors and tourism businesses, and awareness of residents' wishes for a popular destination.

To summarize, tourism management focuses on ways and means to influence visitors' choices of location, access, timing and product provision, and to develop local understanding and knowledge of tourism. It is concerned with judgements of an appropriate balance between demand and supply. It is traditionally problem orientated but it could and should be opportunity and solution focused. An answer to the question, 'what is tourism management?' begs the related questions:

- Who is to do it?
- Who decides what goals?
- Using what controls and influences?

The principle of selective influence and control

Chapter 5 outlined the argument that effective forms of visitor management commence by targeting selected visitor groups. It explained that large parts of total visitor volume at destinations, even for leisure purposes, are outside the direct influence of tourist boards and the private sector. Social visits, visits to friends and relatives, and most same-day visits cannot be controlled except by relatively draconian measures of physically restricting access and/or imposing charging systems for access at prices high enough to have a significant impact on visitor movement. Such measures are theoretically possible and could – with political will and support – be implemented. In practice they are unlikely to be implemented in most destinations because they would be politically unacceptable and the management information needed to target them selectively does not exist. Fortunately there is a staging post between *laissez-faire* and draconian measures which may be called *selective influence and control*. It refers to relatively 'soft' forms of control designed to achieve objectives by persuasion rather than force and it can be summarized as: 'Managing demand in relation to supply, selectively ... to achieve stated and quantified objectives ... at the destination.' In practice this means:

- Specifying sustainable objectives for a destination including judgements on capacity.
- Selecting and targeting particular groups of visitors or market segments who may be influenced in relation to specified products.
- Identifying partner organizations involved in planning and marketing for tourism and supplying the products.
- Developing a combination of management techniques to be applied to the targeted segments and products.
- Systematically monitoring the results achieved and adapting the segments, the products, and the management techniques accordingly.

Although it is usually possible to make initial progress for any destination, using judgement and local knowledge, it will be clear from the five points above that research information for targeting and monitoring at local level is an essential requirement for effective use of the principle of selective influence and control. Bearing in mind that sustainability without tourism management is impossible, and that management requires adequate information, it is hardly surprising that tourism management at destinations is still in its infancy in the 1990s. It will remain so until the local information gaps are tackled.

The interaction of visitors, places and host communities – at the destination

Figure 7.1 indicates the triangular interaction between visitors, places and host communities

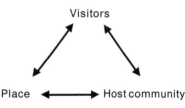

Figure 7.1 *The interaction of visitors, places and host communities. Source: ETB (1992)*

which lies at the heart of all approaches to tourism management. Developed in 1991 for the English Tourist Board (ETB) following extensive consultation in the UK and internationally, the diagram neatly encapsulates the three main focal points for management decisions. The triangle has the obvious advantage of simplicity for both communicating and understanding but it needs some development for the purposes of this chapter.

The essential need is to recognize that there are not just two principal forces which impact upon place (visitors and host communities in the diagram), but four distinctively separate forces or *players* in the management decision process. The idea of players is important since it expresses the continuing competition – and often dispute – between those who determine the goals for a destination and those who have to live with the consequences of the goals. In practice, success or

failure in progress towards sustainable patterns of tourism is the outcome of a network of forces discussed in the next section. The four groups of 'players' outlined below are entirely compatible with the ETB triangle, but take the concept one stage further. The use of a wheel in Figure 7.2 carries with it the idea of movement, of interactive decisions revolving around a hub, and shifting direction.

Four parties involved in the wheel of tourism management at the destination

Figure 7.2 indicates the players as spokes of a wheel with visitor activities at the hub. Some visitors purchase their activities as commercial products and others consume them with only

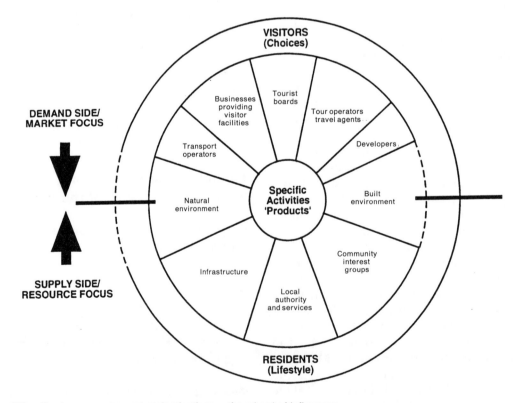

Figure 7.2   *Tourism management at destinations – the wheel of influences*

limited use of the private sector, as in the case of visitors to friends and relatives. Destination management decisions influence the volume and type of activities that a destination provides and, for management purposes, so it is important to group all these activities as 'products'. Grouping destination activities into products for sale or non-commercial use is one of the core techniques available to manage visitors. (See product formulation in Chapter 6.)

The wheel is divided horizontally with the upper half designated as the visitor demand or market side and the lower half, supply or resource side including 'residents' interests. The wheel has ten separate spokes but these may be broadly aggregated for discussion purposes into four groups of 'players'. These are the four main parties involved in decisions at visitor destinations in any country, although they are by no means homogeneous groups. Each of them comprises conflicting interests:

• Residents (community interest groups and local resources) whose lives and – for some their livelihoods – are involved. For holiday tourism especially, the attraction of a destination typically reflects scenic resources and climate, and the arts, heritage, culture and lifestyles of a local population. In some places the lifestyle of the residents may be a primary attraction to visitors and a principal feature in image promotion. Some (usually a minority) of residents are typically represented by community interest groups, some of which are likely to favour tourism activities while others do not.

• Elected representatives and appointed officials of local government (local authority and services, natural and built environment, and infrastructure) responsible to residents for the overall goals and management of the destination. Tourism is typically only one part of a much wider range of responsibilities covering, for example, aspects of housing, transport, education, policing, social security provision, and recreation, sport and the arts. Typically, a local authority has statutory

responsibility for the built environment, natural environment and infrastructure, and it may also be a direct provider of some of the attractions such as museums, theatres, conference facilities and so on. For many destinations the local tourist board is likely to be managed by the local authority although many of its functions will involve direct liaison and need the funding support and cooperation of the private sector.

• Businesses providing directly and indirectly for visitors to the destination. Mostly in the private sector, these include hotels and other accommodation providers, restaurants and cafés, coaches and other local transport, amusement centres, recreation and arts-related attractions. Also directly involved, although mostly not locally based, are the tour operators and transport companies serving particular destinations. Included too are private-sector developers. As noted above, local tourist boards are likely to include commercial as well as local authority players within their organization structure, and to play a dual role. Increasingly at the end of the twentieth century the private sector is involved in operating parts of the built and natural environment for profit, and the market forces/resource focus line in Figure 7.2 is drawn to include both private and public sector.

• Visitors, understood as a group of identified market segments, whose individual decisions collectively determine the volume and type of demand for any destination. Although not all visitors purchase commercial products or respond to commercial marketing, the provision of commercial products is typically the major determinant of the overall volume and type of tourist demand.

The main tourism management controls and influences

With some fifty or more years of development behind them, there are well-established manage-

Table 7.1   *Resource constraints and market forces – tourism management controls and influences at destinations*

Resource constraints (supply orientation) mainly public sector	Market forces (demand orientation) mainly commercial sector
Regulation of land use	Knowledge of visitor profiles, behaviour, needs and trends
Regulation of buildings	Design of visitor products (quality and satisfaction)
Regulation of environmental impacts	Capacity (products marketed)
Provision of infrastructure	Promotion (image/ positioning)
Control by licensing	Distribution of products/ access for customers
Provision of information	Provision of information
Fiscal controls and incentives	Price

ment and marketing techniques available to the players represented in the destination wheel (Figure 7.2). These are summarized in Table 7.1 and based on Middleton (1979) and Pearce (1989), recognizing that numerous other authors cover the same techniques in their own terms.

It can be seen that the management controls or techniques listed under 'resource constraints' are those which are typically associated with the powers of local government. In other words, they are the primary public sector controls. The management controls listed as 'market forces' are typically associated with the private sector. These techniques are defined in Chapters 8 and 9 but they are summarized in parallel in Table 7.1 to stress:

- That tourism management is concerned equally with aspects of supply and demand.
- The way the two sets of controls operate in practice reflects the management orientation or dominant culture ruling in the organizations which use them.

It is true of any form of modern management in both the public and private sector that there is invariably a dominant philosophy or management style practised by senior managers, many of whom learned it in their formative years as junior managers. The dominant philosophy has to be appreciated because it strongly influences the way in which managers behave and make strategic decisions. Although one of the most encouraging developments in international tourism in the 1990s is the breaking down of traditional barriers between the public and private sectors, it would be naive to overlook the deeply rooted and continuing power of the two distinctive management orientations, explained below.

Public sector – supply-side orientation for local government planners

The resource-based or supply-side management philosophy commences, with apparent logic, from an understanding of the nature of the resource for which plans are required. Outside the tourism domain, for example in local government housing policies, there is obvious logic in first establishing how many houses of a certain type can be constructed to meet demand on any given area of land deemed appropriate for housing development, based on an acceptable number of houses per hectare. The number of existing houses, plus any new ones to be built, determines the number of residents and all else follows from there – provision for shopping, local transport, recreation facilities, capacity of schools and so on. Thus, concepts of capacity, based on known area densities and easily quantified standards of provision per thousand head of population, are the basis for strategic decisions and comparisons with other areas. Quantification is precise, based on census data and systems for collecting local taxes, and the measurement process is continuously updated, nowadays with all the relevant information held on computer databases.

Closely quantified capacity-based planning strategies have been developed steadily for over a century in economically developed countries and the issues are well understood and explained in the massive literature associated with local government planning procedures. It does not follow that capacity-based planning is necessarily always successful. In all countries one may find evidence of planning failures and political distortion of the planning procedures, as well as evidence of significant successes. A principal danger arises if local government planners, typically with no commercial experience, become inward-looking to the nature of the resource and preoccupied with *existing uses* because that is what is quantified and understood. Problems invariably arise where planners are required by elected politicians to act as social engineers and to second-guess business development decisions. Human nature generally resists the processes of change and there is little evidence, with a few honourable exceptions, that local planners or indeed the great majority of politicians are also visionaries capable of perceiving future scenarios for post-industrial communities, and orchestrating the changes needed to achieve *new uses* for existing resources. Politicians also tend to have short-term horizons bounded by the need to seek re-election. It was for such reasons that, in the UK for example, Development Corporations were established in areas selected for major redevelopment, deliberately to engineer change and cope with resource needs and long-term planning processes that existing democratically elected local governments and their planning systems could not achieve.

The principal criticism of a supply-based orientation for tourism is that it tends to be backward-looking to existing use notions of resources, rather than forward-looking toward trends and new uses emerging in fast-changing markets. In its tourism application it is often attempting to match people who have many places to choose from with poorly articulated products and notions of 'capacity' that cannot be measured. A difficult task.

Private sector – demand-side orientation for commercially run businesses

The modern demand-side or market-orientated management philosophy, typically associated with the private sector, commences with an understanding of the characteristics of the customers with which an organization seeks to do business. Invariably the focus is on potential as well as existing customers. Outside the tourism domain, for example in the motor industry, the dominant logic is to understand as much as possible about existing users, especially those who purchase new vehicles, and to research the market continuously to develop and refine knowledge of customer needs, wishes and behaviour. Detailed information is available on the profile of customers – their own and of those who buy competitors' products – the purchase choices customers make, the way they finance their purchases and their servicing behaviour during a vehicle's life. Without such management information to supplement commercial judgement it is no longer possible to compete successfully in the private sector.

The concept of capacity is obviously a key issue for manufacturers. For the motor industry it is production-line capacity in factories, and distribution capacity in sales outlets. But it is not calculated or influenced, except in the short run of, say, 1 to 2 years, by any limiting 'existing-use' notions of what a factory can produce. Capacity is geared to a forecast of the volume of cars of specified types which will be purchased at prices producing acceptable profits. If the forecast suggests the number will double over a five-year period, one may be sure that capacity will be increased to meet the new demand. When Ford of UK say in their consumer advertising 'Everything we do, is driven by you' they are expressing succinctly the philosophy of modern market orientation. Most commercial organizations bring the same philosophy to bear on tourism and they have very different ideas of capacity from those in the public sector.

Travel and tourism businesses have been relatively late adopters of modern market-orientated management concepts, but the customer-focused philosophy now motivates international airlines, large tour operators, sea ferries, international hotel groups, car rental organizations and the major players in theme parks. An outward-looking commitment to market research and a continuous concern for forecasting future demand is always a characteristic of such firms. As with planning, there are inevitably many examples of management incompetence and commercial strategies which did not work in practice. The main difference in the private sector is that information systems make it possible to detect incompetence relatively quickly, competition drives out weak managers, and business failures and take-overs by competitors are common, ensuring a continuous flow of new thinking.

The principal criticism of a commercial orientation in tourism is that, at least in the short run, it does not obviously have to take account of environmental issues, either in destination resources or in the broader realm of commercial operations which generate waste and pollution. It is accused of giving customers what they are prepared to pay for today without concern for environmental damage, in order to maximize short-run profits. We return to these issues in Part Three to asses how relevant they are for the next decade.

Tourism management partnerships

From this brief review of the strengths and weaknesses of the two principal management orientations at work within the destination wheel (Figure 7.2) the importance of developing partnerships to achieve synergy between the private and public sector is inescapable. *Partnership for sustainability means jointly negotiated and agreed approaches to tourism management in which the goals are mutually defined and endorsed, and the techniques designed to achieve matching of demand and supply are jointly operated.* The private sector invariably has the best continuous information about demand and the most powerful of the management techniques for persuasive influence (see Chapter 9). The public sector has the ultimate sanctions over the agreed capacity and use of the resources that support leisure tourism, and ultimately reflects the political possibilities of limits to growth and acceptable impact on residents' lives.

In theory, the powers already available to most local governments are sufficient to achieve sustainable goals for tourism. Given determined public sector managers and political support, control over land use, building regulations, car parking and licensing procedures are strictly all that is necessary. In practice, the public sector does not and cannot have the flexibility to innovate continuously and promote change that is inherent in the private sector. It does not have access to the vital flows of information about customers which is a powerful tool for all who deal with them directly. In theory, the powers available to the commercial sector are also sufficient to achieve sustainable goals for tourism. Where a commercial organization operates enclosed resorts, such as Disneyland Paris or Center Parcs, and there are no residents except employees, this is already achievable. In the enclosed resorts, once original planning permissions have been negotiated, the operator acts in lieu of the public sector and it is no surprise that some of the leading examples of good practice in destination management are to be found in enclosed resorts. So too are some of the worst, especially where there is no planned integration with local communities in the surrounding area.

In the majority of established destinations, where tourism co-exists with residents and other forms of economic activity, public/private partnerships have been developing in all parts of the world over the last decade. Part Four provides specific case studies, all of which are partnership based around sustainable goals.

Economically developed or developing countries

It may be supposed that the management of tourism is very different in economically developed and developing countries. In fact some of the more sophisticated approaches to modern planning and sustainable issues are to be found in new destinations in economically developing countries, and the principles of visitor management at the destination are the same. Some differences do lie, however, in the relative power of the two sectors. In economically developed countries the institutions of local government and associated planning techniques are typically well developed. Local residents of tourism destinations and their elected representatives are generally articulate and, with media support, can achieve a strong measure of influence over local development processes. The bargaining position of the public sector against the private sector is, therefore, relatively strong.

In developing countries the institutions of local government and the associated planning techniques are typically weaker and, even where planning laws and regulations exist, they may not be operated in the face of a powerful developer or operator who holds the economic purse strings. This is true, of course, for all forms of industrial development and it happens often enough in economically developed nations too. Tourism development just happens to be a modern example of a much more deeply rooted phenomenon. On the other hand, many developing countries are relatively small, often their tourism industry is relatively less developed, and their national governments may well be able to take a more direct role in destination development, thus reinforcing the local bargaining power. In the *real politik* of achieving inward investment and of earning foreign currency, however, national governments of smaller coun-

tries have little real power against multinational corporations with choices to exercise. Again, this would be true for any major inward investor.

The worst excesses in tourism development over the last two decades have typically occurred where powerful commercial operators have been able to exploit their economic muscle to achieve developments which breach what are now understood to be sustainable principles, and were never planned with sustainable goals in mind. Paradoxically some of the worst excesses are also associated with small, locally owned, resident business entrepreneurs who own or acquire land cheaply and use it to tap into the early rapid growth phases of a tourism destination. Where traditionally deprived populations are offered a prospect of gaining rapid access to wealth, there is no evidence that they tend not to take it. On the contrary, coastal developments, for example in Cyprus, Greece and Turkey, originated in large foreign companies' investment. But the opportunity was quickly seized by local residents seeking, understandably, to join a scramble for profit. Small businesses in developing countries may ignore such planning systems as exist and are certainly the least likely to accept wider concerns for the cumulative environmental damage that their individual actions cause. Concepts of so-called community planning, often hailed as the only logical way forward for tourism, may be just as destructive in practice as the alternatives and may open the door for wider development to follow. There is no evidence that residents' choices and democracy will automatically guarantee sustainable development.

Chapter summary

This chapter has emphasized the growing importance of local destinations as the primary source of energy and development of good practice in the management of tourism demand and supply to meet sustainable goals. It identifies the main players that control the techniques available for managing and influencing tourism and draws the key distinctions between a resource or supply-side orientation and a consumer or market-side orientation. Recognizing that sustainable tourism always means achieving a targeted balance between demand and supply, and influencing what we call 'normally occurring behaviour' of individuals and businesses, the need for partnerships to harness the strengths and techniques available within the public and private sector is introduced. This is demonstrated in Part Four of the book, in the case studies. The principle of selective influence and control has special relevance for tourism management at local destinations, but it requires better research information than presently exists to be effective.

The chapter expresses the authors' view that, apart from a few very special circumstances, sustainable tourism will not emerge from what we know of community-led developments. The case for destination partnerships, and responsibility on the part of large commercial sector organizations is, therefore, powerful and unavoidable. So too is the issue of how large organizations can bring sustainable influence to bear on smaller enterprises.

Three fundamental principles underlying management of sustainable development for tourism at local destinations are developed within the chapter:

- That setting sustainable goals is necessarily associated with specific aspects of demand and supply experienced locally, and that measurement is the essential basis for developing sustainable management techniques.
- That targeted groups of visitors have to be managed in relation to a supply of products, using a range of techniques mostly already available in the public and private sectors.
- That effective management cannot take place without forms of partnership between those who market products at a destination, those who produce them on the ground, and those who are responsible for the local implementation of statutory planning and regulatory powers.

Further reading

Inskeep, E., *National and Regional Tourism Planning*, Routledge, London, 1994 (for a contrast with this chapter).

Murphy, P. E., *Tourism: A Community Approach*, Methuen, New York, 1985.

8

Managing tourism at local destinations – the public sector role

The success of a destination in terms of satisfaction of the tourist is a function of several interdependent components. This underscores the need for strategic and integrated planning in respect of tourist destinations, together with the selective use of specific tools and techniques to address integrated quality management (including quality control) of the destination. (European Commission, 1997).

Chapter 7 focused on the growing importance of managing both demand and supply for tourism at local visitor destinations. It stressed that sustainability involves setting goals for destinations and developing specific techniques or 'tools' to achieve the goals through the processes of tourism management. Some of these tools are in the hands of the public sector and focus mainly on the supply side. Others are controlled by the range of commercial businesses in the private sector and relate mainly to demand. In this chapter *public sector role* means the regulatory and other powers exercised by local government, with support and sometimes with direction from central or federal government and the tourism agencies they appoint. Locally, public sector bodies have statutory responsibility and usually some form of political accountability, for planning and managing economic activity generally, including tourism, providing services to residents, and for key infrastructure services in their area. Local government typically acts as

an agency for implementing nationally and internationally agreed regulations and law, and in this context their role in local implementation of the AGENDA 21 agreements for sustainable development in all countries is especially important.

This chapter highlights five of the principal regulatory/management tools available in the public sector, stressing the extensive power of the tools over tourism – *if* they are coordinated and used systematically. It provides examples relevant to tourism and further illustrations will be found in the case study material in Part Four of the book. We stress in the final part of the chapter that the role of the public sector has been changing rapidly over recent years, partly as a result of growing pressure on the financial resources available to achieve objectives and partly in response to AGENDA 21. Modern partnership activities with the private sector are particularly relevant to the themes of this book and the chapter notes the growing recognition of a marketing perspective, increasingly adopted by local authorities to deal with tourism.

The potential power of public sector control over tourism

The core proposition in this chapter is that there are massive supply-side powers within the public sector in most parts of the world, available *now* to achieve sustainable tourism, provided only that there is first, the knowledge to apply the available powers selectively, and second, the will to enact and enforce regulations. To illustrate the proposition, the following synopsis extracted from the Bermuda Development Plan published more than twenty years ago (1974) shows that there is nothing very new in the rationale for sustainable goals, or in the basic techniques of land use and building regulations for controlling unwanted development. Both flow logically from the provisions for town and country planning legislation, sensibly adapted for tourism purposes. What is new is the growing weight of evidence that the issues identified in Bermuda a quarter of a century ago in a small island context, are now global in their implications and cannot be ignored without the risk of significant environmental damage.

> The following matters shall be at the discretion of the Planning Board – in areas already designated for development for hotels and cottage colonies, working within an overall requirement that hotel and cottage colony developments shall be integrated into the surrounding rural environment. The numbers of rooms permitted; maximum height and bulk of structures; ancillary uses to be permitted or expressly prohibited on site; maximum site coverage; number and location of parking places; amount, type and location of landscaping required; number and location of all points of pedestrian and vehicular ingress and egress.

The full range of matters at the discretion of the Board is actually much longer than the extracts quoted above. To add the belt to the braces, the Development Plan, adds 'and all other matters the Board may consider required to provide a development consistent with the Bermuda image'.

One may argue that Bermuda was especially fortunate in that the island is a small, affluent, and sophisticated destination that inherited a well-developed planning system from the UK. Island government and local government effectively coincided and could exercise full control over the destination, and there were developers seeking permission to build for a well-proven demand. It is different where local destinations in developing countries with very limited economic options are seeking to persuade international developers to choose their sites, and wooing them with incentives. In the latter case the balance of power is obviously more likely to lie with the developer but this does not alter the essential point about the potential power within the public sector. The 1974 link between environment and image is highly relevant to the themes of this book.

Bermuda went on subsequently to hone its powers to sustain the environment and by 1994 was reported to 'restrict resident households to one car, prohibit rental cars, restrict the number of cruise ships permitted at any one time in the harbour ... impose heavy fines for anglers or dive boat operators that damage coral reefs, prohibit neon signs,' and so on (WTTC/WTO/Earth Council, 1996, p. 44).

The five main management tools for local government

To simplify the explanation of a highly complex subject to its principles, we present in the main part of this chapter a brief resumé of the five main powers available to control and manage tourism at local destinations. Four of them are resource-based or supply-side measures, and one focuses on demand:

- Land-use planning regulations (reactive and proactive).
- Building regulations (reactive and proactive).
- Provision of infrastructure, especially access.
- Investment incentives and fiscal controls and regulations.
- Influence over demand.

Land-use planning

(a) Protective/reactive/defensive powers for land-use planning

In all parts of the world statutory controls over the use and especially the development of land for economic and social purposes is the most basic and perhaps the most effective of all the management tools available to planners. Land-use planning was established in its modern form around a century ago in economically developed countries as a necessary response to the need to protect the health of the population in towns from the impacts of industrialization and the demands of a growing population, and to provide essential urban infrastructure. It was initially developed primarily to deal with problems stemming from the chaotic and insanitary conditions created by nineteenth-century industrial change. The needs of rural communities and landscape tended to follow a different form of development although the notion of intervention to control the use of land underlies both forms of planning response. The nineteenth-century origins of land-use planning have little or nothing to do with tourism except, interestingly, in environmentally fragile places such as the English Lake District and some national parks in other countries.

In all countries land-use legislation is typically applied either by local government within a statutory planning framework established at national or federal level or by agencies granted local government powers for planning purposes in designated areas. Land-use controls apply to most forms of development and, in a tourism and leisure context, local permission is invariably required before a developer or operator can develop land for a holiday village, for example, or build an hotel or caravan park; extend an existing facility on its agreed site by adding more caravans; or build an hotel extension. Permission is typically also needed to modify the use of an existing site, for example by turning a golf course into a wider leisure complex. For larger developments there is a growing requirement that Environmental Impact Assessments (EIA) are conducted before planning permission is granted. See Chapter 11.

In areas judged fragile for environmental reasons, the protection of natural resources and bio-diversity from the naturally occurring behaviour of people can be traced back in its modern forms for over a century. Developments since the 1970s have made the process more sophisticated, and in the last decade new technology has greatly facilitated the processes, for example using satellite mapping and monitoring combined with computer databases. Although agricultural land has typically not had the same attention as town planning, land-use designation in the UK dating back over fifty years includes the concept of *green belts* around cities and towns to specify areas in which residential and other forms of development will normally not be permitted. UK national parks legislation dates from the 1940s.

Invariably in areas of special scenic quality and biodiversity, the need for protective land-use regulation has been prevalent. Of specific relevance to tourism, protection commences with area designation and well-established examples include designation of national parks such as the Lake District in the UK and Kruger Park in South Africa, and other special areas such as the Great Barrier Reef Marine Park in Australia, and large parts of the Alpine region in South Europe. Protective land-use designation helps to focus, justify and facilitate land-use regulations.

Other protective measures include designation of areas of outstanding landscape value in a national context, for example Heritage Coast in the UK now covering much of south-west England, and the designation of nature reserves and other areas in which the biodiversity is fragile and threatened with serious loss.

(b) Proactive or indicative land-use planning and zoning

With a framework of protective/reactive or defensive measures in place, it is a logical next step to be proactive in employing land-use planning controls to promote and encourage selected forms of development in specified places. In practice this is an issue for a combination of controls and incentives (see later in the chapter). In Europe, North America and Australia, for example, planners commonly identify and *zone* areas of land as suitable for housing, or for offices, for light industry, for retail parks or for a combination of these activities. Similarly, it is normal to designate other areas as suitable for urban or countryside parks, for golf, for marinas or for hotel or other visitor accommodation construction. The Bermuda example noted earlier is a classic example of indicative land-use planning.

As with the reactive measures, positive designation can cover plans to extend and modify existing uses of land as well as new developments. Increasingly, to support compliance with proactive planning guidelines, packages of funds and other measures intended to bring about the designated form of development may be made available if it is assumed that it will not happen solely by planning designation and market forces. Proactive land-use controls are seen at their most effective in the redevelopment plans for derelict or decaying urban areas, such as Baltimore Inner Harbor, USA, Darling Harbour in Australia, or Cardiff Bay in Wales. They are also most effective in protected environments such as The Great Barrier Reef where some development permission has been linked with requirements for developers to fund and provide infrastructure such as water-desalination plant, sewage treatment and waste water disposal, and facilities to consume and dispose of solid wastes. Internationally one of the most developed forms of positive designation relevant to tourism lies with the United Nations Educational, Scientific and Cultural Organization (UNESCO). Since 1975 UNESCO has formally recognized and designated over 300 World Heritage Sites of 'outstanding universal value' in terms of cultural and natural heritage. They are to be found in all parts of the world ranging from the Pyramids of Egypt, the Taj Mahal in India, the Great Barrier

Reef in Australia and cities such as Krakow in Poland and Edinburgh in Scotland.

In some countries, as a key technique for achieving the objectives of land-use planning, it may be judged necessary to take areas of land into public ownership for the better exercise of control. Although public ownership measures for tourism are not common, tourism and leisure are frequently designated as key sectors for development within such areas. Classic examples in Europe of proactive land-use planning can be seen in the Languedoc-Roussillon region of the South of France in which a chain of six coastal resorts was developed in the late 1960s and early 1970s, specifically for tourism and recreational purposes.

(c) Land-use planning – summary

In the context of new developments or in major refurbishment plans for areas designated for redevelopment, land-use planning instruments are more than adequate for controlling the capacity, form, characteristics and environmental impact of tourism in destination areas, especially where EIAs are a prerequisite. They are, obviously, much less effective in changing established patterns of tourism, sometimes developed prior to the implementation of modern planning regimes.

As with all forms of planning, the use of this very powerful tool is highly dependent for its effectiveness on what those who use it know about the phenomenon being planned and on who owns the land. Land-use planning was not designed with tourism applications in mind and the knowledge of tourism and tourism product development among land-use planners is typically very limited until recent years, for example in most cities, small towns and rural areas, a knowledge of travel and tourism by planners was unnecessary. Land-use designation can greatly facilitate forms of sustainable tourism but, as illustrated throughout this book, it cannot ensure that sustainable goals will be met.

Building regulations

(a) Protective/reactive measures for buildings

Controls over buildings are the second principal supply-side tool in the structure of local government planning. They cover buildings for all purposes, including tourism. Building controls mostly work alongside and supplement the intentions of land-use controls – the left/right punch of regulation. As for land use, there are regulations to cover new building developments and to protect existing ones. As for land use, it is always easier to control new developments than to deal with existing ones, especially where the deeply entrenched interests of industry and populations are involved. For new tourism buildings, as for office buildings, for example, it is normal in all parts of the world for regulations to cover the size of buildings, their height, the density of the structures in relation to a site (for example, the number of holiday villas which may be built on a hectare of designated land), plus access and car parking arrangements.

(b) Proactive planning for buildings

The distinction between reactive and proactive is less clear for buildings than for land. For example, in addition to specifying the limits to what is acceptable, building regulations may go on to specify requirements for landscaping the areas surrounding buildings, as they do in Bermuda; they may determine the fabric and texture of building materials to be used, the colour, and even the architectural style to be observed. Although there are always dangers of applying existing use criteria to new developments, there are at least some fairly rudimentary published guidelines available for planners as to the number of metres of beach space required per hundred tourist bed spaces, the ratio of parking spaces to bed spaces, and so on.

Roughly equivalent to the designation of land for protective purposes, similar measures typically apply to historic and occasionally to more modern buildings. Formal designation of buildings confers protection upon them by imposing specific obligations on owners for their upkeep and prohibiting significant changes in any applications for planning permission that may be made. It is normal for designated buildings to qualify for grants and subsidies in the same way that provision is made for designated land. This is the 'sticks and carrots' approach to achieving planning goals, in which the regulations are the sticks and the grants and subsidies are the carrots.

Where a particular series of buildings make up the bulk of a town or a historic quarter of it, specific areas may be designated as conservation zones. In that case proactive planning provisions apply to all the heritage buildings to protect the historic character as a whole. Notable examples are Bath or Canterbury in the UK, Bruges in Belgium, Prague in the Czech Republic, or the centre of Munich in Germany, but there are hundreds of examples and the numbers increase every year. The UK alone is estimated to have over 9000 conservation areas in the late 1990s. Over the last decade tourism, especially the economic value it generates, has become a primary reason for protecting buildings and townscapes and sites of cultural interest. The buildings are designated ostensibly for their intrinsic value and role within a community, but it is mostly tourism-related uses which convey the vital economic rationale.

In many countries, the state, regional, or local government may construct, acquire or in other ways provide support for particular buildings and use them for tourism-related purposes as part of a plan to achieve particular forms of tourism development. Examples are convention centres now commonly found in leading cities and resorts around the world, theatres, sports and entertainment complexes and, in some cases, hotels and other visitor accommodation. Buildings for leisure purposes with particular access and facilities for people with disabilities, or whole resorts to cater for the needs of people economically and socially disadvantaged, are also common features of the public sector influence and control over buildings, especially in Europe.

(c) Building regulations – a summary

Proactive building regulations, especially when combined with the power of land-use controls and evidence from EIAs, have a synergy that provides the most powerful of tools for the management of tourism and the achievement of sustainable goals in nearly all countries. Such tools are mostly already in place. As noted for land-use controls, however, building regulations were never designed with the tourism industry in mind; tourism is just an application. Everything depends on the knowledge of tourism which lies in the hands of the planners and the elected representatives that take the planning decisions. If they are relatively well informed as they are in Bermuda, although the number of golf courses built there has been criticized as not sustainable in the long run, the two techniques together are capable of nearly all the guidance that is needed in any destination to achieve sustainable new development and to modify existing development toward greater sustainability. As for land-use, the key issue for sustainability is not one of designing new public sector tools to manage tourism development. It is developing knowledge to use the existing tools to their full effect, drawing on good practice internationally.

Provision of infrastructure

Apart from enclosed resorts built by developers, the planning, provision and funding of infrastructure for a destination has traditionally rested mainly in the hands of the public sector. Broadly defined, infrastructure covers the means of access, the maintenance of natural resources and the construction of the publicly accessible parts of the built environment, the provision of tourist facilities such as marinas, and the provision of utilities on which the tourism industry depends such as gas, water, electricity, sewerage and drainage services.

Illustrated, for example, by the development of motorway toll systems and the Channel Tunnel, there is growing evidence that both local and central government in many countries are actively seeking to hive off to the private sector as much as possible of their traditional provision and funding of infrastructure. This is especially likely to apply to tourism where specific new or additional provision is needed, over and above residential need. Some projects are likely to be jointly planned, funded and operated, and infrastructure provision is a logical target for joint or partnership approaches. The public sector is not likely to relinquish its primary role in controlling the planning process, however, nor can it avoid its contribution, at least in part, to funding most major projects for the foreseeable future.

(a) Access to destinations – provision or denial

- *Provision* – In most countries construction of airports, seaports, roads, railways and terminals for public transport, and the provision of car parking spaces and public transport systems, are typically provided and mostly also paid for by a combination of local government with central government and its various agencies. In other words, a destination's overall *capacity* to receive and absorb visitors is heavily influenced by public sector decisions. For most tourism destinations with a significant residential population, such infrastructure is provided primarily to sustain the local economy and for residents' use. Except for purpose-built resorts, or where tourism is a major sector of the local economy, usage for day visits and staying visits is often marginal in most destinations for most times of the year. When infrastructure such as roads and parking provision is already used to approaching maximum capacity, however, tourism uses are often identified as an important issue, not least because of the high visibility of modern visitors' dress and behaviour.

- *Denial* – the opposite side of the coin to providing infrastructure to facilitate access is to use the same powers to deny it, thereby physically choking off demand. For example, it is normal for local government to decide the volume of publicly available car parking spaces to be provided in its area, directly or under licence, and to protect such spaces for residents if that is the wish. It is possible to prohibit certain types of vehicle such as caravans or camper trucks on roads and in areas judged unsuitable for them, and to limit the size of the camp sites and holiday parks provided for such vehicles. In certain cases it is also possible to close roads completely to prevent visitor access by car to environmentally fragile areas or to restrict moorings for pleasure craft. Other controls can be applied, as in Salzburg in the 1990s, to restrict the provision of access and parking spaces for coaches. Although not popular, it is certain that denial and limitation of access by local government will be used increasingly over the next decade where certain types of tourism are judged to have exceeded saturation point.

(b) The maintenance of natural resources and the built environment

As outlined in Chapter 6, much of leisure tourism is motivated by the quality of a destination's environmental attractions. Beaches, lakes, mountains, rivers, forests, countryside, and parks and gardens are all typically the responsibility of the local government in whose areas they are located, working with central government and its appointed agencies. Protection of natural resources is covered by the land-use regulations described earlier in the chapter with much of the cost of maintenance and any enhancement typically funded by the public sector. Where natural resources are developed for tourism use, for example in the construction of pistes for skiing, or the development of long-distance walking routes in national parks, or of yacht harbours,

there is a continuing role for the public sector in the majority of countries, increasingly with the partnership of commercial enterprises.

Large parts of the built environment are also the responsibility of local government, acting in the interests of residents and in accordance with their view of the economic base and future prospects of the locality. Part Four of the book includes a case study of Edinburgh Old Town, the historic quarter of Edinburgh including the castle, on which Edinburgh's image and much of its tourism depends. It fell to agencies in the public sector to motivate, plan, fund and execute this major infrastructure project.

(c) Related infrastructure services

In many parts of the world the provision of water, electricity, gas, sewerage and waste-disposal services are funded and controlled by local governments. Without them the provision of tourism accommodation and other facilities would not be possible. Drinking water in particular, now a scarce commodity in many of the destinations favoured by visitors, has become a major infrastructure issue related to tourism. In the developed world, one may point to the fact that agriculture and poor maintenance of water supply systems exacerbate the drain on scarce resources, but in many destinations in developing countries visitor consumption of water typically far exceeds that of local residents. If golf courses, swimming pools and water-intensive landscaping are provided as part of the tourism industry, in addition to the frequent showers and baths and laundry facilities that modern guests expect, the pressures on available water supply may become a source of local resentment and conflict.

In such cases the problem lies less with tourism developers, however, and more with the capacity judgements that are invariably made, or deliberately avoided, by the public sector. We include in Part Four of the book one example of a commercially operated reservoir originally designed to meet the needs of local residents. It does that and has in addition been developed with new uses to become an award-winning tourism destination and conservation area in its own right.

(d) Infrastructure – a summary

In its role of planning and providing much of the infrastructure of visitor destinations, the public sector ultimately controls two of the key variables for tourism management. The first is *capacity* because, although it is a crude and very blunt instrument for this purpose, the capacity of the infrastructure, especially access arrangements, ultimately determines the capacity of tourism. Equally important, the *quality* of the infrastructure, especially of the natural and built resources which attract leisure tourism, is strongly influenced by the public sector. To suggest that infrastructure *determines* product quality may seem too strong to some readers but the direct linkage is undeniably there. It is judged to be a critical issue for the management of tourism to meet sustainable goals and it lies primarily in the hands of the public sector.

Investment incentives and fiscal controls

'Short of the Minister of Tourism personally undertaking to change the sheets [in hotel bedrooms] it is difficult to imagine more favourable treatment ...' (Young, 1973, p. 137). The quote from *Tourism: Blessing or Blight?* describing a particularly blatant attempt to encourage tourism development is chosen to reinforce the message that there is nothing new in the use of investment incentives or 'carrots' to encourage tourism. Epitomized in the example from Bermuda, land-use and building regulations were described earlier as the essential 'sticks' with which the public sector may persuade developers and tourism businesses to meet planning regulations. No compliance, no permission.

Very often, however, especially in parts of the world which are desperate to attract tourism for the economic benefits associated with it, developers have many choices. Instead of would-be destinations dealing with a queue of applicants for permission to develop, many may find themselves in a queue of supplicants seeking to persuade developers to choose their sites. It is at this point that a range of public sector incentives or 'sweeteners' are brought into play. They are perhaps most vividly witnessed in a modern tourism context in the remarkable effort and investment promises put forward internationally in bids to host the Olympic Games and the other major international sporting events.

Incentives are not, of course, a phenomenon peculiar to tourism development. The urgent need for all forms of industrial development (manufacturing and services) means that national and local governments around the world are now accustomed to active marketing and promotion of their planned development areas, and the tourism industry is just one illustration of a modern search for inward investment. Medlik (1996, p. 148) distinguishes between financial, quasi-financial, and fiscal incentives covering a wide range of potential incentives. They are not all likely to apply in the same place at the same time, although it would be normal for more than one of the following to apply to areas promoting economic development opportunities through tourism. Incentives include:

- Grants towards the capital cost of tourism accommodation and attractions.
- Loans at very favourable rates not available commercially.
- Public sector acting as guarantors for corporate bank loans.
- Initial work in clearing land and preparing it for development.
- Provision of infrastructure services such as access and utilities to the site paid for by the public sector.
- Peppercorn rents for the use of a site for a fixed number of years or until profits reach an agreed level.

- Tax concessions offered against capital development costs.
- Exemption for a specified period from corporation tax on profits and right to carry forward losses.
- Guarantees to ensure that existing exchange rates are maintained (if they should deteriorate against the developer).
- Relief from import duties on materials and equipment needed to build tourism facilities.
- Subsidies to developers for taking on local labour.
- Training provision for local labour at public sector expense.

Fiscal controls are the opposite side of the coin to incentives and may be used as ways to curb tourism by influencing the prices charged by suppliers in the commercial sector. Common examples are taxes imposed at airports, sales taxes and value-added taxes levied on accommodation and food provision, and the imposition of local taxes or rates levied on buildings and land in tourism destinations. There is a growing recognition of the *polluter pays* principle in which governments, local, regional and national, identify the source of specific forms of pollution and levy charges accordingly. Over the last decade there has been growing interest in using fiscal methods to influence the commercial sector of tourism. It is a short step from there to contemplate business charges for the tourism use of environmental resources previously considered to be 'free'. (See also below.)

Investment incentives and fiscal controls – a summary

If the monetary and fiscal 'sticks and carrots' are applied in a way that is supportive of land-use controls and building regulations, and *if* all three are organized in parallel to the provision of infrastructure, the four principal tools or techniques outlined in this chapter provide a public sector armoury for tourism management which is virtually impregnable. What is obvious on paper does not always work in practice, how-

ever, and the big '*if*' in this paragraph concerns the achievement of coordination around agreed goals. 'Agreed goals' assumes public sector knowledge of the demand-side patterns of tourism they seek to manage and, as noted in Chapters 6 and 7, this is usually an unfounded assumption.

Public sector influence over demand

The first four management tools discussed in this chapter are supply-side influences and the capacity and characteristics of supply clearly influence demand. In addition, however, the public sector also wields extensive direct influence over demand. The following examples comprise a menu of influences over tourism demand, all of which are in use around the world at the present time.

Influence on price

In addition to the indirect fiscal methods noted above, the public sector has other ways to influence price directly. For example, charges levied at publicly owned and operated buildings, and at attractions and facilities used by visitors including car parks, have a direct effect. Other ways of influencing the price customers pay include tourist exchange rates and airport charges levied on airlines (and passed on to customers). If local government are the owners of environmentally fragile sites, such as coastal dunes systems, they may control demand by a combination of both access limitations and price.

Control by licensing

Demand can also be controlled by the application of licensing procedures to the main businesses which serve visitors. In many countries, although not at present in the UK, hotels and other forms of accommodation have to be registered in order to obtain permission to operate and, in addition, may be officially classified and graded by public sector agencies such as tourist boards. Taxis, bars, casinos, tourist coaches, sports facilities and sometimes brothels too are required to operate under licences granted by the public sector. Direct licensing may apply also to the owners and use of pleasure craft, those who wish to fish, shoot, or dive on coral reefs, and so on. Large parts of the licensed capacity of tourism businesses, and often the prices the licensed businesses can charge, are thus also under public sector control. The fact that many countries, for example Greece and Cyprus, tolerate a large volume of unofficial accommodation is a comment on the unwillingness of governments to impose their own systems, not a comment on the potential power of the licensing tool to determine total capacity at a destination. Changing licensing criteria in order to ensure sustainable practice is an obvious development.

Influence over demand through marketing and information

The growing influence of marketing for achieving sustainable tourism goals is dealt with in Chapters 9 and 10. It is appropriate to note here, however, that the public sector, both nationally and especially at local level, has become increasingly involved with marketing efforts over the last decade. Destination marketing is designed to motivate particular groups of visitors and influence their behaviour, including the activities they choose (types of product), the times of the year they visit, the type of accommodation they choose, and their expenditure patterns. It is increasingly the case that destination marketing is funded and carried out jointly as a partnership activity between the public and private sector, working to agreed goals.

In the marketing process for destinations there is a particular role for local authorities in the production, promotion, and distribution of information. This includes brochures distributed before a visit and a wide range of information available within the destination for visitors to obtain after arrival. Particularly relevant to this chapter is the provision of visitor information

centres, which is commonly a public sector-funded activity. At the margin, for first-time visitors to an area and for overseas visitors especially, the provision of targeted information is an important tool in the armoury of the public sector for influencing visitor demand. In the case of the island of Jersey, for example, research indicates for 1995 that some 33 per cent of commercially accommodated holiday visitors to the island had seen the tourist board brochure before arrival and almost half of them brought it with them on their visit. The ability of the Island tourist board to get its messages to one in three of its visitors – in addition to influencing their behaviour by information provided on the island – is an important potential contribution to sustainable tourism. Other brochures are likely to be seen by at least three-quarters of visitors at the airport/seaport, in hotels, at attractions, and in information bureaux. The main brochure is produced in a form of partnership with the commercial sector on the island, especially providers of accommodation.

The evolution of the local authority planning role in the last two decades

A very important evolution is at work in the way that the local authority planning role has been changing over the last fifty years, especially since the 1980s. Change has been brought about partly through growing pressure on public sector budgets and the need for greater accountability, and partly because traditional planning methods are no longer adequate for coping with rapidly moving social and economic forces and dealing with the needs of post-industrial societies. Change has forced the pace in privatizing parts of what were previously considered to be public sector roles, and in forging proactive partnerships with the private sector to achieve wider strategic goals that cannot be achieved by the public sector alone.

Table 8.1 summarizes the evolution over three periods since the 1950s, drawing on UK experi-

Table 8.1 *The evolution of local government attitudes to planning and development control*

	1950s *Control & regulation*	1970s Economic regeneration *and facilitation*	1990s Sustainable development *and private sector partnerships*
Primary objectives	Enforcement of regulations for land-use, buildings and infrastructures. Development control focus	Identification of *ad hoc* opportunities for economic development, including planning support and financial incentives where possible	Clearer focus on overall area development plans and mission statements, incorporating quality of life and a sustainable environment for residents
Focus for action	Specific controls for protection of health and safety including water, waste, pollution and air quality. Land-use and building controls	Concern for securing employment and protecting the physical environment. Greater concern for public access and recreational use of the physical environment	Wider concerns for sustainable development, AGENDA 21 and achieving economic growth while reducing the impacts. Growing recognition of heritage, culture and tourism as an economic sector
Principal procedures	Control of businesses through enforcement of regulations operated by local government staff. Public sector planned redevelopment schemes such as town centres	Targeting of business activities, creation of support packages with the commercial sector, indicative planning and better information for decisions. Urban regeneration schemes led by development corporations	Partnership development procedures emerging rapidly, drawing on public sector agencies and the private sector. Increasing use of EIAs, multi-funding investment packages and joint planning procedures
Ethos	Essentially reactive, protective, defensive with relatively inflexible local plans. Clear separation between public and private sector	More proactive, seeking specific growth opportunities with more flexible concepts of structure and local plans and more private sector involvement	Proactive and innovative, developing new forms of public/private sector partnership in which local government is more enabler/facilitator than provider

ence. The evolution has little or nothing to do with tourism as an industry, of course, but it is highly relevant to it. Many other developed countries have followed a broadly similar pattern although the time scales are not the same as for the UK. The evolution is summarized in terms of the objectives of local government powers, the focus for action, principal proce-

dures, and the ethos or corporate philosophy underlying the exercise of powers. The core message in the table is that there has been what amounts to a major shift in attitudes, over the last decade in particular, in the way that local government approaches its powers – a very short period in this context. It is an attitude change that is still in progress but it augurs

AGENDA 21 for the travel & tourism industry

Actions identified for government departments and local authorities, national tourist administrations and trade associations, with the overriding aim of establishing systems and procedures which incorporate sustainable development at the core of the decision-making process for tourism.

(i) Assessing the capacity of the existing regulatory, economic and voluntary framework to bring about sustainable tourism.

(ii) Assessing the economic, social, cultural and environmental implications of tourism industry operations.

(iii) Training, education, and public awareness.

(iv) Planning for sustainable tourism development.

(v) Facilitating exchange of information, skills and technology relating to sustainable tourism between developed and developing countries.

(vi) Providing for the participation of all sectors of society.

(vii) Design of new tourism products with sustainability at their core as an integral part of the tourism development process.

(viii) Measuring progress in achieving sustainable development at local level.

(ix) Partnerships for sustainable development.

Source: Based on press release of February 1997 issued by WTTC/WTO/Earth Council

Figure 8.1   *AGENDA 21 – public sector roles*

well for tackling sustainable development in general and sustainable tourism in particular. It is an attitude shift that embraces commercial partners to help define specified goals, play a major part in implementation, and measure progress.

In forward-thinking local authorities new attitudes underlie the ability to refine, coordinate and implement in partnership the five significant powers discussed in this chapter in ways that were impossible at any time previously. It augurs well for sustainable development.

Chapter summary

Stressing the remarkable *potential* power of local public sector techniques for controlling, regulating, and influencing tourism, this chapter specifies the five main tools in use in most parts of the world. In dealing with environmental matters, local government acts on behalf of national governments, for example in specifying and implementing AGENDA 21 commitments entered into by governments. Figure 8.1 summarizes the AGENDA 21 action identified for the public sector with local authorities typically supported in their role and part-funded by national government and public sector agencies. Local government has direct influence over all the major supply-side decisions that both directly and indirectly influence demand. For new tourism developments these powers provide all the armoury necessary for achieving sustainability, *if* local government has the necessary knowledge to use and coordinate the tools at their command and the political will to implement them in practice. For existing destinations with long-established uses and practices, for example Venice or London, the same powers are available but cannot be so effective in the short run.

For agreed new developments the public sector powers at local level can effectively determine the *capacity* of a destination (by providing infrastructure up to a determined level and through licensing businesses), and control its *product quality*. Product quality, discussed in the next chapter, is influenced partly by maintaining the high standards of environmental attractions that draw leisure visitors in the first place, and partly through licence procedures specifying the types of tourism businesses that are allowed or encouraged to locate at the destination. In our view, shifting towards more sustainable tourism at destinations does not require more regulatory powers – they are there already. It does require much more intelligent and knowledgeable use of the powers and establishing achievable goals which are realistic in the context of current and potential demand. We have chosen to concentrate in this chapter on the five main powers rather than recite the well-worn methodology of master plans for tourism. In our experience most so-called master plans are based on wholly inadequate data and focus too much on theoretical product conceptualizations intended to achieve aspirational objectives based on unproven assumptions – at the expense of defining the methodology of implementation and monitoring addressed in this chapter.

In this and in other chapters the current 'knowledge deficit' about tourism in the public sector is stressed. It is the biggest weakness and block to sustainable tourism development in most countries and is nowhere more evident than in local destinations. In the final part of the chapter important changes at local level in the attitudes of public sector planning are noted (Table 8.1), together with the emergence of partnership planning with the commercial sector. This shift of emphasis is structural, appears to be permanent, and offers genuine scope for future progress.

Further reading

Hall, P., *Urban and Regional Planning*, 2nd edn, Routledge, London, 1992.

9

Managing tourism at local destinations – the private sector role

A clean and healthy environment is the core of the travel & tourism product, and environmental quality ... is vital to the success of the industry. With increasing numbers of consumers becoming more environmentally conscious in their purchasing behaviour, environmental practices will become a decisive factor in travel and tourism purchases (Lipman, 1994, p. 1).

A tourism product which deteriorates or becomes damaged will instantly pay the price of any other uncompetitive commodity. Its customers will abandon it for a rival which is better value (Hughes, 1994, p. 7).

Chapter 8 concluded that the public sector possesses extensive and potentially powerful planning techniques and tourism management 'tools' but they are not yet well coordinated and targeted in the 1990s. The public sector is typically not equipped at local level to use its five main management techniques proactively to influence demand, and respond rapidly to changing demand patterns in national and international tourism markets. It lacks the necessary management information. This chapter considers the role and five equally powerful tools available to three types of private sector businesses whose decisions affect tourism destinations. The first group are destination based providing accommodation, attractions, transport and other visitor services and facilities – from art

galleries to zoos; the second group are directly involved in marketing destinations but not based locally, such as transport operators, tour operators and travel agents; the third group comprises developers, banks and other investing agencies providing the development capital for tourism-related businesses. All these businesses are responsible for generating tourism demand and supplying attractive products. The first two are also the bodies most directly involved in the day-to-day management of visitors at destinations.

This chapter fully acknowledges the environmental damage associated with private sector firms in tourism. It identifies a forward-looking marketing rationale relevant to sustainable business practices at the destination and defines the five main marketing management tools available, which utilize the extensive and growing knowledge of customers available to commercial businesses in the industry. Running through the chapter, two important characteristics distinguish the private sector from the public sector. The first is that it responds directly to market forces and its decisions are determined by extensive knowledge of customers as well as a short- and long-term view of profits. The second is the sheer number and diversity of players in the private sector, many of them not recognizing that they are part of the same industry. At visitor destinations, local governments typically field one team although they may be drawn from different departments and backgrounds. By contrast, the multiple players in local tourism typically do not yet even recognize they are a team.

The potentially damaging power of commercial sector control over tourism development

In the late 1990s, with some notable and increasing exceptions among both the largest and the smallest players and their trade associations, there is still only limited evidence internationally that commercial businesses in tourism yet recognize and accept any real sense of vested interest in sustaining environmental quality at destinations. Developing practical ways to change business attitudes is an essential prerequisite for achieving more sustainable tourism. If economically deprived populations and their governments are hungry enough for economic development for political and social reasons, and there are profits to be made, the cumulative force of the commercial sector will nearly always be able to overwhelm public sector controls, however carefully they are specified. This is not because the public sector lacks the tools, it is because a economically hungry government will not apply them or will allow them to be evaded with impunity. Commercial organizations such as airlines and tour operators may have it in their power to 'make or break' many holiday destinations simply by the decision to include or exclude them from their schedules and/or brochures. Unless they are enclosed destinations in the ownership and management of one organization such as Center Parcs, there is usually no collective commercial mechanism at work in destinations capable of setting capacity limits and protecting the environment until long after serious damage is done. By that time consumers with choices are likely to have rejected eroded environments in favour of alternative destinations and the case for sustainable development will have been lost, at least in the short run.

Despite the previous point the private sector collectively *could* play the most powerful role in managing tourism at local destinations. Its potential powers or management *tools* for achieving and maintaining or managing sustainability through tourism are ultimately more powerful *in practice* than the tools available to the public sector because of the depth of commercial knowledge of customers and market forces, and skills inherent in demand management.

Rationale for sustainable practice in the private sector in travel and tourism

The rationale for sustainable practice in the private sector deserves careful thought. It is now normal to stress that long-run profit and business survival depends upon maintaining an attractive and healthy environment, and that specific operational cost savings can be achieved with improved technology for energy, waste reduction and lower water consumption. Although true, these advantages are not immediately very convincing to most businesses. In Figure 9.1 we offer a wholly pragmatic list of ten good business reasons for shifting attitudes toward more sustainable practice. From a marketing perspective we stress:

- The need to attract and satisfy increasingly sophisticated consumer segments in tourism demanding all aspects of high product quality, especially the quality of the environment.
- The competitive and PR/image advantages that flow from more sustainable practice.
- Investment in the maintenance of environmental resources for the same reasons that all businesses maintain and enhance their capital assets.

While the authors fully recognize there is a moral or ethical case for sustainable practice in tourism, we have excluded it deliberately from Figure 9.1 because we also recognize that it

Compliance with the law

An increasing volume and complexity of health and safety regulations, and the environment protection measures identified in AGENDA 21 are being applied by most countries to all forms of business enterprise, including tourism. Meeting standards ahead of compliance may confer competitive advantage

Avoidance of negative PR

Inevitably associated with polluting businesses targeted for media exposure, with immediate consequences for loss of customers and profit

Meeting growing customer expectations and demands

Demands for better quality and value for money are now experienced by all businesses. For leisure tourism environmental quality is already a direct and major component of product quality, and is vital for the all important retention of loyal/repeat customers

Achieving competitive advantage

By focusing on delivery of the specified environmental benefits associated with place and business operations that most modern leisure travellers seek, not just through variants of ecotourism. Marketing advantage is also associated with award schemes for good environmental practice

Reducing operational costs

Initially at least there is ample evidence that substantial savings can be gained by developing environmental management systems for more efficient use of energy, waste treatments, and re-use and recycling generally. Insurance costs may also be reduced for lower-risk operations.

Maintaining good-neighbour policies locally

Always valuable for positive PR; possibly essential in securing local planning permission for extension and development plans – includes business participation in local partnership schemes

Compliance with business to business procurement policies

Where one business supplies to another, it is normal for the purchasing business to specify conditions to be met in the contracts it places. Environmental good practice criteria as part of this process are in their early stages, but they will grow in line with customer demands noted above

Meeting membership criteria

Trade associations, professional bodies and many tourist boards specify the good practice criteria on which they accept businesses and individuals into membership. Environmental good practice is a logical addition to the criteria, especially if membership classification and grading is involved

Compliance with investors' funding criteria and investment risk reduction

Funding agencies and stock market investors are increasingly stipulating environmental good practice criteria and design standards as part of their conditions for offering financial support and reducing the risks of new investment

Conservation of business assets/resources

Contributing to investment in the quality of the destination environment for exactly the same reasons it is standard business practice continuously to refurbish, upgrade, maintain and replace as necessary the buildings, fittings, vehicles and other equipment on which profit depends

Figure 9.1 *Ten pragmatic reasons shifting private sector tourism businesses toward sustainability in the 1990s*

features last and least for most tourism businesses in the 1990s, especially small businesses. For large companies, where shareholders and published accounts are involved, an ethical stance may be required or at least be perceived as pragmatic for good PR reasons. Such reasons do not influence most small operators. Inevitably, the rationale set out in Figure 9.1 is primarily relevant to larger organizations whose business practices are subject to third-party scrutiny and who face serious business loss if they are identified in the media as causing environmental damage. As always, very small businesses have the least to lose and the most to gain in the short run from ignoring good practice on the grounds that individually their operations are so small they cannot make any significant difference to the environment. Individually this is usually true; collectively, of course, it is not. In practice leading edge small business trade associations and the procurement policies of larger companies can exercise leverage over small businesses and we return to this point later.

Homogeneous or segmented demand? The customer knowledge inherent in the commercial sector

A major difference between the market orientation discussed in this chapter and the resource or supply-side orientation explained in Chapter 8 is that local government and public sector agencies usually deal only in aggregates of tourism, treating visitors *en masse*. They have to. As noted elsewhere, the statistics of tourism available to them for decision making rarely permit any other approach and, with the limited exceptions of visitor information bureaux and responses to media advertising, there is typically little direct public sector contact with visitors. In considering official tourism policies and strategies for destinations, therefore, it is always a relevant consideration to examine how far they are organized around specific segments and products, and how far they are loosely based on nebulous

goals for 'tourists' as a whole. To be effective, local tourism policies must contain specific targets and include the means of measuring achievement by sub-totals of the overall market.

All private sector organizations deal directly with customers as people, not as statistical abstractions. They have no choice. They know exactly who their buyers are, where they live, when and what they purchase. Most have detailed records of repeat customers and every product type can be quantified and analysed. Customer and product knowledge is the basis of modern competition for market share for all forms of commercial enterprise. Using modern computerized database techniques widely available only since the 1990s, larger companies have full access to records of customers and from that knowledge can access the range of geodemographic analysis now available at low cost to identify the marketing potential for any given residential neighbourhood in most of Europe and North America. Geodemographics is an ugly label for a highly valuable modern research tool. On the basis of postal address codes, national census data may be analysed and supplemented by highly detailed information from a range of major national sample surveys of purchasing behaviour of all types. If a tourist business knows the post codes of its visitors and enquirers, it can gain instant access to extensive information about their behaviour generally.

Detailed customer knowledge is the source of commercial companies' principal advantages in using the key tools covered in this chapter. It is to be doubted if any successful commercial organisation ever refers to 'mass tourists' or 'mass markets'. They deal with segments of particular customers for their particular products and the latter are constantly adjusted to customer requirements and expectations. Commercial success depends upon the speed and sensitivity of their response. The extraordinarily rapid development of techniques available for ever more sophisticated analyses and marketing use of customer databases is a striking characteristic of modern management in the last decade of the twentieth century. As a result, although received wisdom has it that the public sector is the proper source for the statistics of tourism, the commercial sectors in tourism are far ahead of the public sector in knowledge of customers. Private sector companies possess, therefore, the fundamental requirement for influencing demand in sustainable ways – adequate, up-to-date information for targeting, using relevant visitor management techniques, and monitoring achievement.

Summarizing the rationale for a segmented approach to visitor management

Away from the abstract world of sociological analysis based on concepts of mass packaged tours for mass packaged people, the tourism industry operates on the principle that visitors vary by characteristics that are crucial to practical management decisions; fortunately they are crucial also to any endeavour to move toward sustainability of visited destinations.

The following are the ten principal common variables:

- Profile of customers for marketing purposes – geodemographic and psychographic variables.
- Customer awareness of/interest in environmental quality as a basis for choice of destination and choice of product at the destination.
- Products purchased – reflecting different purposes of visit and choice of activity: conferences, golf, weekend breaks, cultural activity, adventure, nature or eco-tourism, shopping, and so on.
- Prices paid (tourism revenue generated locally).
- Usage of fragile natural and built resources.
- Time of visit – by year, time of week, time of day.
- Choice of location (within a destination area).
- Prior knowledge of a destination before a

visit – varying from first-time visitors to regular repeat customers.
- Media by which new visitors obtain information about the destination and perceive its image (including advertising, publicity, brochures and information from other sources).
- Means of purchasing their chosen products – from direct contacts with suppliers to use of tour operators, travel agents and other intermediaries.

The five main management tools available to commercial organizations

Set out in the next sections of this chapter are the five principal marketing management techniques or *tools* which all commercial organizations use to manage their chosen segments of demand in relation to the products they supply at destinations. They are the 'four Ps', known to marketing students and practitioners around the world as the *marketing mix*, with the addition of a fifth P, *people*, meaning the employees of tourism businesses who come face to face with visitors in the provision of services and play a vital role in influencing their behaviour.

1 Product
2 Price
3 Promotion
4 Place (or distribution)
5 People

The fifth P is logically a subset of *Product* since people are always involved at some level in the provision of travel and tourism services, but the specific role of staff in communicating environmental awareness and facilitating changes in the behaviour of visitors warrants a separate item as a management *tool* for this purpose. The marketing mix is defined as *the mixture of controllable marketing variables that the firm uses to pursue the sought level of sales in the target market* (Kotler, 1994, p. 68). Middleton (1994, p. 63) likened the four controllable variables or levers to the brake, accelerator, steering wheel and gear shift controls of a car, which have to be manipulated continuously and in coordination in order to control and move any vehicle in a chosen direction. Any commercial organization can thus be conceived as 'driving' itself in a chosen direction, having regard to the demand and supply conditions and competitors operating in the same market places. The marketing mix represents the principal set of decisions an organization uses in the process of achieving commercial objectives and responding to the daily changes in market conditions.

The overall tourism product and the specific offers of commercial companies

Chapter 6 explained the concept of the *overall tourism product* as a 'combination of all the service elements a visitor consumes from the time he or she leaves home to the time of return'. The overall tourism product typically combines the *specific product offers* of more than one company including, for example, the services of airlines, tour operators, travel agents, hotels and attractions. It also includes the quality of the infrastructure at a destination and access to the natural and built environment which are mostly the responsibility of the public sector. These separate service offers may be purchased as a whole, as in a package tour, or separately. This chapter is concerned with products as they are defined by individual commercial businesses providing tourism services at the destination on their own premises with their own staff. *Product* in this sense comprises the designed shape or form of a service offer, or product characteristics, that a business offers to targeted customers. Product characteristics include:

- Design of facilities, such as size of hotels, number of rooms, facilities included, aimed at luxury or economy.

- Sustainability designed into business operations (see Chapter 11 and Part Three).
- Presentation of the product, mainly reflecting the atmosphere and ambience created on the producer's premises (also drawing on access to a destination's resources over which they have only limited influence).
- Service elements including numbers of staff, training, and the attitudes and appearance of those dealing directly with customers (see 'People', below).
- Branding, which represents the designed image of the product as it is communicated and promoted to targeted customers.

The private sector is responsible for providing the bulk of all products at most destinations, organized around the activities chosen by visitors. This is obviously the case for visitors staying in commercial accommodation, but most visitors to friends and relatives or visitors who own and stay in their holiday accommodation may also purchase products provided by businesses variously supplying catering, attractions, local transport, the arts and culture, recreational activities and entertainment. The number of visitors a destination receives is, therefore, strongly influenced by commercial decisions, especially the volume of products offered for sale.

The types of product offered to the visiting public at a destination respond to commercial perceptions of what customers are prepared to pay at any given time. Over the years the established supply of products also influences potential demand because they become an essential element of a destination's image. For example, if a destination has an established image based on popular, budget-priced self-catering, it will be very hard and possibly counterproductive for a company to develop up-market, high-cost products, because many prospective customers for such products would be put off by the destination image. It is, of course, possible to change images, but it is always a long-term project for a destination and the associated cost of marketing would undermine profitability. Commercially successful established resorts such as Blackpool in the UK, the Gold Coast in Australia, Honolulu in Hawaii, or Mallorca in the Balearics have evolved over time and now provide what is in effect, a commercially calculated volume capacity for particular segments. Although capacity is in theory a decision for the public sector, the reality in tourism to established destinations has mostly lain with private sector decisions.

It has to be said that, with some notable but mostly recent exceptions, commercial companies in tourism destinations have traditionally exploited for profit the environment in which they operate without incurring any cost. They build into the products they market the resource base and the image which any given destination affords. Small businesses in particular typically assume full (mostly free) access for visitors to the quality of the environment in which they are based, and expect full access to all services such as water, sewerage and waste disposal. They expect car parking and other visitor infrastructure to be provided but accept no obligation to respect their environment or protect it from erosion by overvisitation if that becomes an issue. Each small business makes its own individual guesstimate of whether or not it can profit from operation in a particular destination.

The competitive quality of the products provided to visitors is, of course, the basis on which long-term prosperity of tourism or any other commercial businesses depends. If the quality falls, as it undoubtedly did, for example in the Balearics in the 1980s as a result of commercial decisions, customers simply choose to go elsewhere. The public sector can and frequently does influence quality by maintaining high standards in parks and gardens and other facilities owned or controlled directly by local government, and sometimes in setting and monitoring standards of accommodation and through criteria attached to licences to operators. But what most visitors experience of product quality in all its dimensions lies essentially in the day-to-day operations of commercial businesses, which also generate the bulk of the waste products and pollution associated with tourism activity.

Specific products – summary

For established destinations, the private sector is directly responsible for much of the design, capacity, and quality standards of products provided. Each business makes its own decisions and coordination is comparatively rare in matters other than promotion, but cumulatively these decisions tend to establish the product base, the image, and therefore influence the nature or characteristics of future demand as well as the overall visitor capacity. Other than in planned new resorts, the ways in which environmental resources and environmental quality controls are built into products and 'used' are also primarily commercial decisions in practice, currently incurring no additional short-run costs.

Price

Price is the second of the four basic Ps, obviously linked directly with product design decisions and the quality to be delivered. Price denotes the published or negotiated terms of the exchange transaction for a product between a producer aiming to achieve predetermined sales volume and revenue objectives, and prospective customers seeking to maximize their perceptions of value for money and quality among competing alternatives.

At least for leisure tourism, and especially for package holidays, price has been proven many times to be a principal determinant of international tourism volume. High volume has tended to sell on low prices, not on value-added elements of product quality, which are harder to communicate. Prices may vary internationally by exchange rate fluctuations or through significant technology-inspired cost–benefits, but the price to be charged for a product is logically related first and foremost to its design and inherent operating costs, second, to revenue objectives, and third, to what a market segment will pay. Where tour operators are involved, they will effectively determine what market segments pay, using their judgement and a highly competitive bidding process to minimize the agreed price. (See Chapter 15.) Budget hotels are designed to sell at budget prices; luxury resorts are designed to sell at high prices and so on, but, as noted above, assumptions that the environment is 'free' mean that environmental protection and contributions are seldom part of pricing decisions.

It is a characteristic of most forms of holiday tourism, however, that the intended price as published in brochures is often not achievable in practice. The actual price in the short run is dictated more by tactics than strategy. It is the price which enables a business to match its competitors' offers and shift as much as possible of any unsold capacity at the last minute. To operate an airline, an hotel or a theme park involves incurring heavy fixed costs of purchasing and operating equipment, training and paying staff, and contracting for supplies necessary to run the business. As accountants put it, the fixed costs of operating a tourism business are high, but the additional or variable cost of handling one or even a few additional customers is relatively low, assuming there is unsold capacity at the margin. It costs virtually the same to fly a 350-seat aeroplane with 250 seats filled as it does with 300 seats filled. If 250 seat sales covers the fixed costs, almost any revenue achieved from selling another 50 seats represents contribution toward gross profit – hence the ability to discount heavily to last-minute customers as soon as it becomes obvious that sales at the full price will not be achieved. Following the Gulf War and the American economic downturn in 1991/2, for example, the price of beds in London hotels was effectively at least halved for customers willing to bargain on the day of arrival. Three years later the same bed and the same quality would have effectively more than tripled in price because demand had recovered and hotel companies could be confident of selling all their rooms at the full price.

Price – summary

Price, a key element of product design, is the most influential tool in the hands of the commercial sector for influencing demand, especially in the short run. The public sector may influence prices through taxes, licence fees and incentives, but the basic decisions on product design and published price reflect commercial judgements of what the market will bear and they effectively determine the nature of the segments to be attracted and the volume or capacity to be offered. Pricing is used by commercial operators both strategically and tactically to manage demand around the available supply of products. It is not an exact science but its power as a management tool is not in doubt. For environmental access and protection to be factored effectively into product prices requires regulation and private sector collaboration to ensure that it applies evenly to all competing in the same market. Such regulation is still in its infancy in the late 1990s.

Promotion and information

The third element in the marketing mix used to manage visitor demand is promotion and publicity, the most visible of the basic four Ps in the tourism industry. The bulk of promotional effort is designed to increase product awareness and the number of possible buyers in a potential market who are favourably disposed to purchase. An extensive range of communication techniques has been developed over several decades to influence customer behaviour, including advertising, the production of brochures and other information material, direct marketing to target groups, sales promotion, merchandising, the operation of sales teams and PR activity. All promotion communicates messages containing images, motivation, and incentives about destinations to customers making choices. For international leisure tourism, especially for those visiting destinations for the first time, the effectiveness of information and the motivation stimulated by commercial brochures are likely to have a major influence over customer choice of destination product. Much of what first-time visitors learn about a destination's environmental qualities that may influence their choice lies in the hands of the private sector.

For many decades it has been common practice for the public sector, for example local government tourism managers and tourist boards, to take a lead in destination promotion, often providing opportunities for commercial businesses to participate by inserting their own advertisements, as in a resort brochure. Increasingly, as local government reacts to financial pressures, the commercial sector as local partners are likely to be more involved in devising and implementing jointly agreed promotional campaigns.

Promotion and information – summary

Promotion, backed by targeted information, is the most powerful of the commercial sector tools for communicating messages and, in leisure tourism, for selling 'dreams'. Marketing managers and their advertising agencies have been honing their skills in the communication process for over 100 years. It would be surprising if they had not achieved extensive professionalism in the process. Marketing communications are usually associated with sales advocacy but there is nothing in the techniques that cannot be used for other goals. Because achieving sustainable development requires a shift in behaviour on the part of both customers and tourism businesses, those responsible for achieving it will need to use the powerful communication tools already available in the commercial sector. In markets with choices, coercion to change behaviour is usually impossible but influence through targeting selective messages is always an option. The power of promotional tools to create more positive attitudes to the environment is potentially immense but it has yet to be developed in tourism.

Place/distribution/marketing access

The fourth of the P's of the marketing mix, place or access, does not just mean the location or destination where a product is produced and consumed (although it is included if the location is also one of the places of sale); it means all the places at which a customer may gain access to the product. Product design and pricing are aimed at satisfying the wants and needs of targeted customers at economically viable prices; promotional messages are aimed to ensure awareness and motivation in sufficient numbers to absorb capacity, and points of access have to be provided so that aware and motivated customers can easily transact their purchasing decisions.

For much of holiday tourism, access is mostly provided by marketing directly to customers or through retail travel agents. But these are only two of the distribution options linking producers to prospective consumers. Tourism businesses may also seek to provide access via international computerized reservations systems, through sites accessible on the Internet, through linking directly with transport operators, or via clubs, schools and societies. Each of these linkages represent places through which targeted customer groups can gain access to the products that have been designed to meet their needs. Since the 1980s, the role of information technology in widening access opportunities and increasing the flow of information to potential customers has increased the number of places for accessing tourism products. It has facilitated the amount and quality of information which can be communicated.

Distribution and access – summary

Often underestimated, even within the tourism industry, the provision of convenient access for prospective customers is a powerful tool in the marketing mix. An adequate product, competitively priced but not offering excellent value for money and satisfaction, can be sold if a well-developed distribution system provides easy access where and when it is needed. On the other hand, brilliant product design, high environmental quality, competitive pricing and even award-winning promotions can all fail if motivated customers find it difficult to access the products they desire. Increasingly, as a result of global developments in information technology, distribution channels can now be used to provide access to better product information, including graphics and aspects of environmental quality. Distribution systems can be used as allies in programmes to communicate environmental qualities to targeted buyers.

People

Service products in the commercial sectors of tourism involve people, self-employed or employees at all levels, who deal with customers face to face, on the phone, and through letters in the normal conduct of their work. Staff–visitor ratios may be high, as in luxury hotels or a cruise ship, or minimal, as in self-catering. In all cases there are contacts or visible clues in which tone of voice, choice of words, the body language of welcome or indifference, the appearance and look of staff and the way they behave to each other, are part of a tourism product. Communication may be restricted solely to an information search and booking procedure but it is still an important process where undecided customers are making difficult choices. Staff behaviour individually and when communicating with other staff, even when customers are present but not directly involved, also conveys messages which are part of a product experience.

From doctors and hairdressers to banks and buses, all service products have a people element, but travel and tourism is special because of the potential environmental influence of employees. Staff not only represent a company in selling and delivering products, they often also have knowledge and information which few visitors are likely to have about the places they visit. Staff at destinations are, or easily could be

with low-cost training, a primary source of information and advice about the local environment. They are a powerful means of modifying customer behaviour in environmentally sensitive places, likely to be much more 'natural' and influential than printed advice or codes of conduct, however carefully written.

Evidence collected by WTTERC demonstrated that staff in many larger travel and tourism organizations in the 1990s were not only aware of environmental issues but were willing to contribute voluntarily to company programmes designed to reduce waste, re-use and recycle materials, and generally promote the causes of the environment. For example, a Canadian Pacific Hotels and Resorts questionnaire was distributed to all 10 000 employees in the early 1990s revealing that 'more than 90 per cent were favourably disposed to environmental programmes in hotels and 82 per cent indicated a willingness to commit extra time and [unpaid] effort to participate in corporate environmental improvements' (Middleton and Hawkins, 1993, p. 74).

Continuous manipulation of the marketing mix – at a cost

Coordinated use of the management tools in the marketing mix is never an easy task and it is always easy to point to failures in practice. Human nature and judgement is involved. But success is greatly facilitated where the primary tools are controlled by one management team in an organization and adjusted continuously to achieve targets that are set and closely monitored on a daily or weekly basis. Once commercial product specifications and production capacity have been agreed, there is normally little room to alter them in the short run, even if the sales volume objectives are not met. With modern computerized on-line distribution and reservations systems, however, there is scope to vary price, on an hourly basis if need be. There is also scope to adjust the promotional programme at short notice and scope to increase the level of sales promotion incentives offered through distribution/access systems. The marketing mix tools can mostly be rapidly adjusted to market conditions and even product capacity can be massively adjusted in crisis conditions, for example when hotels close whole floors or even complete units to cope with a major fall in demand.

The use of marketing tools does not come without a significant cost, however. Making allowance for use of retail travel agencies and including discounts, the costs of brochures, and of regularly servicing the distribution systems, the full cost of marketing in holiday tourism may be as high as 30–40 per cent of the nominal (published) sales price. This allows for advertising, distribution, reservations systems and all the associated costs of materials and sales staff. Tourism businesses have every incentive to control costs and maximize the efficiency with which they approach their marketing, and the processes are under more or less continuous management review and evaluation. Continuing heavy investment in marketing in price-sensitive markets is the clearest possible acknowledgement of its power to influence demand. We consider the use of this power to support environmental quality in the next chapter.

Two additional marketing advantages inherent in private sector operations at tourism destinations

In addition to the synergy created through coordinating the marketing tools within one management team, there are two further advantages in the private sector, typically not found in the public sector.

Customer databases

Most large tourism businesses in the private sector have developed sophisticated customer databases in the 1990s. Such databases look set for further development in the next decade, providing detailed information on existing customers and those who make enquiries in response to advertising. Less expensive but more powerful computers and software have greatly facilitated the processes of direct-response marketing, which in turn yields added information about the effectiveness of marketing tools. For tour operators and others using customer-satisfaction questionnaires, there is an added stream of data about customer responses to all the many elements of products, which can be analysed by customer type. Modern databases are continuously updated and provide the basis for efficient segmentation, target setting, product adjustment, and monitoring of results. They make it possible to target prospective customers with a similar profile to existing users and give access to extensive customer research available in many countries, based on geodemographic profiling. They open up the potential for relationship marketing in which businesses develop and maintain a continuing relationship with their repeat customers.

Linkages within the private sector

Because overall tourism products are an amalgam of multiple components supplied by a range of businesses it is increasingly clear, at least to larger operators of accommodation, attractions, and transport and other facilities at destinations, that their interests are often best served by some form of collaboration, especially joint marketing. The more mature the market and the greater the level of overall capacity and competition for market share, the greater the incentive for the individual players at destinations to seek the benefits of partnership synergy. Collaboration in the commercial sector is driven initially and most obviously by motives of protecting or enhancing profitability. But successful collaboration may lead on to coordinating targets and marketing mixes between commercial companies which, once established, can be used for other purposes including programmes for sustainability as the partners identify their long-run profit interest in the destination asset base. Collaboration between public sector and private sector is a logical development of the same process.

Chapter summary

This chapter identifies the five principal marketing management tools used globally in the private sector for controlling and influencing tourism at local destinations. It stresses the massive power over destination decisions inherent in private sector business practices. The five tools have a completely different orientation and source of energy from those in the public sector noted in Chapter 8, but there are now ten potential management tools which *could* be brought to bear on tourism to achieve sustainable objectives at the destination, if only they can be harnessed and focused. It hardly happens yet, in the late 1990s, but it represents a major opportunity for the next decade.

In the late 1990s, awareness of the need for sustainable tourism goals, and for changes of behaviour on the part of businesses and visitors at destinations, are still in the early stages. *The key problem is that the ten principal tourism management tools lie in multiple hands and will continue to do so*. Especially in the private sector, the many hands using the same tool (for example, product formulation, capacity and pricing) may be pulling in opposite directions. Most businesses have thus far avoided the key issues of sustainability because each business is only one player in a cast of tens or hundreds of businesses and there is no effective coordination of effort. We stress that international companies are not the worst environmental offenders. Such evidence as exists suggests that small businesses resident in the local community with no concerns about media interest and exposure, and few incentives to shift toward sustainable goals may be the principal problem.

The next chapter aims to provide a logical, coherent framework within which a wholly practical approach to sustainability can emerge jointly between the public and private sector, using a marketing perspective to coordinate and focus the power of the available tools for managing supply and demand in tourism.

Further reading

Lipman, G.H., *The Environment and Your Business*, Green Globe Publications, Oxford, 1994.

Middleton V.T.C., *Marketing in Travel and Tourism*, 2nd edn, Butterworth-Heinemann, Oxford, 1994.

10

The marketing process for sustainable tourism at destinations

This chapter aims to pull together the theme of the book that *a marketing perspective provides the optimum management process for achieving sustainability at tourism destinations into the next century.*

This statement will be an anathema to some readers. It runs counter to most received wisdom in this field but it underlies our standpoint. The concept of a 'management process' is stressed because marketing is too often narrowly identified with commercial objectives and profit motives. The traditional role of marketing in generating revenue from tourism remains vital, especially where such revenue may be used to help cover the costs of sustainable programmes, but sustainable goals are unlikely to be wholly commercial, at least in the foreseeable future. It is as the best available coordinated management process that modern marketing can deliver a contribution to sustainability worthy of the best professional skills.

This chapter identifies tourism as a source of massive global energy and specifies the processes that may be harnessed to achieve sustainable goals. Conceptually, and in practice, the harness combines a marketing perspective and marketing management tools. The chapter outlines the symbiotic balance between commercial prosperity and environmental health and focuses on six specific issues through which sus-

tainability influences tourist choices and marketing decisions. It develops a view on partnerships and collaboration at tourism destinations which brings together the issues identified in Chapters 7, 8 and 9.

Sustainable progress – by harnessing the energy of the world's largest industry

In reviewing the international development of tourism over recent decades it is all too easy to become preoccupied with the problems arising from negative impacts noted in Chapter 6. Measured in terms of global economic activity, employment opportunities and contributions to the world's arts, heritage and culture, travel and tourism has an astonishing global record of unparalleled growth and success over the last quarter-century. Now at around 10 per cent of world GDP (on WTTC estimates), there is no other growth industry of comparable size and geographic coverage that comes near to its performance. Its growth prospects are equally impressive looking ahead well into the next century and, together with creative and cultural industries, tourism is increasingly identified as a lead sector of post-industrial economies and urban regeneration.

In the face of this remarkable success story, readers may wonder why so many books and articles on travel and tourism take for granted the past achievements and future growth, as if it happened automatically by some form of spontaneous combustion peculiar to the tourism industry. Too many authors *assume* continued growth, and focus almost exclusively on negative impacts and regulatory measures needed to establish public sector control over the private sector. We are invited by many opinion leaders to demonize tourism as sowing 'the unstoppable seeds of destruction for the unspoiled parts of our world which drives the quest for travel in the first place' (HRH Prince Charles, September 1996).

This book is concerned with identifying proactive responses to the damage and pollution at destinations associated with tourism development, and learning from the methods now being developed around the world to create solutions. To do better now and in the future the industry needs a creative vision to harness and influence the global energy which marketing represents, not a barren backward-looking preoccupation with what has happened over the last twenty-five years. It is essential to start by understanding that there was nothing automatic about tourism growth; it happened because of a combination of growing global tourism demand and the remarkable energy and vitality with which the private sector recognised the opportunities and developed and adapted to meet them.

Every second, every minute, every day in all parts of the world, that energy is poured out in a vast, continuous flow of marketing decisions and activity – adjusting supply to demand *and* vice versa. By contrast, the energy, industry knowledge and adaptability inherent in the public sector and the whole regulatory process is minuscule. *It is surely no more than common sense, therefore, that this continuous marketing expenditure and energy should be harnessed and adapted to meet*

sustainable goals recognising the two inescapable facts of tourism that:

- Environmental goals and commercial goals have to coincide in the long run – healthy environments create healthy businesses; polluted environments destroy businesses.
- As long as customers have choices, sustainability can only be achieved through the products that consumers are willing to buy, and businesses are willing to market.

These two core facts make sustainability an achievable task because the essential mechanisms are already there in daily business operations. Progress does not lie in concocting ever more complex regulatory powers; it lies in refocusing and channelling the overwhelming energy that already exits. Marketing is the key that opens the way.

The modern definition of marketing

The organization's task is to determine the needs, wants and interests of target markets and to deliver the desired satisfactions more effectively and efficiently than competitors in a way that preserves or enhances the customers' and the society's well being (Kotler, 1994, p. 26).

Traditional approaches to marketing evolved for some seventy-five years or so around relatively narrow ideas of profit-maximization and somewhat sexist notions of treating the customer as 'king'. Kotler's definition, widely accepted internationally, shifts the paradigm by stressing the modern need for balance between company profits and consumer satisfaction, and stressing the overall goal of society's wellbeing. Although Kotler does not use the word 'sustainability' in this context it is fully implied both in this definition and what he elsewhere terms the 'societal marketing concept'. 'Societal' includes the wider interests of all stakeholders ranging from investors and shareholders to staff and residents of local communities. The British author, Hugh Davidson (1987) expresses a related point in his emphasis on *asset-based* marketing. It means marketing in the present, having full regard to sustaining and enhancing the core assets on which the long-run competitive advantage and future prosperity of a businesses depends. The interpretation of the environment as a core asset in marketing travel and tourism is already common ground, at least among larger

organizations in the tourism industry. While critics of commercial enterprise in tourism continue to attack an outdated sales-orientated view of marketing, we have to stress that modern marketing concepts and processes fully encompass sustainable goals.

For marketing in travel and tourism we believe the major issue for the next decade is to define and attempt to balance the often competing needs of the three E's, *Economy, Ecology, Equity – Globally* (Middleton, 1994, p. 373). Econ-

Table 10.1 *Public and private sector processes – directly associated with marketing management – essential to sustainability in tourism*

Understanding demand and supply at local destinations		
• Knowledge of visitor segments	Numbers, expenditure, characteristics, motivations and behaviour patterns of customers/users.	The basic requirement for all modern marketing, directly relevant to public sector planning
• Development of products	Matching and sometimes leading segments expectations – determines core business decisions	

Influencing the behaviour of individuals and businesses		
• Setting targets (by time)	Optimising chosen segments and products to meet targets	Negotiated by local public sector/private sector partnerships
• Influencing customer/user behaviour	Through information, product development, quality controls, consumer research.	Normal product delivery processes
• Influencing business behaviour	By codes of conduct, award schemes, trade association membership criteria, planning and licensing controls, and by purchasing policies requiring suppliers to meet environmental criteria	Role for trade associations, regulatory bodies, planning control, and professional bodies

Monitoring progress		
• Customer research by tourism businesses	Through information collected primarily as a byproduct of marketing and other business processes (e.g. accommodation occupancy studies)	Role for partnership between public and private sector
• Destination research by partnership process		

Note: These processes underlie the effective use and co-ordination of the ten tourism management tools explained in Chapters 8 and 9.

omy in this context means profit (or contribution of revenue to cover cost in the case of non-commercial organizations). *Ecology* means environmental constraints and goals recognizing that high environmental quality is the core asset on which future leisure tourism depends. *Equity* means a shift towards a fairer distribution of the use of Earth's resources between groups within a population and between nations. In the tourism context equity also means recognition and response to the needs and interests of residents of visited destinations balanced against those of visitors. *Globally* stresses that these issues are international.

Whatever an organization's goals, marketing tools offer the most developed and tested management process for specifying achievable targets, measuring success against them and for moulding and managing customer demand and behaviour around a specified supply of products. Marketing is the global *lingua franca* of tourism management.

Harnessing industry energy and marketing processes to sustainable tourism management

Table 10.1 summarizes the various ways that existing marketing processes can be harnessed to achieve more effective management of tourism at destinations. We stress that all the processes noted in the table exist now, although some need developing, and they represent a practical framework for harnessing and guiding existing energy. From a marketing management perspective there is relatively little additional cost involved in adapting these processes to sustainability; the significant costs relate to decisions to forgo growth in some places and invest in environmental improvements in others. The following points amplify the three sections of the table:

- Knowledge of segments and product formulation are covered in earlier chapters. All modern businesses in competitive conditions regard these processes as the cornerstone of marketing management. They are also the basis for sustainable development. Product decisions within a destination are critical in determining tourism capacity and volume.

- Setting targets locally is the essential first step in moving toward sustainable goals. Initially this may be a somewhat judgemental process but it can be refined continuously as research improves. Targets have to be set by segments and product types, having regard to seasonality. They can only be negotiated and agreed locally between the public sector responsible for much of the key environmental resources and the commercial sector responsible for the bulk of marketing activity for destinations. Influencing customers' behaviour in the ways shown is a normal part of marketing activity and was covered in Chapter 9, which also stressed that environmental quality can and should be promoted and delivered as an integral part of product quality.

- Influencing business behaviour may be practised internally by large organizations when they incorporate Environmental Management Systems (EMS) into their daily business operations (see Chapter 11). Environmental criteria may also be set for their purchasing policies, which all operators (small as well as large) must meet to obtain a contract. It is feasible for tour operators to deal only with accommodation and transport operators that meet minimum standards of sound environmental practice, for example, for scheduled airlines to deal only with tour operators meeting minimum standards, and for hotels to specify food and other products which directly benefit the locality in which they are based. This provides a direct or 'jugular' means of influencing the practice, especially of smaller suppliers which we identified as a particular problem in travel and tourism in Chapter 5. Practical models come from the automotive industry where Japanese companies revolutionized the quality standards of their component suppliers. The TUI case in Chapter 15 indicates a way ahead in tourism.

- In addition to the purchasing policies of individual businesses there is a growing role for trade associations, professional bodies, and local tourist boards to develop and coordinate their own codes of environmental conduct and to incorporate them into their membership criteria. For caravan parks, for example, compliance with an agreed code of environmental conduct could be a formal requirement for membership and for access to all joint marketing carried out by trade bodies. Tourist boards in their evaluations of accommodation standards can build in good environmental practice as part of their criteria for classification and grading, and in due course as part of the process through which accommodation and attractions can gain access to tourist board brochures and information centres. Both of these forms of influence can be summarised as *network influences* and are certain to grow in importance over the next decade. Access to networks is increasingly a vital part of marketing in tourism for small businesses in competitive conditions, especially for businesses seeking access to international markets.
- Finally, the systematic monitoring of progress is the only way to assess how far targets are achieved in practice. Monitoring is common to all forms of marketing and planning, of course, and commercial operators in tourism are a vital potential source of continuous information which is in practice a byproduct of normal business operations, for example satisfaction with product and environment quality at the destination. Coordinated sharing of such information at destinations would be a practical way of reducing the total cost of destination research that otherwise falls to the public sector and, as we have noted, is not systematically undertaken because of the cost.

Sustainability – symbiotic balance between prosperity and environmental quality

The objective of all plans and programmes intended to lead to the sustainability of economic activities generally, not just tourism, is to secure continuing benefits for resident populations in economic, social and physical environment terms. And to do this without creating damage to the long term health of either the social and physical environment on the one hand, or to the competitiveness and prosperity of the industry, on the other, on which those economic benefits depend. In other words, to achieve *net* benefit in which any damage is not permanent and any gains can be maintained by management action into the foreseeable future. Defined succinctly by Murphy (1985, p. 167) as 'the symbiotic relationship between prosperity and a healthy environment', sustainability is a delicate balance to be achieved between economic development and its inevitable impacts on the environment. This seductively simple truth is easily stated. Achieving balance in practice is a matter for informed management decisions, harnessing industry energy, and better coordination between partners in the processes dealing with demand and supply.

In an ideal world science and technology would be available to measure the desired balance of sustainability. In the late 1990s, as a result of scientific programmes around the world costing many millions of dollars a year, knowledge of environmental impacts is constantly developing, although the trade-offs or balances between gain and damage at specific destinations are still matters more for judgement than fact. The use of scientific evidence to measure pollution and environmental damage underlies wide-ranging existing agreements to measure water quality, soil erosion and pollution, bathing water quality, air quality, noise, and so on. Increasingly these measures, promulgated by international organizations such as the World Health Organization and the European Union as well as by national governments, are the basis for setting acceptable standards and stimulating local action to ameliorate problems. Invariably, however, it is impossible to unravel the specific input of travel and tourism within the total impact. The level of pollution in the Mediterranean, for example, is precisely measurable and at crisis point in places. Tourism contributes to it. But it is not possible to quantify the tourism element within the overall pollution, the bulk of which is not tourism related at all. Where pollution such as acid rain crosses national frontiers, it is especially difficult to isolate the contributions of specific industries, even more so with an 'industry' as diverse as travel and tourism. Environmental indicators are with us now on a permanent basis and will influence economic activity generally including tourism, but they do not amount yet to an adequate means of assessing the impact of tourism activity. The World Tourism Organization is working on specific environmental indicators for tourism (Manning *et al.*, 1995), but no output was available as this book goes to press.

Thus, although scientific measures provide an overall mechanism for alerting industries to modify existing behaviour they do not provide a primary route for achieving the necessary balance between tourism benefits and environmental damage. The need remains, therefore, for a wholly practical process for analysing and reorganizing tourism development in ways which shift a destination towards the desirable balance implicit in sustainability – moving along a path which identifies the reduction of negative impacts on the environment, and targets specific benefits to be achieved. The cumulative effect of reducing damage and increasing positive impacts may not add up to sustainability in the short run (bearing in mind that it cannot be accurately measured) but it most certainly represents a shift toward achieving net benefit. It reflects also the well-established precautionary principle of acting now on the basis of generally accepted judgement rather than waiting for scientific proofs which may not be achieved until major, perhaps irreparable, environmental damage has been done.

Sustainability not achieved by current tourism management methods

Whatever else is contentious about this book, most readers will agree that the holy grail of sustainable development for tourism has not yet been discovered or even understood. As the end of the twentieth century approaches many developed resorts have produced and published some form of goals which relate to sustainability. Current evidence suggests, however that such goals, typically developed by national and area tourist boards with local government partners, are likely to be statements of good intent, not amounting to a practical programme for achievement. The firm ground in the debate about how to achieve sustainability at tourism destinations is that balance must be found between demand and supply. Demand means the volume of particular types or segments of customers at particular times in particular places doing specific things/activities. Supply means the type and volume of products which are supplied to the customer/user groups. Unravelling the complications of demand and supply and influencing them locally is the essence of the debate. It is also the essence of a marketing perspective.

> Tourism is elaborately complicated. ... The success of tourism is measured in perceptions by the degree of relaxation, satisfaction, happiness, enlightenment, romance, stimulation, entertainment, contentment, adventure, fulfilment and excitement it imparts to its clients, **each of whom will gauge those impressions differently**. The same goes for inhabitants of a destination and the way they assess what is acceptable about the benefits and deficits of tourism. (Hughes, 1994, p. 4; authors' emphasis in bold type).

This report, developed from an initiative by the International Federation of Tour Operators (IFTO), summarizes succinctly the problem of dealing effectively with a complex international holiday industry serving multiple motivations. It is interesting to consider that the quality of the environment (as perceived) could influence directly all eleven of the perceptions listed – for example, on a holiday in a ski resort or in a national park or wild-life park.

The report stresses the importance of perceptions. Customers' perceptions, images and beliefs are paramount issues for all marketing managers and one of the principal reasons why sustainability is so hard to define – it is ultimately a matter of perception, or rather a mixture of multiple perceptions, often conflicting and changing over time. The report also spells out the issues for sustainability where they are most acute – at developed resorts needing to balance multiple tourism perceptions with those of their residents. ECOMOST dealt with two such destinations, Mallorca in the Balearic Islands of Spain, and Rhodes, another island which is part of Greece. Other destinations with very similar sustainability issues to tackle are the beach resorts along the Costa Brava in Spain, the Italian Adriatic resorts, ski resorts in the European Alps, island resorts in the Caribbean, beach resorts in Hawaii, Goa in India, the Gold Coast in Australia, and Phuket in Thailand. The pragmatic approach of the ECOMOST research analyses existing resorts with known problems in order to develop tourism management models that can be adapted to any particular set of local circumstances.

Six points at which sustainability issues enter commercial marketing decisions

Sustainability assures the profitable future of tourism ... Tourism cannot destroy the environment without destroying itself. (Hughes, 1994, p. 7)

As a principle for international tourism in the long run, the statement above is clearly true. Unfortunately it is also a brutal statement of the destruction that can be wrought in the short run and cold comfort for many destinations and residents whose environments are eroded by commercial interests and uncoordinated tourism growth. It is an unacceptable principle for those whose lives may be turned into 'uncompetitive commodities,' meaning, bluntly, expendable casualties.

Many argue there is little convincing evidence that commercial decisions generally in travel and tourism will significantly reflect environmental goals until the public as consumers of specific products and investors in companies demand evidence of such goals and adjust their purchasing and investment decisions accordingly. Yet there are at least six points at which sustainability enters commercial marketing decisions now, influencing the products offered for sale. The first three, representing commercial opportunities, are based on customer demands for higher environmental quality. The next three are threats which may turn customers away from products perceived as uncompetitive for environmental reasons. It has to be stressed in the late 1990s, however, that with notable exceptions such as Canada, Germany, and Switzerland, relatively very few people express, or even recognize, a demand for 'environmental quality' *in those terms* because that is not the way they think about such issues. Marketing thinking, which is concerned with seeking insights into what motivates customers' behaviour, suggests the following points are all highly powerful motivations acting for and against destination choices in the 1990s. Each of them has a significant but largely unacknowledged environmental dimension in the late 1990s.

- *Customer interest in and demand for peace, quiet, tranquillity, and opportunities to relax and unwind from the stress of modern living.* Market research indicates repeatedly that these are already the principal requirements of holidays for a majority of people in developed countries. This holds good for domestic holidays as well as for international travel. In northern countries such requirements are often related to destinations providing sunshine and warm weather and to beach-based holidays but the same motivations may be satisfied by a range of environment based activities such as walking, skiing, sailing, cycling or fishing. These motivations are directly related to experiences provided by the quality of a chosen destination's environment, especially its natural and built resources. Ample research evidence exists to demonstrate that at least a half of all European holiday makers have such need and expectations when they make their destination and product choices (see Chapter 1).

- *Customer interest in and demand for access to culture, social customs, the way of life of residents, heritage, museums, and the visual and performing arts* is the second major group of leisure travel motivations. In Europe and North America, interest in the heritage and culture of the visited destination is revealed as a principal motivator for international travel for visits to cities, towns and rural areas away from traditional beach resorts. Market research indicates that for countries such as the UK, Netherlands, Scandinavia and Germany, such motivations account for well over half the tourism demand by visitors from other countries.

- *Customer interest in particular ecotourism products.* Although it is often seen as the principal indicator of new customer interest in and demand for environmental quality, so-called *ecotourism* or green products are notoriously difficult to define and represent only a small minority of what is purchased in total – typically less than 10 per cent of all international holiday purchases, much less of domestic tourism. From EarthWatch and archaeological tours, cycling and walking holidays to whale watching, however, there is growing evidence that the number of people seeking leisure products that deliver specifically targeted environmental benefits has increased very rapidly in the 1990s. Such demand reflects the interests of more sophisticated niche-market customers emerging internationally, as discussed in Chapter 6. The label

'ecotourism' has been heavily overworked since 1992, however, and may well rebound on its users. There is no evidence that it symbolizes positive perceptions to most people and a danger that unsustainable practices may be taking place in ecologically fragile areas, masked by a superficially beneficial label.

The first three points above are aspects of consumer choice based on positive expectations and reactions to the perceived quality of the environment – given delivery, of course, of what customers regard as value for money. The next three identify aspects of visitors' negative reactions to environmental quality which are possibly even more powerful in determining customer choices in the long run.

- *Customer avoidance of intrusive environmental negatives based on pollution or evident damage to natural resources.* Customer perception of what constitutes a deteriorated product are polluted bathing water and beaches, obtrusive and insensitive buildings out of scale and sympathy with natural environments, extensive litter in areas used by visitors, air quality concerns through traffic fumes, eroded landscapes and intrusive noise from all sources such as aircraft movements, traffic, and late-night bars.

- *Customer avoidance of ugly, overbuilt, overcrowded and inadequately kept resorts.* Associated with the point above, and especially related to the architectural style (or lack of it) of brutally stark concrete hotel blocks, such negatives are partly a result of *laissez-faire* commercialism and equally a failure to enforce the public sector controls covered in Chapter 8. One of the most interesting developments in the 1990s has been the level of investment in Spanish and Balearic resorts to rectify some of the acknowledged development problems of the 1960s and 1970s, including the demolition on environmental grounds of specific hotels such as the Hotel Playa at Palma Nova in

Mallorca in 1996. The Spanish response is a proactive 1990s recognition of the power of environmental negatives even among the so-called mass market resorts.

- *Customer avoidance of destinations where the attitudes and lack of welcome from residents and the quality of service indicates resentment and dislike.* An international concern, it is very evident that unwelcoming or actively hostile attitudes to visitors on the part of local residents and employees in the tourism industry (however justified in the perceptions of the players involved) are a major negative to all forms of tourism.

Although the point cannot be proved statistically, judgement suggests that somewhere in the six points above are positive and negative motivations affecting the choices and perceived satisfactions of at last seven out of ten leisure customers – some customers are likely to be affected by all six points. Other evidence indicates that such motivations will grow stronger over the next decade, both enhancing the opportunities and underlining the threats to commercial businesses at tourism destinations. In the highly competitive world of marketing tourism destinations, many of them with more capacity than they can easily sell, the growing power of environmental factors will become more evident and require the kinds of urgent redevelopment response now emerging in Spain. Even in the short run the *realpolitik* of environmentally uncompetitive products is a potent reminder of consumer power.

Public and private sector involvement in tourism management – at the destination

Having identified the need for collaboration and new forms of destination partnership for tourism management in Chapters 7, 8 and 9, this section looks at the three principal models available.

Some type of coordinating framework is necessary to develop tourism's potential and its contribution to the well-being of host communities ... the lack of coordination ... has reduced the effectiveness and rewards of destination planning. The growing emphasis on community responsibility should continue, since this industry (tourism) uses the community as a resource, sells it as a product, and in the process affects the lives of everyone. (Murphy, 1985, pp. 152 and 165.)

Community-led planning

Long before the present concepts of sustainability were articulated in the late 1980s and in the Earth Summit Conference of 1992, the issue of balance between tourism development and environment was well recognized. Baud Bovey Butler, Gunn, De Kadt, Inskeep, Murphy, Pearce, and many others in recent years have looked at the impact of uncontrolled tourism development and concluded that there is an urgent need for better planning. One of the best argued cases was put by Murphy, in *Tourism: A Community Approach* (1985), quoted above. In that book, recognizing and emphasizing the important distinction between planning (goals) and management (control of visitors) Murphy argued logically that because the tourism industry markets a community's resources, the community should be a leading player in the process of planning and management of tourism. The logic is not in question. Murphy's focus on the destination is critical to sustainability and is reflected in this book. If effective community-led planning for tourism could be implemented in practice, however, the sophisticated, affluent communities of Canada are better placed than most to do it. But it has not been done in Canada. The community concepts remain influential but the debate on how to achieve sustainability rumbles on in Canada as in other parts of the world. There is no doubt that a coordinating framework is needed, but community planning approaches seem unlikely to supply it in ways that meet the needs of a global growth industry.

Some will argue that community planning and decision making has not worked because it hasn't really been tried. Much the same is said by apologists for Communism but the arguments are not convincing. Community decision making does not work in practice because, as Taylor (1995) argued perceptively, communities are an appealing concept but often impossible to define for practical purposes. The notion of 'consensus' on issues such as tourism is bogus; some residents are for it, others are against. Moreover, any form of consensus would inevitably be ill-informed because the research information which the 'community' would need to participate effectively mostly doesn't exist. Finding representatives who can speak for a 'community' often proves impossible in practice, and such as may be found generally have no control and little practical knowledge of commercial operations and management constraints. It is undoubtedly true, as Murphy states, that the tourism industry cannot succeed in the face of determined local opposition. 'Where development and planning does not fit in with local aspirations and capacities, resistance and hostility can raise the cost of business or destroy the industry's potential altogether.' But organizing local opposition to a proposed development must not be confused with a community's ability to conceptualize, agree and then achieve its own long-run tourism future, or to evaluate tourism sensibly against other forms of needed economic development. Recent work in the UK to develop a community planning model (Godfrey, 1993) confirms this judgement.

Public sector led planning and the failure of regulators

As outlined in Chapter 8, the traditional approach to planning is led by planners in the public sector aiming to generate appropriate development within the estimated capacity of resources for an area controlled by a locally elected government. Working within guidelines and statutory controls provided at national level, local government planners have all the tools they need for planning purposes. What they and often the elected politicians to whom they report lack is the commercial knowledge and judgement needed to generate and mould demand and adapt products in a changing and fiercely competitive market. They have statutory controls over land and buildings that are vital components for tourism products, but they certainly do not have the powers to manage demand or control the forms in which products are delivered to customers.

The idea, heavily promoted by sustainable tourism lobby groups, that tourism must have a regulatory framework imposed on it by the public sector appears logical and very attractive – in theory. With only a few notable exceptions in small areas with easily defined boundaries, such as islands and some national parks, it generally fails in practice. It fails because the 'public sector' is not an autonomous force equivalent to market forces. It is a small number of politicians, government officials and lawyers in central government, and an equivalent group in local government, responsible for devising and applying international, national and locally established regulations and policies. Experience reveals time and again that neither politicians nor officials have any training or background in the industry for which they have nominal responsibility. Their intentions may be honourable but the research information available to them of a highly complex and fragmented industry is minuscule. By the time they achieve some understanding of the issues it is probable that they will be shifted to another post, or the volatile market will have moved on. At worst, regulation for today's tourism will be devised using yesterday's inadequate data, and it will be irrelevant for tomorrow's conditions. Lawyers and regulators working with dated information can never realistically expect to predict business conditions five years ahead or even keep pace with the dynamic shifts of market forces of international tourism. The UK, for example, changed its minister responsible for tourism about every 18 months on average in the last ten years, and the civil servants on whom the ministers rely tend to change with a similar rapidity that inhibits the development of industry knowledge.

Private sector-led planning

The powers and tools of the private sector are outlined in Chapter 9. If the long-run objectives of businesses are to prosper – the symbiotic relationship referred to earlier – there should be little difference between the interests expressed as goals of the public sector and the long-run objectives of the private sector at the destination. In the last two decades, often because the public sector has not used its available powers, the shape of international leisure tourism as we see it around the world has been largely determined by the short-run *laissez-faire* activities of developers and businesses aiming to generate and maximize profit from an expanding tourism demand.

With the benefit of hindsight one can see that the quarter century of tourism development since the 1960s was driven by a form of *Klondyke* mentality having much in common with the hectic growth phases at different times in the nineteenth and early twentieth centuries of industries such as coal mining, textiles, car manufacturing, chemicals production, oil extraction, logging and speculative housing. None of these industries were concerned with environmental impacts at the time. They saw no reason to be. Demand was buoyant, prices were profitable, and there was no shared perception of the negatives of such development. Is it so surprising that tourism has thus far followed a similar path for essentially the same opportunistic reasons? Would it not have been flying in the face of all we know of industrial/economic and human behaviour if tourism interests had adopted an ethical stance at the outset? Do not all great industries have to reach crisis conditions before facing squarely the social and physical environment implications of their growth phases – and taking action?

Although some of the leading commercial players in tourism have adopted environmental goals and EMS since the early 1990s, these are still early days. Short-term interests may continue to outweigh long-term evaluation if national governments feel forced to seek the economic benefits of tourism as a priority goal and are willing to cut corners to achieve them. This book identifies a watershed that occurred in the late 1980s, forcing larger tourism interests to face environmental issues for the first time. It is fair to complain that the changes to commercial practice have not been immediate or always thorough, and mostly they have not yet filtered down to the majority of smaller businesses which dominate the tourism industry numerically. But the unique strength of the commercial sector lies in its inherent customer knowledge and the management of day-to-day operations in travel and tourism.

Partnership models – for tourism planning and management

Unless effective regulatory powers and working partnerships between public and private sector are established at a destination, *laissez-faire* industry-led commercial practices are never likely to produce sustainable tourism at destinations. The industry/environment symbiosis is not self-generating; it needs direction. It can only be achieved on collaborative basis. Examples of public and commercial sector collaboration at destinations can be found going back to the 1950s, but traditional partnerships were often narrowly focused on joint promotion campaigns or on collaboration to fund and build particular developments which the public sector identified or accepted as advantageous. In the last decade it has become increasingly obvious that the optimum route to effective planning and management lies somewhere between the resource responsibility and orientation of the public sector and the asset responsibility and market orientation of the commercial sector. Participation of both parties is essential. The most exciting development in tourism in the 1990s is new forms of partnership, formed not just for undertaking specific tasks or programmes but for dealing with tourism planning and management for a destination as a collaborative *process*. The best forms of partnership are based on shared participation in the tourism management process which includes all the processes summarized in Figure 10.1. Several examples will be found in Part Four of the book.

If the processes indicated in Figure 10.1 are adequately specified, the actual source of the initiative that drives the coordination process hardly matters. There clearly has to be an organization or coordinating framework which controls the process but, while it must gain full public sector participation and local residents' support to secure the optimum use of available statutory levers, it does not have to be community-led or even public sector-led as Murphy and most other authors have assumed. In practice, leadership is likely to reflect the availability of locally respected personalities with the energy and vision to drive the process and this may come from either sector or from independent locally elected leaders. It should be clear from Figure 10.1 that effective partnership has to be able to devise a *voluntary* process for harnessing commercial sector energy, because marketing is in practice the primary means of achieving the functional processes noted. These are also the processes essential to achieving the balance implicit in the more responsible conduct of tourism businesses.

Chapter summary

Underlying this chapter is a positive focus on the remarkable global success of tourism development and the potential opportunities it conveys for the environment. The need is to harness marketing energy to shift towards a working balance between commercial interests in a highly competitive world and respect and support for the integrity of environmental resources and

- Jointly agreed planning goals and targets to be used as the framework for public consultation and participation, and for tourism management programmes.
- Joint participation in the essential research information on which to base goals and action.
- Jointly agreed targets and capacity projections for a destination (expressed as segments and product volume limits).
- Programmes and monitoring – recognizing that the best information lies with the commercial sector as a byproduct of routine businesses operations.
- Jointly agreed development plans, possibly with joint funding arrangements and coordinated investment programmes – infrastructure and superstructure provided jointly by the two sectors.
- Coordinated action in visitor management programmes drawing on the powerful synergy of the full set of management tools defined in Chapters 8 and 9.
- Coordinated communication of interesting, stimulating 'user-friendly' environmental messages and signals to visitors both before and after arrival at the destination – to interest, educate, and entertain them and shift their behaviour in ways designed to minimize negative environmental impacts.
- Cooperation of larger companies and trade associations in regulating the environmental standards of small businesses through purchasing policies, enforcing codes of conduct, and controlling access to destination marketing.
- Jointly coordinated research to monitor the achievement of targets and measure customer and resident satisfaction.
- Jointly agreed images reflecting and respecting the characteristics of the destination.

Figure 10.1 *Partnership processes for tourism management at destinations*

residents at tourism destinations. Balance is not a static concept. It changes continuously according to the perceptions of residents, visitors, businesses, politicians and all the other players explained in Chapter 7. It shifts according to the latest scientific evidence. It requires a dynamic process to identify and respond to such changes. In practice, the volatility of free markets and the businesses which provide for market needs are the main agent of change. Modern marketing, in its societal context, is the most dynamic and powerful management process able to control and influence change.

Marketing as a process is traditionally associated with short-term, profit maximization that has led to most of the damage attributed to the holiday sector of travel and tourism. But such damage is not the result of marketing as defined in its modern sense by Kotler. Overdevelopment in tourism responds to the same human behaviour as that which drove the Klondyke gold rush, mid-nineteenth-century urbanization, and dust bowls in the USA; and which drives much of hardwood logging and the poaching and slaughter of tigers and rhinoceroses today. Readers may put their own interpretation on human motivations and greed but it assuredly was not a marketing philosophy at work in any of these cases.

The marketing perspective is always founded on a deep and continuous understanding of visitors and their behaviour, identified as segments and products. If it is undertaken collaboratively, negotiated and implemented jointly between the public and private sector, marketing provides the most fertile route for harnessing the professionalism and energy of modern management thinking to the achievement of sustainable goals. Marketing processes can also bridge the otherwise catastrophic chasm between the hundreds of large businesses that can be made responsible for their own environmental actions and the millions of smaller businesses that otherwise cannot.

Of course, every tourism destination is different. Each has a unique natural and built environ-ment, on the one hand, and a unique set of economic and social characteristics, on the other. There are similarities between destinations, but most are at different stages in their development. Fortunately, if the actual sustainable formula to be applied has to be unique to each destination's circumstances, the methodology, tools and solutions for shifting toward sustainability in tourism activity are global. Applying Naisbitt's (1994) memorable aphorism, *think local; act global* (p. 24) to travel and tourism, it is the partnerships that must 'think local.' It is encouraging to note the growing evidence from around the world in the late 1990s that destination partnerships are emerging and flourishing everywhere in a logical but largely spontaneous reaction to acknowledged problems. This is an exciting, vibrant and fertile process out of which we predict that internationally valid criteria for successful sustainable development will emerge over the next decade. 'Act global' in this context requires a marketing perspective, the universal constant in the methodology for sustainability that recognizes no geographical boundaries either as a management philosophy or as a coordinated set of management techniques.

Further reading

Godfrey, K., *Tourism and Sustainable Development: Towards a Community Framework*, Oxford Brookes University, Oxford, 1993 (unpublished PhD Thesis).

Middleton, V.T.C., *Marketing in Travel & Tourism*, 2nd edn, Butterworth-Heinemann, Oxford, 1994.

Murphy, P.E., *Tourism: A Community Approach*, Methuen, London, 1985.

IHEI (International Hotels Environment Initiative), *Environmental Management for Hotels*, Butterworth-Heinemann, Oxford, 1993.

Hughes, P., *Planning for Sustainable Tourism: the ECOMOST Project*, International Federation of Tour Operators (IFTO), Lewes, 1994.

Part Three

The Issues and Cases of Good Management Practice in the Main Sectors of Travel and Tourism

11

The 'R Word' guide to corporate action on sustainability

The first two Parts of this book examine the main environmental opportunities and impacts of travel and tourism, first, as an industry within the overall context of the global environment, and second, in terms of managing demand and supply at specific destinations. This Part considers how individual businesses in the private sector of travel and tourism can make progress to ameliorate the negative aspects of their operations, and play the more responsible part in development and operations which is a necessary requirement of any significant shift to sustainability in the industry. In practice this means decreasing the existing usage of scarce resources, reducing current outputs of waste and pollution, promoting awareness of environmental qualities at destinations and influencing the ways in which their customers understand and respond to the quality of their environment away from home.

Many readers will be reasonably familiar with the concept of the 'Three Rs'. Applied to environmental tasks within both the public and private sector they have become the watchwords of managers concerned since the late 1980s to promote better environmental practice. The words are used to encapsulate an appropriate and memorable management response for shifting necessary business processes toward long-run sustainability. The three Rs are:

- Reduce
- Re-use
- Recycle

All three Rs are important and are explained below. Taken seriously they reflect an important shift in corporate perceptions, attitudes and behaviour toward the environment. They are, however, rather too restricted for practical guidance on sustainable action and for the purposes of this book we identify *Ten Rs*, summarized in Figure 11.1.

This chapter offers an overall introduction to immediately available environmentally friendly procedures common to all businesses in travel and tourism, at all levels from the smallest to the international giants. It also outlines the growing use of Environmental Impact Assessments (EIA), Environmental Impact Statements (EIS) and Environmental Management Systems (EMS), which now influence the business operations of large companies in most parts of the world. The *Ten Rs* approach to sustainable action programmes in the main business sectors of travel and tourism is covered in more detail in Chapters 12 to 15, which also explain the current market context within which they operate. The *Ten Rs* operate primarily on the supply side rather than the demand side, especially on achieving more

- Recognize

- Refuse

- Replace

- Reduce

- Re-use

- Recycle

- Re-engineer

- Retrain

- Reward

- Re-educate

Figure 11.1   *The Ten Rs criteria for environmental good
practice in tourism business operations*

efficient use of resources, and controlling business costs and the output of wastes. There is, of course, a strong connection between the *Ten Rs* criteria for good environmental practice and the modern marketing perspective of this book, identified as product design and quality engineering to gain competitive advantage, influence customers' attitudes and behaviour, and deliver satisfaction.

To facilitate the explanation, the *Ten Rs* are treated in sequence as if they were separate self-contained processes. In practice, especially when being implemented following a systematic audit procedure, several of the processes are logically linked, and may be introduced and developed simultaneously. Larger companies find it relevant to implement all ten procedures together, integrated within a corporate environmental management system (EMS – see below), and increasingly such companies develop operations manuals as part of their routine staff training programmes. The International Hotels Environ-

ment Initiative was derived initially from just such a manual (see Chapter 12). The Green Globe initiative sponsored by the World Travel and Tourism Council also distributes guidelines for good environmental practice. Smaller companies may follow up on just one or two of the processes. For each of the *Ten Rs* it is a relatively straightforward task to target and trace the potential environmental benefits, and in many cases there are likely to be some cost savings to be achieved as well. It is not suggested, however, that environmental good practice is just another form of cost saving. The processes in this chapter are associated with higher-quality outputs, in some cases requiring significant investment, and in the long run they will mean higher prices for consumers justified by the value added to product quality through environmental improvements.

1 Recognize

Recognition of the nature of the issues, the problems and the opportunities surrounding environmental impact and sustainability has to come before action. Recognition underlies awareness and understanding and it covers the vital research and analytical functions which logically precede any effective design and implementation of programmes – and become the basis for monitoring and evaluating results. Because practical solutions to negative environmental impacts are often issues for science and technology, technical as well as consumer research is required. Large multinational companies, such as airlines, are likely to have research and development departments (R&D) responsible for corporate environmental issues, and some work closely with supplier companies manufacturing the inputs used in the airline business. R&D is relevant to all major purchase decisions such as new aircraft, new engines, modified fuels, maintenance supplies, chemicals used in cleaning and de-icing and so on. In the late 1990s, although some large hotel chains have also developed environmental programmes, very few tourism businesses have access to formal R&D departments for analysing the purchase of materials and other inputs needed for the conduct of business. Yet the requirements of building design, landscaping materials, heating and lighting systems, laundry equipment, water usage, and waste water treatment and so on are very similar in principle to those facing airlines.

At all levels research is the basis for *recognition* and it underlies all forms of environmental assessments and audits. It is also the basis for corporate mission statements concerning the environment and providing a framework for defining achievable targets. It includes the identification of relevant environmental indicators which can be routinely monitored and assessed. Examples are indicators for estimating the output of high-altitude emissions for airlines, estimating the sustainable density of visitors per hectare of beach at a beach resort, or measuring the level of water pollution associated with tourism activities. If there is no systematic recognition of environmental impact, there is little realistic prospect of achieving sustainable progress. Smaller businesses cannot afford R&D departments for environmental work and the research for them can only come through trade associations, the purchasing specifications of larger companies they deal with and through other networks such as tourist boards. In all cases, recognition and awareness, increasingly likely to be based on research and/or formal environmental audits, has to be the first of the *Ten Rs.*

2 Refuse

Perhaps the simplest of all action programmes is to refuse to engage in activities as soon as possible when they are recognised to be environmentally damaging, for example the use of CFCs. Refusal should also embrace the *precautionary principle* of refusing to engage in activities for which there is good cause for suspecting sig-

nificant damage to the environment, even if the scientific proof is still lacking. For an airline it may mean refusing (or being refused permission) to operate night flights in order to limit noise pollution over residential areas surrounding airports. For a holiday village it may mean refusing (or being refused permission) to extend the existing range of accommodation because the access roads around the village are already seriously congested at peak times, or because the available water supplies cannot cope without loss of amenity to other users. It may mean refusing to introduce non-native plant species among indigenous plants for landscaping purposes because the long-run implications of the mix could be damaging to local ecosystems.

3 Reduce

What cannot be refused, because in the short run there is no available alternative resource, can often be tackled by a targeted reduction from current levels of usage. Research and audit processes can be expected to identify potential reductions to achieve cost savings as well as to improve overall environmental performance. For hotels and restaurants, for example, reduction of food waste by better portion control saves costs. New computerized systems make it easy to isolate rooms and public spaces and switch off heating and lighting automatically when the spaces are not in use, reducing fuel consumption. In cold climates, even the simple expedient of reducing temperatures by one or two degrees is likely to produce significant cost savings on heating bills over a period of months without affecting consumer satisfaction. The 'brick in the loo' is perhaps the best-known example of easy cost savings through reduction of water waste over a twelve-month period. All such reductions are readily quantifiable over time.

As part of an overall programme to reduce and control waste in all areas of operations, reductions in the use of plastic and paper packaging are normally easily targeted by most accommodation suppliers, ranging from installing dispensers for salt and pepper, and soaps and shampoos, instead of using the ubiquitous disposable plastic mini-pouches. A tour operator using up to twenty brochures per booking may well be able to reduce the number wasted, cut costs, and save tons of paper over a holiday season by introducing better targeted distribution systems now greatly facilitated by new database marketing technology. We stress that the process of achieving reductions in the use of resources is first and foremost a matter of changing attitudes and training for staff at all levels. Only second is it a matter of investing in new technology, at least in the early stages.

A more challenging application of the reduce principle would be the introduction of a strategy for scaling down of accommodation capacity in a resort where overdevelopment can be shown either to be damaging the local environment or lowering customer satisfaction through perceptions of overcrowding, or both.

4 Replace

Once refusal and reduction procedures have been implemented the next logical consideration is replacement. Increasingly identified and recognized as part of the output of a systematic audit process, it is often comparatively easy, at least initially, to replace existing supplies or processes with other products or processes which are demonstrably more environmentally friendly or measurably less toxic. In some cases replacement may reduce the existing costs of necessary business operations. Transport operations use thousands of tons of toxic materials such as paints, engineering fluids and chemicals. In some cases there are replacements or substitute products available or being developed which do the same job with less environmental damage. Hotels also use large quantities of chemicals for laundries, swimming pools and cleansing, some of which have less toxic replacements. Hotels typically also use and dispose of

thousands of plastic bags for collecting and returning laundry items which could be replaced profitably by re-usable fabric bags and covers, or no covers at all. Replacements of this nature may be achievable simply through an effective awareness initiative with customers.

Driven by a search for cost savings, the measurement of inefficiencies in heating and lighting equipment and in the usage of water and chemicals is the obvious logical starting place for audits of routine business operations. There is now solid international evidence available to demonstrate that real bottom-line savings can be achieved from efficiency programmes which are more environmentally friendly at the same time. The replacement of inefficient insulation, for example, is proven to pay back over a short period. Replacement programmes may follow from the introduction of systematic environmental criteria into the budgets allocated for purchasing business supplies, replacing suppliers as necessary with others better matching revised specifications. It is a simple step, once these criteria are established, to review them continuously from the standpoint of both cost efficiency and environmental impact.

5 Re-use

When targeted improvements to operations and associated savings have been made by replacements and reduction of unnecessary and inefficient uses the next logical step in tackling waste is to see what supplies can be economically reused. Obvious examples, although trivial individually, are wire coat hangers, delegate badges at conferences, cotton laundry bags, re-usable dispensers rather than disposable sachets for catering supplies, and so on. For operations such as transport systems requiring large volumes of chemicals for engineering and equipment maintenance there are some supplies that can be used again if they are collected systematically and not simply disposed of. Individually the re-use savings may appear relatively trivial, but collectively over twelve months can produce quantifiable benefits if a monitoring system is in place. Such savings are dependent upon new attitudes towards costs and the environment on the part of management and staff, continuously applied.

6 Recycle

Recycle is the logical next step beyond re-use. Where re-use is not an option, outputs which represent traditional waste at the end of one cycle of business operations can sometimes be salvaged and recycled for further uses thus easing the pressure on the environment for supplies of natural materials. Although currently largely confined mainly to developed countries where recycling plant is available, the recycling of paper, cardboard, clothing, glass, and aluminium drink cans are among the most obvious examples, now drilled into most schoolchildren as part of their education process from a very young age. The recycling and re-use of waste water and waste heat has been noted earlier. The opening of bottle, paper, tin and clothing banks at supermarket sites over the last five years has been a remarkable development in the UK. As a result, virtually all children and most young adults are accustomed to the weekly trip to dispose sensibly of unwanted items for recycling. A decade ago such materials were burned or buried in the ground with no salvage for further use. Office systems for collecting waste paper and other materials for recycling are also now commonplace.

In North America both restaurants and hotels have introduced procedures to save significant parts of their food waste so that it can be recycled for animal foodstuffs and organic composts. In some cases, where the food is still safe and hygienic for human consumption although not at the peak level of freshness required for commercial purposes, some items may be distributed free or at very low cost through community distribution systems provided for local people in need.

In developed countries generally there is now growing concern over the lack of space to dump or otherwise dispose of all forms of waste by traditional methods. Rising charges can be expected for business waste in particular, deliberately to alter traditional attitudes to waste disposal in favour of re-use and recycling where it is an option.

7 Re-engineer

In its modern business management sense *re-engineering* means introducing change to traditional corporate management structures and operations to reduce costs and achieve growth in ever more competitive conditions. In its original technical sense, re-engineering is part of the ethos of R&D programmes operated by most large companies for their purchases of expensive and significant supplies and for the introduction of new plant. Re-engineering applies especially to the design and purchase of new equipment and buildings and for major refurbishment plans. All large companies have to work to some system of formalized purchasing criteria. Using environmental audits there is an obvious opportunity and logical development in adopting and specifying environmental criteria with the other requirements. In this sense, environmental criteria are one aspect of overall product quality requirements of suppliers. Re-engineering runs across an almost limitless range of purchase requirements, from the redesign of more fuel-efficient and quieter aircraft, through the redesign and operation of waste water treatment plants, all the way down to redesigned plastic trays and cutlery required to service delegates at a conference. For global organizations such as McDonald's restaurants, once serving millions of customers every day with polystyrene food containers, the decision to re-engineer operations using recyclable cardboard made from renewable resources was a vital corporate decision with a major impact on the bottomline.

In the broader, non-technological sense, it is a valuable insight to perceive the decisions of tour operators as a form of 'product engineering' (see Chapter 6). What tour operators do, and any other business that buys in and puts together different components of leisure tourism products, is to design and specify component inputs in the context of an overall product for sale, typically in brochures. Tour operators select certain services to combine with others, rejecting or *refusing* other options in the process. They may persuade their suppliers to provide or adapt services they consider to be marketable along with other elements. Since the tour operators already have clearly defined purchasing criteria for most of the components or 'supplies' they build into their brochures, there is an obvious role for developing environmental criteria as part of expected product quality, drawing on research into consumer needs, wants and expectations – and measurement of satisfaction with product delivery. There is not much evidence of this happening in the late 1990s, but the processes are well established if the management will exists to use them.

8 Retrain

Because most travel and tourism businesses are relatively labour intensive, and much consumption of tourist products takes place over several hours or days on the producers' premises, the role of staff is critical to the delivery of the services on which customer satisfaction depends. As greater competition in travel and tourism becomes a global reality, and as more businesses seek to compete on quality rather than price, the processes of training and retraining become more important. It is already very well established among service businesses generally that all staff dealing with customers require training in specific personal and communication skills such as personal presentation, answering enquiries from customers, solving customer problems, and providing information. Many are also trained to perform a promotional or selling role by drawing customers' attention to the services available on the premises – in other words, they are already trained to influence customer behaviour in targeted ways.

If a service business dealing closely and continuously with customers on its premises seeks to provide them with environmental information and advice, its staff will become the primary medium for communication and persuasion. Such information may be positive in the sense of making customers aware of environmental quality and attractions and the opportunities they provide, or negative in seeking to modify customer behaviour that could cause unnecessary environmental impact at the destination. Examples of the latter could include reducing the use of water if it is scarce, the form of dress which fits appropriately with local customs, or not disturbing wild life. The way that Center Parcs in Europe manages to detach visitors from their cars, to create a largely traffic-free environment in its villages, is a good example of targeted communication, backed up with the relevant facilities, which combines both positive and negative information. Many visitors are introduced to cycling for the first time or use cycles for the first time in years. The Quicksilver Connections case in Part Four of this book provides other practical examples of positive and negative communication by staff. Training programmes reflect the way a company at senior level understands and implements the environmental elements of its mission statement.

9 Reward

There is interesting evidence, for example from the programmes operated in North America in the early 1990s by Canadian Pacific Hotels, that many staff are sufficiently interested in the environment and the impact of their employment upon it to give at least some of their time freely to achieve more sustainable operations. Doing business in more sustainable ways generates job satisfaction for many employees and creates its own rewards. To harness such inherent good-will it is vital that clear targets are set and agreed and that results are known and communicated. Beyond the level of good-will, which in any case is likely to need supporting after an initial period of response, it is widely recognized that staff motivation is heightened by some form of recognition, monetary and other, for targets achieved or exceeded. For example, Inter-Continental Hotels and Resorts sets and pub-lishes its environmental targets, and rewards both hotels and individuals with cash and re-cognition for excellent performance.

For large service organizations, defining staff tasks, setting measurable targets for achievement and monitoring and communicating results throughout the organization and to customers and stakeholders is part of the process of En-vironmental Management Systems (EMS) out-lined below. In their operational principles, environmental management procedures are closely related in their approach to the better-known procedures for Quality Management or Total Quality Management (TQM). Auditing job functions, specifying appropriate routines, iden-tifying targets to achieve, devising programmes and recognizing performance is the normal and well-established approach to TQM. It is also the logical approach for targeting and achieving corporate environmental objectives and the two procedures overlap and can be organized to operate in tandem.

10 Re-educate

The Preface to this book stresses the overwhelm-ing global need to change the existing patterns of people's attitudes and behaviour toward their environment, especially in the relatively affluent developed world where the bulk of environ-mental damage is initiated and done. Changing behaviour is the focus of the last of the R words, re-educate. This relates to the special responsi-bility and opportunities that many businesses

dealing with leisure tourism have to introduce and develop their customers' awareness of the environmental qualities of the products they buy. This involves informing, interesting, per-haps enthusing, and in the process 'educating' those who purchase tourism services. More than any other major international activity, through face-to-face communication of employees with millions of visitors, businesses in travel and tourism have a major opportunity to target and communicate positive environmental influences to audiences on their premises, often at their most receptive when at leisure. The world's largest industry is uniquely positioned to fulfil an awareness and educational role, often at low cost, recognizing and to some extent helping to compensate for the unavoidable fact that busi-nesses in travel and leisure consume scarce resources and can cause extensive environ-mental damage.

It is characteristic of leisure tourism that most customers have paid for the opportunity to visit a destination to pursue their own personal goals, such as relaxation, entertainment and recreation away from their daily world of work and cares. There are, of course, thriving and growing seg-ments of the leisure market that also choose to participate in courses or cruises and other packages in which education, arts and crafts are featured as the major attraction. These are, however, minority markets and there is no evidence that the bulk of all visitors are in any mood for education in the formal sense. Most would certainly resent any forms of intrusive communication or perceived 'instructions'. On the other hand, the leisure industry deals with people who have time to devote to experiences which capture for a while their interest and imagination. The evidence of growing visitor numbers to tens of thousands of new museums and heritage/culture-based attractions created all over the world reveals a remarkable level of international curiosity and interest in aspects of people and place. It is easy to criticize the quality of some of these heritage attractions and be cynical about the so-called commoditization of culture, but it is a remarkable manifestation of a real visitor interest. The need and the opportunity is to develop the quality of such attractions so that they can play a better role in meeting their objectives and *at the same time* play a role in shifting the environmental understanding of their visitors at local level. In mature tourism markets cultural and heritage attractions are already clearly identified as core element of tourism motivation and visited by at least a half of all international visitors.

It is a core belief of this book that relevant environmental messages and understanding, appropriately interpreted and presented, can be delivered to the majority of visitors who will be interested in them. Such a process will not require major and costly new procedures; the main elements are already in place as aspects of normal business operations. This represents a major corporate opportunity by any standard. Not immediately, perhaps, and not for all, but if the messages are correctly targeted and delivered, customer behaviour can be modified over time. Businesses in the travel and tourism industry and their staffs are vital elements in the communication process and such a process cannot be left to chance. It has to be organized and delivered within a framework created by companies for that purpose.

Environmental evaluation processes and auditing: EIA, EIS and EMS

Around the world since the 1970s, but given added weight and urgency since the Rio Summit of 1992, many governments have made it a statutory/regulatory requirement that the potential environmental impacts of all significant new development proposals for all purposes are first evaluated as part of the process of achieving planning consent. The underlying theme is detailed *coordinated* assessment of all the environmental implications of large new developments. It includes scrutiny of the measures included to mitigate negative effects, having regard to the massive network of specific international and

national environmental regulations enacted over the last twenty five years. In the USA, the Environment Protection Agency was established as a federal agency as far back as 1970 to coordinate environmental programmes then undertaken by some fifteen separate agencies. Its responsibilities include EIA procedures. In Europe, the first EC Directive on Environmental Impact Assessments was agreed in 1985, and the first comprehensive EC Declaration on the Environment took place in 1990. Environment Impact Assessment Acts are in place in most European countries explicitly aiming to foster sustainable development.

In reading this section, it should be noted that the three environmental procedures outlined are interrelated and complementary. They are not at all specific to travel and tourism but cover industrial and public sector activities generally, both for new developments and for existing operations. Although international and national in their origin, they apply at local level where impacts are experienced. They reflect state-of-the-art knowledge of sustainability and regulatory practice in the public and private sector, and many of the procedures are technically complex. In the 1990s they apply only to large developments, and small and medium-sized businesses are not covered, although their collective impact on the environment is typically significant in travel and tourism because of the sheer numbers involved.

Environmental Impact Assessments (EIAs)

EIAs, now a mandatory requirement for large new public and private sector projects in most developed and some developing countries, are 'a critical appraisal of the likely effects of a policy, programme, project, or activity on the environment.' (Gilpin, 1996, p. 76) EIAs may be required for the decision purposes of local, state or federal government and are carried out independently of those seeking approval for development, although proponents are responsible for preparing and submitting the case for assessment (see 'EIS' below). EIA extends to the whole process from the inception of a proposal to environmental analysis of impacts and post-project evaluation, and it promotes public consultation and participation. An assessment is intended to cover all adverse (as well as beneficial) outcomes, including impact on ecosystems; on the community; on aesthetic, recreational and scientific values of a locality; on significant local buildings; and arising from the disposal of wastes. An EIA also covers the quality, range and depth of the environmental management systems to be implemented in a proposed development.

A full EIA is a complex procedure and Gilpin lists no less than thirty-three separate principles derived from Australian practice which cover the various roles of assessing authorities, proponents, the public, and government.

Environmental Impact Statements (EIS)

An EIS is the direct responsibility of a developer and typically prepared as an input to EIA procedures. It is a 'document, prepared by a proponent, describing: a proposed activity or development and identifying the possible, probable, or certain effects of the proposal on the environment; examining the possible alternatives; ... proposing a programme of environmental management including provisions for monitoring, post project analysis, or auditing; and plans for rehabilitation' (at the end of the project) (Gilpin, 1996, p. 78) This is also a complex process, normally undertaken by consultants, and Gilpin lists twenty-six separate stages in the process of drawing up an EIS. Where large developments are concerned, the processes of EIS are likely to be used to evaluate more than one site to achieve the best possible match between a developer's proposals and a specified site.

Environmental Management Systems (EMS)

EMS applies to the conduct of existing, day-to-day business operations and is a useful label for the range of programmes undertaken by a public or private sector organization to protect, enhance, or reduce its impacts on the environment. It is a corporate approach usually based on auditing procedures and it involves setting objectives, measurable targets, a detailed programme for the *Ten Rs*, and a monitoring and evaluation process. An EMS typically involves management arrangements (organization, budgets and staff) as part of specifying programmes and tasks. In larger companies EMS may be formally linked with annual reports in providing information to stakeholders, and in the future, if the technical obstacles are overcome, it could be linked to new forms of environmental accounting, as part of routine corporate accounting processes.

Within the UK, there is a standard procedure for corporate environmental management systems, developed and promoted by The British Standards Institute (known BS 7750 in the UK and ISO 14000 internationally), which involves assessment of company practice by professional independent assessors and the granting of certification (renewable annually) for companies whose procedures meet or exceed the BSI requirements. The European Union adopted an Eco-Management and Audit Regulation (EMAR) in 1993 as a voluntary scheme to encourage companies to set environmental targets and use external auditors to verify compliance. As noted earlier although there are similarities in principle between the conduct of EMS and the more widely known Total Quality Management procedures, in the late 1990s EMS procedures adopted are being increasingly used in manufacturing industry, but have not made much impact on travel and tourism companies at the time of going to press. Companies such as British Airways and Inter-Continental Hotels are notable leaders in this field, however, and further information will be found in Chapters 12 and 14. We can confidently predict that the momentum now building for the implementation of EMS will embrace most large travel and tourism companies over the next decade.

AGENDA 21 for the travel & tourism industry

Actions identified for travel and tourism companies, with the main aim of establishing systems and procedures which incorporate sustainable development at the core of the decision-making process for business operations. (Applies also to public sector business operations)

   (i) Waste minimization, re-use, and recycling.

  (ii) Energy efficiency, conservation, and management.

 (iii) Management of fresh water resources.

 (iv) Waste water management.

  (v) Management of hazardous substances.

 (vi) Use of more environmentally friendly transport.

 (vii) Land-use planning and management.

(viii) Involving staff, customers, and local communities in environmental issues.

 (ix) Design for sustainability.

  (x) Developing partnerships for sustainable development.

Source: Extracted from press release of February 1997 issued by WTTC/WTO/Earth Council

Figure 11.2   *AGENDA 21 – the private sector role*

AGENDA 21

Figure 11.2, which may be compared with Figure 8.1 covering the public sector role in tackling AGENDA 21, sets out the agreed WTTC/WTO/Earth Council recommendations on action identified for travel and tourism companies to incorporate sustainable development principles at the core of their decision-making process. The *Ten Rs* in this chapter provide ample illustrations relevant to the recommended processes.

Chapter summary

For a given level of tourism the overall effect of working through the *Ten Rs* will:

- *Reduce* the level of consumption of natural resources and other inputs required in the travel and tourism industry for a given volume of visitors.
- *Reduce* the level of wastage and pollution generated by business operations.
- *Generate* cost savings through greater efficiency and the introduction of new technology.
- *Develop* staff and management awareness and interest in the environmental implications of their work.
- *Oblige* suppliers to adopt more effective environmental practices in order to stay in business.
- *Enhance* the quality of the experience received by visitors and their satisfaction.
- *Shift* customer awareness and be part of the process of shifting consumer behaviour into more sustainable ways.
- *Facilitate* more positive contributions from the industry to the quality of the physical, social and cultural environment at visited destinations.

Marketing techniques are not usually associated with environmental good practice, especially in travel and tourism. Of all the management skills available within the sectors of the tourism industry, however, it is a marketing perspective which provides the most developed techniques for conveying information, adapting products and moulding and monitoring customer behaviour. Customer attitudes and behaviour are often the most sensitive variables in achieving a more sustainable approach to business. There are important links also between marketing, especially the management and monitoring of service quality and satisfaction, relationship marketing aimed at developing repeat business, total quality management (TQM) procedures, and the more recent environmental management systems (EMS). These links are only just being explored in the late 1990s but we expect the connections to develop strongly in the next decade.

Further reading

The technical information drawn upon in the section on EIA, EIS, and EMS can be fully referenced in *The Dictionary of Environment and Sustainable Development*, by Alan Gilpin, Wiley, Chichester, 1996.

See also *AGENDA 21 for the Travel & Tourism Industry: Towards Environmentally Sustainable Development*, WTTC with WTO and The Earth Council, London, 1996.

12

Sustainability in the accommodation sector – with international illustrations

Since 1990, in common with leading players in other sectors of the world economy ... Inter-Continental Hotels and Resorts has positioned itself with WTTC at the forefront of implementing the principles of sustainable development (Robert Collier, see Foreword).

Apart from same-day visitors, tourists by definition stay one or more nights in the places they visit. Accommodation is, therefore, one of the five integral components of tourism products identified in Chapter 6. This holds good whether the accommodation is commercial – such as hotels or holiday villages – quasi-commercial – such as youth hostels or university accommodation operated on a non-profit basis, or non-commercial – for example, when visitors stay overnight with friends and relatives. There is a very wide range of both serviced and self-catering commercial accommodation types available around the world.

It is important to make a distinction between holiday accommodation provided essentially to give tourist access to the resource attractions of a destination, and accommodation provided for other reasons. Historically, inns and the fore-runners of modern hotels were not provided for leisure but for business travel purposes at ports, towns and cities and at staging locations on the main road network. The railway and steamship era in the nineteenth century promoted extensive hotel development, first at stations and ports and then in purpose-built resorts, for exactly the same reasons that airline expansion in the twentieth century has produced its own parallel developments. Around the world, business travel was and still is a vital element of the accommodation business in many destinations, and for many hotels the per-capita revenue contribution of non-leisure travel far exceeds that of leisure travel. Outside purpose-built resorts, relatively low-yielding leisure products are often built onto the back of higher-yielding business visitors, utilizing the space available at times when it cannot more profitably be sold for business and other non-leisure uses. In the 1990s, conferences, seminars, training and business meetings are increasingly targeted by leisure hotels and resorts for the higher yield they provide.

In many countries accommodation businesses are by far the largest group of employers in the tourism industry. Not surprisingly, large accommodation businesses and trade associations representing them together with smaller businesses often play a major role in tourism destination politics and wield important influence over tourist board and local government decisions. In the UK, for example, many locally elected politicians in tourist destinations are hoteliers, and most businesses in membership of area tourist boards are drawn from the accommodation sector.

Overall role of accommodation in the environment of the destination

Decisions taken by commercially provided accommodation critically influence the practice of sustainable development at any destination. *Collectively*, at the end of the twentieth century, including the decision whether or not and to what extent to put destination marketing in the hands of tour operators, accommodation businesses have perhaps the major influence over two key factors:

- Volume and type (segments) of staying visitors that any given destination attracts.
- Quality of the destination environment as perceived by visitors, especially its physical appearance and image.

Decisions to build particular categories of accommodation, such as five-star or two-star in serviced or self-serviced units, together with the related marketing decisions, means accommodation businesses directly influence and in many cases effectively decide the profile of staying visitors. They largely determine the type of products visitors buy, their behaviour patterns at the destination, how long they stay, the amount of money they spend, and the seasonality of visitor flows. Because each customer segment has a different level of economic and social impact, the characteristics of the accommodation provided for them directly influences local environmental impact.

In other words, the design of accommodation and its marketing may largely determine not only the profile and characteristics of the visitors attracted to it but also the whole character and image of a destination. The bed capacity provided (mainly a commercial decision) is usually the principal determinant of the volume of tourists. This is easy to see in the case of new hotels or time-share properties which are purpose-built to supply products closely matching the researched needs of an identified group of target market segments. The position is less obvious for an established hotel if it has to adjust its marketing to new types of clients, but the principle of targeting market segments is the same. In all cases, the role of accommodation, and the mix and price range of serviced and unserviced accommodation at any particular location, are crucial to the achievement or failure of sustainability locally.

Although accommodation is, by definition, always part of the tourism product, it may not necessarily be part of the environmental attractions or quality of the places in which it is located. Accommodation often plays just a facilitating role which makes it possible for visitors living beyond a convenient day-visit return distance to gain access to a destination's attractions or to do their business. A growing sector of modern accommodation is provided on or adjacent to airports or along major motor routes for use *en-route* to the primary attractions of a chosen destination. This functional role traditionally has not involved either environmental or aesthetic considerations. Many modern accommodation blocks for tourism constructed since the 1960s are downright ugly from the outside, having all the architectural charms of high-rise blocks of municipal housing or car parks. This is true from the Gold Coast in Australia, through Florida, Hawaii and the coastal resorts in Spain, and it can be seen also in the emerging destinations in the Pacific Rim. Thus far, developers have been able to build and sell ugly functional hotels because it was usually cheaper (more profitable) to do so, and for decades tourists showed no signs of caring if the price was right. In response to the growing influence and changing attitudes of better-educated, more experienced and more demanding customers of the late 1990s, this now appears to be changing.

In the short run at least, ugly structures, even blots on the landscape, are able to perform an adequate role in the functional provision of accommodation and food and beverage, and they can be sold. The authors of this book do not believe this will be a sustainable position, however, looking ahead to the next century. The architecture of a hotel makes the most highly visible statement about its owners' environmental awareness and commitment, especially if it is located in an area of high environmental quality. It is interesting to see the very different new approaches to hotel and resort architecture being pursued since the 1990s.

The size of business influences environmental impact

The section above notes the overall or *collective* influence of accommodation on the environment. In practice, accommodation provision and marketing decisions are made not collectively but separately by hundreds or even thousands of mostly small and medium sized enterprises, with no collective vision. To understand the impact of accommodation on sustainability it is vital to draw distinctions by size of operation.

First, for large businesses in the international holiday market, where a self-contained integrated resort hotel is built on its own island or in an area surrounded by its own grounds and with its own leisure facilities on-site, the destination, the attraction, the environment, and the accommodation provided may coincide within one enterprise. This is clearly the case with large hotel resorts such as the Sheraton on Maui (Hawaii), with Center Parcs in Europe, and with Club Méditerranée villages and with most time-share resorts. It is true of many island resorts in the South Pacific and the Caribbean where environmental quality is under direct private sector control. At this level, the resort effectively is the destination. It is also designed to be an attractive product in its own right and it may matter little to many customers where it is actually located geographically. Such resorts are typically operated by international corporations providing products at premium prices and they have a heavy investment in the quality of the environment as the core asset of their business. They are committed to it. Market forces and commercial self-interest are likely to encourage such corporations to develop sustainable policies – especially if their customers expect high standards and active pressure groups with easy media access are monitoring developments and seeking to expose any perceived transgression. Increasingly, in the future all such large new developments are likely to have to undergo an environmental impact assessment study (EIA) before construction and to modify their building designs and EMS to enhance as well as to protect the environmental resources at the destination.

Second, among the thousands of medium and smaller accommodation businesses, such as those to be found in the large resorts around the coasts of the Mediterranean, different considerations apply. Most such businesses are independently owned and many have become wholly or largely dependent on international tour operators and retail travel agents for their marketing in the last two decades. These resorts are an important phenomenon in the international tourism industry at the close of the twentieth century, although measured in global terms they comprise only a minor part of commercially provided accommodation in the travel and tourism industry. Allowing corporate responsibility for marketing to be divided from corporate responsibility for designing and providing accommodation facilities, especially when the marketers have no vested interest in the environment of the places they include in their brochures, has been a recipe for environmental degradation in many places. It has led to reckless short-term attitudes to profit and overcapacity of beds (see Chapter 15) and it is potentially disastrous in environmentally sensitive areas.

Such a division of responsibility is not an inherent characteristic of the tourism industry, however, merely a reflection of business opportunities in tourism resorts in a particular era of tourism development. The division represents a failure in tourism to comprehend the nature of modern marketing and we believe it reflects a temporary phase in the progress of the world's largest industry.

Third, at the small and very small end of the accommodation scale the direct links between accommodation and environment appear to be rather more clear, at least in principle. Most farmhouse accommodation, many bed-and-breakfast establishments in rural areas of high scenic quality, and holiday cottages in rural areas such as national parks combine environmental resource, attraction and accommodation in the same accommodation product offer. In this case the operators appear to be providing on a micro scale exactly what the large resort corporations provide on a much bigger scale. But in doing it the small businesses do not take responsibility for the resource; they draw on, one might say feed off, the environment and other local visitor facilities and attractions in the same location. They are typically part of a 'local community' but they make their profits by trading on an attractive environment to which many make no direct contribution.

The operations of a few dozen bed-and-breakfast places, even a few hundred holiday cottages, may have only a very minor impact on a scenically attractive area such as a national park. They can easily be absorbed by the environment and the visitors they attract are part of the tourism economy and may help to provide economic uses that sustain traditional buildings in good repair and provide much-needed local employment. But when dozens become hundreds, and hundreds become thousands, and they are concentrated in areas which are the most scenically attractive and environmentally

fragile, the issue looks different. The authors believe that for many countries it is at this scale of operation, where very few official regulations can be effectively enforced and monitored, and where individuals make decisions on how to make short-run profit from a 'freely' available resource base, that *collectively* the worst excesses of environmental damage are likely to occur.

It would be naive indeed to suppose that such decisions, taken individually by tens of thousands of small businesses or *micro-operators*, ever considered environmental sustainability as part of the process. But the impact collectively is massive. In many of the attractive villages in the Lake District National Park of England, for example, much of what is now holiday accommodation was bought by people who live elsewhere as an investment and is rented out for holiday purposes. The families of many local residents cannot afford the prices that properties fetch on an open property market; many incoming visitors with cars have no obvious reason to respect the social and cultural environment of the remaining residents; they have paid for a holiday home providing 'free' and unrestricted access to the environment; and the scene is set for resentment of tourists by a local community. It was not planned as such. It was not a commercial conspiracy. It is not an inevitable consequence of tourism. It was simply the working of opportunism in a free society with consequences which none could foresee. To place the blame for this on 'tourism' or to see it as an unalterable characteristic of the accommodation industry is foolish and impedes the sensible route to finding solutions.

Formulating the accommodation product for environmental purposes

From a marketing standpoint, the simplest way to understand the formulation of any commercial product, including accommodation, is to 'deconstruct' it into its component parts (see also Chapter 6). Environmental considerations can be built into each element of the product as indicated in the two case studies in this chapter. The quality of the resources at a destination is frequently the most important element of the core product or *promise* which accommodation providers make to holiday visitors in their advertising and promotional work. It is the promise which influences the expectations of first-time buyers and strongly influences their perceptions of satisfaction and value for money. We have argued throughout this book that environmental qualities – although not using those words – are increasingly the element that determines customer satisfaction, repeat visits and competitive advantage.

For hotels and other forms of holiday accommodation a key issue for designing and landscaping buildings is the extent to which they blend into and respect the local environment and minimize environmental impact. Apart from the capacity of the chosen location to absorb the number of people to be provided for, this includes technology for the efficient use of energy and water, and control of waste. Safari Parks are a good example of sensitive product formulation because the over-intrusive participation of visitors into a natural environment may bring about changes in the behaviour of animals and alter the habitat. It could destroy the resource. Bed capacity is the key judgement reflected in the product formulation decisions taken at Kruger National Park, for example, where the Park authorities have successfully restricted accommodation capacity, contained it within enclosed camps, and managed visitor flows for over sixty years in accordance with their judgement of how many visitors the Park can sustainably absorb. (See Part Four.)

In the next section – pages 148–151 we summarize the specific environmental management issues for the accommodation sector.

Sustainability for accommodation purposes – the environmental management perspective

Reflecting the issues identified in Chapter 2, and the overall approach to environmental management programmes set out in Chapter 11, the main environmental impacts to which the sector has responded include the following.

Specific environmental impacts

Resource depletion:

- Use of energy generated from fossil fuels.
- Use of non-renewable natural resources such as oil, coal, and natural gas for heating or the production of manufactured goods.
- Consumption of fresh water, especially conspicuous consumption in areas of water shortage for swimming pools and golf course irrigation.

Pollution:

- Contribution to global warming and acid rain through the consumption of energy.
- Contribution to global warming, acid rain, low-level smog, and potentially ozone depletion through the use of transport both directly and by visitors travelling to destinations, and the import of goods to service visitors' needs.
- Pollution of watercourses through the discharge of sewage, untreated waste water from laundries, kitchens, guest rooms, swimming pools, and run-off from chemically treated golf courses.
- Production of solid wastes for landfill sites, and sometimes landscape deterioration from illegal dumping.
- Contribution to ozone depletion through the use of CFCs, halons, etc.

Degradation:

- Of local footpaths, heritage sites or cultures caused by a large number of people visiting sensitive areas.
- Reduction in species diversity as a result of infrastructure development, building, or landscaping work such as golf courses, plus direct interference by visitors as on coral reefs.
- Reduction in landscape quality as a result of creeping urbanization associated with in-fill development which has characterized many large tourist resort areas.
- Of local cultures in economically developing countries through disruption of traditional male/female employment modes and commercialization of traditional ceremonies as visitor entertainment.

Environmental opportunities for the sector

The opportunities that can be gained from environmental improvement programmes in the accommodation sector include:

- *Cost savings.* Programmes to reduce consumption of energy and water and reduce waste production have cut the total utilities bill by up to one-fifth for some companies. For a large international hotel chain this can equate to a saving of many millions of dollars (see the Inter-Continental example below).
- *Increased staff motivation and loyalty.* The travel and tourism industry generally, especially the accommodation sector, suffers from a rapid turnover of staff. This results in relatively high recruitment and training costs that, in some cases, affects service quality. The companies that have adopted a proactive environmental approach – especially where staff are rewarded for their initiative – have found that staff turnover has decreased and staff motivation is increased. Indeed, many accommodation establishments have initiated their environmental programmes with little or no

financial investment, relying entirely upon the voluntary efforts of staff.

- *Improvements in product quality.* Companies which have developed detailed environmental programmes have found that perceived service quality increases. Appropriately lit and heated rooms, for example, are often associated with programmes to manage energy; water management programmes detect and fix leaking taps before they become an irritant; waste management programmes replace paper napkins with fabric ones; and interpretative tours or cycle hire facilities offer additional attraction to guests.
- *Improvements in community relations.* Established environmental programmes almost always extend to incorporate the local community in some way. Local welfare hostels, for example, may be the beneficiaries of a recycling programme or a local landscape may be cleaned up as a part of a landscape quality programme. Such programmes often help to integrate the accommodation facility into the community and may ensure that guests at the facility are a welcome addition to the local area.
- *Improvement in relations with local authorities.* Authorities and local regulators will often look more favourably upon development applications from companies which have a firm and longstanding environmental commitment, especially in sensitive environments. Government authorities in some areas, for example, New Zealand's national parks, have developed a series of development permits which must be renewed periodically. The value of the permit will vary with market prices and these reflect the environmental quality around the establishment as well as location. Operators who ensure that environmental quality is enhanced are, therefore, rewarded financially when they seek to sell on their permits.
- *Reduction in liability to prosecution.* In the developed countries of Europe, North America,

Australia and New Zealand programmes to mitigate negative environmental impacts reduce liability to prosecution. Such prosecutions can now result in heavy financial penalties, considerable clean-up costs, or in the worst instances gaol sentences.

- *Increased attraction to customers.* A recent MORI poll in the USA found that 85 per cent of respondents stated that they would prefer to buy products that did not damage the environment. Such preferences are not usually accompanied by willingness to pay premium prices (for that purpose) but growth in so-called 'ecotourism' products is significant and points to changing customer expectations about the quality of the products that they purchase, and the likelihood of an increase in the number of clients that respond to accommodation establishments with green credentials.

- *Long-term resort development.* With the exception of a small number of very large companies, individual accommodation establishments have little potential to influence the nature of resort development if they act alone. Acting together in partnership with local authorities they can influence resort quality and the long-term security of their investment. In some cases the life-cycle evolution of resorts, from growth to decline when the quality of the environment is damaged through overdevelopment, may take as little as fifteen years. To some extent, some of the larger hotel chains have already protected their interests through the development of *Integrated Tourist Resorts* (see Chapters 3 and 4). Predominant in South Asia, these resorts are typically constructed by a development company and operated by three or four large hotel chains. Ownership of the land provides complete control over environmental quality and the guest experience. Most of these resorts, however, exclude residents of the area, thus earning them a reputation among some critics as 'neo-colonial enclaves'.

Regulatory background

Environmental regulations have not been developed specifically for the accommodation sector. It is instead subject to the wide range of more general environmental and environmental health and safety regulations that exist in all countries. For larger establishments in developed countries, the regulations which impact on the accommodation sector include:

- *Planning and building regulations.* These regulations encompass the broad range of planning and building issues from the need to gain planning permission to extend or change the use of a building for small hotels, to the requirement that large hotel developers go through a full environmental impact assessment (EIA) prior to gaining permission to go ahead.

- *Environmental health and safety regulations* which encompass all aspects of the safety of employees while at work and guests while on the premises.

- *Regulations governing the use and disposal of potentially hazardous materials.* Like any other business, hotels are obliged to ensure that potentially hazardous materials are stored and disposed of appropriately after use. When detected, discharges to landfill or watercourses are penalized by heavy fines, or in some countries, gaol sentences.

- *Regulations governing the responsible disposal of wastes.* Failure to dispose of wastes appropriately is increasingly penalized by regulators and many countries have now introduced a 'duty of care' system whereby the originator of the waste is liable for its responsible disposal, even if this final disposal is undertaken by a contractor. Increasingly in the EU, accommodation establishments are subject to a range of regulations that require waste separation and recycling. The Packaging Waste Directive due to come into force in the UK in 1997 requires that a high percentage of packaging waste is recycled, which will necessitate increased levels of waste separation by accommodation establishments.

Self-regulation in the sector

Beyond the normal processes of compliance with the law, self-regulation initiatives are more responsible for shaping the environmental credentials of the hotel industry than regulation and the sector has already achieved some progress. The International Hotels Environment Initiative (IHEI) has been particularly successful at driving the agenda forward with membership and funding from eleven of the world's leading hotel chains. Regional hotel associations such as the Finnish Hotel and Restaurant Council, the Thai Hotel Association, and the Caribbean Hotels Association have also been successful at encouraging hotels – especially larger ones – to adopt environmental programmes. A 1996 report from the International Hotel & Restaurant Association with UNEP (Green Hotelier) lists fifteen good practice case studies from eleven countries around the world and includes reference to environmental programmes developed by fourteen different national hotel associations. None of these were in place before the early 1990s. Specific issues which have been covered by voluntary programmes include:

- Purchasing policies, especially as regards favouring locally produced products, selecting non-chemical cleaners wherever possible and the use of organically grown agricultural produce.
- Use and disposal of potentially hazardous materials, such as chlorine bleaches, PCBs and CFCs.
- Use of transport for company purposes.
- Development of alternative cycle routes, etc. for visitors.
- Integration of the community into the company's environmental programme, through local educational initiatives, donations to local charities, or initiatives to clean up local landscape areas

- Cost saving areas of energy, waste, and water management.

A number of guidelines and manuals have been developed in different parts of the world to help accommodation establishments improve their environmental performance and good practice examples have been widely publicized, in some cases by the government department responsible for environmental issues. Some of the 'green' labels which have been developed for the tourism industry are applicable to the accommodation sector and these include WTTC's Green Globe and PATA's Green Leaf.

Summarizing the environmental issues for accommodation businesses – the way ahead

The key issue for accommodation businesses, even though comparatively few have formally recognized it at the present time, is that the future value of their capital assets as well as their earning potential is at risk in a deteriorating environment. Since 1991, through the International Hotels Environmental Initiative and WTTC, the large international corporations have begun to demonstrate their awareness through mission statements, environmental audits of operations and implementation of environmental programmes (EMS) as noted above. EMS procedures are still rare in this sector, however, has only evolved since 1990 and are still typically focused only on cost savings. Most accommodation businesses have been reluctant to involve clients in their environmental programmes, fearful that guests may perceive they are being offered a reduced level of service. Apart from marketing approaches, four primary avenues of development for sustainability are open to accommodation businesses at local level:

- A programmed approach to the *Ten R's*, which is a logical extension of traditional controls of waste and costs and leads into a formal purchasing or procurement policy to deal as far as possible with suppliers who operate on environmentally sustainable principles.

- Design and building of new accommodation units which are environmentally sensitive in the obvious dimensions of architectural features and visual impact, technological efficiency, attractive and locally relevant landscaping, and regard for the recognised capacity limits at a destination. Although new buildings are easier to handle from the design point of view, the same principles apply to modification and refurbishment of existing buildings – especially where there are important heritage features of structures that merit preservation.

- Proactive use of the time that visitors, especially holiday visitors, spend in their accommodation, to communicate environmentally interesting as well as functional messages ranging from appreciating something of the history of the local culture and natural resources at the destination, to encouraging a more economical approach to the use of fresh water and bath towels.

- Participating in destination partnerships to formulate goals and objectives in the long-run interests of all the stakeholders in the destination's environment and collaborating on mutual marketing and development objectives with tour operators. This partnership process is likely to include both the negotiation and application of any regulatory agreements, and forms of trade association and marketing consortia to influence, monitor and self-regulate the activities of smaller and medium sized enterprises which will otherwise tend to slip through the established networks of environmental control.

In the next section – pages 152–158 we outline specific examples of current good practice in the accommodation sector.

Accommodation business examples

Inter-Continental Hotels and Resorts

Led by a small number of international hotel chains, there are now several sectoral guides that help companies to address many of the major environmental impacts associated with their business activities. Taking a leading role within this group, with more than 200 hotels in over seventy countries around the world and some 71 000 bedrooms, Inter-Continental Hotels and Resorts is one of the longest-established international hotel companies. Of the total, 124 hotels are first-class Inter-Continental properties, twenty-six are mid-market Forum hotels, and some fifty-five are affiliated hotels designated as Global Partners. The hotels cater for the needs of both business and leisure travellers. The company employs in the region of 40 000 personnel and had an annual turnover approaching US$2 billion in the late 1990s.

Environmental improvement is a core tenet of the company's overall mission:

To establish Inter-Continental as the leading and preferred hospitality outlet by the year 2000. This will be achieved through consistent improvements in the commercial and leisure services that we provide to the global business traveller. We aim to achieve our goal while consistently enhancing returns for our stakeholders and preserving our ethic of being an environmentally conscious corporation and a responsible employer.

To fulfil this mission, the company was the first international hotel company to develop a comprehensive approach to environmental management and this programme was fundamental to the subsequent creation of the International Hotels Environment Initiative (IHEl).

Rationale for a Sustainable Strategy

Inter-Continental Hotels and Resorts' environmental programme was developed from both a business and an ethical standpoint. On the one hand, in line with the aims of AGENDA 21, the company recognized that 'real improvements in the global environment will only be realized when all stakeholders take steps to improve their environmental performance'. On the other hand, the company was aware that significant cost savings could be made through the adoption of a systematic environmental programme.

Partnerships involved

Partnerships have been essential to the programme, both internally to motivate staff and externally to pass on the message of sustainable development to the other companies with which Inter-Continental Hotels and Resorts interacts. Partnerships have been formed between individual hotels, between hotel employees and community groups, with financial institutions such as the World Bank, with conservation groups, with local authorities, and with competing international hotel chains. Within its environmental programme, the company is one of the few in the travel and tourism industry to make information available to its competitors which can actually help them to cut costs and gain market advantage.

Environmental programmes

(a) Environmental management

Flexibility has been essential to the establishment of a programme which can be adapted and implemented by a committed staff throughout hotels in vastly different cultural, physical, and political environments around the world, and at the same time be monitored at head office level.

Head office commitment has been essential and a General Manager has been designated with responsibility for environmental issues. The General Manager chairs a world-wide Environmental Committee that coordinates regional programmes through ten Regional Environmental Chairmen (one for each of the global regions into which the company's operations are divided). Each individual hotel has an environmental chairman who is responsible for convening an environmental committee. Individual hotels can then report progress or problems to this Chairman, who either provides answers, or passes them to the World-wide Environmental Committee for solutions. Good practice examples, or solutions to problems, are regularly published and distributed to staff and clients through the environmental news bulletin, *The Daily Planet.*

This environmental management process has been extremely effective in facilitating the monitoring achievement of the six point environmental commitment described below, which lays out the company's aims and objectives concerning overall environmental improvement. The commitment is supported by annual improvement targets which provide short-term objectives company-wide. Compliance with these targets is carefully monitored and reported.

Individual hotels are provided with an environmental reference manual and a 134-point environmental checklist which helps them to monitor compliance with the environmental commitment, achieve targets, and ensure that they address the range of environmental impacts generated by a major international hotel company.

(b) Inter-Continental Hotels and Resorts environmental programme goals for 1997

1 *Energy conservation.* Inter-Continental is committed to reduce global energy costs by 2 per cent over 1996 actual costs:
   Base: 1996 Actual $79 500 million
   1997 Goal $77 900 million

2 *Refrigerant management.* Inter-Continental will implement refrigerant containment techniques for existing equipment operating with CFCs:
   (i) Wherever low-pressure chillers are installed, the purge units are to be replaced with high-efficiency units.
   (ii) Install centralized leak monitoring and detection equipment in mechanical

rooms where CTC plant and equipment is located.

3 *Environmental audit/review.* Inter-Continental will improve its environmental audit rating world-wide by 2 percentage points.

Base 1996 – actual average rating world wide 77 per cent

Target	From	To
UK/ Scandinavia	73.0%	76.0%
France/Mediterranean	57.5%	62.5%
Forum/Benelux	64.8%	68.0%
Germany	82.4%	84.4%
Austria/Eastern Europe	94.5%	95.0%
North America	78.1%	81.0%
Latin America	84.6%	86.6%
Middle East	75.9%	78.5%
Africa	64.0%	67.0%
Asia/Pacific	83.3%	85.5%

(c) Inter-Continental Hotels and Resorts six-point environment commitment and how it is implementing action

1 *Conservation of natural resources and energy in its hotels without sacrificing safety standards or jeopardising guest satisfaction* Progress in implementing this area of the mission statement has been outstanding. By adopting a comprehensive approach to management and measurement of resource use, and by allocating resource costs to individual department heads, Inter-Continental Hotels and Resorts have significantly cut overall energy and water costs over a seven-year period.

2 *To select only product and materials from environmentally responsible sources whose use – wherever possible – has positive and beneficial effects* Many products have been replaced as a result of initiatives to seek benign alternatives for potentially damaging materials. Wherever possible, for example, individually packaged food items have been replaced and paper products are recycled and recyclable. German hotels have led the field in developing a Product and Purchase List and have identified

more than 500 products which are regularly used and targeted 100 of these for phase-out and replacement.

3 *To minimize and efficiently manage waste production, ensuring the least possible negative impact on the environment* Measurement of waste throughout the chain has proved problematic with currently available methods, but some hotels have managed significantly to reduce their total waste output.

4 *To acknowledge regional differences in environmental needs and practices by establishing adaptable local programmes designed to improve the performance of each individual hotel* The key to the success of the Inter-Continental environmental approach has been flexibility and a number of hotels have adopted particularly innovative approaches to environmental management. The Regional Chief Engineer at the Nairobi Inter-Continental, Kenya, has been particularly innovative, producing an environmental management guide and supporting video to help other hotels in developing countries to adopt suitable environmental programmes.

5 *To identify ways to participate in local community action on the environment world-wide* A hotel cannot operate sustainably in isolation from the community in which it is based; to do so is to risk the quality of the product. Community programmes have been a great motivator in the Inter-Continental approach and more than twenty-eight new programmes were initiated in 1995 alone, ranging from a community-based waste composting programme in Bali, Indonesia, and an Environmental Olympiad for schoolchildren in Abu Dhabi, to support for a homeless shelter in the centre of London.

6 *To develop awareness of environmental initiatives internally and externally through a variety of education and training initiatives* There can be no doubt that the environmental programme has been very successful in raising awareness and shifting attitudes. Within the company, all staff now have access to environmental information and are given some form of relevant training. Externally, significant media cover-

age and PR benefits have been achieved through the leading role the company has played in IHEI, through the specific publicity achieved by the programme locally and internationally, and through the outreach activities undertaken by individual hotel managers.

In support of its six commitments, Inter-Continental Hotels and Resorts has developed a comprehensive monitoring system to measure achievement and ensure that progress is quantified where possible.

Summary – Inter-Continental Hotels and Resorts

The approach to environmental management taken by Inter-Continental has been innovative and successful, reflecting management commitment to the programmes at all levels, starting at the top. The company has invested in financial and personnel terms to develop the programmes and this has resulted in pay-back in terms of improvement in overall staff morale, cost savings working through to the bottom line, partnerships with local authorities in the destinations where the hotels are located, and partnership with the World Bank. It has also generated valuable positive PR.

Although there is no solid evidence that the programme is of itself generating new customers, it is now part of the product quality approach the company adopts. The company sees potential growth in niche markets such as the increasing international environment conference circuit and, as many more companies develop the relevant technology and good practice, business clients whose companies have established their own environmental programmes prefer to deal with like-minded companies. The Olympic Games Committee, for example, is incorporating environmental criteria into its location decision processes.

The company remains aware that the full benefits of its programme will only be achieved as more travel and tourism companies participate in programmes such as IHEI and Green Globe, as part of the drive to improve the en-

vironmental performance of the whole accommodation sector. In early 1997, the company announced that it would invest US$1 million over the next five years in the development and implementation of travel and tourism environmental programmes generally, responding to the challenge of the Earth Council which called on the industry to implement AGENDA 21. All the company's hotels are now Green Globe members.

Grecotel SA

Catering mainly for holiday travellers who select their accommodation as a part of a package tour, Grecotel offers a quite different product from Inter-Continental Hotels and Resorts. It has also fully incorporated environmental management into its corporate philosophy, however, and has pioneered a very comprehensive and successful environmental programme. Grecotel is the leading hotel chain in Greece. It owns fifteen luxury and four-star hotels and manages six other units under different corporate labels, comprising a total of over 10 000 bed spaces based mainly in the Greek islands. In 1995 Grecotel recorded some 1.3 million guest nights and had over 3000 employees.

Grecotel drew up an environmental policy statement in November 1992, stating the company's intention to develop comprehensive environmental programmes with the aim of becoming the 'environmental champion' of the hotel industry, and to act as an example for resort hotel groups throughout the Mediterranean. European Commission funding was sought by the company for these initiatives and a grant was provided for environmental improvements within the hotels themselves, within the local communities in which they operate, and for developing an awareness of environmental issues among other tourism managers.

Rationale for a sustainable strategy

Primarily attracting holiday markets, Grecotel's management were well aware that deterioration of the physical/cultural environment could damage their business interests. With Greek ownership, the company also felt a strong moral responsibility towards environmental protection and enhancement of the communities in which it operates. In 1996 the company stated:

'Environment is one of Grecotels most determinant factors in all its activities, including renovations and new buildings, operating standards, applied technology, fixtures and fittings, food and beverage purchasing, sales promotion and advertising material, and ... guest entertainment programmes.' (Grecotel Environment Progress Report, 1996).

Partnerships involved

Partnerships have been the key to the success of the Grecotel strategy. At one end of the scale, the partnership achieved EC funding, which was fundamental to the establishment of a professional programme, and at the other, partnerships with suppliers have been essential in reducing the resource impacts of the operation.

Partnerships with tour operators have also been important. Both Thomson (UK) and TUI (Germany) have been involved in the programme and have great potential to influence other hotels in the region to adopt similar programmes, as well as communicating with tourists prior to their holidays. TUI is part-owner of Grecotel but the group was dealing with some sixty different tour operators in the late 1990s.

Local authorities in the Mediterranean area have been stimulated into action by the programme and the partnerships have not ended once the programme has demonstrated its success. Through the link with the IHEI, Grecotel will continue to be a champion to help the resort hotel sector improve its environmental performance.

Environmental programme

(a) Environmental management

Environmental initiatives are managed within individual hotels by an environmental coordinator who reports to the Environmental and Cultural Department at head office, first established in 1990 and the first such department for Mediterranean hotel groups. Hotel staff are fully involved in the programme and, as of 1993, Grecotel's management consultancy, Ergoplan SA, had incorporated environmental duties into all hotel personnel job descriptions. This ensures that central policy is implemented in each hotel unit. An environmental manual was developed and provided to all staff, explaining the importance of the environment to the industry and indicating ways in which staff could become good environmental citizens.

The environmental programme aims to achieve gradual improvements for the hotels and areas affected by them resulting in a low-cost basic programme which can also be implemented by other hoteliers without specialist expertise. The company aims to share the experience it has gained from developing its programme with other hotel companies.

(b) Staff and guest awareness

Initiatives currently under way include internal eco-audits, staff and guest awareness programmes, educational seminars with local schools and colleges, provision of information to potential employees, improved purchasing policy and pressure on suppliers, close cooperation with major tour operators in Europe, and sponsorship of non-profit organizations affected by tourism.

(c) Improvements in operational areas

By 1996, eco-audits under the EC (EMAR) regulation had been completed in six of the hotels and were being extended. The steps taken to manage day-to-day business operations are extensive and include measures to conserve and manage water now implemented in all hotels, including a scheme to change guest linen on request; re-use of water from biological waste water plants for garden irrigation wherever possible; metering of water use and analysis of usage for individual departments; weekly analysis of the quality of pool, sea, and drinking water; instructions issued to all staff about water saving; use of throughput regulators wherever practical; and use of environmentally friendly cleaners in all hotels where possible to minimize water pollution. All hotels also use commercial water softening plants thereby reducing the amount of detergent necessary for washing and cleaning.

Sewage treatment is an important part of the programme. All Grecotels operate biological waste-water treatment plants and the company has worked closely with the municipality in its head office town of Rethymnon in Crete to assist in the construction of a waste-water treatment and refuse landfill plant.

Despite the fact that most Greek islands do not have a municipal recycling programme or facilities, the group has made considerable progress in waste management: bottled water is now provided in glass rather than plastic bottles; individually wrapped catering supplies have been replaced by re-usables, where possible, and manufacturers pressured to find alternatives; all cocktail decorations have been replaced with fruit or flowers; recycling boxes have been provided for aluminium cans; guest soaps are issued without packaging and dispensers are increasingly used; paper is always used on both sides for photocopying and waste paper is re-used as memo pads; kitchen waste is separated into organic and non-organic categories and waste food is donated to local farmers as animal feed. Recycled paper is not widely available in Greece, but is used whenever possible – recycled photocopier paper has now been introduced into all head office departments and some hotel units. In addition, the group is supporting the establishment of a private glass recycling plant for the island of Crete, thus encouraging the development of appropriate infrastructure for use by other industries.

Energy conservation has been a priority in all hotels and an investment of some 10 million drachmas has replaced all incandescent lamps with energy-saving units; water is now heated by solar panels (accounting for 70 per cent of all hot water in the group); gas appliances are purchased in favour of solid fuel, thus minimizing atmospheric pollution. In addition, all new facilities are designed to be fuel efficient and use double-glazing and thermal insulation; bedrooms have master switches which automatically turn power on and off as guests arrive and leave; condensers are used on electric circuits for the efficient use of energy; air conditioning and heating is controlled by thermostats and all bedrooms have shutters or heat insulation curtains.

Landscape and outdoor facilities are important to the tourism product and environmental quality. Wherever possible, local materials are used in hotel construction and renovation; larger hotels are built in a style reflecting that of traditional Greek villages; environmentally friendly materials are used throughout; gardens use local species of flora and fauna and areas have been allocated for special endemic species; synthetic fertilizers and pesticides have been replaced by environmentally friendly products and organic fertilizers. In addition, local arts and crafts are used extensively in the interior of all hotels.

(d) Programmes to involve local people and support the local economy

Efforts are made to sustain the local economy and minimize the transport of goods: fruit and vegetables are brought freshly from local producers; most wines, soft drinks and beers are local, and fresh bread is baked daily; all produce is preferred in returnable wooden crates; Greek specialities are always available in the restaurants and locally produced foodstuffs are sold in hotel shops.

Cultural and environmental activities are also a part of the programme and the hotel chain actively encourages environmental conservation. For example, Grecotel has sponsored a major archaeological exhibition which is now promoted through tour operators and has also supported the Sea Turtle Protection Society of

Greece since 1991. Guests are encouraged to visit small villages and staff have been trained in flora, fauna and cultural interest. Local crafts are actively supported and increased awareness of the environmental quality of the islands is encouraged in local people by the development of posters and visits to local schools.

(e) Spreading the sustainable message

The group has a commitment to encourage environmental awareness among other Mediterranean tourism businesses. It hosted a seminar highlighting the need for private sector Greek companies to solve environmental problems which affect tourism. Staff and local people are involved in programmes promoting the economic value of green tourism. Guests are invited to slide shows of local flora and fauna and provided with copies of Grecotel news with details of the environment programme.

Summary – Grecotel

The comprehensive approach adopted by Grecotel has brought promising results, including an increase in awareness of environmental issues among local people, increased environmental activity with some local authorities, an effective partnership between tour operators and the hotel chain, an improvement in guest communication, and an improvement in the local cultural and physical environment. Through its communication programme, the hotel chain hopes to be able to encourage other hotel companies in the region to adopt sustainable methods which will help to preserve the attraction and viability of the Mediterranean coastline as a tourism destination.

In recognition of its achievements, Grecotel has been awarded over forty-five international awards by guests, tourism organizations, tour operators and international associations, for the quality of its hotels, its contribution to upgrading the Greek tourism product, and for its initiatives in the environmental and cultural field.

Sustainability – the marketing perspective

Figure 12.1 summarizes in note form the extensive role and the massive power of marketing influences which accommodation businesses are in a position to bring to bear on achieving a more sustainable approach to tourism at any destination. As with tour operators the leverage of accommodation businesses is still mostly poten-

tial rather than actual; partly because most are not yet organized to orchestrate their efforts within a partnership approach; partly because the larger players and trade bodies have also to accept and exercise collective responsibility and influence over the smaller players who are quite capable of frustrating local environmental initiatives for their own reasons. As always, the development of proactive partnership organizations point the way to a more sustainable future.

By the nature of their operations, especially where hotels and other accommodation structures are built in environmentally sensitive areas, accommodation suppliers are generally the most powerful players in the overall quality of the environment at destinations, as it is perceived and experienced by visitors.

Their marketing decisions strongly influence and in some cases directly control:

- Customer segments targeted for promotion and distribution to optimize yield.
- Product design and quality of the accommodation provided.
- Price levels to be charged for the accommodation on offer, including promotional tariffs and discounts (approximate price bands are also established by design decisions, such as five-star or two-star accommodation).
- The capacity to be offered at a destination (a function of bedspaces available).
- Architectural/visual impact (for good or ill) on destinations including the architectural styles adopted and their 'fit' with a destination's cultural/physical environment – influencing a tourism destination's image.
- The quality of the building and design and the landscaping quality around accommodation.

- The distribution process, including the decision to market direct or with selected partner organizations, for example in transport, or to pass the marketing task over to tour operators.
- The information flow to customers on the premises about the destination and its special environmental/cultural qualities, including the opportunities it affords to visitors and their responsibilities in the way they treat it.
- A major part of what most visitors experience of host–guest encounters at destinations.
- The level of repeat customers, reflecting satisfaction and perceived value for money.
- Customer knowledge through profiles held on databases for analysis and future marketing.
- Marketing objectives, budgets and programmes.

Accommodation suppliers in particular have a vital role for the environment in that most visitors spend more hours within and around their holiday accommodation than in any other tourism facility. They could use this power to better effect than at present by working more closely with their logical destination partners such as tourist boards, tour operators, transport operators and the larger visitor attractions.

Figure 12.1 *Sustainability – the marketing perspective for accommodation businesses*

13

Sustainability in the visitor attractions sector

As the spring invasion of Tuscany gets under way, the authorities in Florence are planning 'drastic measures' to limit the number of visitors allowed into the city centre (The Times, 6 April 1996).

It is a widely held view in most societies that much of the physical, social, and cultural environment inherited by current generations comprises intrinsic values that ought to be protected and conserved for future generations. It is a very short step from concepts of protection and conservation to the logic of public access and the management of resources as visitor attractions. Protection obviously applies first to the intrinsic and life-sustaining aspects of the natural and built environment, and the need to avoid erosion or destruction for short-run economic advantages. It applies also to the quality of life and recreation-sustaining aspects of the environment. Some argue that modern, stressful post-industrial life-styles, without the compensating aspects of holidays, leisure and recreation, would not be sustainable. Certainly a vital part of modern leisure and recreation focuses on the quality of natural and cultural resources and rights of public access, which increasingly involves the management of resources as visitor attractions. Its not an easy process, as the authorities in Florence know.

Although we tend to be obsessed with the environmental issues of our own time, one should not forget the long-established recognition of intrinsic values. Such recognition can be traced back in modern times to the eighteenth century and the development of cultural tourism in Europe, the so-called Grand Tour. By the late nineteenth century, travel motivated by what we would now call environmental purposes was well established, ranging from cities and the Alps to antiquities in the Middle East. In America and Britain the origins of national parks can be traced to conservation movements in the late nineteenth century and to farsighted thinkers such as Ruskin. Even in South Africa, where one might have supposed the environment would be taken for granted given the size of the land and the smallness of the population, the origins of the Kruger National Park can be traced to a nineteenth-century concern for the protection of wildlife from indiscriminate hunting.

In the late 1990s, although not recognized as such by most tourists, the perceived quality of the environment is the primary rationale for most forms of holiday tourism. Resource qualities, perceived and used as visitor attractions, are the basis for much of the 'world's largest industry'. It is one of the many paradoxes of modern travel and tourism that the environment is at the same time the victim of tourism through overexploitation of access, and its major beneficiary. Reducing the negative effects and increasing the benefits of tourism through systematic management action is the principal concern of this book. It is especially relevant to managing resource-based visitor attractions.

The tourism role of resource-based visitor attractions at destinations

Visitors need to be transported and accommodated, with or without the intermediary role of tour operators and travel agents, but it is their awareness and perception of a destination's attractions on which the other components of leisure tourism are based. The fact that visitor attractions and environmental resources tend to coincide in practice led one leading contributor to conclude that tourism is a *resource industry* (Murphy, 1985, p. 12). 'Resource' is a very broad term in this context, however, and it covers the widely disparate resources that reflect society and culture, ranging from geographically extensive areas of natural environment, cultivated sites such as parks and gardens, heritage areas such historic cities and villages, to specific buildings and collections including palaces, local museums, and zoos. It also covers a wide range of cultural provision. Figure 13.1 notes twenty types of resource-based visitor attractions grouped in four categories.

The first three categories in 13.1 are resource-based attractions with intrinsic values specifically related to the communities in which they are located. They typically serve an important role, acting as guardians and communicators of what exists of a sense of place and history, and they are managed as much for the benefit of residents as for visitors. This distinguishes resource-based attractions from accommodation, tour operators and much of the transport sector, which are essentially facilities provided solely for the benefit of tourism. The management and marketing decisions for sustainable development noted in this chapter typically have to balance the needs of the resource with the demands and usage patterns of residents and visitors, as in Florence or Venice (see the quote introducing this chapter). Many tourism destinations also have other attractions such as amusement parks and theme parks, constructed primarily to appeal to day- and staying-visitor markets, but many of them are economically viable only because they are built in or adjacent to areas with intrinsic environmental values.

Reasons for growth in the provision of resource-based visitor attractions

Around the world, throughout the 1980s and 1990s, there has been what amounts to an explosive growth in the provision of resource-related visitor attractions of all the types noted in Figure 13.1. This development appears certain to continue well into the twenty-first century. Not only is the number of managed visitor attractions increasing, but the great majority of them are seeking more visitors and, crucially, more revenue. Most cannot survive without visitor expenditure. The reasons for the growth of resource-based attractions are not hard to discern. Briefly they are as follows:

- The economic role of the natural and cultural environment in securing sustainable growth and jobs in both developed and developing countries.
- The strong association of an attractive natural, built and cultural environment with quality of life for residents.
- The powerful role of heritage and culture in motivating tourism – perceived as a growth sector in all parts of the world.
- The perceived relevance of cultural/entertainment provision in helping to break down barriers in multi-cultural societies.
- The need to preserve important buildings and townscapes for which tourism uses are often the only economically viable options.
- The need to foster a sense and pride of place for local communities.
- The acknowledged role of managed attractions based on environment, heritage and culture as lead sectors in urban regeneration schemes.

All these reasons are potentially very positive for the continuing development of resource

Countryside/coastal resources of scenic, social, and ecological value

National parks
Areas of outstanding beauty, heritage landscapes, preserved coasts
Preserved parks and gardens
Ancient monuments and archaeological sites – pre-eighteenth century
Historic houses
Designated heritage villages
Rural industries and crafts

Urban resources – sites, buildings, objects and collections

Castles, palaces, major historic houses
Cathedrals, temples, mosques and major churches
Other historic properties such as government buildings, town halls and covered markets
Historic city/townscapes – areas rather than specific buildings
Industrial archaeology – post-eighteenth century – especially water-related structures
Historic transport, ships, trains, trams, buses and other
Museums and galleries

Royal parks and gardens

Performance-related attractions drawing on cultural and heritage themes

Festivals
Drama, music, dance
Pageants
Carnivals
Events based on natural and cultural themes

Heritage-related retail parks

Although not part of natural, built or cultural resources there has been a remarkable growth of retailing centres utilizing heritage themes in North America, Europe, Australia and New Zealand. City examples are: Baltimore and Boston (USA); Covent Garden and Nottingham lace market (UK); and Darling Harbour, Sydney (Australia). Such 'Retail Parks' are developed specifically for visitor use and they represent an important form of modern tourism in which heritage themes are likely to become more important because they signify 'Place' and provide the distinctiveness and image appeal which the operators need to achieve their retail marketing goals

Figure 13.1 *Twenty types of resource-based visitor attractions – The Spectrum of Provision*

attractions and provide a powerful economic and social rationale (especially where subsidies are involved) for creating more. As with the accommodation sector, a country's resource based attractions usually comprise a wide variety of types and sizes and ownership patterns. An important destination management problem arises, however, because the individual organizations in the *spectrum of provision* set out in Figure 13.1 are mostly in competition with each other and seldom perceive mutual goals or act in collaboration. Each player within the spectrum makes decisions about its own development and marketing, usually with only the most limited knowledge about its competitors. Typically in the late 1990s there are no effective area or

destination strategies for the sustainable development of resource-based visitor attractions across the spectrum.

For most of the twenty or so main types of visitor attraction shown in Figure 13.1 it is possible to control visitor access to their areas/sites and some charge the public for admission. But controlled access and pricing are not defining characteristics of resource-based attractions. The principal characteristic which links and moves them inevitably in the direction of more effective environmental policies and action is the fact that they are designated and managed for visitor-related purposes and ultimately survive or fail according to the relative quality of the experience and satisfaction they provide.

Management and control of resource based attractions

With a few significant exceptions such as national parks, most of the natural or built resources attracting day- and staying-visitors could be enjoyed until recent times without much intervention or need for management. It is only as the number of visitors increases, and other pressures of modern living are exerted as in Florence, that it becomes increasingly necessary to control and manage resources so that their qualities and values are not eroded by over-use. Intervention justified initially to control visitors (essentially negative and reactive) translates into management to sustain and enhance resources (essentially positive and proactive). The shift towards management is increasing in the 1990s because the better the perceived quality of the environmental resources, the greater the prospect of generating and retaining visitor expenditure in an ever more competitive world. The greater the level of expenditure by visitors, the better the prospect of managing and sustaining the quality of the environmental resource – if part of the expenditure is used for resource conservation purposes. Management and sustainable goals may be linked in a virtuous circle.

Management in this context means that a body, whether it be public sector, commercial, trust or an individual, has accepted responsibility and statutory obligations for the resource. That body typically makes decisions that influence directly the key aspects of visitor capacity/volume, price, and products to be provided, and determines which groups or segments of the public are to be encouraged or discouraged. The particular combination of these elements achieved in practice, which readers should recognize as the primary responsibility of marketing management (see Chapter 10) ultimately determines whether or not any given attraction is sustainable in terms of its visitor use.

In the negative/reactive control phase for resource attractions, attention focuses primarily on estimates of the capacity of supply. In other words, assuming existing visitor uses, what is the perceived visitor capacity at the busiest times? That appears to be the position in Florence and Venice in the late 1990s. In the positive/proactive management phase, much more important is the knowledge, vigour and professionalism with which the resource is actively managed and marketed to the visitor groups it aims to attract. That requires research knowledge of visitors.

From ancient monuments to zoos the need to draw in more visitors and the income they generate has become the dominant agenda for competition in the 1990s and it has created a revolution in management terms. For example, historic royal palaces and the royal parks in the UK, a highly significant element of London's heritage, were relatively passive state-owned and controlled resources for most of the twentieth century. Not any more. There is no new capacity in the palaces or parks but, under the stimulus of their new management arrangements created at the end of the 1980s, they are creating and staging events, refurbishing and interpreting their attractions, and vigorously exploring new ways to attract more visitors and generate more revenue. With their massive intrinsic appeal, the flexing of the management and marketing muscles of London's royal parks and palaces is capable of doubling visitor numbers and tripling visitor revenue within *existing* notions of capacity. Their core mission to protect and sustain vital heritage resources remains pre-eminent.

Product formulation and design for visitor attractions

Biologists, archaeologists, anthropologists, sociologists, planners and geographers apply their science or methodology to define and measure the values of environmental resources. Scientifically defined criteria are usually essential for the systematic evaluation of resource quality, but such criteria do not explain the appeal or attractiveness of a resource as a tourism product.

Tourism products can only be understood in terms of the experiences they provide for visitors.

A mountain range in a national park, for example, may provide the benefit of spectacular views amounting to an uplifting spiritual experience for those who contemplate them with an artist's eye. The hills may provide a precious and disappearing habitat for wildlife such as eagles and other birds of prey. For others the visitor benefits afforded by the same mountains could include an exciting location for rock climbing, for hang-gliding, for mountain biking or walking, or in winter for skiing. The same range may serve as the visual backdrop and a unique selling proposition for a conference venue or for sybarites contemplating a gourmet weekend, or others visiting a health resort to relax and recuperate their energy. It may serve as a routine, daily recreational facility for the residents of an area within, say, 30 miles – for them a good place for walking dogs, riding horses, using cycles or motor cycles, shooting, golfing and fishing.

The essential point for management purposes is that the visitor experience or recreational role for residents provided by a mountain range does not lie solely in its intrinsic environmental qualities, even if they can be evaluated scientifically. It lies in the minds of those who find it attractive. There is not just one type of consumer benefit or experience or product being sought but many, and these may only be identified accurately by market research among the main groups or segments of users. This does not deny the ultimate significance of the intrinsic values in any way but suggests that understanding and managing what visitors perceive and experience is the most productive route for achieving more sustainable forms of tourism.

As with accommodation and transport, designing resource-based visitor attraction products is best perceived as a form of 'component engineering', accepting that the components to be assembled are based as much on images and expectations of benefits as on physical elements. Explained in the context of a first-time visit to an historic temple in a developing country, for example, the visitor experience:

- Begins with images and anticipation of an experience, stimulated by effective advertising and promotion, especially printed materials to capture and communicate the benefit which users can expect to find.
- Commences formally through the quality of signposting and the initial physical impact and attractiveness of the entrance to the site.
- Continues through the ambience and layout of the point of entry to a site or building where visitors are especially open to influence by being introduced to or reminded of what is available. For example, why a temple is important, its history, any dress codes which should be observed by visitors, and so on.
- Includes the process of paying if appropriate and the provision of any information to read and take away, or audio equipment to carry within a building or site.
- Proceeds with the interpretation of the resource, explanations and any routes designed for visitors, and includes displays and the appearance, knowledge and friendliness of guides, if they are provided. It also includes the cleanliness of the building, state of repair of the fabric and any objects, use of music and lighting and other influences on a visitor's appreciation and satisfaction.
- Comprises also the range of ancillary facilities which support the basic satisfaction or experience being sought, including toilets, refreshments, and shopping facilities.

It is always helpful to view these product elements both separately for management purposes and as part of a bundle or an 'engineered package' of components marketed as an overall experience for visitors. Every element in the package noted above is capable of development and change by management decisions.

In the next section – pages 165–167 we summarize the specific environmental management issues for the visitor attractions sector.

Sustainability for attractions – the environmental perspective

The environmental impacts, responsibilities and opportunities for visitor attractions cannot be compared directly with those for accommodation, transport and tour operation. Essentially most resource-based attractions are established to protect and interpret natural, built and cultural resources and to provide and manage public access. In that sense they are already part of the visitor management solution to environmental impact at destinations and have a special role to play in communications, interpretation and influencing visitors' behaviour. On the other hand, many attractions are also very large businesses, typically established in sensitive environmental areas, operating on commercial principles with some of them attracting over a million visitors a year. They are, therefore, also part of the problem and require environmental management programmes in the same way that any other business operating in fragile areas does. This point applies especially to large commercial theme parks such as Disneyland Paris or Alton Towers in the UK.

Because attractions are such a disparate group (see Figure 13.1), as well as a special case, there is no international trade association forum equivalent to the IHEI for accommodation, or IATA for air transport, to drive the environmental agenda forward in this sector. With the major exception of national parks, some of which are managed as visitor attractions as in the USA, and all of which have special planning status (see the Kruger Park case in Part Four) specific visitor-related environmental regulations only affect most attraction operations at the fringe. The main environmental impacts which the sector generates are broadly similar to those for the accommodation sector and include the following.

Specific environmental impacts

Resource depletion:

- Use of energy generated from fossil fuels involved in bringing visitors to sites.
- Use of non-renewable natural resources such as oil, natural gas, and coal for heating and lighting, and the production of manufactured goods needed at attractions and for sale.
- Consumption of fresh water, especially for large landscaped attractions.
- Consumption of natural resources, such as coral reef systems, in the conduct of their operations.

Pollution:

- Contribution to global warming, acid rain, low-level smog, and potentially to ozone depletion through the use of transport by visitors travelling to the area.
- Contribution to global warming and acid rain through the consumption of energy.
- Pollution of watercourses through the production of untreated sewage, waste water from kitchens, guest facilities, run-off from chemically treated landscapes, and in the case of aquariums, from fish tanks which may have specific consequences for local marine ecology.
- Production of solid wastes for landfill sites.
- Contribution to ozone depletion through the use of CFCs, halons, etc.
- Indirect pollution arising from increased demand for agricultural or manufactured goods in the area, thus stimulating pesticide and nitrate use or industrial pollutants.

Degradation:

- Of natural resources, heritage sites and cultures caused by influx of a large number of people visiting sensitive areas.
- Through construction of car parks, buildings, landscaping work and visitor facilities in fragile areas, which may lead to a

reduction in species diversity and disruption of local ecosystems.

- Reduction in landscape quality as a result of steady urbanization and commercialization in areas otherwise not affected – including building and widening of access routes.
- Of local cultures through commercialization and artificial re-enactment of local traditions and rights.

Environmental opportunities for the sector

The major opportunity is to act positively as guardians of a destination's environmental resources in the broadest sense that many attractions reflect and communicate a society's values. In terms of business operations, cost savings are the major impetus behind the development of many voluntary programmes in large-scale commercially operated attractions, but for major environment resources such as Olympia in Greece, the Uffizi museum in Florence, or the Pyramids in Egypt, conservation of the attraction depends heavily upon which visitor revenue generation depends plays a stronger role. (See the Ironbridge Gorge Museum case in Part Four.) Specific opportunities that can be gained from environmental improvement programmes in this sector include:

- *Improvements in product quality.* This is the primary opportunity for all resource-based attractions. For some sites, such as the Horniman Museum in London, environmental interpretation and technology programmes have offered an opportunity to diversify the 'visitor product' elements, for others they have offered an opportunity to improve the quality of service in a similar way to that identified for the accommodation sector.
- *Increased staff motivation and loyalty.* Evidence from resorts such as Disneyland indicate that significant improvements in staff morale can be gained from environmental programmes in this sector as well as the accommodation sector (see Chapter 12).
- *Cost savings.* Programmes to reduce consumption of energy and water and reduce

waste production will cut the utilities bill significantly, especially for attractions which include leisure rides.

- *Improvements in community relations.* For some companies, such as the visitor centre established at the Sellafield Nuclear Plant in Cumbria, tackling environmental issues head-on has offered an excellent opportunity to improve customer communications, for others it has opened routes to undertake presentations in local schools or involve local people in recycling or landscape improvement programmes. The majority of visitor attractions run special programmes designed to draw in as many schools as possible as part of an outreach and educational programme.
- *Improvement in relations with local authorities.* See Chapter 12, although most attractions are much better placed to be proactive and some are owned or part-funded by local authorities.
- *Reduction in liability to prosecution.* See Chapter 12.
- *Increased attraction to customers.* The increase in interest in environmental and cultural issues has presented visitor attractions with a considerable marketing opportunity. From the proposed Earth Dome in Leicestershire (UK) and the Sea World attraction in Florida, the environment in all its forms provides a powerful motivation for visitors and seems certain to continue to do so.
- *Long-term destination development.* Most visitor attractions rely on leisure tourism for a major percentage of their revenue generation and have an even larger vested interest than accommodation businesses in partnership activities to ensure that their area remains environmentally attractive into the future.

Regulatory background

Environmental regulations have not been adopted specifically for visitor attractions. As for accommodation, the activities of this sector are subject to the wide range of more general environmental and environmental health and safety regulations that exist. For attractions aiming to display and use traditional machinery and processes, modern legislation can create significant obstacles, however, and normal disability access requirements may not be feasible in heritage structures. The regulations which impact on the attractions sector are essentially the same as those affecting accommodation (see Chapter 12). They include:

- Planning and building regulations.
- Environmental health and safety regulations.
- Regulations governing the use and disposal of potentially hazardous materials.
- Regulations governing the responsible disposal of wastes.

Self-regulation in the sector

As noted above, the characteristics of the sector mean that coordinated self-regulatory initiatives for environmental purposes have been slow to emerge in the visitor attraction sector, and those which have emerged have been pioneered by individual companies, rather than through trade associations and their equivalents. On the other hand, in most developed countries, there are long established national and regional statutory bodies and/or membership associations for specific groups within the sector, such as national parks, museums and galleries, and historic houses. Most visitor attractions are also members of destination and area marketing consortia, including those established by local or area tourist boards. In other words, the principles of collaboration and the exchange of information and communication of good practice for sector purposes are well established. The future lies in developing the existing links more proactively for environmental purposes. Specific self-regulation procedures include:

- Developing, monitoring, and communicat-

ing examples of good environmental practice for the benefit of all attractions.
- Developing codes of environmental conduct equivalent to those already produced for the accommodation sector.
- Purchasing policies, especially as regards favouring locally produced products for sale in retail and catering outlets, selecting non-chemical cleaners wherever possible, and the use of organically grown agricultural produce.
- Advice on the use and disposal of potentially hazardous materials, such as chlorine bleaches, PCBs and CFCs involved in operating visitor facilities.
- Development of alternative transport modes, park and ride, etc. to reduce the impact and pollution of car traffic.
- Integration of the community into the attraction's environmental programme, through local educational initiatives, organization of volunteers and friends, donations to local charities, or initiatives to clean up local landscape areas.
- Collaboration with other partners to promote environmental interpretation both on- and off-site.
- Cost saving areas of energy, waste, and water management.

Only a small number of guidelines and manuals have so far been specifically developed for visitor attractions, largely under the aegis of broader environmental initiatives such as WTTC's Green Globe programme, which applies the principles developed elsewhere for visitor business operations more generally.

Summarizing the environmental issues for visitor attractions – the way ahead

It is no accident that most of the managed visitor attractions developed internationally in the last decade are based on environmental or cultural resources. It is no accident either that the attractions identified in Figure 13.1 are increasing rapidly in most countries. It demonstrates the real strength of the motivating power of the natural and cultural environment for visitors, and their interest and healthy curiosity in knowing more about it. The construction of new attractions specifically designed to communicate environmental themes, and the adaptation of many existing attractions to incorporate such themes, is one of the most interesting developments in this field. In the UK it has been greatly stimulated in the last five years by the availability of national lottery and Millenium Commission funding intended to facilitate environmental awareness generally.

Within this buoyant demand context, the main issue for the environment reflects the fact that managed attractions have a most important role to play in interpreting, explaining, enthusing and interesting visitors so that they better understand what and why the environment at particular destinations is important and how best to appreciate and enjoy it without causing damage. From a tourism perspective, resource attractions have the greatest vested interest in the long-run health and quality of the environment at a destination. They are, in effect, standard bearers or leading organizations for sustainable goals, which most of them typically express in their mission statements and objectives. They are in the vanguard of shifting visitor attitudes and behaviour in sustainable ways.

Four specific environmental roles are identified:

- To develop and channel their special knowledge as inputs to destination partnerships reflecting their responsibilities as guardians of local heritage resources. For example, taking initiatives with accommodation businesses reflecting their joint commitment to a destination. There is much more that managed attractions could do to develop their main messages which could be communicated initially to visitors by partners in transport and accommodation businesses and by tour operators. Resource-based attractions have the most to lose if the partner organizations, which they cannot control, do not deliver their own sustainable strategies for a destination.

- To extend their knowledge of visitors and marketing processes (see Figure 13.2) in order to improve their level of influence and control over the selection and management of targeted visitor segments. Typically, most resource-based attractions have not yet developed their marketing skills because they feel their first commitment is not to a market but to the resource. The growing nature of competition in tourism suggests that marketing skills provide the best available set of tools for achieving their resource objectives.

- To participate with other local resource-based attractions to achieve mutually sustainable objectives for a destination, cooperate in marketing, and to influence and support the management skills of smaller attractions.

- To maximize and use the revenue that is gained from receiving and communicating with visitors to underpin the long-run sustainability of the resources they manage (preserving the intrinsic values).

Sustainability – the marketing perspective

Figure 13.2 summarizes in note form the extensive role and power of marketing available to managed visitor attractions to support their sustainable objectives. Larger attractions with more than, say, 150 000 visits a year are generally capable of developing and using all the marketing tools directly. Most smaller attractions will only be able to draw on professional marketing skills when networked with larger attractions and local tourist board, but all need to collaborate as they all have a common interest in sustainability of resources at the destination.

By the nature of their operations resource-based visitor attractions are key players in sustainable development from a marketing perspective. Their marketing decisions strongly influenced and in some cases directly control:

- The specific customers targeted for promotion and distribution (from among those staying at a destination and others within easy day-travelling distance).
- Overall design and quality of the experience which the attraction provides.
- The most direct 'hands on' experience of environmental resources accessible to most visitors.
- Communication of information explaining and interpreting the nature of the attraction/resource and its significance.
- The specific presentation of objects, stories and themes, and all the forms of display provided for visitors.
- Opportunites for visitors and residents to meet on equal terms; qualified local guides and interpreters can perform a key role in this process.

- Prices at which visitors are admitted including any promotional and discounted offers.
- Product offers put together with other destination partners such as accommodation and local public transport operators.
- Evaluation of customer profiles and satisfaction through customer research.
- Customer profiles held on databases for analysis and future marketing.
- Marketing objectives, visitor volume targets, budgets and programmes.

This combination of influences, all of them part of the modern process of marketing for visitor attractions, is especially important where the attraction being managed is a core part of the environmental quality and appeal of a destination, for example a castle, a cathedral, a museum or a national park. Non-commercial attractions such as museums have a special role to play because of the authority and extra credibility often attached to their communications.

Figure 13.2 *Sustainability – the marketing perspective for resource-based visitor attractions*

14

Sustainability in the transport sector – with international illustrations

The company formally incorporated environmental responsibility into its corporate philosophy in 1989 ... Environmental issues are now important company wide from top management to individual departments and staff members (Hugh Somerville – see British Airways example).

Because all tourism involves travelling to and from a chosen destination, transport makes possible all forms of overnight and same-day visits. For any given destination, the type of transport used and the current state of its technology plays a vital part in determining the capacity, volume, segments, value and characteristics of tourism. Tranport operators also have a major role to play in the development of more sustainable tourism through reducing and controlling their substantial contributions to international pollution and waste.

This chapter is concerned with public transport operated by airlines, sea ferries, railway companies and coach operators, and the interactions between them and the other sectors of the travel and tourism industry. Given their dominant role in international tourism, this chapter tends to focus more on airlines than other forms of transport but the conclusions drawn broadly hold good for the other forms too. It has to be noted, however, that the bulk of the world's international and domestic tourism as defined in Chapter 5 is, and will continue to be, dominated by private transport. Cars are the transport choice for much of international as well as domestic tourism. In the late 1990s, for example, some three-quarters of domestic staying visitors in the UK used private transport for their journeys, and a similar proportion applies to most countries in continental Europe where land frontiers greatly facilitate international tourism by car. Even higher proportions of car usage apply in North America.

Historically, public transport was not developed for leisure and holiday purposes. Ocean liners carried passengers on business and for emigration, mail and freight; trains carried freight, mail and travellers on business and for social purposes; airlines also were originally provided to carry business and government passengers, mail, and valuable freight. Elements of leisure travel existed but most transport companies did not fully recognize tourism as their primary growth market until around the 1970s. In the last two decades of the twentieth century, leisure and holiday tourism segments have become the dominant marketing concern on most airlines and ferries, although not yet on rail, and there are large parts of the coach operators' markets that are not tourism related. As for hotels, business- and work-related travel markets remain vital for the profitability of most transport companies in terms of how much they contribute per passenger. Differential contribution by market segments, known technically as *revenue yield* (see below), means that some travellers such as business markets may be worth twice or three times as much per capita as leisure segments.

Technology determines the impact of transport on the environment

In the latter half of the twentieth century rapid developments in air transport technology produced remarkable improvements in the size, speed, range, comfort and the seat-mile costs of operating medium-size jet aircraft capable of linking tourism markets to destinations within a range of around 600 miles and some 2 hours' flying time. Developers were, as always, quick to see the potential and create the tourist facilities the markets demanded. The Mediterranean coastline was thus made accessible from north Europe, the Caribbean for North America, and parts of the South Pacific for Australia and New Zealand. In the last two decades especially, the ability conferred by developments in large long-haul aircraft, allied to developments in information technology, made it possible to target leisure traffic and develop holiday markets for long-haul flight destinations, for example from Europe to Australia/New Zealand and the Far East, and from North America to all parts of the Asia-Pacific area. Currently, the same process is at work within the Asia-Pacific region as potential tourism markets expand with economic development.

It is sometimes supposed that modern tourism grew and developed around the world as a result of government and other public sector policies and strategies, and the promotional work of national tourist offices. In fact most development was simply opportunistic, aiming to exploit the market advantages provided by each state-of-the-art breakthrough in transport technology. It is interesting to speculate that the modern geography of international travel and tourism owes as much to global competition between transport technologists and engineers as it does to climatic and scenic advantages or cultural differences of destinations. In wind tunnels, in research laboratories for materials such as carbon fibre and in engineering workshops, there is intensive constant competition to find technological breakthroughs with commercial advantages and to reduce the cost of every part of transport systems. Technology focuses on:

- Increases in the fuel efficiency of engines (especially airlines) to travel greater distances for the same fuel payload cost or shorter distances for less cost.
- Development of power output from engines to give greater speed and range and, for example, the use of twin-engined airplanes to perform the same journeys as four-engined planes at less cost.
- Reduction in the weight of transport vehicles and all components, leading to greater efficiency and lower seat-mile costs.
- Reduction in the output of emissions and noise, and the use and control of hazardous chemicals and waste.

In the technology race, the design engineers and technicians at Seattle (Boeing headquarters), and Toulouse (Airbus headquarters) may have had a greater net impact in the last quarter of a century on the international structure of tourism and its impacts of the environment of visited destinations, as hoteliers, tour operators and travel agents put together.

Transport industry economics are a second major source of environmental influence

Together with the impact of technological progress, a simple appreciation of basic transport economics is also needed to understand the patterns of world international tourism in the last half of the twentieth century. The key elements are:

- *High fixed cost* and low variable cost of operating public transport means that the fixed cost of operating a scheduled flight, a sea ferry passage or a train journey, includes the full cost of using the vehicle, comprising landing/terminal costs, crew cost, share of overheads for administration and salaries, marketing, engineering/servicing and allowance for vehicle depreciation costs. The *additional* or variable cost of fuel and passenger consumables represented by seat occupancy of, say, 65 per cent compared with seat occupancy of, say, 50 per cent is invariably low, usually marginal. But the revenue generation differential is very large indeed. Elliot estimated that if one less passenger had travelled on each one of American Airlines 854 461 flights in 1991, the airline would have increased its loss in that year from $240 to $315 million. Two extra passengers per flight would have virtually eliminated the loss; three extra would have generated net profit (*The Times*, 22 February 1992). In other words, profit or loss may be dependent on plus or minus just 1 per cent of seat occupancy for modern airlines. The incremental variable cost of one to three extra passengers is negligible for aircraft carrying 200 or more passengers.
- *Seat occupancy or passenger load factor* means the number of seats or available passenger spaces sold on any given journey.
- *Peaks and troughs* are a normal operational issue for public transport operators. Flights, trains or ferries which may be fully sold for,

say, 30 per cent of their journeys are likely to be little more than a quarter full for at least another 30 per cent. Peaks reflect months of the year, days of the week, and hours of the day or night. Marketing is aimed at reducing the effects of these troughs and low pricing is the easiest method to do that. Applying the high fixed cost argument, almost any price achieved, even $50 for what is normally sold as a $250 seat, makes a financial contribution to offset committed fixed costs and is logically better than an empty, totally unproductive seat.

- *Passenger revenue yield* means the sum of the prices paid to occupy each of the seats/spaces utilized on any given journey. In practice passenger revenue yield is a fairly complex measure as most public transport vehicles provide seats at different prices. On long-haul airline flights there are typically 'high-yield' first-class passengers who may pay ten times as much or even more for a return journey as a passenger in economy class taking advantage of a low-cost promotional fare. There are business-class passengers some of whom may be using some form of promotional fare. There are full-fare economy passengers purchasing flexible tickets with an option to change departure times, and 'low-yield' economy passengers buying one or other form of advance purchase fare (APEX) restricted to specific journey times and dates with no flexibility for change. In an ideal world for passenger transport, all passengers would pay full fares. In practice they do not and the art of filling the available seats on each vehicle journey with optimum revenue generation (optimum yield) is a continuous preoccupation for transport marketing managers. Information technology makes it easier in the late 1990s than at any time previously to target and forecast the capacity likely to be sold on each journey, and to organize marketing to fill the predicted load factor gaps. Holiday segments are logical targets.
- *Social and environmental costs* reflect the fact that all forms of public transport impose

costs on society which ultimately have to be paid for. Air transport produces emissions which pollute the atmosphere, noise which affects people living within the noise 'footprint' of an airport, while the construction of airports takes away green space and countryside and is likely to affect the local ecology. At a lesser level measured in national terms, although the effects may be just as great in areas affected locally, trains and sea ferries impose equivalent environmental and social costs. Buses and coaches, especially those running their engines continuously to operate heating and air conditioning while parked at tourist destinations, can contribute significantly to atmospheric pollution at popular sites. Such costs are to some extent controlled and partly paid for by the imposition of strict regulatory controls on noise and emissions, which oblige operators to work within stated limits and invest as necessary in technology to do so. But many believe that the full costs of transport operations generally are only partly met by operators at the present time, the remainder is paid for by the general public. In particular, the environmental costs resulting from transporting more visitors to a destination than it can manage sustainably are typically not currently addressed by transport operators. There are many uneasy and temporary compromises in responding to these environmental costs, but they will become more explicit in the next decade.

Environmental implications of transport decisions on profit and capacity

One might suppose that any industry able to demonstrate the remarkable growth record of transport for international tourism in the last forty years must be profitable. It is important to note that to date it has not been so. Writing at the beginning of the 1990s, before the further

massive losses following the most recent international economic crisis in 1991–93 were known, Doganis (1991) discussed the international 'conundrum of high growth and poor financial performance' of airlines. He noted that 'only in the period 1963–8 were significant profits achieved, and again in 1987–9'. Significant profits have been achieved again since 1994, but only against a record of massive losses internationally made possible in part because of widespread government subsidy and writing off of debt. The subsidies on rail networks internationally are, of course, well known.

The reason for the losses is that most public transport operators, like most tour operators, are locked into an intensely competitive business. The leading players are forced into a matching strategy in which the dominant leisure traffic is secured almost exclusively on the basis of price competition. To take the example of sea ferries between the UK and France, the crippling price competition between the ferry operators and the Channel Tunnel since the tunnel opened in 1994 provides a classic illustration of price wars from which none of the leading players could extricate themselves in the short run without committing commercial suicide. The social and environmental costs of transport in these circumstances are borne by taxpayers generally and out of state revenues since they obviously cannot be paid for out of losses.

In terms of capacity, it is by now widely recognized that growing visitor numbers pose the greatest tourism threat to the environment at many holiday destinations. Increasing numbers is just another way of looking at growth in public transport capacity. Especially in developing countries dependent on air transport for tourism arrivals, capacity is effectively controlled by route capacity, fleet utilization and load factor decisions made by transport companies. The fact that tour operator capacity is often linked to transport capacity decisions, and that aircraft can be switched easily between destinations, makes the transport decisions vital to any understanding of destination capacity. Like many tour operators, most transport operators have no vested interests in the quality of the environment at the destinations they use.

The economics of public transport, especially the need to utilize expensive equipment for the maximum possible number of hours every day, oblige companies to concentrate on filling seats on every route they operate. If load factors reach around 80 per cent there is always a temptation put on extra departures and or increase the size of the vehicles provided. Such decisions are not made with the quality and sustainability of a destination's environment in mind; only the pressure to maximize route and vehicle yield. One can safely assume that achieving additional passenger revenue takes priority over any concerns for the carrying capacity of destinations served.

There is always an issue in both public and private transport as to what extent capacity follows demand and to what extent it creates it. Capacity can be doubled or halved to a destination by decisions which interpret potential trends in markets of origin but have no concern for environment. Thus a new motorway typically increases traffic in the early stages when its use represents a significant time/cost saving. The Channel Tunnel served to increase cross-Channel traffic significantly from the position before it opened. Airline capacity on routes tends to make the traffic grow, if only because once it is available marketing energy and money has to be put behind it. Since the mid-1970s, the introduction of wide-bodied jumbo jets on long-haul routes has undoubtedly served to generate its own massive growth in demand.

In the next section – pages 174–177 we summarize the specific environment management issues for the transport sector.

Sustainability – the environmental management perspective

Within the travel and tourism industry as a whole, the transport sector has undergone the greatest scrutiny about its environmental impacts. As a result, in addition to stringent safety requirements, its activities are specifically regulated, especially as regards noise and emissions, and there is a great deal of progress to report. Rail and bus attract rather less attention but the rail sector has been making progress on environmental issues such as noise and energy conservation for many years. Technology has a major role to play in transport generally and, driven as much by competition as by regulation, some of the most impressive progress has been in the fuel efficiency and emissions control of aircraft. The progress in the pipeline is even more impressive. When considering environmental issues in general, it is important to bear in mind that rail, bus and coach transport stand to gain from the environmental movement, because they reduce the range of impacts associated with personal car travel for leisure, now widely targeted as a principal source of environmental pollution.

The main environmental impacts to which the sector has responded include the following.

Specific environmental impacts

Resource depletion:

- Use of energy generated from fossil fuels – especially by long-haul air transport and use of cars.
- Use of non-renewable natural resources, notably oil, natural gas and coal for heating and lighting, and the production of manufactured goods used in tourism.
- Consumption of fresh water at airports, for example.

Pollution:

- Contribution to global warming and acid rain through the consumption of energy.
- Contribution to acid rain through to the production of oxides of nitrogen and sulphur in exhaust fumes.
- Contribution to the formation of low-level smog from exhaust fumes, especially from cars in city centres.
- Production of volatile organic compounds (VOCs) from the refuelling process.
- Potential contribution to high-level ozone depletion, especially by the airline sector.
- Pollution of watercourses through the production of untreated waste water from airport facilities, contamination from fuel storage, run-off from chemically treated roads and landing strips, and pollution from heavy chemical processes such as paint stripping and de-icing.
- Noise and vibration, especially near major roads, high-speed rail tracks and airports.

Degradation:

- Of landscapes primarily as a result of insensitive/inappropriate siting and development of transport infrastructure.
- Of marine environments from cruise shipping and some pleasure-boat operations.

Environmental opportunities for the sector

Cost savings are still the obvious impetus behind the development of many of the programmes implemented by transport operators but the sector has also been driven by a desire to improve its public image and reduce the threat of more prohibitive regulation. The opportunities that can be gained from environmental improvement programmes in this sector include:

- *Cost savings.* Programmes to reduce consumption of energy are a logical preoccupation. Other work to reduce water consumption and waste production in facil-

ities have provided significant cost-saving opportunities. Initiatives to reduce emission of pollutants have also invariably resulted in cost savings as fuel efficiency increases. Innovation has brought about unexpected savings too. Some airlines, for example, now strip aircraft using environmentally benign high-powered water jets, rather than costly and environmentally harmful chemicals.
- *Increased staff motivation and loyalty.* Some airlines now have well-known programmes to reward staff that take the initiative in certain environmental areas. British Airways has a *Green Waves* scheme through which staff contribute ideas into the environmental programme, and a network of appointed 'environmental champions' within the company to ensure that those ideas are put into action.
- *Improvements in product quality.* See Chapter 12.
- *Improvements in community relations.* Environmental programmes almost always extend to incorporate the local community in some way, who may be invited to use local recycling facilities, schools may be provided with educational materials, or residents' housing fitted with double-glazing to reduce noise nuisance near airports.
- *Improvement in relations with local authorities.* See Chapter 12.
- *Reduction in liability to prosecution.* The threat of prosecution for environmental damage is probably greater for the transport sector than any other part of the travel and tourism industry. When imposed, fines can be large, and the increasing use of the mechanisms of the market ensure that costs rise for those with the least efficient response.
- *Increased attraction to customers.* See 'Accommodation sector'.

Regulatory background

Environmental regulations have been specifically developed for the transport sector, which is also subject to the wide range of more general environmental and environmental health and safety regulations and increasingly the focus of market mechanisms. For larger companies in developed countries, the regulations which impact on the transport sector include:

- *Noise restrictions.* Concorde was a *cause célèbre* in the 1960s but most airlines, railway companies and motor vehicles now have to comply with basic noise regulations. The way in which these are applied and the specific noise level permitted for specific countries varies around a maximum noise standard specified by the World Health Organization. In the airline sector, for example, maximum noise on take-off and landing is specified within the regulations of the International Civil Aviation Organization, but more stringent measures are adopted by some airports. Non-compliance is usually met with heavy financial penalties.
- *Restrictions on emissions.* Concern about smog and other low-level pollutants, especially in city centres, has resulted in the development of a range of regulations which limit emissions from motor vehicles. These regulations are often evolved on a regional basis (for example, within the USA or the EU) and then adapted by federal or state governments. The requirement for all cars built after a certain date to be fitted with a catalytic converter or for all cars to pass a periodic emission test are two examples of such regulations.
- *Planning and building regulations.* Like most other forms of major development, transport requires infrastructure, and the development of such infrastructure is usually guided by planning and building regulations. In most countries, major transport projects are the subject of some form of planning enquiry, and increasingly the subject of environmental impact assessments (EIA) or strategic environmental assessments (SEA).
- *Environmental health and safety regulations* which encompass all aspects of the safety

of employees while at work, and of clients while in transit.

- *Regulations governing the use and disposal of potentially hazardous materials.* Like other business sectors, transport companies are obliged to ensure that potentially hazardous materials are stored and disposed of appropriately after use. Where chemicals are used for de-icing buses, trains or airlines, these must also be prevented from entering into watercourses or contaminating groundwater. When detected, discharges to landfill or watercourses are penalized by heavy fines or, in some countries, gaol sentences.
- *Regulations governing the responsible disposal of wastes.* Failure to dispose of wastes appropriately is increasingly penalized by regulators and many countries have now introduced a 'duty of care' system whereby the originator of the waste is liable for its responsible disposal, even if this final disposal is undertaken by a contractor. (See also Chapter 12.)
- *Regulations governing access.* Most public transport route decisions, including night flying, are subject to agreement and formal ratification, even in a 'deregulatory' era. Congestion of historic cities and conflict between the needs of coach parties and residents has recently brought about restrictions in bus access to some historic towns. The Salzburg case in Chapter 3 illustrates a recent approach to rectify some of these problems.

Self regulation in the sector

Voluntary industry initiatives have not received the same level of attention by the media as the regulatory requirements faced by transport companies, although they have been influential in shaping the response of the sector to many of the issues raised in the Rio process. Such initiatives have largely been pioneered by individual companies through a sense of corporate responsibility. Details have, however, been coordinated and circulated by trade associations, such as the International Air Transport Association and the International Union of Railways. Among the larger and more profitable airlines which are committed to demonstrating their 'green' credentials, British Airways has one of the most respected corporate environmental management programmes in the UK. American Airlines, Canadian Airlines, US Air and the manufacturers Boeing and Airbus, have each developed their own detailed proactive programmes.

The following issues have been the focus of these programmes:

- Cost saving areas of energy, waste, and water management.
- Purchasing policies, especially as regards favouring replacement of chemical processes with more environmentally sound alternatives.
- Technological developments to reduce, for example, fuel consumption (and thus emissions) and noise.
- Technological developments to replace chemical intensive processes (for example, paint stripping) with more benign alternatives.
- Sponsorship/involvement in scientific studies to examine, for example, ozone depletion.
- Involvement in programmes to interpret specific destination wildlife or cultural attributes to clients. For example, the development of destination specific in-flight videos, and the sale of WWF products.
- Use and disposal of potentially hazardous materials, such as chlorine bleaches, PCBs and CFCs.

A number of examples of good practice have been well publicized to promote the range of programmes which are in progress and help transport operators improve their environmental performance. Some of the 'green' labels which have been developed for the industry are applicable for the transport sector and these include WTTC's Green Globe and PATA's Green Leaf.

Summarizing the environmental issues for public transport companies – the way ahead

Because transport companies are such major users of energy and have a well-understood impact on the environment through emissions, noise and production of waste in their normal operations, they have an obvious requirement to undertake a systematic, programmed response to the *Ten R's* outlined in Chapter 11. Compliance with current and expected future international regulation reinforces this requirement. Airlines have for decades pursued rigorous safety audits and procedures, of course, and have developed their management systems and programmes to cope with environmental regulations emerging in the 1990s. The leading companies have mostly drawn up formal mission statements for their environmental responsibilities and through regulation and agreement with trade and regulatory bodies such as IATA and ICAO, these processes are certain to continue. They are at the forefront overall in the environmental responses of the travel and tourism industry. They have made significant progress in energy use, emissions, noise control and control of wastes, and they have a massive commitment to technological developments.

Important though this progress is, the major issue for the next decade is as much about the impact of transport management decisions on the environment of the destinations served as it is about greater efficiency in operations. Recognizing the growing leisure market focus of transport operators, and the immense leverage they exercise with their marketing policies and programmes (see Summary below) we believe it is essential for transport operators to join with others to recognize and reflect destination impact concerns within the routing, capacity, and pricing decisions that are the principal outputs of transport management decisions. Five specific steps are identified:

- Acceptance of the environmental impact of

operational routing and capacity decisions by adding destination impact assessments into the existing range of environmental audits increasingly undertaken for routine operational purposes.

- Cooperation in destination partnership activities to help formulate practical sustainable capacity goals and objectives in the long run interests of all the stakeholders in the destination's environment, and collaboration in mutual marketing programmes designed to achieve them.
- Programmed initiatives within the *Ten R's*, developed from existing compliance monitoring and more traditional cost-reduction programmes. As major purchasers of goods and services from other suppliers, there is a logical role for formal environmental criteria to be built into procurement policies, as for accommodation businesses.
- Where transport operators sell their services to third-party tour operators, link with accommodation businesses for seat sales, or operate part- or whole-vehicle charter, they have an opportunity to use the power of their own branding and route network to ensure that such third parties observe basic environmental good practice in relation to the destinations they serve. In other words, they deal only with businesses for which the code and practice of environmental conduct matches the same high standards as those adopted by the transport operator.
- Proactive use of the time that holiday travellers spend in transit, to communicate environmentally interesting as well as functional messages about the destinations they have chosen to visit. This is likely to include use and distribution of third-party information as well as that provided by the transport company.

In the next section – pages 178–182 we outline specific examples of current good practice in the transport sector.

Transport operator examples

British Airways

British Airways, the first major European scheduled carrier to be privatized in 1987 is one of the world's largest and most efficient airlines. In total, the company carried around 30 million people (passenger journeys) in the late 1990s, with a total fleet size of over 240 aircraft, flying to more than 180 destinations in eighty-five countries.

The company formally incorporated environmental responsibility into its corporate philosophy in April 1989, although recognition of the significance of environmental issues such as noise and emissions has been prominent within the airline since the 1970s. Environmental initiatives are led and coordinated by an Environment Department and initially the airline was the only one in the world to have a team dedicated to bringing about environmental improvements in both technical and non-technical aspects of the operation. Environmental issues are now important company-wide from top management to individual departments and staff members. Involvement is encouraged by a scheme of 'Environmental Champions' (a designated network of staff to promote environmental activity within their particular departments) and by inclusion of environmental issues in a range of training schemes.

As a sign of its corporate commitment to the environmental programme, BA published its first Annual Environmental Report in 1992, one of the first British companies of its size to undertake a detailed assessment of the impacts of its operations on the environment and deliver its findings for public scrutiny. The report illustrated that sound environmental practice is not only a necessary response to AGENDA 21 but also results in considerable savings.

The airline's environmental programmes have been widely recognized by other organizations with awards achieved from, *inter alia*, the Smithsonian Institution, the Royal Geographical Society, the Pacific Asia Travel Association and the American Society of Travel Agents. Three awards have been achieved from ACCA (the Chartered Association of Certified Accountants) for environmental reporting, including the overall winner's award for 1996. Also in 1996, a Premier Award from Business Commitment to the Community recognized the breadth of the airline's environmental commitment.

Rationale for sustainability

A core part of the company's mission statement is to be a 'Good Neighbour' concerned for the community and environment, and this aim underlies the company's environmental programme. Action is largely driven by a clear corporate recognition of the finite nature of natural resources and a determination to mitigate unavoidable pollution and improve the environment where possible. The company has a significant programme of philanthropic activities and award initiatives to help others participate in environmental improvement programmes as well as the obvious focus on efficiency and cost savings. The 'Good Neighbour' goal has been retained as one of the key values in the recently restated Mission and Goal package of the airline.

Environmental management

(a) The environmental management system

Company-wide environmental awareness is promoted by the Environment Department through an Environment Council involving directors from departments most involved in environmental matters. A supporting network of environmental focal points and working groups also exists to support the environmental programme at senior management level. External consultants are employed as appropriate for particular aspects of the programme, such as auditing, and employees at all levels are involved as part of a network of 'environmental champions'.

Each year there is a formal process in place (EMS) through which environmental targets are set, and progress against these is reviewed with designation of responsibility for improvements. In 1996 there were some fifty published environmental targets. This is part of a formal approach to environmental management and the airline has recently embarked on a major (the second) review of its activities based at Heathrow, using the company's environmental policy and the ISO 14001 EMS as yardsticks. In 1997 one part of the company, British Airways Avionics Engineering located at Llantrisant in Wales, has achieved certification to ISO 14001.

(b) Stakeholder consultation

BA's annual environmental report is evidence of the airline's wish to consult with all its stakeholders. In 1996 the airline published a booklet, *Aviation and the Environment*, in which space was allocated for comments from the Aviation Environment Federation, which represents a number of interest groups. The airline published a separate Community Relations report in 1997, reflecting initiatives in the communities around its main operational locations.

Passengers are informed of the environmental programme by in-flight information and attitudes are monitored regularly as part of BA's market research programme. Approach and departure procedures are under ongoing review with a view to identifying changes that can reduce the noise impact on communities without compromising safety.

Recent research illustrated that stakeholders – including the public – are well informed about the programme. A surprising 25 per cent of passengers questioned at Heathrow in the late 1990s were aware of BA's initiatives and many of these expressed an interest in receiving further information.

(c) Environmental management

In developing its approach, the company retains its primary focus of minimizing the impacts of its day-to-day business operations on the environment. The staff-based activity programme 'Environmental Champions' has been recognized as an outstanding success. Champions monitor environmental performance in specific aspects of the operation, generating ideas for improvement as well as helping to motivate all employees, and communicating the aims and results of the environmental programme.

The aircraft fleet is constantly monitored and is among the most modern and efficient in the world, thus reducing noise disturbance, emissions and pollution. Environmental factors are high on the list when agreeing specifications for aircraft purchase. For example, the most recent acquisition, the Boeing 777, has a noise 'footprint' or impact much less than the smaller Boeing 767 and is, in fact, close to the even smaller Boeing 737-400. There are regular meetings and exchanges with manufacturers to review the environmental factors influencing fleet performance.

Operational areas are carefully monitored to ensure that resources are not wasted and energy efficiency, waste minimization, water management, and effluent management programmes have been in place for some years. Innovative programmes have helped to tackle issues such as congestion around the airport and special days have been hosted to encourage staff to use public transport where possible or to share cars in order to reduce pollution.

It is difficult to assess the exact costs and savings from the many environmental projects introduced in the 1990s and most are not measurable in financial terms. Some programmes have, however, brought tangible savings. For instance, £2 million was cut from the energy bill (resulting in a reduction of carbon dioxide emissions), and £150 000 was saved on waste-disposal costs (with obvious environmental benefits). Savings have also been made in effluent disposal and water costs.

These savings have to be balanced, of course, against the costs of running the Environment Department, implementing the technology to reduce noise, and upgrading aircraft to reduce emissions. BA aims to keep ahead of regulatory minimum standards which apply to all airlines, and such a lead requires investment.

(d) Awards programmes

The company operates a wide range of internal and external awards programmes. The internal programmes provide an important motivation for employees, and are complemented by on-going suggestion schemes, such as the *Green Waves* programme. There are specific environmental Awards for Excellence, recognizing contributions from individuals, both within the airline and its main suppliers, who have made an extraordinary contribution to the environmental progress.

Many of the external programmes seek to encourage the wider travel and tourism industry to develop good practice and incorporate environmental management into their business decisions. The most widely publicized awards programme is the British Airways *Tourism For Tomorrow Awards*, organized with partner organizations, which receives in excess of 100 entries annually from all around the world. Collaboration with one of the most popular holiday programmes on national television ensures that the award winners, and the practical meaning of sustainable tourism, is communicated to millions of consumers every year. The 1996 winner was Taybet Zaman village in Jordan, a project which rejuvenated and rebuilt a dying village into a modern tourist development without changing the historic character of the location.

(e) Philanthropic activities

The company has a well-developed programme of philanthropic activities, largely under the auspices of its *Assisting Conservation Programme*. Through this programme, travel assistance worth many hundred thousands of pounds has been given to individuals working in conservation and other environmental programmes around the world, including Belize, India, Jamaica, Venezuela, Mauritius, the Seychelles, and the Caribbean.

Summary – British Airways

British Airways now operate one of the most widely respected and comprehensive environmental programmes in the travel and tourism industry. It has achieved impressive results in terms of internal cost savings and is justified on those grounds. More important for sustainable tourism are its achievements in widely communicating the ideas and news of environmental management among the company's staff and stakeholders, especially its customers. It also supports nature conservation. Although the company does not attribute a financial label to the environmental programme, which is seen as a part of a quality management approach, the programme helps to differentiate British Airways from its competitors and complements the image of the its chosen advertising strap-line 'The *world's favourite airline'*.

British Airways Holidays, a leading long-haul tour operator linked to British Airways, produced its own first environmental statement based on an external audit in 1993 and has been subsequently evaluating and aiming to recognize good environmental practices among the hotels with which it contracts.

The Pacific & Oriental Steam Navigation Company (P&O)

P&O operates a diverse range of tourism interests from cross-channel ferries and cruise ships to resorts. With annual turnover in the region of £7000 million, the company carried some 10 million passengers (passenger journeys) in the late 1990s employing some 50 000 staff. The head office for the company is in the UK, but its operations are spread world-wide.

P&O formally indicated its commitment to the environment by the issue of its first Group Environmental Policy in February 1991, which was subsequently revised and reissued in 1994 and 1997. Environmental issues had been important from an earlier date as a part of the quality management concept, and closely related to the Group's health and safety policies. Many operating companies within the Group have been awarded the BS 5750/1SO 9000 certification and

a number of the Group's companies have embarked on the trial period of the new ISO 14001 Environmental Management System.

The importance of environmental issues both within the company and within the shipping industry is indicated by P&O's leading role in the development of an Environmental Code for the General Council of British Shipping (now British Shipping).

Environmental management

(a) Environmental audits

The Group is committed to an environmental auditing programme for all its activities, to set baseline environmental performance criteria. Auditing guidelines have been issued to all operating companies and approximately 100 executives have attended two-day residential seminars to equip them for carrying out their own environmental audits. In addition, each company is required to submit an annual report to the Group on its environmental performance and progress.

(b) Raising staff awareness

Staff are made aware of environment issues through a regular Environment Briefing and an Environmental Legal Briefing, plus regular updates in the company's newspaper *Wavelength*. Training is given to designated staff as a part of the implementation process for the environmental programme.

Each P&O vessel has appointed an environmental officer and P&O established its own course for these officers, as they could not find one that met its standards. The Group's environmental manager and a team of managers from the ship-operating companies have created a programme which covers issues such as legislation compliance, CFCs, oil pollution, garbage, hazardous chemicals and the roles of the environmental officers. To date, two residential seminars have taken place involving fifty ship's officers.

(c) Improvements in operational performance

A wide range of improvements in operational performance have been achieved, and these include:

- A reduction in water consumption of up to one-quarter on the large ferries operated by P&O European Ferries on the Dover–Calais route. These ferries carry thousands of passengers each year and use substantial quantities of fresh water. A reduction in use has reduced fuel consumption, resource use, and effluent production.
- Working with a local company to take away old paint and chemical containers which would previously have contributed to the hazardous waste stream. The company cleans the containers out and refurbishes them for re-use, thus bringing about a double improvement (a cost-effective and environmentally friendly way to dispose of hazardous wastes in proximity to their generation and a contribution to the recycling chain).

(d) Utilizing the Best Available Technology (BAT) to dispose of wastes responsibly

The company has been operating recycling programmes as a part of its environmental commitment for some years. The company realizes, however, that recycling is not a panacea to all ills and that in some instances alternative methods of waste disposal are more appropriate.

Combined heat and power technology (CHP) is one option that the company has explored. This can significantly reduce the volume of waste while providing both electricity and community heating. P&O's Olympia Exhibition Centre now sends much of its annual 1200 tons of waste to a local South London CHP plant.

(e) Ensuring new purchases match environmental objectives

P&O's newest cruise ship, *Oriana*, has many environmental attributes. The engines consume approximately one-third of the fuel used by older ships, reducing emissions of carbon dioxide. The ship has a sophisticated rubbish-disposal programme which will enable it to achieve a zero dumping policy. There are also on-board facilities for recycling of aluminium, glass, and other re-usable materials. The paint used on the ship has a low solvent content, while the hull is partly painted with tin-free anti-fouling paint to reduce pollution to the marine environment.

(f) Environmental awards

The Group's US Cruise company recently won the prestigious Smithsonian Environmental Award, the first time that this has been won by a cruise ship company.

Summary – P&O

P&O's comprehensive programme was developed as a response to the issues set out in AGENDA 21. It addresses the major environmental impacts of corporate business operations and the Group issued an Environmental Report in 1996 with a further report planned for 1998.

Sustainability – the marketing perspective

Figure 14.1 summarizes the immense marketing leverage which public transport operators can bring to bear on many destinations served by their route networks. For smaller, newer destinations in developing countries, this leverage effectively amounts to control over development because the capacity decisions rest in the transport operators' hands. Most transport operators have some level of commitment to the destinations they serve, especially to the countries and the regions that are an integral part of their route networks. But, in common with most tour operators, they currently recognize very few commitments to the environment of the individual resort destinations they serve. The all-important capacity issue is typically not addressed at all.

It is a major challenge for transport operators to accept the long-run health of destinations as one of their sustainable business assets, and to use their great leverage and professional skills to work in support of the environment, not to leave those resources to chance and the efforts of other stakeholders. The processes are all in place to do this and the lead already established in operational environmental programmes by the larger companies suggests that logical extensions would not be too difficult to implement. What is lacking is the type of participative partnership arrangements noted throughout this book, through

---

By the nature of their operations especially for destinations geared to international markets, public transport operators have a key marketing role to play in the sustainable development of tourism. Their marketing decisions strongly influence and in some cases directly control:

- Access to destinations through the routes on which they decide to operate.
- The segments of the market they target for promotion and distribution in order to optimize passenger yield on chosen routes.
- The product quality available on routes, related to the vehicles* they use.
- Their investment policies for future equipment, especially in its greater contribution to minimizing environmental pollution.
- The daily capacity available for tourism (especially for airlines – more or less capacity via frequency of operation and the use of larger/smaller, faster/slower vehicles).
- Seat prices to be charged including promotional offers and discounts.
- Seasonality factors influenced by the level of services provided and promotional offers.

* 'vehicles' is used variously in this context to cover aircraft, trains, sea ferries and coaches.

- The activities of tour operators contracting space on scheduled airlines, or chartering whole aircraft (for tour operators not owning their own airlines).
- Part of destination marketing, sometimes in collaboration with destination organizations
- Provision of on-board information which may contain environmental information.
- Product offers put together directly with accommodation suppliers in initiatives controlled by transport companies (not involving tour operators).
- Customer knowledge through profiles held on databases for analysis and future marketing.
- Marketing objectives, visitor volume targets, budgets and programmes.

This combination of influences, all of them part of the modern transport marketing process, puts extensive leverage for sustainable tourism into the hands of transport operators. This is especially true where one or two transport companies have an influence over at least half the total visitor traffic, as is the case for many islands and tourist resorts in developing countries.

Figure 14.1   *Sustainability – the marketing perspective for transport operators*

15

Sustainability in the tour operator sector – with international illustrations

Our principal destinations in Europe are among the most threatened by the growth of tourism. It is inevitable that anyone supplying holidays is going to have their activities scrutinized for their compatibility with the ethic of sustainable tourism (President of the International Federation of Tour Operators, 1993).

The history of entrepreneurial tour operators putting together and selling holiday packages can be traced back to the activities of the British pioneer Thomas Cook in the 1840s, and to travel by rail and sea. Modern tour operation is related to developments in the airline industry in the late 1950s and the 1960s, in north Europe generally and especially in the UK. At that time scheduled airlines were rapidly upgrading their fleets to jet aircraft, releasing dozens of very serviceable and inexpensive piston-engined aircraft perfectly able to perform holiday charter flights. The post-war economic circumstances were right for rapid tourism market growth. There was a pent-up and relatively undiscriminating demand for holidays in the sun; the available aircraft could carry loads which the new destinations could readily accommodate in their new hotels; the distances from north European markets to the new resorts on the Mediter-

ranean coasts were within the normal range of the available aircraft; and if approaching 100 per cent seat occupancy could be sold, the prices compared with traditional scheduled airline prices were very low and highly attractive.

Energetic, entrepreneurs saw the growth opportunity and a boom industry began. Quickly adopting the latest jet aircraft, the demand continued to expand through the 1970s and 1980s, when market expansion seemed limitless. In the sun-belt countries around the world, notably in the Mediterranean and more recently in the Caribbean and South Pacific, governments encouraged rapid development of their resorts in order to take full economic advantage of the growth market, and hotel owners looked naturally to tour operators as the easiest way to generate their business. The era of so-called mass tourism is associated with large tour operators catering especially for first-time and travel-inexperienced customers, in about a twenty-year period between the 1960s and 1980s. It was the fortuitous combination of aircraft technology and airline economics, continuous growth in demand for international holidays, and increasing resort capacity that stimulated the emergence of large-scale tour operations. It endowed operators with the massive marketing leverage they now enjoy. In their turn, tour operators further stimulated market growth through their promotional activities and aggressive pricing policies. Importantly, at least until the 1990s, the large operators could take for granted the environment at individual destinations, using it as a 'free' resource to be exploited for profit.

Out of the UK the summer market for air package tours abroad appears to have stabilized in the late 1990s at between 8 and 10 million packages, with four operators controlling and dominating around two-thirds of this total. The total UK holidays market for destinations abroad in 1995 was estimated at 28 million, however, and it is important not to confuse summer packages by air with all holidays. Packages abroad for the whole year, by all forms of air and surface transport, account for just over half of all holidays out of the U.K. making it the most developed market for inclusive tours in Europe. Packages account for less than half of all holidays in the major European markets of Germany, France and Scandinavia. Of tourism for all purposes, including domestic tourism, it is clear that packaged tours are crucial to many resorts but only a minority sector of world tourism.

The positive role of tour operators in the tourism industry

In Chapter 6, overall tourism products as they are perceived and experienced by customers were introduced as comprising the five main components of attractions, destination facilities and services, accessibility of the destination, images and perceptions, and price. Environmental considerations are inextricably bound up in four of the components. Drawing on Burkart and Medlik's (1981) succinct view, a tour operator is a *manufacturer* who 'buys the components of the package, the inclusive tour (transport, accommodation, etc.) from the suppliers of the individual tourist services and

packages and brands them into a single entity' (p. 216).

Product packages may be more formally defined as:

Quality controlled, repeatable offers comprising two or more elements of transport to the destination, accommodation, food, destination attractions and excursions, and other facilities and services (such as travel insurance and car hire). Product packages are marketed to the general public, described in print or other communication media, and offered for sale at a published, inclusive price in which the costs of the individual product components cannot be separately identified (Middleton, 1994a).

As a manufacturer, a tour operator performs a valuable and often indispensable service to the three main parties concerned; visitors, tourism businesses located at destinations, and destination marketing interests:

- *For customers*, tour operators provide reliable information and easy access to nationally branded products, mostly through national networks of high-street retailers. The retail network offers choices, details of the product offers, facilitates bookings, provides tickets, travel insurance, and offers various forms of guarantee of product quality and assurances of personal security. These services simplify customers' decisions and for many represent the only way they can travel abroad with confidence. They are wholly functional contributions to the travel market and, in addition, tour operators provide their customers with greater convenience and a significantly lower inclusive price than they could conceivably obtain for themselves by direct negotiation with several different suppliers. Small wonder that tour operators have built such a strong market.
- *For suppliers at destinations*, especially hotels, tour operators provide product design expertise through the contracting process, international access to market segments in many

countries using global distribution systems mostly not accessible to small local suppliers, fill otherwise unsold capacity, operate forms of product control by monitoring customer satisfaction, and they reduce or obviate the need for separate marketing expenditure. Once a local supplier has contracted with an operator, the latter effectively takes over the marketing task. As customers' traditional patterns of booking holidays six months or more before departure become less and less relevant, with many now preferring to book their travel within a few weeks or even a few days of departure, tour operators and their retail networks provide a vital late booking service which most individual suppliers cannot possibly match.

- *For destination marketing interests*, a small number of tour operators can effectively handle the costly international marketing task by determining through the contracting processes the product design, the market segments to be reached, quality control, and the development of ancillary services provided such as excursions. In the production and dissemination of information about a destination, including information about the quality of its environment, a tour operator can be an important ally.

And a cost for the environment

When considering the environmental downside of tour operations it is important not to lose sight of the powerful real benefits for the three main parties. But, inevitably in the real world, there is a price to be paid for them. The price is an important one from the environmental standpoint and it is paid if local suppliers and destination managers lose control over marketing, product development, and capacity decisions, and are continuously squeezed on prices through the highly competitive contracting process.

Worst of all, a destination may lose control over which customer segments it attracts. All too often the tour operator link, which may appear as a marketing lifeline offering easy access to market growth and international business, can become a ligature throttling local profit and eroding environmental quality as a trade-off for greater capacity and the lowest possible short-run price. The large independent contracting agencies with their airline links typically have no vested interests in the destinations they serve. Most take no direct responsibility for environmental quality and they can move on to other resorts if the environment at currently featured destinations becomes damaged and polluted by the usual combination of overdevelopment, unsustainably low prices, and the lowest common denominator market segments.

To date, big operators argue that a broadly acceptable level of product quality in consumer terms has been achieved and is demonstrated in consumer responses to customer satisfaction questionnaires and a relatively low level of complaints. But the low price/high volume approach is self evidently not a sustainable position for the twenty-first century. Sustainability and protection of the environment requires a value-added, higher yield per customer basis for competition which is the opposite of the traditional tour operators' approach to business. There are clear indications in the late 1990s that this supply-led attitude is now changing in favour of a modern marketing philosophy but it is a slow process.

Three types of tour operation

The *manufacturer* concept most accurately describes the business activities of the large, independent entrepreneurial tour operators such as Thomson in the UK or TUI in Germany. These operators, whose activities capture popular media interest, are most obviously associated with what is known as 'mass tourism'. They are able to exercise significant influence over destinations and some also own their own airlines. Importantly, responding to the growing sophistication and experience of the travelling public in all the main markets of origin, the larger operators have increasingly segmented their product offers over the last decade. Each now produces several brochures where once it was possible to produce only one or two. Growing competition and the flexibility of the new information technology has speeded up the pace at which the former mass markets are segmenting, and this seems certain to continue.

Second, the manufacturer principle holds good for smaller independent operators and one of the most interesting developments of recent years has been the growth of hundreds of small specialist tour operators dealing with niche markets, benefiting from the overall segmentation trend noted above. Although individually they command only small shares of the total holiday market, many of these small operators flourish by developing close working relationships with their suppliers in chosen destinations and are equally close to their customers. The products include eco, adventure, activity and cultural packages, most of them specifically focused on aspects of the natural, built or cultural environment. For the most part these operators cannot and do not attempt to compete head-on in the popular end of the market, and they are able to charge higher prices on average for their specialist product knowledge. Reflecting the personal knowledge and commitment they have to local suppliers and customers, the level of environmental awareness among this group is typically higher than that of the large tour operators.

The third form of package or inclusive tours, also reflecting the growing segmentation of what were formerly mass markets, are put together by the owners of one or more of the product components. Thus sea ferries, cruise lines and railway companies, on the one hand, and hotels, consortia of holiday cottages, sports and recreation activity centres or universities aiming to market their accommodation during student vacations, on the other, may all act as tour operators. They put together packages of components and offer them for sale as product

entities, especially targeting customers by direct marketing. A distinguishing characteristic of the package operations of the component suppliers, which they share with smaller tour operators, is that most have a vested interest in the environment of the destination they are packaging – through local ownership or through local business relationships.

From the customer's viewpoint, packages generally look the same when presented in brochures and who owns or contracts for the different components may be neither evident nor relevant to the buyer. For example, Club Méditerranée and Center Parcs own holiday villages which are an inclusive, integrated combination of resort, environmental attractions, accommodation and related facilities. Club Med, largely dealing with an international market, also acts as a tour operator and travel agent, contracting with transport operators. Center Parcs, dealing mainly with domestic markets, does the same although its brochures reflect the fact that the majority of its customers will arrive by car and not need packaged transport. So are Club Med and Center Parcs tour operators or resorts? Does it matter to the customer? Both companies are certainly manufacturing key components and presenting them in a brochure at a range of prices as a package, but the resorts have a vested interest in the environment of the sites they own. They take direct responsibility for managing the environment, and protecting it into the future as their primary business asset. They are increasingly responsible in law for the quality of the environment in the places in which they operate and may be sued for compensation if clients have legitimate complaints.

A hybrid operator in this context is RCI, an independent contractor with strong commitments to businesses in particular destinations, and the largest of the international time-share exchange companies. RCI is a marketing network that acts as a tour operator for customers owning one or more time-shares in the resorts who wish to exchange them for holidays in other resorts in the network. RCI does not own any resorts and is not directly responsible for the environmental quality of the resorts it deals with, but it is responsible for deciding which resorts may, and which may not, join its network and gain the benefits of the RCI brand. It does this by operating quality standards for its resorts and grades and prices them accordingly. The resorts have to agree to work to minimum standards and RCI can both set and monitor environmental standards as part of its overall quality-recognition approach. Its operational systems provide an excellent example of good practice for the development of an explicit environmental role for other large tour operators.

Environmental negatives of product orientated large-scale tour operation

It has become a major global challenge for sustainable development in holiday tourism that, right from the beginning, package tours by air were typically not marketing-led in the modern sense (see Chapter 10) but supply- or product-led. They were developed on a basic and often intuitive knowledge of customer needs, interests and benefits sought, but not on any understanding of environmental pressures and costs at destinations. This was possible because holiday products were self-evidently in demand if the price was low enough, and initially environment problems were not apparent. It was not necessary in a booming growth market to work hard on demand, only on cost. Accordingly, and logically from a short-term business point of view, large-scale inclusive tours were developed primarily around the maximum utilization of aircraft and this was easiest to achieve with the lowest possible price.

In the UK especially, large-scale independent tour operators have operated on the three concepts of maximum aircraft load factors, the lowest possible prices for the contracted product elements, and the perceived advantages of market share. It is an approach to business neatly summarized as *pile it high and sell it cheap*. The economics of tour operation (see, for example,

Middleton, 1994a, and Josephides, 1996) provide inducements to add more beds, more seats and more volume, if the demand exists. This leads to a vicious cycle from an environmental standpoint of ever greater capacity, lower prices, and last minute deep discounts to achieve some return to offset committed costs. In conditions of the fiercest competition for market share between a handful of big operators, research evidence suggests that a difference of just £10 on a package tour price of £300 was sufficient in the mid-1990s to shift consumer demand in significant volume from one operator to another – and from one destination area to another. The tourism fortunes of mainland Spain, the Balearics, Greece, Turkey and Cyprus swayed to the rhythm of cost cutting and relative exchange rate advantages. The destination environment has paid the price.

Over the last two decades, the development of larger aircraft and larger hotels further fuelled the classic vicious business cycle of competition on price and last-minute discounting to move unsold capacity, from which none of the players can extricate themselves. In a free market, with no environmental standards in place at destinations, none of the main players can pursue premium prices. The profits of tour operating have always been wafer-thin, with the margin between profit and loss typically dependent on less than two or three percentage points on aircraft load factors. Clarksons in the 1970s and Intasun in the 1990s are just two of the biggest UK players crushed on the anvil of their own market-share ambitions because they were overextended at the point when an unforeseen market downturn left them financially overexposed.

In the next section – pages 189–192 we summarize the specific environment management issues for the tour operators sector.

Sustainability, the environmental management perspective

Since the 1990s there has been increasing awareness of the environmental impacts associated with the travel industry among tour operators. With the exception of a few pioneering companies and a few isolated projects, however, there is still a relative lack of action in this sector. When tour operators have adopted environmental improvement programmes, they have fallen into two quite distinct groups: (1) the larger tour operators that dominate the market have set up a small number of impressive partnership projects or in-house environmental improvement schemes (see the TUI case at the end of this chapter); (2) the smaller operators (and especially those providing so-called 'ecotours') who have donated money to conservation initiatives and changed their own management practices to reduce environmental impacts. Driven by an increase in consumer pressure for certain products, the threat of increased regulation, and – for the smaller companies at least – recognition of the potential environmental decay of the destinations on which business success depends, the sector has begun to play a more proactive role in addressing the impacts associated with its activities over the last two or three years. These impacts include the following.

Specific environmental impacts

Resource depletion:

- Use of energy generated from fossil fuels, especially associated with transport and accommodation.
- Use of non-renewable natural resources such as oil, coal, and natural gas for heating or the production of manufactured goods.
- Consumption of fresh water – see also Chapter 12.
- Use of paper (mainly from non-recycled sources) for brochure production.

Pollution:

- Contribution to global warming and acid rain through the consumption of energy.
- Contribution to global warming, acid rain, low-level smog, and potential ozone depletion through the use of transport both directly and by visitors travelling to the resort and the import of goods to service visitors needs.
- Production of solid wastes for landfill sites.
- Indirect pollution arising from increased demand for agricultural or manufactured goods in the area, thus stimulating pesticide and nitrate use or industrial pollutants.

Degradation:

- Of sensitive environments, heritage sites, or local cultures caused by a large number of people visiting fragile resource areas, especially in the developing 'ecotourism' resorts.
- Reduction in species diversity as a result of infrastructure development, building, or landscaping work, and direct interference by visitors, for example on coral reefs.
- Reduction in landscape quality as a result of steady urbanization associated with in-fill development which has characterized many large tourist resort areas.

Environmental opportunities for the sector

In terms of business operations, the opportunities for tour operators and travel agencies from environmental improvement programmes are less direct than for other sectors of the industry. In the UK, many operators do not own the facilities in which their clients are accommodated or entertained and cannot, therefore, gain the significant benefits from cost savings in the areas of energy, waste and water management which have spurred other sectors into action. The opportunities from environmental improvement programmes for this sector are more directly associated with consumer communication, satisfaction and value for money, and marketing.

The main environmental opportunities for the sector are:

- *Increased attraction to customers.* There is little solid evidence that most customers will pay more for travel products which do not damage the environment. There is, however, massive evidence that customers prefer to travel to environments which are not scarred by modern urbanization or industrialization. The progression of leisure tourists in Europe from the Mediterranean coastal resorts of Spain and Italy, to the Algarve, Greece, and latterly to Turkey and long-haul destinations, illustrates the way in which tourists select destinations which are perceived not to be 'damaged' or 'over-commercialized'. For the smaller operators, the huge growth in demand for 'ecotourism' holidays is further evidence of the attraction and business success that can be associated with well-maintained natural environments. (See also Chapter 1.)
- *Increased ability to retain customers.* Achieving repeat custom and personally recommended business is one of the most efficient uses that can be made of marketing resources. Satisfied customers will return to the same operator and the same resort time and again and there is considerable evidence that customers prefer to return to destinations which provide a high-quality experience in which the environment is an essential element.
- *Increased staff motivation and loyalty.* See Chapter 12.
- *Improvements in product quality.* See Chapter 12.
- *Improvements in community relations.* Through the locally employed representatives and the excursions they arrange, tour operators probably have more dealings with the local community than any other sector of the industry. Involvement of the community in itineraries, as guides or interpreters, all help to enhance the quality of the guest experience and the acceptance of tourism in the local area. There is considerable evidence that 'friendly locals' are one of the major elements of the tourism experience and one which cannot be controlled by the operator. Careful outreach programmes can, thus, help to underpin business success.

- *Improvement in relations with local authorities.* As countries become increasingly aware of the potential negative impacts associated with tourism development, they are likely to evaluate the activities of tour operators and those with excellent environmental credentials are more likely to benefit in terms of treatment, securing licences, and so on. Cox and Kings, for example, have benefited from their excellent environmental credentials by being invited to partner Programme for Belize in opening up parts of the rain forest to environmentally sensitive tourism.
- *Reduction in liability to prosecution.* Increasingly, operators have found themselves taken to arbitration by clients over a range of issues which can be broadly termed as environmental. Congestion, noise, polluted sea water, and filthy beaches are all issues which have involved tour operators in recent disputes with clients. Effective local area partnership programmes can help to reduce these problems and thus reduce liabilities.
- *Long-term resort development.* Some of the larger operators have great potential to influence long term resort development and ultimately sustainability. Operators have the greatest potential to exert such an influence in areas where they cumulatively account for the majority of bed spaces, where they can require the accommodation establishments and other facilities that they contract to introduce initiatives to improve certain aspects of their environmental performance. To date only one large operator, TUI, is known to have fully adopted such an approach and this is described in the case study below.

Regulatory background

With the exception of a small number of local areas, environmental regulations have not been developed and applied specifically for tour operators. They are subject to the wide range of more general environmental and environmental health and safety regulations that exist in most countries, of course, and for larger operators in developed countries, the regulations include:

- *Package Holiday Directive.* Implemented through-out the EU, this directive has no direct environmental criteria. It requires, however, that holidays are accurately described in brochures and tour operators can be sued on environmental grounds where photographs or text avoid mention of specific environmental issues which affect the overall holiday quality.
- *Planning and building regulations.* These only apply directly in the rare instances that operators own facilities in which clients are accommodated – see Chapter 12 for full details.
- *Environmental health and safety regulations.* See Chapter 12.
- *Regulations governing the responsible disposal of wastes.* See Chapter 12.
- *Regulations governing visitor flows.* Some countries and national parks have implemented quota or permit systems which provide guidance on the number of visitors allowed in an area at a specified time or the activities in which they can engage. Tour operators must gain the specified number of permits etc. prior to operating into those areas. See, for example, the Quicksilver Connections case in Part Four.

Self-regulation in the sector

Voluntary industry initiatives have played a more significant role thus far than regulations in shaping the approach of at least some tour operators to the environment. The International Association of Antarctic Tour Operators set their programme in motion in 1992 by establishing a code of conduct which was agreed by all those operating cruises to the area and copied to all clients. The International Federation of Tour Operators (IFTO) then led the field by pioneering a partnership environmental improvement programme in the Balearic Islands (Spain) and Rhodes (Greece) in 1993 (see the ECOMOST case at the end of this chapter). TUI, the leading German tour operator, established a partnership programme with Greece's leading hotel chain, Grecotel, bringing about significant environmental improvements and improving client communication. More recently the Association of Independent Tour Operators (AITO) undertook a study of the environmental impacts associated with ski tourism, and the European Tour Operators Association has joined forces with Green Globe to assess the impacts and potential solutions to tourism management in Europe's cities. The Green Globe, Green Leaf, and CERT* environmental initiatives also each offer advice to help companies improve environmental performance. Specific issues which have been addressed by voluntary programmes include:

- Partnership programmes between destination authorities, the accommodation sector, transport operators and tour operators to identify targets for joint environmental improvement.
- Programmes to establish environmental policies and staff training initiatives (largely pioneered by CERT).
- Programmes to fund the clean-up and operation of certain landscapes (largely led by CERT and tour operator Abercrombie and Kent's charity, Friends of Conservation).
- Programmes to encourage clients to reduce the volume of packaging on products prior to going on holiday, or to persuade them to take biodegradable detergents, thus reducing local environmental impacts.

* CERT (Campaign for Environmentally Responsible Tourism) is a UK organization formed in 1994 aiming to undertake environmental improvements from which both tourism and destination interests benefit. In 1996, membership was less than fifty mostly small tour operators who fund the campaign by small per-capita contributions (per passenger carried).

- Programmes to tell clients about the nature of their environmental impacts while on holiday and to help them reduce those impacts (largely led by CERT).
- Programmes to encourage clients to consider alternative modes of transport while on holiday.
- Integration of local communities into the company's environmental programme, through local educational initiatives, donations to local charities and initiatives to clean up local landscape areas.

Summarizing the environmental issues for tour operators – the way ahead

With the relatively unsophisticated, inexperienced holiday tourists of the 1960s and 1970s, and with a strongly growing demand for what were then new and fashionable resorts, it was possible for tour operators to take for granted the quality of the environment. But, however unacknowledged, environmental quality was always a very powerful motivation in the majority of visitors' minds. We predict that more sophisticated buyers in the mature market conditions of the next decade will shift environmental quality toward the forefront of their decision processes (see the TUI example, below). Marketing logic indicates that, in the growing competition for the leisure tourism market, the quality of the environment is a leading factor for product and destination differentiation and for customer choice. Value-added product formulation and premium pricing is the only available way to produce good profits and surpluses for environmental protection. It is the credible and sustainable approach for modern market circumstances.

By the late 1990s, the more farsighted tour operators clearly recognize the issue. As Martin Brackenbury (President of IFTO) put it in the quote that introduces this chapter, anyone supplying holidays is going to have their activities scrutinized for their compatibility with the ethic of sustainable tourism. To put those words into effective action, it follows logically that for any destination where tour operators' packages represent more than, say, 25 per cent of the total leisure market and are growing, it is essential to:

- Develop local partnerships to link tour operators with hotels and other suppliers of tourism services having vested interests in the future of the destination, and with the other stakeholders in the destination's future, especially municipal authorities and the representatives of local residents
- Develop specific environmental targets through the partnerships, including capacity limits, codes of conduct, and regulatory agreements applying as ground rules to *all* tour operators and suppliers. These agreements will incorporate international and national regulations as well as any developed especially for the local environment. In other words creating a level playing field on which all the competing tour operators and suppliers must play
- Develop as part of tour operators' procurement policies environmental performance standards expected of local suppliers, recognizing the vitally important product specification and capacity-contracting role the operators play. Such an approach would mirror that of leading retail chains and car manufacturers, which now specify and monitor the environmental standards required of their suppliers.
- Provide incentives that reward auditing of tour operators' business practices, especially if they include an airline and travel agents within their operation, applying the *Ten R's* introduced in Chapter 11.

A proactive partnership approach as outlined above provides the practical means whereby private sector businesses can be obliged to meet minimum environmental standards, which they will otherwise tend to ignore.

In the next section – pages 193–197 we outline specific examples of current good practice in the tour operator sector.

Tour operator examples

Touristik Union International (TUI)

Based in Germany, TUI is the largest tour operating company in Europe with business activities extending to hotel chains, incoming agencies, and foreign tour operators in which it has a significant ownership stake. Its traditional business has lain with marketing package tours to clients from north Europe looking for holidays in the sun in the Mediterranean but, while the bulk of its volume still lies in that region, its scope now extends virtually world-wide. In the late 1990s TUI carried some 5 million visitors to 145 destinations in more than sixty different countries.

As a major private-sector player in a country which is in the forefront of the environmental movement with a well-established Green political party, TUI were well aware by the late 1980s of the implications for tourism of eroded environments and the threat to their business interests. In 1990 a senior management appointment was made to spearhead the company's environmental responses, reporting directly to the Executive Board. Detailed knowledge of German consumers' interests and expectations in environmental matters underlies the operator's responses, and they have access to comprehensive information on market trends. Bearing in mind that Germany is now an affluent mature market with many very experienced international travellers, the data included in Chapter 1 of this book showing how environmental expectations increases with frequency of travel are especially relevant to this case.

Partnerships involved

Stating that 'any scope for cooperation should be exploited to the full', and recognizing the need to work with local authorities as well as with non-governmental organizations (NGOs) at its destinations, TUI identify productive partnerships with their own subsidiary and part-subsidiary companies, with the Environment and Culture Committee established by the German Travel Agents Association (DRV) and with the International Federation of Tour Operators (IFTO). Utilizing its environmental database (see below) TUI has also established an international Environment Network (TEN) collating information flows derived from its subsidiaries and contracted hotels for all the countries with which it deals, from Antigua to Zimbabwe. TEN is the quantitative and qualitative expression for the people, institutions, organizations – internal and external – cooperating in terms of reporting and working practically on the process of reducing environmental impacts worldwide.

Rationale for a sustainable strategy

TUI ask their own question: 'How can even a large tour operator justify expenditure of millions of D-marks on environmental activities? The reason is obvious; holiday regions and resort hotels cannot remain successful in the long term without clean beaches, clean water, and unspoiled landscape ... Changing values and customer expectations show that traditional ideas of what constitutes [product] quality are outdated. Environmental compatibility, or to be more precise, minimum pollution is very high on the list of holiday essentials. Tour operators wishing to survive need to offer unspoiled landscape and nature.'

TUI make it perfectly clear that they are in business to make a targeted return on investment and that any environmental efforts and investment must be subjected to the kind of cost-benefit analysis that is 'an essential element in today's corporate development'.

Environmental programme

(a) TUI environmental criteria for destinations

Obviously reflecting customer demands and expectations, the operator uses ten criteria for formally evaluating the quality of the environment at destinations. It includes waste-water management, landscape and nature; air quality and levels of noise; garbage-disposal practices; fresh water supplies; sea and shoreline; the nature of environmental activities (statutory and proactive) undertaken at the destination; and the quality of 'surroundings', or the overall ambience provided by a resort. The implications that the operator will not contract with destinations that do not match their criteria developed on a comparative/competitive basis are ominous for destinations that allow their environment to deteriorate. Over the years, dealing with dozens of competing destinations, the company has built its information flows into a database referred to earlier as the TUI Environmental Information System. This database, even for just one large international tour operator, is a potential goldmine for evaluating and communicating good practice.

For new resorts under consideration for investment by TUI, their project managers are drawing up formal environmental impact statements (EIS), recognizing that any major project is increasingly likely to undergo an environmental impact assessment (EIA) before it gains permission.

(b) TUI criteria for hotels and other accommodation

Again reflecting its customers' demands and expectations, TUI operate an eight-point assessment for evaluating the environmental credentials of the accommodation suppliers with which it deals. The detailed criteria are explained and presented to hoteliers as checklists which are analysed by the Group's database. Seminars are conducted to explain the process. The checklist includes operational issues such as waste-water treatment; waste-disposal practices; energy- and water-saving measures; noise levels in the hotel; and broader 'environmental ambience' factors such as architecture and building materials of the hotel; location and immediate surroundings of the hotel grounds. Interestingly, TUI add 'other aspects of the hotel either causing concern or being particularly environment-friendly'.

(c) Head office operations

Although of lesser immediate impact on sustainable tourism, TUI has nevertheless audited its head office operations and by changing the paper used for brochure production, for example, was able to reduce the environmental impact on the water used in the process by 90 per cent. It operates the normal systems for controlling energy use, waste separation and recycling, re-use, etc.

(d) Influencing the behaviour of tourists on holiday

TUI recognize the need to influence the behaviour of its customers at the destination using carefully prepared information designed to stimulate interest in sustainable issues and the options open to visitors on holiday. They are also clearly aware that this is not an easy process. 'Persuading hedonistic citizens of the leisure era to save water and energy and to avoid discarding litter is by no means impossible.' More than 600 million pieces of environmental information in TUI brochures are distributed by the German package tours market every year and a complex system of different ways and means provides guest information after arrival in the hotels.

Summary – TUI

Large, independent, so-called 'mass tour operators' have been heavily criticized for their failure to act in support of the environment, especially at destinations. This case, with its important stress on precise environmental criteria developed and applied by a commercial operator in determining with which destinations and with which accommodation suppliers it will work, provides a striking indication of post-1990 corporate thinking which we consider to be a clear indication of the direction of market trends. It is especially relevant that the operator's business is based in one of Europe's most sophisticated and demanding populations, but we judge it to be equally relevant to the more affluent half at least of the other major mature tourism markets in north Europe. A key section of TUI's published corporate principles is noted below.

'The protection of an intact environment is of the utmost importance to all of us. It helps us to safeguard our natural resources and ensures the future of our enterprise. Each of our corporate divisions bears responsibility for the environment. Each employee is called upon to come up with helpful ideas, since environmental protection begins with each of us. The environmental compatibility of our product is an integral part of our standard of quality.'

TUI Corporate Principles, 1996

This corporate principle is part of the Group's *Strategy 2001*. It is applied to all other group members in other tourism-generating countries, such as the Netherlands, Belgium, Switzerland and Austria. TUI is thus using its strategic influence proactively as a major purchaser to influence its suppliers and contractors in environmentally sustainable ways. It illustrates neatly the principles by which larger businesses can influence the sustainable actions of smaller ones addressed in Chapters 9 and 10 of this book.

International Federation of Tour Operators: The ECOMOST Project

The International Federation of Tour Operators (IFTO) is a representative trade body with some nineteen members drawn from tour operators associations throughout Europe. Collectively, IFTO members carried some 44 million international inclusive tour passengers a year in the late 1990s; the bulk of these continue to be attracted to the resorts around the Mediterranean coast and many of them are repeat customers with the same operators. IFTO meets regularly with national and regional governments, airlines, hotel groups and local tourist handling agents to deal with tourism matters. It has pursued policies for securing environmental health and safety among its suppliers and developing criteria for customer protection more generally.

ECOMOST is an acronym for European Community Models Of Sustainable Tourism. Described below, this is a research-based model

developed over two years and tested in prime tourist destination areas in the Balearics and Greece. The model was designed to be applicable in all parts of the world where the volume of leisure tourism affects the local environment.

Rationale for sustainable tourism

Leading IFTO members were well aware during the 1980s of a significant consumer backlash against overdeveloped, environmentally degraded resorts in their primary Mediterranean destination areas and the need to confront the problems and take appropriate action. They were equally aware of the long-term implications for profitability if their primary resources/business assets were further eroded. As individual tour operators they were aware they could not act separately and would need to collaborate with other operators and tourist businesses and in particular with public sector interests having direct political and planning responsibility for the resort areas.

There was nothing altruistic about IFTO's motives. These are internationally competitive marketing organizations and their interests are business and profit related. But the more farsighted are clearly looking to future prosperity and all are highly sensitive to their customer's needs and interests, especially their changing preferences as demands for higher product quality emerge. As tour operators, all the big players conduct their own continuous research into customer satisfaction, both overall and in terms of specific aspects of holidays, including consumer perceptions of environmental factors.

The ECOMOST research

In 1992, following detailed discussions, IFTO were able to specify research and seek support from the European Commission, which at that time was developing its more focused environmental critieria expressed in the Maastricht Treaty. The Spanish government and the government of the Balearics agreed to collaborate and the Dodecanese Chamber of Commerce participated for Rhodes. Two specific destination areas – Mallorca and the island of Rhodes – were selected for study. An essential point is that all the principal private and public sector parties were involved in the research.

The overall research objective was to develop practical models and methodologies for achieving sustainable tourism. Mallorca is believed to have one of the highest concentrations of tourists in the world, attracting some 6 million visitors a year and generating around half of its economy from tourism. Rhodes as an island was rather less intensively developed although the town of Rhodes had been highly developed in the 1980s and was still expanding its capacity at the time of the research. In tourism terms, the key question for the research to answer was, 'how can the lifecycle of mature resorts be extended on a sustainable basis?' Carried out primarily by Dr Alfred Koch and a German research Institute, DWIF, the research was completed in 1993 and a management summary was published by IFTO in 1994 (Hughes, 1994).

The ECOMOST approach has been dubbed 'tourism's stethoscope', against which to gauge a destination's achievements against the ideal of sustainability. 'Instead of listening to heart beat it gauges a tourist destination's attainments against the ideal of sustainability.' (Hughes, 1994, p. 6). The approach is based on three simple goals relevant to long-run sustainability and success in any tourism destination: first, that the local residents should remain prosperous and maintain their cultural identity; second, that the destination should remain attractive to prospective visitors; third, that any damage to the environment is minimized, contained and reversed where possible. These three goals require a fourth, an effective political and planning framework developed in collaboration with the principal business and residents' interests in a destination.

Following the preliminary analysis the research, and the model focused on four elements:

- The prosperity of the population – economically and in cultural terms.
- The attractiveness of the tourist product.

- The health of the local ecology (and quality of the environment).
- The effectiveness of the political/regulatory framework.

The model was developed by breaking down each of those four elements into a range of specific components for which it was possible to devise measurable indicators. The indicators can be used to check the performance of the destination and, based on experience, it is possible to broadly identify when critical points are reached at which remedial action is required. Obvious examples are the tourism use of fresh water measured against available capacity, or bathing water quality; or customer satisfaction and perceptions of overcrowding expressed in relation to competitive resorts. Less obvious examples are estimates of the quality and efficiency of regional planning and the satisfaction of resident populations with tourism development. The bulk of the research work lay in finding appropriate measures for the component parts of the four elements, and testing them in the two areas chosen for the project. Inevitably some of the measures are based as much or more on judgement as on statistics, but that reflects the current state of the art.

(a) Prosperity of the population

The main indicators assessed are per-capita income and unemployment rates (against national averages); employment structure and level of qualifications and training in the tourism industry; seasonality of employment; infiltration of foreign investment and ownership; crime rates; bed occupancy in the local tourist industry; and price levels (higher than average prices indicate higher quality products warranting premium payments – and higher wages).

(b) Attractiveness of the tourist product

The main indicators assessed are tour operator customers' perceptions of product quality (see also below); average age of tourist accommodation; levels of investment overall; and investment in management.

(c) State of the ecology

The word 'ecology' is used in the research to cover all the physical environment factors and the main indicators assessed are carrying capacity and level of use of airport and attractions; capacity of resources/infrastructure for drinking water, and sewage treatment and disposal; preservation of species, level of emissions into the atmosphere, and the landscape aesthetics of the coastline. Also included are guest satisfaction comments/criticisms on the standards of the local environment (including aesthetics) and guest awareness and perceptions of environmental problems.

(d) Political framework

The main indicators assessed are the range of legislative powers available to maintain environmental standards relevant to the tourism industry; the development of unambiguous regional and local plans for tourism and the use of adequate planning tools and enforcement of planning regulations; and participation by the tourist industry and the public (local residents) in the planning process.

Summary – ECOMOST

The report notes that the negative case against tourism is well known, commenting that the case is all too often an emotive one, however, founded in prejudices and preconceptions. 'Precious little science has been brought to bear, largely because there is precious little science available. The purpose of the ECOMOST model was to supply that science. From the analysis of one industry – in this case Mallorca's – was distilled a series of tests which could be used in the design of a new industry or to determine the condition of, and if necessary propose remedies for, an existing one.' The research was, therefore, both diagnostic and predictive. The intention was to design a set of measures that could be used anywhere in the world to evaluate the impact of tourism and highlight what needed to be done to shift towards sustainability, and who would be responsible (including the private sector) for doing it.

The report concludes 'it is perhaps the overriding lesson from the report that only if the political structures are developed early enough can errors be avoided or their effects at least be minimized'. It emerges clearly in the report that 'political structures' means a collaborative planning process between the public and private sector at local level with joint responsibility for implementing goals and targets using the respective instruments and market mechanisms outlined in Chapters 8 and 9 of this book.

As a pioneering industry-led approach to the measurement of tourism impact, and implementing visitor planning and management and partnership principles at local level, the ECOMOST approach deserves the widest attention. Inevitably the model is not perfect, the science is not complete, and most resorts do not have the measurement processes and skills to implement the model effectively in practice. But it does address all the main issues reflected throughout this book and provides an ideal case study for further development.

Sustainability – the marketing perspective

Figure 15.1 summarizes the remarkably powerful marketing leverage which tour operators are able to bring to bear on many destinations. Much of this power is still potential rather than actual because most tour operators are still at the stage of selling what they can produce, and large operators in particular have accepted very few commitments to individual destinations. Many are still competing on price rather than marketing the benefits that underlie most customers expectations. It is a major challenge for tour operators to use their leverage to work for rather than against the environment of visited destinations, but the levers are all in place to do it. What is lacking is the type of destination partnership organizational arrangements noted in this chapter.

By the nature of their operations as contractors, especially where tour operators in developed countries send clients to developing countries to enjoy the quality of the environment, they are very powerful players from a marketing perspective. Their marketing decisions strongly influence and in some cases directly control:

- Customer segments targeted for promotion and distribution.
- Product design and quality in terms of what they think their customers will buy in accommodation, ground facilities and excursions.
- Product design (and a major cost element) in their airline contracting or operating role.
- The capacity to be offered for sale – number of beds in the accommodation units contracted.
- Prices at which the capacity they contract for will be sold, including special offers and discounts.
- The destination images and positioning (usually focused directly or indirectly on the environment) to be projected in brochures and other promotional materials.
- The distribution process, whether through travel agents or direct.
- The information flow to customers about the destination and its environmental/cultural qualities.
- Evaluation of customer reaction through customer-satisfaction questionnaires.
- Customer knowledge and profiles held on databases for analysis and future marketing.
- Marketing objectives, target volume, budgets and programmes.

By participating with others responsible for a destination's environment, tour operators could share some of the costs and tasks involved in sustainable development. The pay-off would be that by participating in regulatory processes to avoid environmental damage they could influence the scope of future regulation, establish commercially viable ground rules, and shift from existing counterproductive competition on price towards competition on environmental quality and value added.

Figure 15.1 *Sustainability – the marketing perspective for tour operators*

Part Four

International Cases of Good Management Practice for Sustainability

Kruger National Park, South Africa

Introduction

The year 1996 saw the 70th anniversary of Kruger National Park in South Africa and in that time it has undergone tremendous changes. There have been great advances in conservation and tourism management techniques to make this one of the top ten national parks in the world, yet its original inspiration – conservation of ecosystems in a natural but managed environment permitting and promoting access to visitors – is as modern today as it was in 1926. The Park provided one of the earliest forms of what is now considered *ecotourism*. The key features of the first visitor areas pre-dated good practice in modern design by at least half a century. The Park provides models of thoroughly tested visitor interpretation and management techniques and generates over 70 per cent of its operating costs from tourism. Not eligible for consideration under the former South African government, the Kruger National Park submitted its proposal in 1996 to be designated a World Heritage Site.

The Kruger Park is also very modern in the 1990s in the sense that its future is by no means secure. Adjacent to its boundaries have settled tens of thousands of people in the last twenty years, mostly subsisting by the most basic unsustainable agricultural practices causing soil erosion, over extraction of fresh water and pollution of watercourses now affecting the Park's ecosystems. The Makuleka tribe, forcefully displaced when the Park was fully enclosed in the late 1960s, is in the process of claiming restoration of lands, or compensation under the Restitution of Land Rights Act of 1994 introduced under the new South African government. In 1995 a proposal was launched by politicians and businesses from the Northern Province for a new road and gas pipeline to link the Province with Mozambique. If it happens it would bisect the Park and could affect the long-established movement and breeding patterns of the animal life. It would inevitably facilitate the activities of poachers of ivory and rhino horn which is decimating the big mammals in much of Southern Africa.

Although it is also vulnerable because, especially pre-1994, it was generally seen as a leisure facility for white South Africans, the Kruger National Park is a striking example of what management in enclosed boundaries can achieve in forging a sustainable partnership between tourism, the conservation of wildlife, and a natural ecosystem in one of the largest protected environments in the World. If threats to the Park are clear, so too are the opportunities to draw in more international visitors to generate needed foreign currency, and to build effective partnerships for the benefit of adjacent local communities.

Background

The Kruger National Park, situated in the north-eastern corner of the Republic of South Africa, is bordered to the north by Zimbabwe and to the east by Mozambique. The park is some 4 hours' drive from Johannesburg and Pretoria, both of which are major tourism-generating areas. Visitor entrance to the wholly enclosed and fenced Park is from South Africa only, and controlled via seven entry gates and an airport at the main rest camp of Skukuza.

Named in 1926 after Paul Kruger, President of the former Zuid Afrikaansche Republiek, the Park was first proclaimed in Kruger's time in 1898 as the Sabie and Shingwedzi Nature Reserves. At the end of the nineteenth century, as a result of years of uncontrolled hunting, mining, and farming, as well as shooting of animals to sustain troops in the Anglo-Boer War, there had been a drastic decline in the animal life. In 1912 it was estimated there were only twenty-five elephants, six black rhino, 200 hippos, 250 giraffe, and so on within the reserves. Conservation action was essential. These two reserves were later combined and expanded and, under the National Parks Act of 1926 the area was officially named the Kruger National Park, to be managed by a board of trustees. Public access was considered to be an integral part of life for the national parks under the Act although only three cars visited in 1927, generating an income of £3.

The Park is significant for several reasons. Its sheer size of 19 485 km² means it is larger than the state of Israel or the principality of Wales in the UK and it has been described as a model of nature conservation and a natural laboratory. The Park has a remarkable ecosystem currently comprising more than 2000 different forms of plant life, 146 types of mammal, more than 490 species of birds; 114 species of reptiles, forty-nine types of fish and innumerable insects and other forms of life, many of which are not found elsewhere in the world. The Park can be divided into sixteen ecozones, each supporting a different spectrum of plants and animals.

In the 1920s roads were poor, rivers could be crossed only by pontoon, and visitor facilities apart from very basic camp-sites were almost non-existent other than rangers controlling access and patrolling the Park for poachers and snares. In 1927 a beginning was made to make the Park more accessible to visitors. By end 1929 the Park had seventy-eight *rondavels* (round huts built in clusters using local materials and adopting traditional African designs to sleep four or more visitors with simple sanitation and cooking facilities). To this day, seventy years on, the rondavel concept is maintained and much appreciated by visitors. By 1930, six stockaded rest camps were completed, with over 100 rondavels, already incorporating concrete within the traditional design. The control of the larger camps was contracted out to the private sector responsible for catering, selling petrol, and maintaining trading stores.

Rationale for and foundations of a sustainable strategy; programmes for maintaining the integrity of the resource base

Up to 1951 the Park was managed without formal scientific research. In that year the Parks Board initiated an extensive building programme to improve tourist facilities and a research division and an educational service was created, with headquarters in Skukuza, the main rest camp and the site of the airport which also serves adjacent private sector reserves. Scientific management of the Park may be traced, therefore, to the 1950s. Since then, the following main management and conservation developments have taken place:

- 1951 (ongoing) – work on the first planned network of firebreaks to combat accidental veldt fires (very common in the tinder-dry conditions of the Park for much of the year) was started, and a scientifically founded policy of rotation fires was implemented. Later the Park developed a computer program to measure the interaction of variables such as rainfall, soil types, and even underground rock formations in determining which areas needed to be burnt (to replicate nature but avoid massive destruction). Current policy permits most natural fires (caused by lightning, for example) but controls others, especially where human life, Park property, and areas of particular scientific importance are threatened.

- 1959–1960 – fencing the southern and western borders of the Park to exercise better control over foot and mouth disease entering the park from farmed animals in the border areas.

- 1961 (ongoing) – reintroducing various animal species that had previously existed in the Park and become extinct, including 336 white rhino, black rhino, oribi, grey rhebok, samango monkeys, and Lichstein's hartbeest. Over the years the numbers of certain species were replenished, for example of red duiker, mountain reedbuck, cheetah, nyala, eland, suni, sable antelope and roan antelope.

- 1964 (ongoing) – the first organized wild life census of the bigger mammals (elephants and buffalo) using helicopters. These operations are now carried out annually, supplemented by extensive ground surveys undertaken by research personnel and game rangers. In earlier years, for reasons such as overgrazing, overcrowding and excessive predation on some species, large herbivores such as elephant, buffalo and hippo were culled. Present culling policy states that only animal populations that do not respond to short-term (±20 years) climatic cycles are controlled. Upper and lower 'acceptable' population limits have been set for buffalo and elephant. Culling operations are carried out under strict supervision and methods are constantly refined to reduce the level of stress on the animals selected. The culling policy was due for review in 1996 after extensive consultation and consideration of other options.

- 1971 (ongoing) – following serious anthrax epidemics in 1959, 1960, 1962 and 1970 researchers advised immunization of roan antelope. Immunization is carried out annually by helicopter, using darts containing the vaccine and has been successful.

- Over the years great progress has been made

with immobilizing animals in the Park, allowing researchers to fit radio transmitters used to track the movement of animals and relocate them if necessary. Some larger animals have been relocated to other game reserves and to other countries to help build stocks and create new founder populations.

- 1974–1976 – erection of an elephant-resistant fence along the international border with Mozambique, thus creating a fully enclosed boundary system for the first time.

- 1994 – parts of the Western boundary fence were removed, permitting animals to move between Kruger Park and neighbouring reserves of Sabie-Sand, Klaserie, Timbavati and Umbabat.

- With the aid of 500 fixed-point photography sites and 530 veldt monitoring sites surveyed at regular intervals, researchers monitor vegetation changes allowing them to manage veldt conditions.

These developments, as well as the sinking of boreholes to ensure a constant water supply for the animals (which commenced in 1933), have contributed to a firm foundation of Park management in which the natural environment is pre-eminent and upon which the Park can sustain tourism, the financial life blood of the Park.

Tourism and visitor management techniques

Visitor arrivals to the Kruger National Park have remained fairly stable since 1989/90 at around 700 000 per annum, although there was an increase to 835 000 in 1995/6. Most of these are white South African domestic tourists with the educational culture to appreciate natural environments, and the relative affluence needed to have a car, purchase entry to the park, and pay for overnight stays and subsistence. For 1995/6 tourism and commercial income was just under 180 million rand (approximately £25 million at

1996 exchange rates), an average of around £31 per visitor trip (day and staying visits combined).

In 1996 there were fourteen public rest camps of varying sizes for visitors, open around the year and offering approximately 4000 bed spaces within the Park. Another five small camps have been established by donations from private sector organizations for some twelve to nineteen people per camp and these are available to the general public for 11 months of the year. Finally there are six secluded bush camps sleeping up to seventy people a night with no shops, restaurants or petrol stations, although the huts are fully equipped. Employment for some 3500 people is created.

To preserve the integrity of the ecosystem and the wildlife experience for visitors, the Park's management decided to fix bed capacity at around 4000. All these have to be booked in advance and demand significantly exceeds supply in the popular months. A typical average length of stay is around 3–4 nights and most visitors move between rest camps during the day to explore the Park and observe wildlife. Day visits are possible, but given the travel distance from major catchment areas the demand is not as great as it would be closer to urban centres, and in the peak season day visits are limited to give an estimated average capacity of 0.75 vehicles per kilometre of road space. This strict capacity regulation compares favourably, for example, with the Masai Mara Reserve in Kenya where the number of visitor beds was allowed to increase sevenfold between 1990 and 1996, so that 'the most visible herds migrating across the plains are ... minibuses' (*The Economist*, 1996).

Over several decades the Park management developed and clearly communicate the following seven rules covering visitor behaviour. Visitors are required:

- To remain in their cars when in the Park. The animals have became familiar since birth with motor vehicles and do not recognize humans inside the cars. If the car silhouette is broken and humans become visible to animals, for example if people get out to take photo-graphs, the animals flee, or worse, they may charge the person.
- Stay on visitor roads and not venture onto firebreaks, which are not regularly patrolled. The park has 1739 kn of gravel roads and 885 km of tarred roads.
- Keep the park clean by not throwing away papers, cans, etc. when driving in the Park. Garbage is not only unsightly but, for example, plastic and cans can kill the animals. Each vehicle is provided with a paper refuse bag on entry to the Park. Recycling facilities are available for glass, cans, and some waste paper.
- Obey speed limits, which apply throughout the Park to protect animals, reduce disturbance, and avoid excessive dust on untarred roads.
- Not disturb or feed animals thus altering the natural systems. Monkey and baboons and hyenas lose their fear of humans if fed and they may become aggressive and a nuisance at picnic sites and rest camps.
- Make minimum noise which can disturb the wildlife and other visitors. Visitors are typically motivated by the wish to escape urban living and to enjoy nature. It is an unwritten rule that there must be silence in rest camps after 9 p.m.
- Observe camp hours. Rest camp gates are opened and closed at clearly stated hours and visitors must be off the roads in the hours of darkness. This is to protect the wildlife, much of which hunts at night, is very difficult to see, and sometimes sleeps on tarred roads that retain day-time heat during the cold nights.

Apart from the above basic visitor rules enforced throughout the Park, other visitor-related techniques contribute to sustainable tourism. The following are examples:

- Rondavels are thatched with grass collected in the Park to blend with the environment. Two brickworks are located within the Park and managed by the Park's Board to provide building and paving bricks. The Park is now self-sufficient in this regard and creates local jobs.

- Road signs and other signboards are made from materials found within the Park and designed to blend in with the environment. Road signs are constructed from rock, which serves to make them elephant-proof. Inside the rest camps, signboards are mostly engraved on wood.
- Wood for fires – South Africans are as committed to barbecues as Australians, and most cook their own food in the camps. Wood has been imported into the Park since the 1970s so that naturally occurring dead wood rots and lies *in situ*, playing its own part in the local ecosystem. Fallen trees also prevent soil erosion and create natural seedbeds for grass.

Rest camp design and visitor interpretation

Most of the rest camps in the Park were established long before 1990s notions of sophisticated visitor management were considered. Some of the core concepts originate from the 1930s and it is remarkable with hindsight to see how far the early camps reflected what are now considered to be models of good practice. The Skukuza Camp design includes:

- The use of traditional architecture for the rondavels.
- Accommodation units adequately spaced to ensure privacy and laid out on circular or fork-shaped routes to minimize car traffic disturbance.
- All huts within easy walking access to the central facilities of shops and restaurants.
- The use of well-designed attractive visitor reception areas where arrivals are greeted and registered and good use is made of the key interpretation techniques.
- Provision of information packs, literature which may be purchased, and maps, photo-

graphs, posters and displays around the reception area – Skukuza also has its own museum.
- Maintenance of security systems at Park gates where visitors' pre-booked accommodation permits are checked and capacity controls are maintained.

One of the newer rest camps, Berg-en-dal, was completed in 1983. This camp is zoned to accommodate the various visitor types in different areas. Day visitors, camp residents and staff are separated so as to avoid the groups impinging on others. Experience has shown that different visitor groups may have negative impacts on each other. The central facilities are shared by all and strategically sited for maximum accessibility.

To provide visitors to the Park with greater opportunities to achieve closer contact with nature, the following initiatives were introduced:

- 1979 – Introduction of guided wilderness trails. There are now seven such trails for eight visitors a time in a group which departs from a base camp on foot under the guidance of two armed game rangers. Bush camps, which provide these trails, are built to be in harmony with the environment and this form of tourism has the minimum impact on nature yet allows for the highest form of visitor interpretation. The trails must be pre-booked and are extremely popular, often achieving 100 per cent occupancy rates.
- 1994 – Guided night rides were introduced. Just before nightfall, one of the main hunting times for wildlife, ten vehicles specially equipped for the purpose and carrying twenty visitors each leave the main rest camps to give visitors the opportunity to observe the Park at night. These tours have minimum environmental impact and are profitable as well as increasing visitor appreciation of the Park.
- Educational bush drives can be arranged at three of the rest camps. A maximum of seven visitors can be taken out by an experi-

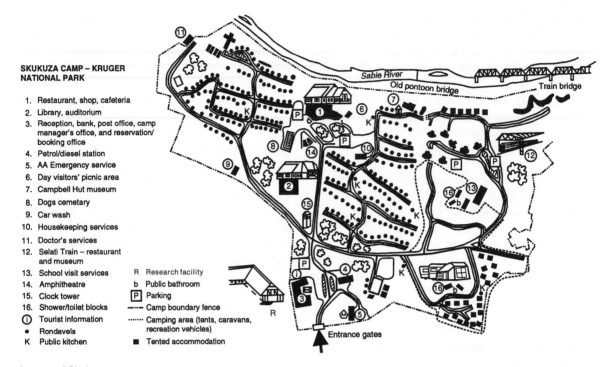

SKUKUZA CAMP – KRUGER NATIONAL PARK

1. Restaurant, shop, cafeteria
2. Library, auditorium
3. Reception, bank, post office, camp manager's office, and reservation/booking office
4. Petrol/diesel station
5. AA Emergency service
6. Day visitors' picnic area
7. Campbell Hut museum
8. Dogs cemetary
9. Car wash
10. Housekeeping services
11. Doctor's services
12. Selati Train – restaurant and museum
13. School visit services
14. Amphitheatre
15. Clock tower
16. Shower/toilet blocks
   ⓘ Tourist information
   • Rondavels
   K Public kitchen

R   Research facility
b   Public bathroom
P   Parking
---   Camp boundary fence
·····   Camping area (tents, caravans, recreation vehicles)
■   Tented accommodation

Layout of Skukuza camp

Current issues, opportunities and threats for the future

The Kruger Park has survived various threats to its continued existence as a dedicated nature reserve. In 1992 a prominent ANC leader, subsequently to be Minister of Land Affairs, hinted that state-owned land such as the Park should be considered for farming purposes. The statement was quoted out of context but it set in motion a large-scale lobbying process by the National Parks Board. ANC leaders were invited to the Kruger and other national parks to show not only the significance of the ecosystem protected in the parks but also the benefits of tourism to

enced and trained game ranger providing an opportunity to learn some of the intricacies of the Park's ecosystems.

host communities. One of the results of this effort is the current drive to involve the adjacent (mostly deprived) communities on a greater scale, and to make a contribution to the quality of their lives. This project is still in its early days but the success or failure of community partnerships in delivering quantifiable benefits is certain to influence whether or not the Kruger Park survives in its present form.

Bearing in mind that over 95 per cent of Park visitors up to the late 1990s have been relatively prosperous white South Africans, and that the National Parks Board management were all white, with segregation of staff living quarters in the Park, the Kruger Park was clearly vulnerable to change in the new South Africa. In mid-1996 the National Parks Board had grown from twelve to eighteen members and four were black South Africans including the Chairman. The Parks Board has committed itself to affirmative action to change its current staff composition.

More black South Africans will be appointed to management and other positions, and formerly separate staff living areas are being integrated.

The pipeline and road proposal across the Park is noted in the Introduction. The other major threat facing the Park is to its water supply. In the early 1960s the rivers in the Park started to show signs of stress. Increased irrigation, forestry, industrial and mining activities, as well as urbanization in neighbouring areas, led to a heavier load of pollutants in the rivers. As more people settle outside the Park but in the catchment area of the rivers, the demand for water increases. The lack of treatment of waste materials from what are mainly rural settlements raises the nutrient level in the rivers, altering the local ecosystem. Aggravating the water problem, the Park had its worst ever recorded drought in 1992/3, when all the perennial rivers either stopped flowing or experienced tremendous pressure. Water shortages also affect visitors and the Park's contingency plans date back to the 1960s when boreholes were first sunk and emergency storage dams built. Water-saving devices have been installed in the rest camps but the problems remain.

In the late 1990s Park managers have succeeded in developing and implementing sustainable tourism policies and practices over the years, involving government, the Parks Board and private sector partners. They have thus far resisted the easy option of overdevelopment by building to satisfy demand and have an enviable record of revenue generation from tourism, and good practice in visitor information and interpretation. Late in 1996 the Chief Executive of the Parks Board resigned in response to the board's policy decision to further develop revenue-earning activities and this may cause a rift between the conservationists and those responsible for commercial decisions.

The three main challenges facing the Park are to involve the adjacent local communities in the benefits of sustainable tourism, to successfully complete the affirmative action programme, and to generate more revenue in such a way that the wilderness character remains intact. All will be easier to achieve if the Park gains World Heritage Site status.

(Case contributed by Professor J. Alfred Bennett, Rand Afrikaans University, South Africa with contributions from the National Parks Board and Kruger Park personnel)

Main sources used

Carruthers, J., *The Kruger National Park: A Social and Political History*, Pietermaritzburg, University of Natal Press, 1995.

The Economist, London, 6 July 1996.

National Parks Board, *Kruger National Park: A World Heritage Site* (Proposals of 1995), Pretoria.

National Parks Board, *Annual Reports* from 1989/90 to 1994/5.

Stevenson-Hamilton, J., *South African Eden*, Struik, Cape Town, 1993.

Selected articles from several editions of *Custos*, the National Parks Board journal.

Quicksilver Connections Ltd, Great Barrier Reef, Australia

Introduction

Quicksilver Connections Ltd is a large marine day-tour operator based in Port Douglas some 70 km North of Cairns in Queensland, Australia. It is a commercially run business, a market leader in its sector of a very competitive industry, and its operations are based in the Cairns sector of the Great Barrier Reef Marine Park. From its beginnings in 1979 as a small family-owned business it has grown into a multi-million-dollar firm, developing with the rapid growth of the tourism industry to North Queensland.

In particular, Quicksilver Connections grew in the last decade with the international growth of tourist interest in the environment and ecology generally, which Australia has taken very seriously. The company now takes almost 200 000 visitors a year to experience directly the quality of the environment at the Great Barrier Reef, one of the world's most precious and irreplaceable marine environments, designated a World Heritage Site.

This case is of particular interest because it demonstrates a close working partnership between a commercial operator based on a highly sensitive natural resource and a public-sector authority responsible for the integrity of the local environment. It is focused on a combination of high product quality and sustainable practices that are the principal themes of this book. As the case shows, the practical linkages between the operator and other bodies concerned with the Reef are extensive. The balance achieved in the late 1990s between regulation by the Marine Park Authority and self-regulation by the operator is impressive.

The attention to detail in applying the *Ten R's* (see Chapter 11) is of particular interest. The creative use of Reef Biosearch, an arm of the company which simultaneously conducts research into the reef environment and whose personnel act as interpreter/guides to inform and educate visitors, appears to be in the vanguard of practical and attractive methods for influencing visitor behaviour on sensitive sites.

Background

Quicksilver's company philosophy or *mission* is a commercial commitment to leadership in product quality within a declared and practical approach to the environment. It is summarized as 'to provide an unsurpassed Great Barrier Reef experience'. To that end there has been a major investment in the vessels, pontoons and other hardware used for the operations which amounted to some A$10 million in 1995. Although the operations are capital intensive, economies of scale help to contain the per capita cost. In no sense is this a mass market product. All product options are focused on the quality of the environment available on the Reef, catering for a series of upmarket niche segments, and providing access to the Reef. There is a range of visitors from qualified scuba divers seeking to experience one of the world's most precious marine environments, through those requiring a more general ecotourism experience through snorkelling, to others content with viewing the Reef from glass bottomed boats or from the pontoons.

In 1995 there were two permanently moored floating reef platforms or pontoons, with one to follow in 1996, two state-of-the art wave-piercing catamarans with a total capacity for some 1000 visitors per day, and a sailing catamaran for a further 150 visitors. The day excursions operate to dedicated sites on both the outer Reef and an inshore coral cay not far from the site where Captain Cook ran aground in *Endeavour* on a coral reef in 1770.

The Great Barrier Reef is the core resource on which all of Quicksilver's products are based. It is both the major attraction and principal long-run business asset. Self-interest at least as much as regulatory pressure dictates that Reef protection and conservation are integral aspects of its operations.

Rationale for a sustainable strategy

The Great Barrier Reef Marine Park was established by the Australian Government in 1975 to manage the various uses of the very large area off its East Coast which, in total, comprises some 2900 individual reefs, 300 coral cays and 618 continental islands extending for around 2300 km. In recognition of its international ecological significance and biodiversity, the Reef was designated a World Heritage Area by UNESCO in 1981. The Reef provides a natural habitat for some 1500 species of fish and 350 species of coral including some endangered species. It is a fragile area clearly in need of responsible management to control its various uses which included shipping and commercial fisheries.

An important part of the management strategy for the Marine Park is the zoning of specific areas for recreational and tourism uses based on specific commitments to sustainability. Operators such as Quicksilver Connections Ltd are licensed for such purposes with a requirement to meet agreed environmental standards.

Partnerships involved

To some extent the fact of operating within a designated and closely regulated Marine Park automatically ensures that there is close collaboration between the commercial operators and the Authority. In the case of Quicksilver, the managing director in 1995 was a member of the Barrier Reef Consultative Committee; board member of the Cooperative Research Centre for the Great Barrier Reef; and board member for the Association of Marine Park Tour Operators. On the wider scene he was also a board member of the Tourism Council of Australia, a member of the Queensland Government's Regional Tourism Ministerial Advisory Council; the Maritime Industries and Science Council, and Chairman of the Far North Queensland Promotion Bureau. The Reef Biosearch team (see below) is also linked with the Marine Park Authority and operates courses for other organizations. Forms of partnership have been developed with the residential community around Port Douglas and with local suppliers in Queensland (also noted below).

Programmes for sustainability

It is inevitable that taking over 200 000 visitors a year to dedicated sites within a delicate ecological system will have some impact on the natural environment. Quicksilver operations are, of course, confined to a small area of the Barrier Reef already zoned for visitor purposes by the Marine Park Authority. To minimize the impact in those locations to manageable proportions the following five specific management programmes are in place.

(1) The management of daily operations

- The use of permanently moored pontoons, originally capable of handling 100 persons but now developed to handle 450 persons each after transfer from the catamarans. These are complex ecofriendly structures costing some A$1.8 million to construct.
- Mooring is a sophisticated process, mainly in sandy areas, aimed at minimizing damage to the coral – the visiting boats are not separately anchored. The pontoons are designed to withstand cyclone force winds to prevent damage from dragging moorings. Separate day moorings are laid for use by boats taking groups for accompanied dives.
- Pontoons are placed in areas where water depth minimizes physical damage from people standing on or knocking into the coral.
- Provision of non-contact access to the reef through the use of semi-submersibles and glass-bottomed boats.
- Supervision of groups by diving instructors/ marine biologists as well as the interpretation lectures to prevent unnecessary contact with the reef and minimize as far as possible the taking of souvenir coral or shells. Underwater signs are also used to guide divers away from fragile places.
- Use of the time taken to reach the Reef to show an audiovisual of the Reef and its environment and lectures by the Biosearch team (see below) to explain its importance and how to get the best from a visit without causing damage to ecosystems. The lectures are backed up by the distribution of leaflets in seven different languages.
- Daily monitoring of the Reef's ecosystem such as water temperature, water quality, level of nutrients, state of the coral and so

on, as part of routine operations and to contribute to ongoing research noted below.

(2) The formation of Reef Biosearch

Reef Biosearch is an arm of Quicksilver which employs a team of professional marine biologists to conduct daily monitoring and research operations on the coral and also to implement the education and interpretation programme noted in (3) below. The research is designed to evaluate natural changes occurring on the Reef as well as the effects of visitor impact on the local environment around the pontoons. It also monitors the impact of other influences such as the nutrient-rich run-off from rivers and streams that flow into the sea and the high nutrient output of sewage-disposal plants serving local industries and residents (including the shore-based tourism industry), which currently provide only primary or secondary level treatments. Such research is seen as vital to ensure the preservation of the Reef and also to sustain the long-term future for cruise operators.

Biosearch also acts as a research contractor for other organizations concerned with the biology of the Reef. It is linked with the Great Barrier Reef Marine Park Authority and the Department of National Parks and Wildlife. GBRMPA appoints an independent company to oversee monitoring work that is directly related to Quicksilver Operations. The overall effect of its daily research and monitoring programmes helps Quicksilver to put itself at the leading edge of best practice in sustainable management of the Reef environment.

(3) Education and interpretation

Quicksilver work on the principle that 'the more that people understand about the delicate structure of coral reefs and the creatures that inhabit them, the more they will care' (Max Shepherd, Director of Operations). Every tour participant is provided with an audiovisual explanation of the Reef and lectures from the team of biologists who travel on all tours and combine their monitoring activities with other duties of guiding visitors and helping them to get the most value from a visit by personal explanation and provision of information. There is already a short course on the biology of the Barrier Reef for which accreditation is being sought from the Australian Tourism Training Review Panel. Quicksilver induction training is conducted on a one-to-one basis covering all aspects of the operation including vessel handling, safety, reef interpretation and environmental best practices.

In addition to the education and interpretation programmes for visitors, and as part of the programme to support the local community, lectures and reef trips are conducted for secondary schools, technical and further education colleges, and university groups.

(4) Waste management

Quicksilver use a systematic audit-based waste-management programme designed where possible to re-use materials, to recycle waste, and prevent the use of any toxic chemicals (for example, by sterilizing snorkelling equipment ashore). Waste products are carried away from the Reef for disposal. The vessels use non-toxic types of antifouling for the hulls requiring weekly scrubbing and there are no discharges onto the reef apart from small quantities of fresh water from showering. No soaps and shampoos are permitted and showers are unheated and hand pumped to discourage waste. To minimize pollution arising from visitors and staff on-site, all vessels and the platforms are provided with holding tanks for sewage and detergent-charged water, which is returned to the vessels and released in deep water distant from the Reef. In 1996 there was not an option for onshore discharge although operators and government were working towards the early development of onshore discharge facilities. Pollution and nutrient levels on the Reef are, however, monitored continuously as noted above. Crockery and cutlery are mostly re-usable and the use of plastics and superfluous packaging is limited.

(5) Local product purchasing policies

Local purchasing is significant with some A$28 000 and A$16 000, respectively being spent, for example, every week on food and fuel. All Quicksilver vessels and other structures are constructed in Cairns and a policy to purchase locally wherever possible is in place.

Budgets and staffing

The annual turnover of the operation based at Port Douglas was of the order of A$20 million in 1995 and Quicksilver employed a staff of 145 across a range of occupations including boat crews, catering, marketing, administration and some ten marine biologists/interpreters. The exact cost of the environmental management systems cannot be specified precisely because it has become an integral part of the quality of operations. The overall cost of operating according to long-run sustainable principles is nevertheless estimated at between 10 per cent and 20 per cent of annual costs although a proportion of this is offset through economies of scale and marketing efficiency – it is not simply passed on in additional prices charged to visitors.

All staff receive training to develop their understanding of sustainable operations and develop their interest and skills. The team of biologists set a standard which all staff strive for, and the idea of 'ownership' of the Reef is instilled into staff who become very protective of the Reef sites.

Achievements and lessons learned

Quicksilver Connections is operating at the leading edge of sustainable practice for the recreational/tourism use of the Barrier Reef for which there are no precedents. The company's determination to ensure the sustainability of its operations, combined with the lack of existing information on best practice in the marine tourism industry, 'has meant that it had to pioneer by trial (and sometimes error), equipment design innovations and site management practices. Primarily these innovations and practices have been in the area of mooring designs, floating reef platforms, and control of in-water activities'. As noted above, the combination of five separate programmes to achieve sustainability lies at the heart of the endeavour. This is a form of self-regulation, imposed out of concern for the sustainability of the operations and achieved at considerable cost. But it has meant that the operator can often act ahead of but in line with the direction of the regulatory process established and controlled by the Marine Park Authority. In this way, self-regulation and regulatory practice become mutually informing and reinforcing over time.

As of 1995 Quicksilver detected no clear customer preference leading to a measurable financial advantage for operators who manage their business operations sustainably. This is expected to change over the next decade as the level of customer awareness of environmental issues increases and it may be boosted by a possible Australian scheme to recognize and promote through formal accreditation those operators who achieve agreed standards. In this context, perhaps, because environmental quality is built into and energetically marketed within the overall Quicksilver concept of product quality, the company will be a leader in the field. This is likely to be true in the Cairns area of the Barrier Reef but also in Australia more generally. In that broad context, a marketing advantage is likely to flow from leadership status.

'Sustainable use of a given site for tourism purposes is sometimes seen as a contradiction in terms, especially if large operators like Quicksilver are involved. Admittedly sustainable use does pose a complex management problem for which well-thought out strategies are required. In Quicksilver's case, these strategies have involved the education of passengers as to acceptable and unacceptable practices while on site (influencing their behaviour); non-intrusive but nonetheless present supervision of passengers; design and/or purchase of equipment capable of being used with minimal site damage/modification; the engendering in all staff of a sense of responsibility towards the Reef; and the establishment of systems to allow a two-way flow of information from operations staff to management so that the success of new site practices can be quickly assessed, or site management concerns identified before serious problems arise' (p. 153).

Source: Quotations are from Crabtree, A., 'Quicksilver Connections', in Harris, R. and Leiper, N. (eds), *Sustainable Tourism: An Australian Perspective*, 1995, pp. 145–156. Alice Crabtree is a former marine biologist employee of Quicksilver.

(Case contributed by Max Shepherd, Operations Director of Quicksilver Connections Ltd, Port Douglas, Queensland, Australia)

Edinburgh's Old Town, UK

Introduction

Few cities in the world rank with Edinburgh in terms of its history, architecture, and quality of life for the people who live and work there. It has been a magnet for tourism for many decades and plays a special role as a major attraction for overseas visitors to the U.K. and as the primary gateway to Scotland. But Edinburgh is also a vibrant, modern city preparing itself for the challenges of the twenty-first century, and has to come to terms with its overall economic growth, its traffic congestion and its role for tourism. At its heart is the world famous 'Old Town', including the castle and the Royal Mile, which is Scotland's premier visitor destination attracting over 8 million visitors a year in the late 1990s.

Edinburgh attracts international visitors and visitors from England as well as serving an important role for domestic tourism and recreation within Scotland. The economic impact of this volume of visitors on Edinburgh's and indeed on Scotland's economy is therefore, substantial. The Edinburgh Visitor Survey estimates that visitors to Edinburgh's Old Town contributed over £340 million to the local economy in the late 1990s, and directly and indirectly sustain over 20 000 jobs in the City alone, with additional contributions to the rest of Scotland.

The objectives addressed in this case study are how to revitalize and regenerate the historic, physical and social environment of an international heritage resource that had become a traffic polluted and partly run-down urban area by the end of the 1980s, and restore it in ways that would enhance its own integrity and historic sense of place, at the same time contributing to an important tourism economy.

This case helps to demonstrate the importance of research in identifying the issues to be resolved and, although it is not specifically covered in this case, the Edinburgh Old Town Renewal Trust had access to what is probably the best market research available for any city or town in the UK in the late 1990s. The Old Town redevelopment and the Action Plan addressed in this case are the achievements of a public sector partnership formed for the purpose, embracing community interests and also private sector initiative crucial to economic success. It was selected as a leading, innovative approach to the problem of encouraging tourism while respecting and securing the environment, and recognized as a UK winner in the prestigious European Prize for Tourism and the Environment in 1995, an annual award made by the European Commission to destinations which most innovatively and effectively develop a tourism policy respecting the environment.

Background

Perhaps surprisingly, although there was never any doubt about the importance of Edinburgh for Scottish tourism, prior to 1989 the value and importance of the physical fabric of the Old Town to tourism in Edinburgh and Scotland was largely unrecognized. Its importance was highlighted by the *Edinburgh Tourism Review* (KPMG, 1990, unpublished report), however, which identified threats and pressures on the historic fabric recommending that unless a comprehensive series of physical and environmental improvements were undertaken, Edinburgh's Old Town was in danger of slipping into a spiral of possibly terminal decline.

By the late 1980s Edinburgh's Old Town was characterized by a great number of derelict buildings and gap sites that blighted the area. The internationally famous Royal Mile, with the Castle at the top and the Royal Palace of Holyrood House at the bottom, and another twenty visitor attractions in between, was littered with vacant shopfronts and derelict upper floors which hardly reflected its position as Scotland's most popular visitor destination. Key arterial routes to and from the Old Town were underwhelming in appearance and provided nothing by way of encouragement to visitors to enter and spend time in the area to purchase local goods and services. There was, therefore, little doubt that a comprehensive programme of physical improvements was necessary which, coupled with the increasing recognition of the importance of customer care and staff development training, would serve to transform Edinburgh's Old Town.

The 1990 tourism review and its comprehensive remit was, over time, to prove to be the foundation of many of the successful improvements that have taken place in Edinburgh and thereby ensured its continuing pivotal role for Scottish tourism.

Rationale for a sustainable strategy

No capital city can remain static. Even if there were no faults of the past to correct, there would still be the challenges of the present to provide for. Sustainable development is one of them. In Edinburgh it is widely recognized that it is visitors' perception of the quality of the environment that dictates their economic contribution to the area. One of the most significant differences between Edinburgh's Old Town and many

other traditional inner city areas, however, lies in its continuing role as a vibrant residential and recreational area, which springs to life when its cluster of civic, legal, educational and religious headquarters close for the night.

This variety of uses gives the Old Town its unique character but also generates competing demands on its environment. In order to ensure a productive balance between the needs of residents, visitors and businesses in the area, the Edinburgh Old Town Renewal Trust (EOTRT) was formed in 1990. The Trust is a partnership funded by Lothian and Edinburgh Enterprise Ltd (LEEL, which is part of the Scottish Enterprise Network), the City of Edinburgh District Council, the Lothian Region Council and Historic Scotland, an executive agency within the Scottish Office which advises on various matters relating to historic buildings. While the EOTRT does administer conservation and other grant funding to assist with the improvement of important listed buildings and other visitor services, its remit and role is of far greater strategic importance. Through its three advisory groups: Development Quality, Economic Development and Service Quality, it provides a vital link with the local residential and business communities. These advisory groups have representatives not only of the funding agencies but importantly include local residents, the local business association, the Edinburgh Tourist Board, and the Chamber of Commerce.

- The Development Quality group aims to encourage high-quality new developments and appropriate changes of use of existing properties.
- The Economic Development group seeks to generate new ideas to improve the commercial vitality of the area: for example, late opening initiatives backed by media advertising; public entertainment festivals and events; and marketing campaigns to reinforce the area's appeal.
- The Service Quality group is more concerned with 'housekeeping' issues such as discoura-

ging flyposting, removal of graffiti, street cleaning and licensing issues.

Collectively this forum for partnership and consultation ensures that visitors' demands on the area are balanced with the practical day-to-day requirements of others who live and work in the area. In effect these challenging demands are what give the Old Town its vitality and vibrant character and, providing that a sustainable balance is maintained, its attractiveness as a place to live, work and visit is assured.

Objectives and principal initiatives

While the rejuvenation of Edinburgh's Old Town became a key objective for the public agencies in Edinburgh, its successful transformation resulted from finally recognizing the importance of the Old Town environment to tourism, and the importance of tourism to the local economy. This can be shown diagramatically as follows:

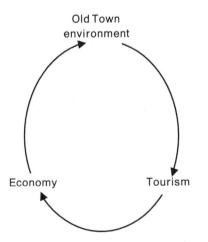

The importance of the environment and tourism to Edinburgh's economy

Today this simple but crucial relationship between the quality of the environment, tourism and the economy underpins the restoration and management of historic cities and towns gener-

ally; or should do so if they are to be commercially successful.

In Edinburgh's Old Town the Royal Mile is the main pedestrian arterial route linking the Castle at the top with the Palace of Holyrood House at the bottom and over twenty other attractions along its route. It is also joined and bisected by a series of streets and closes (lanes) that lead to a host of other places of interest within the Old Town. Prior to 1993 this vital city route was polluted and dominated by vehicular traffic. Today it is well on its way to becoming one of the most attractive public spaces in the United Kingdom.

- Following a series of comprehensive consultations with local residents, businesses, representatives of local authorities and other civic bodies a new high-quality pedestrian-friendly environment has been created. The emphasis is on allowing and encouraging pedestrians to move easily through the area at their leisure.
- Given the annual volume of visitors to the area, around 8 million a year in the late 1990s, the agreed policy of more than doubling the size of the pedestrian carriageway is fully justifiable. It was achieved through the sensitive design and use of high-quality traditional (sustainable) materials, and discouraging through vehicular traffic by altering junction priorities and enforcing traffic management regulations.
- These improvements have in fact served to create a new civic space that is well utilized both day and night. With an atmospheric array of café bars and street entertainment the Royal Mile now has a cosmopolitan feel and look to it that draws on Edinburgh's sense of place and simultaneously enhances it.
- At its heart is the historic Tron Kirk, which now serves as an Old Town visitor information centre and has access into Hunter Square. This square, around which all the buildings have been restored, and in which high-quality works of art are located, has

been given back to pedestrians and a new performance space provided for street entertainment.

- Following the physical improvements, a series of marketing and customer care initiatives are being implemented. These range from the creation of a new Old Town festival, late-night shopping promotions, an *Autumn Gold* short breaks entertainment programme, shopfront improvement assistance, and a series of tourism training initiatives targeted at local retailers and businesses.

These projects are starting to have the desired effect of encouraging more people to visit and explore the Old Town, stay there longer, and purchase more local goods and services. A comprehensive five-year economic impact survey is well into its second year (1995) and although it is too early to make long-term predictions about the success of these initiatives, early results are very encouraging.

Budgets and staff

We believe the successful transformation of Edinburgh's Old Town is primarily due to the coordinated partnership approach taken by the public authorities in making the Old Town a top priority for allocating resources. The allocation of resources through this partnership is facilitated by the development of an Old Town Action Plan, coordinated by the Old Town Renewal Trust, which highlights development opportunities and appropriate uses for sites and buildings that were either derelict or underutilized in the early 1990s. This focus, together with a long-term commitment to the future of the Old Town, ensures that adequate resources are made available for a rolling programme of improvements.

Communicating the value and rationale for these improvements and future proposals is a key feature within such a sensitive area. Following the success of a temporary shopfront exhibition as part of the Royal Mile project, for

example, another derelict shop is being refurbished to give the Old Town Trust a presence on the Royal Mile itself. This will enable visitors, residents, and businesses to see what is going on and planned by the Trust partners.

Results

Edinburgh's Old Town has been substantially refurbished and improved in recent years and every attempt is being made to maintain this momentum through allocating sufficient resources towards a coordinated series of integrated improvements that are designed to enhance and sustain this unique product. The approach was formally recognized as a good example of international best practice when Edinburgh's Old Town achieved an Award as one of the UK winners of the European Commission's Tourism and Environment Awards.

More importantly, the quality and ambience of a visit to the Old Town today shows a remarkable transformation from the late 1980s, with the most encouraging aspect being the number of visitors who are meandering on foot along the Royal Mile and exploring the series of improved streets and closes that lead off it. This is the true test of the success of physical regeneration and environmental improvement projects aimed at visitors to historical cities. In Edinburgh, the Old Town is once again bustling with visitors whose expenditure produces a very substantial contribution to the local economy. The virtuous circle may not yet be complete but the spiral of decline has more than been reversed and the economic prosperity of the Old Town looks assured.

Future developments

Within the next five years it is intended to complete the physical transformation of the Royal Mile and fully extend the traffic-calming measures along its length. This, coupled with the development of a substantial new commercial, leisure and residential development on a former brewery site adjacent to Holyrood Palace, will encourage visitors to explore more of the Old Town, stay longer and purchase more local goods and services. In addition, a comprehensive series of shopfront improvements are currently underway and a new entertainment strategy will be used to develop new events, attractions and exhibitions into the area.

It will also be necessary to establish a more permanent visitor centre in the Old Town if its ambition to achieve World Heritage Site status is to be achieved. Similarly, current proposals to create the post of Manager for the Old Town need to be developed along with a more co-ordinated marketing and signage strategy. The Old Town also has great potential to attract more speciality quality retailers given the number and relative affluence of visitors to the area.

The most important lesson learned in the past five years is that the quality of the environment within historic town centres is of substantial economic importance to the local tourism market. Unless a premier product is created, maintained and enhanced, business will be lost to other competitor cities which may have started with a vastly inferior product but have created a clean, safe and attractive environment in which visitors 'feed good'. Where the 'feel-good' environmental factor exists, visitors will tend to return rather than visit other cities that might previously have been perceived as offering a more attractive product. For a city such as Edinburgh, dependent on a very high level of repeat visits, this is a vital issue for a sustainable future.

(Case contributed by Robert A. Downie, Tourism Manager for Lothian and Edinburgh Enterprise Ltd)

Anglian Water Services Ltd: Rutland Water, UK

Introduction

Rutland Water is Anglian Water Services Ltd's largest reservoir, with a water surface of 1260 hectares surrounded by 500 hectares of land, located in the county of Rutland in England. It lies approximtely 100 miles north of London, and some 35 miles east of Birmingham, meeting the water needs of around half a million people resident in the five counties surrounding it. The reservoir is a man-made lake, created between 1972 and 1977 by constructing an earth dam across the river Gwash to impound two tributaries into a Y-shaped valley. It is the largest artificial lake in England and replenished by water pumped through an extensive system of tunnels and pipelines from two larger rivers, the Nene and the Welland. It is located in an area of considerable natural beauty, mainly used for agricultural purposes, with numerous attractive villages within a 10–15-mile radius.

From early planning stages it was appreciated that the reservoir could become an important venue for countryside leisure and watersports, recognizing that several million people live within around an hour's driving time. Today, Rutland Water has achieved an international reputation for sailing, trout fishing and wildlife through careful development and management of both its natural and built environments, and its visitors. A sustained growth in visitor num-bers, including many who stay overnight, has been achieved in tandem with a programme of internationally recognized environmental improvements to the benefit of local communities and wildlife.

Traditionally in the UK, the provision of water services was a public sector operation. As part of a government decision to privatize large parts of the public sector, Anglian Water became a private limited company in 1989, many years after the original public sector decision to create a reservoir and develop it for tourism and recreation purposes. But it is significant to note how the original plans have been developed by a private sector operator as explained in this case. The provision of water supplies remains the primary objective of Rutland Water, but the current additional mix of facilities and services for recreation and tourism co-exist with a clear commitment to good environmental practice in operations and in creating a scenic amenity of very high standards. Along with Edinburgh Old Town, Rutland Water was selected as a UK winner in the prestigious European Prize for Tourism and the Environment in 1995. It was recognized for its excellence in the development of good practice for balancing sucessful management of water resources, in a site of outstanding 'natural' beauty and scientific interest, with sustainable visitor pressures.

Background

Following completion in 1977, recognizing its natural scenic and wildlife qualities, the whole of Rutland Water and its perimeter was designated as a Site of Special Scientific Interest (SSSI) in 1983. It was further designated a Special Protection Area and an international Ramsar Site for its habitat and waterfowl in 1991, the first man-made site to receive both of these designations.

A Visitor Centre has been built on the south shore of the lake, and is complemented by a more prestigious Birdwatching Centre on the West shore. Combined with seventeen bird hides and nature trails surrounding the lagoons, managed woodland and grassland habitat, these offer high-quality services to birdwatchers from throughout the world.

Anglian Water has widened the appeal of Rutland Water to tourists in the last decade or so by adding interests beyond the original concept of fishing, sailing and birdwatching opportunities which are traditionally provided at UK reservoirs. Participants in these specialist recreation activities are now a minority among visitors who enjoy the excellent access for walking and cycling around the waterside tracks, calling at the varied land-based attractions created along the route.

Day visits from the counties surrounding Rutland are still the predominant visitor group, but the creation of Rutland Water has led to a rapid growth in all grades of tourist accommodation from high-quality hotels, farmhouse bed and breakfasts, to dormitory bunk beds for youth groups. The Rutland area had reached nearly 1000 beds registered with the Area Tourist Board by 1990, mostly within 10 km of the reservoir. Accommodation has continued to grow through new developments and extensions to existing businesses throughout the life of the reservoir. A large time-share resort opened recently, doubtless influenced by the quality of the local environment and the facilities it offers.

Because the site does not have enclosed boundaries and gates for visitor admission, the precise number of visitors is not known, but estimates based on car park income and participation in recreational activities indicates a figure of between 0.6 and 1 million visits annually in the late 1990s. Public transport to the venue is very limited and car parking for 3500 vehicles is fully utilized on several occasions each summer.

Rationale for a sustainable strategy

The County of Rutland has an inscription 'Multum in parvo', meaning so much in so little, and this symbolizes the importance of Rutland Water within the local environment. The reservoir's water surface covers 3 per cent of the County area and places the nation's largest man-made lake in what is its smallest English county. Apart from the obvious obligation to manage and maintain water quality, there are five main aspects of the rationale for sustainable development:

- The relative scale of the reservoir, and the high environmental quality of its surroundings, places a huge responsibility upon Anglian Water to fulfil its statutory obligations in protecting the natural and built environment.
- Through careful planning and management the reservoir has been developed to blend into its surroundings giving the impression that it has always been there. Maintenance of that quality is an important role.
- The local community, which originally opposed the development, now accepts Rutland Water as its greatest asset providing significant employment and enhancing the local environment. This change in attitude has been gradually achieved over twenty-five years from initial consultation to maturation of the reservoir into a natural feature of the landscape.
- Rutland Water was designated as a Site of Special Scientific Interest within seven years

of its completion, primarily in recognition of its value to waterfowl. Since then the Ramsar designation and Special Protection Area under EU directives further recognize the value of the habitat as a whole.

- These designations establish constraints on any development or new activity likely to affect the environment and require additional consultation and agreement with English Nature and the Rutland County Council as the local planning authority.

Having achieved international recognition for Rutland Water's living environment, Anglian Water has invested in facilities enabling visitors to appreciate this aspect of the reservoir without detracting from its value.

Partnerships

The strength of Rutland Water as a recreation and tourist attraction lies primarily in having a wide variety of leisure opportunities set in an attractive natural environment. Reflecting the wide range of interests concerned with the environment surrounding the reservoir, the necessity for partnerships between public and private sector was recognized from the beginning. Accordingly, Anglian Water PLC has developed its links and underpinned the strength of the attraction as follows:

- Working together with Rutland County Council (since 1996, and its predecessor authorities) and the (former) East Midlands Tourist Board in agreeing Local Plans and Tourism Strategies for the area around Rutland Water, in the interests of both local communities and tourists. In particular the adoption and endorsement of these by the Rutland County Council is regarded as an indication of the successful integration of Rutland Water as a tourist attraction within the local community.
- Conservation development has been a 21-year partnership with the Leicestershire and Rutland Trust for Nature Conservation (LRTNC) with guidance from English Nature, a national statutory body which promotes directly and through others the conservation of wildlife and natural features. The LRTNC has played a vital role in establishing the extensive nature reserve funded by Anglian Water, and the success of this aspect has been the key to successfully balancing the pressures of recreation activity with the needs of wildlife.
- Coordination of these interests together with those representing the customers and Anglian Water's business partners at the reservoir, has been through the Rutland Water Users Panel. This group has convened, under the administration of Anglian Water, at least twice a year since before the reservoir's completion in 1977. The Users Panel represents County and former District Council, Rutland sailing and canoe clubs, wind-surfers, Rutland Fly Fishers, Salmon & Trout Association, horse-riders, Ramblers Association, Rutland Water Rescue Service, Leicestershire & Rutland Trust for Nature Conservation, National Farmers Union, and cyclists. The Users Panel is chaired by the Recreation Development Manager for Anglian Water. The success of this Panel has depended upon its members' acceptance of the need to change and enable the diversification of attractions around the reservoir.
- In 1985 Anglian Water's Rutland Water Information Centre became registered with the (former) East Midlands Tourist Board as a networked TIC and it is believed to be the only completely privately funded TIC in the region in the late 1990s.
- More recently a Rutland Tourism Association has been formed to meet the wider interests of the area as a whole and Anglian Water is one of the principal supporters of this organization.

(See also partnership marketing noted under programmes for implementation.)

Specific objectives, and programmes for implementation including marketing

Rutland is essentially a rural environment characterized by small farms, gentle hills, hedgerows bordering arable and grass fields, and localized woodlands. Buildings are mostly of traditional local stone construction with a few more recent brick developments. Accommodating the reservoir and its infrastructure within this setting has been a challenge successfully undertaken with the guidance of Dame Sylvia Crowe, landscape consultant to the scheme.

By using natural and reconstituted stone wherever practicable, planting 250 000 trees, re-shaping ground profiles, establishing new hedges and access routes avoiding residential areas and zoning recreational activity in both time and space, the reservoir has been blended into the environment and added to the value of the vital water resource as a tourist attraction.

Public transport is very weak in the vicinity of the reservoir and it has always been assumed that visitors would always arrive by car or chartered coaches. Parking for 3200 vehicles was originally provided and this has been extended to 3500 places, all carefully screened with landscaping and planting. This capacity partially limits the number of visitors but visitors park outside the site and walk or cycle in when this is reached.

The water environment too requires constant management. The reservoir is dependent on pumping from distant rivers and Anglian Water carefully controls abstraction to protect them and the recreation and wildlife habitat which they too provide. Anglian Water supplies 500 000 people with water continuously from the reservoir and the ability to balance inputs, outputs and water quality is crucial for both consumers and the environment of the reservoir.

Marketing strategies have been developed to recognize the venue's diverse attractions and the wide range of commercial interests. The majority of visitors are family groups seeking a low-cost day trip in attractive outdoor surroundings, and these are attracted through regional campaigns whereas the specialist angling and birdwatching visitors are targeted through specialist national media. The accommodation business targets customers from beyond the day trip radius of approximately 70 km but generally finds anglers and birdwatchers prepared to travel longer distances for a day trip or select lower cost B&B accommodation rather than hotels.

Rutland Water is marketed at three levels by different sectors of the leisure industry.

- As part of a wider tourism product by the County Council, District Council, The Regional Tourist Board and the Rutland Tourism Association
- As a single entity by Anglian Water and accommodation businesses
- As component attractions by Anglian Water and the independent businesses which operate in the vicinity of the reservoir

Joint marketing initiatives have been sponsored by coordination of these groups, for example exhibitions, events, brochures and advertising features in local and national press.

Market research

Visitor surveys have been used for some twenty years by Anglian Water, to identify the origins of visitors, group size, frequency of visits, and interests, and to assess visitor reaction to possible future development to meet customer needs. These have utilized the same personal interview technique on all four car parks with the equivalent five August and September weekend days in 1977, 1983, 1985 and 1991 giving directly comparable information.

Sample size has varied between 1000 and 1600 groups. Results in the 1991 survey showed increasing group size (4.1), more dispersed origins (59 per cent from outside Leicestershire) and a consistently high proportion of first-time visitors (25 per cent). These are important indicators in reviewing the management strategy of the venue. Results from the 1995 survey were not available at the time of preparing this case study.

Budgeting and staffing

Anglian Water has a policy that its recreation services should be self-financing and this is largely achieved through running active elements such as sailing, angling, catering and car parking, in order to support information services and nature reserves. The total turnover from recreation and tourism achieved by all the independent businesses around the reservoir is difficult to estimate but based on disclosed information and estimating from bed-occupancy rates in hotels it was probably approaching £10 million a year in the late 1990s, providing employment for around 250 people on a full- and part-time basis.

In common with other UK outdoor visitor attractions, the venue has a highly seasonal demand with 75 per cent of its visitors within 35 per cent of the year. This has important implications for budgeting and human resource management.

Achieving sustainability

The success of Rutland Water as a tourist attraction is largely attributable to successful integration into the natural environment, acceptance by the resident population and its attraction to a wide sector of the population as an enjoyable low-cost venue for a day-trip or short-break holiday. Specific elements of an overall sustainable programme are:

- Close cooperation with the planning authority and environmental agencies making it possible to meet and broadly balance the demands of anglers, sailors, birdwatchers, cy-

clists and walkers for access to this specially protected environment while enhancing the local economy.
- Maintaining high environmental standards, underpinning customer perceptions of the quality of the natural environment and provision of customer care, recognizing that the market for day-trip tourism is extremely competitive in the East Midlands.
- Managing flexibly to meet the changing market trends, for example a gradual reduction in demand for trout fishing from the bank (through increased competition), increased interest in wind surfing (a relatively new sport), off-road cycling (BMX mountain bikes and subsequent developments) and the highly mobile, modern birdwatcher ('twitchers' who will travel all day for a rare sighting). New and modified facilities have been created to accommodate these developments over the past five years.
- Developing mid-week and low-season business is critical to increase significantly the number of visitors without reducing the quality of their experience. The potential to increase peak-time visitor numbers is restricted by the capacity of the car parks and the cycle route on peak weekends.

Future developments from past experience

Rutland Water is one of the most important single water resources in the UK and the reservoir is still likely to have this status in one hundred years' time. Its value for recreation and tourism will probably be sustained while people are able to visit it, whether this is by solar powered cars or bicycles.

- Rutland Water's attractions, stemming from its high environmental value and education opportunities, will be developed further with the encouragement of the agreed Local

Plan and Tourism Strategy of the County Council.

- Long-distance cycle routes will help change the attraction of Rutland Water from being an enjoyable 2- to 3-hour ride for day trippers arriving by car to become a key stage and stop-over on major routes.
- Areas of existing weakness such as the diffuse marketing efforts of so many independent, varied interests will be tacked by developing more opportunities for coordination.
- The future at Rutland Water will see continued change in the relationship with the local community, which will strengthen its attraction to tourists.
- A key factor will be the development of Rutland County as one of the UK's smallest unitary public authorities (the local authority boundary designation in England and Wales applying from 1996) which will highlight the importance of Rutland Water to its identity and economy.

(Case contributed by David E. Moore, Recreation Development Manager, Anglian Water Services Ltd, UK)

Ironbridge Gorge Museums, UK

Introduction

Symbolized today by a magnificent wrought iron bridge which spans the river Severn over the Gorge that gives the site its name, the bridge itself is the product of what was dramatic new industrial technology when it developed there in the eighteenth century. There are eight museums presenting the restored and conserved remnants of a major industrial site located some 30 miles west of Birmingham. The Gorge is a natural feature of the historic landscape at the upper reaches of the navigable river Severn which provided vital access to the port of Bristol (nearly 100 miles distant) from where industrial products were shipped to the world. The location provided the necessary combination of wood, coal, iron ore, transport links and innovative engineering technology skills, and it is identified as the birthplace of the British industrial revolution whose industrial processes were the forerunners of first the European and then the American and Japanese industrial revolutions of the nineteenth century.

It is not too much to claim the area is the birthplace of global industrial technology and its workers the first skilled labourers of the modern capitalist economy. Although the area of the Gorge is now one of considerable natural beauty and nature conservation, it was a toxic industrial wasteland at the peak of its economic activities and arguably the birthplace too of global pollution and environmental degradation arising from industrial manufacturing processes.

In many ways the whole ethos of the Ironbridge Gorge restoration over the last thirty years reflects what has since become identified as sustainable development. This case debates some of the highly complex issues of managing a World Heritage Site which is adjacent to a large residential area, part of a dynamic diverse modern economy, and obliged by circumstances to blend the needs of conservation and sustainability with economic activities for historic monuments and buildings that make conservation possible. This is a story of partnership collaboration primarily between an independent museum trust using pioneering interpretation methods and public sector bodies and agencies responsible for different parts of sustainability in the Gorge. They all must have regard to commercial enterprises and community interests. The issues of achieving a sustainable balance between a cultural heritage resource of world status, the physical and natural environment, and the local economy and community – constant themes throughout this book – are fully reflected in the following pages.

Background

The heyday of heavy industrial operations in the Gorge was from the mid-eighteenth century to the early 1800s followed by a renaissance in decorative ironwork, tiles and china ware in the latter part of the nineteenth century. The area was an active but declining production site until between the two world wars. By the 1950s new technology and processes, different transport modes and the shift of industry to other areas left Ironbridge to fall into dilapidation and decay. The problems of halting and reversing the decline of such a major national site, and the employment prospects of the resident population it supported, were too great for the resources of locally elected governments. The process of recognizing the values of the site and developing the means of rescuing and restoring important parts of it did not start until a Development Corporation was established by the UK government, first in 1966 and re-formed in 1971. One of several such corporations in Britain, the intention was to create a new town to the west of Birmingham using public sector funding and land controls to leverage private sector investment in the area. The town is called Telford in recognition of the pioneering eighteenth century engineer but it is not located in the Gorge. The historic area serves as an important focus for Telford's image and spirit of place, and it serves as a recreational facility for the new urban population as well as being an international visitor attraction.

The key to Ironbridge's rescue was a partnership of effort reflected in a massive programme of conservation and restoration works by the Telford Development Corporation and the activity of the Ironbridge Gorge Museum Trust. Their joint objective was to rescue key buildings and monuments, repair them, and put them into sympathetic and broadly viable economic reuse, interpreting them as widely as possible to the visiting public and local population. The success of the restoration in preserving and interpreting the site in its impressive natural setting, and the way the remains are managed for the 'benefit of all humanity', led to the designation by UNESCO of Ironbridge Gorge as a World Heritage Site in 1986 for its 'exceptional and universal value'.

The Museum Trust was in the forefront of an international movement in the 1960s and 1970s to create a new type of heritage site, where the core collection was of monuments and buildings, seen as part of an industrial and post-industrial landscape, where interpretation extended to the re-creation and demonstration of historic industries, and where local people are involved as demonstrators, guides, fund-raisers and historians.

The Museum Trust and its sites

Opened to the public in 1967, the Ironbridge Gorge museums attracted some 10 000 visitors in the first year, reaching a peak of over 400 000 in 1988. Although revenue has continued to increase through visitor admissions and spending on-site, visitor numbers dropped at Ironbridge in the 1990s – as they did for most other UK museums – reflecting growing competition between an increasing number of attractions. The total for 1995 was around 300 000 visitors, generating a total turnover of some £10 million within the local community. The museums are the major employer in the heritage areas with some 160 full-time staff, ninety part-time staff in the peak season and over 350 volunteers in all.

The Museum Trust was established as an independent body and has become a model for many subsequent museums of industrial themes. The Trust is able to access funding from a range of national and European Union sources and operates its own trading company, but it is independent of national and local public sector bodies, and essentially the master of its own destiny.

Rationale for a sustainable strategy at Ironbridge and the partners involved

Over the last thirty years the Telford Development Corporation and the Museum Trust, working with local authorities, successfully created a new type of museum in the Gorge and established the dynamic of processes for the rescue of the whole area from dereliction and neglect. It has been transformed into an attractive place to live, work and visit. It continues to support a diverse economy ranging from heavy manufacture at the Coalbrookdale Foundry (using mostly traditional processes), to the numerous tourist enterprises – including eight different museum sites – which together provide most of the local employment.

It is important to understanding Ironbridge

and its development to recognize that a sustainable strategy for the heritage site is not a matter of a single monument or landscape that can be managed by a single enterprise or agency. The legacy of the new town development process is a group of 'leading' agencies, each with a main area of responsibility:

- The Museum Trust and English Heritage, for key monuments and buildings in the eight sites.
- The Severn Gorge Countryside Trust, endowed with land by the former Development Corporation and responsible for large areas of the wooded Gorge including some Special Sites of Scientific Interest (SSSIs).
- The local authorities and planners for the evocative industrial townscapes and residential settlements of the area (the new town Development Corporation was formally wound up in 1991/2 having completed its role and returned local government functions to an elected local authority).

Ten years after the UNESCO designation of World Heritage Site these bodies sat down to consider whether more needed to be done to protect and manage this remarkable testament to early industrialization. It rapidly became apparent that there were few, if any, useful models to help solve the management problems identified. The museum world has debated the idea of an *Eco-Musée*, a term used to describe a heritage site embracing monuments, buildings, landscape, industries and living communities. However, the central idea of an entire community participating as guardians and interpreters of heritage, although conceptually attractive, rapidly melts away in face of the real issues and motivations in a diverse and dynamic economy such as exists in the Gorge. Even in the better-defined area of historic conservation there are few new ideas about how to deal with large groups of redundant industrial buildings and structures, and even less to add to Ironbridge's particular contribution in the use of buildings as context for the

demonstration of historic industries such as iron rolling and founding and tile manufacture.

The conservation of the natural environment is on firmer ground when dealing with SSSIs – of which there are two important sites in the Gorge – but less so when trying to define what should be sustainable in a landscape that has been variously ravaged by industrial pollution, intensely managed and then totally neglected and, most recently, landscaped and made attractive in parts as a public amenity. Theoretical approaches such as Limits to Acceptable Change have little to say about landscapes that have suffered many violent changes over the centuries. Not even the formal planning experience of local authorities has much to offer in the way of a conceptual framework for dealing with the conflicting interests of heavy industry, a dormitory suburb, and tourist businesses such as accommodation, catering and retail, all densely woven into and around the historic fabric.

A strategy exercise which started off as a quest for a management plan has turned into something rather different: a *process* for working more closely together to identify and achieve sustainable solutions. Fundamental to this is the realization that there are three powerful sets of interests in the Gorge and that the task of management is to resolve conflict and seek cooperation to protect the heritage 'for the benefit of all humanity'. These forces are set out in the diagram overleaf.

Objectives and programmes for implementation

What emerged from the debate between the lead agencies is a series of review stages leading back repeatedly to reconsideration of a unifying objective or vision These stages are:

- Detailed enumeration and description of the Gorge in its heritage, natural and economic aspects.
- Agreement on a unifying vision of management.

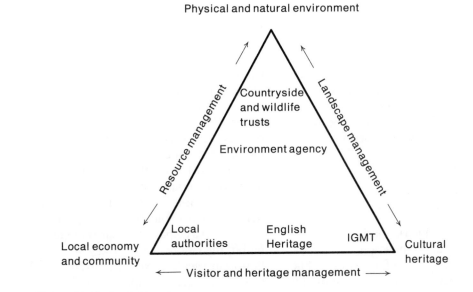

The sets of interest in the Ironbridge Gorge

- Review and evaluation of current management practices
- Analysis of longer term consequences of current management and external influences
- Testing the perceived consequences against the vision statement – and review of vision
- Priority programmes for short- and long-term actions

Description of the Gorge

A wealth of material now exists, ranging from the formal property and infrastructure records of local authorities, through the historical research and archaeological reports of the Museum Trust, to databases on the natural environment. There are exciting possibilities to correlate and handle this mass of data, which through computer systems could be accessible and useful to the general public and expert alike. In this respect, joint work by the agencies could create a new type of resource and interpretation for a historic site.

Meticulous recording of the site is also a good antidote to spurious arguments for conservation.

A perspective of the changes that have occurred, even in the last thirty years, illustrates *change* as a fundamental property and character of the area. The economic description of the Gorge fills in a further part of the argument by revealing a diverse economy and considerable employment, not only in the Coalbrookdale foundries and the obvious heritage and tourism industry but also in multifarious self-employment, craft workshops, etc.

Vision

So far this crucial stage has served mainly to illuminate the limits of the current management exercise. Each agency has its own vision of what it is aiming to do in the Gorge. This is fairly general in the case of the local authority seeking to make Telford a better place to live, but very specific in the case of the Museum Trust seeking to excel in the scope, innovation and breadth of its interpretation of early industrialization. These agencies do not share a detailed vision of how the Gorge might appear in thirty years time. The exercise has, therefore, become one of comparing visions and seeking an overall vision of management which is compatible with these. The result in early 1996 is shown below:

Vision Statement

The Ironbridge Gorge has achieved international recognition for the importance of its monuments to industrialization in their evocative setting and for the pioneering work which has made them widely accessible and celebrated.

As the lead agencies involved with the cultural and natural heritage of the Gorge, we aim to build on this foundation:

- To conserve the industrial heritage in a distinctive semi-natural landscape.
- To interpret it as a whole for a wide public.
- To contribute actively to the economic life of a diverse community.

In our management of the Gorge we will:

- Work together to achieve the highest standards.
- Protect the heritage whilst ensuring that it remains accessible to all.
- Seek to engage people and agencies in our efforts to manage the heritage for the benefit of present and future generations.

Current management programmes

The review between agencies usefully identified three key areas where they need to share common management principles.

Conservation of historic and natural heritage of the Gorge

A review of current preoccupations shows that all the agencies are still grappling with massive problems of stabilising the heritage in their care. This is true of important industrial buildings, such as the offices and workshops of the old Coalbrookdale Company, of prominent parts of the natural environment such as overgrown and neglected river banks and unmanaged woodlands, and of derelict and vacant lots within the townscapes.

The examination of current management issues reveals clearly that the pressures for change on the character of the Gorge are still those of decay and neglect (of historic buildings and landscape features) and of inappropriate development, principally in the erosion of the heritage character by the owners of private dwellings and shops. Such owners have a natural desire to modernize their properties, accommodate motor cars, take advantage of double-glazing and the cost advantages of plastic and other modern materials. There is scope for sensitively handled long-term education of the area's residents, which could be given greater authority with the participation of all the agencies active within the Gorge. Another key area of collaboration is in seeking external funding for heritage restoration, for example from the UK Lottery Fund for heritage

Access

This includes not only the obvious issues of traffic and visitor management, signposting and parking, but also access for disabled or partly abled persons, and access to relevant information.

Interpretation

Bearing in mind that the majority of the interpretation of historic sites in the Gorge is done by the Museum Trust, current management is identifying many areas where all the active agencies are playing a part in managing visitors at the destination, supporting the educational use of the Gorge, and presenting the Gorge as a whole.

Looking to the future – limits of planning

Reviewing the past thirty years, the responses outlined in this case may appear a rather modest response to the challenge of managing a World Heritage Site. It puts forward no great unifying vision of what the Gorge might look like in the future. It supposes no fashionable theory or model for managing the complex interactions of the three main elements:

- Local community – residents and local businesses – and the overall economy.
- The heritage business and
- The natural environment.

By aiming at a collaborative partnership management process rather than a master plan, there is an implicit acceptance of a gradualist and organic future for the Gorge in which the agencies most concerned will agree on some aims on behalf of their constituents, as set out above, and some coordination of their work. It is expected that it will also make it possible to deal sensitively and equitably with the three areas which will continue to generate conflicts of interest that have to be resolved:

- *Involvement of the community* The need to involve the community is clear. The problem is, which community? There are those who identify with tourism futures, and all are affected by it; those who identify with the natural environment in the area, and those who are most concerned with the needs and interests of residents. Community is a matter of perception and in a complex area such as the Gorge one cannot expect unanimity of views.
- *Conservation/heritage* The issue here is, what is to be conserved? What is the character of the heritage? It is difficult to find an acceptable rationale for freezing the post-industrial landscape as it exists today – which after all is an accident of timing. The whole Gorge has gone through several cycles of industrial development and neglect and has changed quite dramatically in appearance over the last thirty years alone. Which period ought to be conserved? Conservation is inseparable from an intelligent and creative view of the interpretation of heritage, but such a view is not without controversy. The current balance of conserving and operating flagship traditional processes in traditional buildings, with other buildings cheaply renovated to provide workshops for craftsmen and additional interest to visitors, imbues the Gorge with new life

and vigour but it is a working compromise and very different from a static view of the character of the area. The current compromise must be tested against the basic principles of conservation of intrinsic values for the sake of posterity.

- *Sustainability* Often based on the reasonable (but often illusory) notion that we can manage the flora and fauna in some way that is balanced and enduring, the application of the concept to historic industrial remains is misleading. Sustainability of a building in economic use can only be guaranteed as long as its use – as a museum, workshop, or youth hostel, for example – is maintained. There is, therefore, a fundamental conflict between a self-sustaining natural environment and a self-sustaining building in economic use which may require it to adapt and develop new uses as circumstances change. Some especially important monuments may be exempt from this because they will be endowed with resources to be maintained just as they were (Abraham Darby's original furnace in Coalbrookdale, for example), but for the rest their management and future poses quite different problems from those of the natural environment and conflicts are inevitable.

Tourism has been a key economic factor in justifying and generating resources put into the Gorge sites to arrest decay and to find ways of bringing parts of the heritage back into the economic life of the area. Not yet a major problem in the late 1990s, in the longer term the needs of visitors could bring new pressures to bear on the character of the area. It is a mutual management issue to study what are the constraints on the capacity of the Gorge to handle increased numbers of visitors without unacceptable loss of its character. We believe the collaborative process now established offers the best chance of success.

(Case contributed by Glen Lawes, Chief Executive of the Ironbridge Gorge Museum Trust)

Epilogue

Positive visions for sustainable tourism

A spectre is haunting our planet: the spectre of (mass) tourism ... In its modern guise ... it can ruin landscapes, destroy communities, pollute the air and water, trivialise cultures ... and generally contribute to the continuing degradation of life on our planet (Croall, 1995, p. 1).

A key conclusion of the Earth Summit (Rio, 1992) was the importance of harnessing the entrepreneurial drive of the private sector in the cause of environmentally compatible development. Travel & Tourism has a primary business as well as a moral interest. The environment is our core asset, the key component of product quality, and an increasing priority for our consumers (Lipman, G., in *AGENDA 21 for the Travel & Tourism Industry*, 1996, p. 3)

Opposing streams of thought about tourism and the environment – is it a blight or a blessing? – are encapsulated in the quotes above and have polarized the debate about the impact of tourism since they were first juxtaposed by George Young in 1973. All concerned with decision making in travel and tourism have to make up their mind where they stand on the issue of sustainability, and what they are going to do about it. Regrettably, but perhaps inevitably, environmental issues slipped down the agenda around the world after the heady commitments of Rio in 1992, as most governments grappled with the priorities of recovery from economic recession. But tackling environmental impact will not go away; it cannot be ignored; it offers endless opportunities for lobby groups to use the media to pillory what they perceive as a destruc-

tive global industry and to target the key players and their customers. As we approach the millennium, sustainable development and how to achieve it is the biggest issue facing all in tourism in the public and private sector, in large and small businesses alike. It is simultaneously the greatest weakness and threat, and the greatest strength and opportunity for global tourism development over the next decade.

The first quote reflects a now powerfully entrenched, doom-laden apocalyptic view, regrettably common among many academics debating the issues and others influential in the media. If anything, this view is probably gaining rather than losing ground. In his book, Croall adopts a typically selective and personal approach to travel and tourism, grandly ignoring the industry definitions worked out internationally since the 1960s, and simply inventing his own: 'I define a tourist as someone who makes a journey for leisure purposes ... to rural, coastal, mountain and wilderness destinations, many of which until recently have been free from an influx of outsiders' (Croall, 1995, p. 3). Fine for Mr Croall, but bogus, misleading and useless as an industry definition. It is, perhaps, akin to publishing a book on human anatomy defined as feet and elbows.

The second quote expresses the pragmatic action-oriented philosophy underlying this book. It treats the whole of travel and tourism as it is defined internationally, focusing on the potential for harnessing the continuous flow of global marketing energy to achieve sustainable goals. The problems of tourism are already well known and do not need restating here. What is needed are solutions and action. It is our view that a marketing perspective provides a well-developed, fully tested international framework for defining and implementing the necessary action, and for achieving solutions. It also provides a functional basis to underpin the local destination-based partnerships that are central to all solutions. Above all else, a marketing perspective opens the route to financial and management resources needed for effective action.

The reader has to choose between a sterile journalistic spectre, 'the haunting thought of an expected calamity', or a robust evolutionary philosophy of management action encompassing the most highly developed, explicit, and efficient set of integrated techniques for influencing the attitudes and behaviour of individuals and organizations that the world has ever known. Marketing is not an end or a goal; it is a means to an end and there is no contradiction whatever between the goal of sustainable development and the use of management methods based on a marketing perspective.

We have no pious expectations that the tens of thousands of human minds responsible for management decisions in travel and tourism will easily or quickly adopt sustainable goals in any altruistic way. We agree with Dawkins (1989), 'Much as we might like to believe otherwise, universal love and the welfare of the species as a whole are concepts that simply do not make evolutionary sense' (p. 2). Harnessing marketing energy to sustainable goals will not happen by spontaneous combustion and politicians' exhortation but fortunately there are no mysteries about the necessary processes. It requires only awareness and the will to act among the clearly identified players – recognizing and seeking to maximize their long-run commercial self-interests in protecting and sustaining the resource or asset base on which their industry futures and profits depend. This book provides ample evidence that this is now happening in many parts of the world and in all parts of the industry.

What follows offers seven positive visions for sustainable tourism in the twenty-first century.

1 If a marketing perspective has such obvious and powerful advantages, why hasn't it supported sustainability thus far?

This is a good question. The answer is, that with few exceptions until around 1990–92, senior managers in the industry outside air transport were either not aware of the environmental issues that have since become all too obvious or they chose to close their eyes because the problems were not generally perceived to be urgent. Tourism was seen as a profitable sector of business with no obvious constraints to growth, few barriers to entry to the market, an almost universal welcome from governments and, for the most part, few effective regulatory requirements to take the environment into account. Commercial organizations, large and small, act on Dawkins' principle of self-interest. They do not make significant changes to the way they do business because of exhortations or out of good intentions, but only in response to the pressure of external factors that cannot be avoided, or to seize a competitive advantage. In the case of tourism as we approach the millennium, many more businesses can be expected to respond to growing international competition, the necessity to deliver higher value-added product quality, and the fear of losing customers and market share. Supported by the evidence in the cases included in this book, the first positive vision suggests that these marketing concerns will create profit motivated action to:

- Enhance the attractiveness of holiday destination images for competitive purposes – in which the environment invariably features, directly or indirectly.
- Develop product quality and value for money, in which perceptions of environmental quality are an integral part of product differentiation and value-added.
- Respond to the diversification of mass markets by more efficient segmentation and the

creation of market niches for which environmental values are a primary motivation.
- Encourage and secure more repeat customers, for whom product satisfaction is essential.
- Halt erosion of the resource or asset base and develop ways to restore and enhance its existing quality.

Every one of these action principles can be traced in the Part Four cases of this book. Market maturity in the principal countries generating domestic and international tourism, leading to greater competition between suppliers for more demanding customers, is providing the powerful dynamic that drives these actions.

2 Tourism's Klondyke era is over

It is essential to take a long-term view of the environment. Although the current global concerns with sustainability and the overall impact of humanity on earth were focused at the World Summit in Rio in 1992, they have been the subject of mounting concern over the last forty years or so, as the growth of international environmental regulation indicates. Despite market maturity in some countries, tourism globally is still an infant industry, albeit a lusty one, and international tourism as we understand it today is little more than 25 years old. Its characteristics and the nature of demand have developed and changed enormously, of course, since the 1960s, and any attempt to draw firm conclusions and make projections about the environmental impact of tourism on so short a history is unlikely to be justified in the perspective of the next 25 years. There is every reason to believe that 1990–92 will prove to be a watershed in the way humanity generally understands and treats its environment, although it is too early to be certain of the pace of change in attitudes and behaviour of governments, businesses and consumers.

For travel and tourism in particular we endorse the view of Poon (1993) that the tour operator-dominated era of mass international holiday tourism, based on traditional standardized packages and lowest achievable prices, will prove to be a temporary model. Such packages were appropriate and inevitable for the early growth stages of the industry, but they are outmoded and irrelevant as a model for future tourism. Tour operations, especially the techniques of packaging components will remain important, but the standardized 'mass' package tour of the 1970s will have as much relevance to future holidays as Henry Ford's Model Ts have to the modern automobile industry. Lowest common denominator tourism is already in decline.

With the benefit of hindsight we suggest that international leisure tourism has been going through its *Klondyke phase*, in which the opportunities for making quick profits from exploiting what were regarded as freely available natural resources dazzled the eyes of governments and businesses, as well as many local residents. The same has been true at different times for logging, mining, whaling, farming and fishing, big-game hunting, rhino-horn poaching and just about every other opportunity to exploit available resources when they appeared to be free and inexhaustible. This is a comment on human nature, however, not on any inherent toxicology of tourism. Although excesses of tourism development exist and are certain to continue in some places, especially those lacking economic development alternatives, our second positive vision suggests there is already widespread recognition that the Klondyke phase has ended and good reasons for believing that the leading players in the industry have moved on and are adapting to cope with new competitive circumstances and consumer expectations.

3 Selectivity based on heterogeneity, not mass consumption

In his series of influential, future looking books since *Third Wave* was published in 1980, Alvin

Toffler has developed a consistent theory of social, industrial, and political change based on what he calls the *Information Society*. In particular, he traces changes from the mass production processes of the industrial era of the nineteenth to mid-twentieth centuries, towards 'demassified processes of production, distribution, education, media and entertainment, creating a highly heterogeneous society in which individuality is celebrated and promoted' (Toffler, 1995). Customer expectations and demands for improved product quality drive the process of demassification in all industry sectors, including welfare provision.

The growth of marketing as the leading approach to the conduct of business in the late twentieth century reflects the Toffler analysis. Modern marketing is a product of the information age and it is based on deep and continuous knowledge of customers and other stakeholders as individuals – and what is now known as *relationship marketing*, especially with repeat customers. With the benefit of hindsight the mass-packaged holiday tourism phase of the 1960s to 1980s can now be seen as a service sector throwback to an earlier phase of mass-production processes – equivalent in its way to the post-war era of the automobile industry. Whenever strongly rising demand exceeds the capacity of production, for as long as the products provide reasonable satisfaction, businesses concentrate less on customer needs and satisfactions and more on ways to process larger numbers. That is simple business logic. But that era ended in the automobile industry around the 1970s. We believe it is ending for the same reasons in the tourism industry in the 1990s. Standardized packages will not disappear as long as they satisfy a continuing demand, but the leading edge of development does not lie there. It lies in bespoke, customized deals in which customers are treated as individuals, not as part of a 'mass'. Information technology makes it possible to target under-utilized capacity for accommodation and transport with precision, and identify the individuals most likely to be interested to buy it in a packaged but individually presented arrangement. The same technology is available for targeted promotion and distribution and especially suitable for encouraging last-minute purchases and stimulating customer loyalty.

As for other consumer industries, selectivity in travel and tourism is based on marketing research, which is increasingly a by-product of information technology and modern marketing databases. Research identifies segments; their profiles and their needs, expectations and perceptions; research identifies the product formulation which matches the needs; and research monitors customer satisfaction and value for money. We have commented throughout the book that, while the leading commercial organizations in the travel and tourism industry now have access to excellent information for marketing purposes, the quality of marketing research for destinations is still wholly inadequate and arguably the greatest single obstacle to the development of sustainable strategies. Our third positive vision is that information sharing, feasible with modern information technology, will provide a powerful modern argument for local partnerships.

4 Large and small firms in tourism – the role for inter-industry relationship marketing

We have stressed the numerical importance of small businesses in most sectors of travel and tourism. With a ratios of around 1000 small businesses and 'micro-operators' for every large player in developed countries, the cumulative power of small operators to block or undermine progress towards sustainability represents a major environmental threat. Against most received wisdom, we do not believe that small local businesses, or the great majority of local communities, are in any position to develop sustainable strategies for destinations and reliance on their contribution appears doomed to failure. Dawkins' view of human nature noted above applies especially to small businesses.

Progress depends partly on the better implementation of planning mechanisms identified in Chapter 8, but more on establishing commercially orientated control mechanisms for small operators. The fourth positive vision identifies two primary routes to achieve this.

The first route lies in the procurement policies developed and used by large organizations when purchasing supplies and product components from their smaller suppliers. Thus hotel chains can specify environmental criteria in the design stages for new units such as energy conservation and waste water treatment; when buying new equipment or supplies for use in routine business operations such as swimming pools, brochure production, catering and laundry facilities; and when dealing with suppliers such as taxi firms and coach operators. Tour operators are especially well placed to specify environmental performance criteria in their contracting negotiations (based on the *Ten Rs* in Chapter 11), and to monitor performance by incorporating environmental criteria in customer satisfaction questionnaires. Both the TUI and the Grecotel cases (Chapters 12 and 15) illustrate the process well.

The second route lies in the self-regulatory activities of membership bodies such as trade associations, local chambers of commerce and tourist boards, of which the travel and tourism industry in most destination countries has dozens. Some are international bodies, such as the World Business Council for Sustainable Development (WBCSD), which includes global companies supplying to travel and tourism, or the World Travel & Tourism Council (WTTC); others are international area organizations such as the Pacific Asia Travel Association (PATA) or sectoral associations, such as the International Air Transport Association (IATA,) the International Federation of Tour Operators (IFTO) or the International Hotel Association (IHA); and some are national, such as the British Hospitality Association (BHA) and the British Holiday & Home Parks Association (BH&HPA), in the UK. All these are examples of membership organizations which already specify criteria against

which they decide whether or not to accept businesses into membership. Such criteria typically reflect business competence, financial stability and professional qualifications. Increasingly they include criteria for minimum standards of business operations and product quality. Incorporating specific criteria for good environmental practice as the basis for membership is just a logical development of existing procedures. In the late 1990s, it is remarkable how few membership-based area and local tourist boards around the world have yet had the courage to develop and apply such critieria to their members, through fear of losing membership revenue.

Looking ahead, our fourth positive vision suggests that a practical combination of procurement policies, on the one hand, and membership criteria for trade and professional bodies, on the other, offers the best means to control the environmentally predatory actions of many small businesses and secure product quality in which the environment features strongly. Such policies would be exactly in line with the AGENDA 21 recommendations developed for travel and tourism. They would involve, encourage and support the activities of the many (but still a small minority of all) small businesses at the leading edge of sustainable good practice in their own right.

5 Destination partnership models for sustainable development and visitor management

We have stressed in this book that sustainable development for tourism depends upon decisions taken locally rather than nationally. Given the inevitable structural diversity of the tourism industry and its domination by small businesses, there is no logical alternative to the development of local partnerships involving:

• Leading local tourism businesses involved in marketing the destination, especially those with substantial vested interests in local property.

- The local authority representing resident communities and controlling statutory planning processes.
- Local trade associations and chambers of commerce representing small businesses.
- Local tourist boards (if different from the local authority).
- Other local interest groups affected by the tourism industry – positively and negatively.

Such partnerships would be ideally placed to involve and liaise with non-local tour operators and transport interests where these are significant enough locally to influence sustainable destination strategies. Our fifth positive vision focuses on the growing role for local partnerships, summarized as:

- Deciding local sustainable goals using information when it is available and common sense judgements and experience where it is not.
- Agreeing and communicating rolling five-year capacity targets (type and volume of products offered for sale and key segments to be attracted).
- Devising and implementing planning guidelines and coordinating the available tools to integrate environmental assessment with planning (see Chapter 8). Where additional legislative/regulatory powers are required, it is essential that these are negotiated and implemented jointly by the public and private sector.
- Devising and implementing local visitor management programmes from the business perspective (see Chapter 9).
- Drawing up community awareness programmes.
- Coordinating visitor-awareness programmes to be implemented by local businesses and their partner organizations such as tour operators.
- Monitoring progress in achieving targets, undertaking research as necessary for this purpose.

In countries with a well-developed tourism industry many of these actions are already undertaken locally, of course, but typically they are led and dominated by local authority interests. Mostly they lack the research information to set and monitor realistic targets, mostly they do not coordinate visitor management programmes as explained in this book, and mostly they do not involve local businesses in the process of setting and achieving agreed targets. National and regional tourist boards typically have a role to provide leadership and support for local authorities and to distribute such national funding for tourism as may be available for environmental purposes. In the UK at least, although policy statements, award schemes and exhortations abound, and some valuable initiatives in establishing pilot local partnerships have been taken in the last decade, national and regional tourist boards have not made major progress in this area. Because sustainable issues are essentially local in their impact, it is part of our positive vision that the energy for action is passing to the local level where the problems lie and solutions must be found.

6 AGENDA 21 and the three available mechanisms for action

AGENDA 21 sets out an internationally agreed framework within which to achieve sustainable development globally. It is the comprehensive programme of recommended action 'adopted' by 182 governments at the United Nations Conference on Environment and Development (UNCED) in 1992. Developed over the months leading up to the Conference, it claims to provide a 'blueprint' for securing the sustainable future of the planet. One may argue that it is not really a blueprint in the accepted engineering meaning of the term as there is no agreement on population control, and it is not legally binding but rather a cohesive set of recommendations for which actions have to be interpreted, developed, and implemented nationally and locally. It is, however, the first document of its kind to achieve widespread international agreement in principle, and perhaps the most complex document ever negotiated at an international conference. The Agenda represents a political commitment to strategic goals and it is grouped around a series of themes comprising forty chapters and 115 separate programme areas – from energy conservation to action to support the status of women.

International agreement notwithstanding, it is a fact that while the objectives of AGENDA 21 are recognized in central and local government, and among the larger international and national trade associations, they are still largely unknown in the private sector generally and have had little direct impact since 1992. It is, therefore, an interesting and significant development that three of the international bodies most concerned with government and industry involvement in travel and tourism have developed an agreed interpretation of the Agenda. Entitled *Agenda 21 for the Travel and Tourism Industry: Towards Environmentally Sustainable Development*, it was published in 1996. Undertaken for WTO, WTTC, and the Earth Council, the report places major emphasis on the need for partnerships and sets out a framework for specific actions by governments, national tourism administrations (NTAs) and trade associations on the one hand, and the specific responsibilities of travel and tourism companies, on the other. (See also Figures 8.1 and 11.2 and Appendix II.)

To achieve its recommendations, AGENDA 21 identifies three primary methods or tools and our sixth positive vision is that these recommendations will be increasingly implemented over the next decade, providing more examples of good business practice that can be applied around the world:

- *Regulation* – for the most part, regulations are highly specific for global issues such as carbon dioxide levels, banning of CFCs for refrigeration, control of hazardous wastes and use of certain chemical pesticides. They are mostly drawn up nationally, using inter-

national comparisons. They are typically not targeted at specific industries such as travel and tourism, although they embrace them as appropriate, and are mostly not specific in adapting regulation to meet local circumstances. There is currently no agreed regulation process for tourism management locally. The Earth Council reported that by the end of 1996, however, some 1200 municipal authorities around the world had already developed their local AGENDA 21s. In the late 1990s, UK local authorities are also developing their responses under the coordination of the Department of Environment.

- *Market mechanisms* – designed to influence the normal operations of mostly unregulated supply and demand, these mechanisms range from incentives such as grants, loans and subsidies, and disincentives such as sales or value added taxes, airport taxes/harbour dues, licence conditions for operators, road tolls and car park charges. They include 'polluter pays' charges where these apply. To be effective, such mechanisms have to be accurately targeted and underpinned by effective market research.

- *Voluntary/self-regulatory mechanisms* – primarily action to be taken by trade associations and commercial operators summarised within the *Ten R's* (Chapter 11) but increasingly concerned also with setting local goals and targets for sustainable action programmes based on destination partnerships. (See also the fourth positive vision.)

7 Risks and hazards and the precautionary principle

Risk and hazard assessment is already an 'essential component of the Environmental Impact Assessment relating to any major project' (Gilpin, 1996, p. 190). More generally, we live in an era in which it is becoming common for individuals and pressure groups to challenge businesses and public sector organizations to take responsibility for their actions, and to sue for alleged environmental damage going back years since events occurred. Tobacco, chemical and oil companies, and providers of utilities such as water and nuclear power, are the obvious targets today. But many companies are potentially now vulnerable to litigation resulting from their environmental decisions, and although the science and technology of measurement and monitoring is developing, it is still far from an exact process. In the USA, at least, directors of companies can in certain circumstances be held personally liable for corporate actions of which they may actually have little direct knowledge.

In these circumstances, the adoption of the *Precautionary Principle* – endorsed at the Earth Summit in 1992 as Principle 15 of the Rio Declaration – is a logical decision for companies. The principle is summarized by Gilpin (1996) as meaning that 'where there are threats of serious or irreversible damage to the environment, lack of full scientific certainty should not be used as a reason for postponing cost-effective measures to prevent environmental degradation'. The precautionary principle is our seventh positive vision and it affects mainly large companies in the 1990s. It is increasingly an issue also for insurance underwriters providing indemnity for corporate actions. But growing corporate awareness generally of the need to evaluate environmental risks and hazards more carefully, and take the necessary action, is beginning to influence decisions in smaller companies too.

Summary

Our overall message is as positive as we can make it. As we approach the millennium there is no other global growth industry that can affect the lives and livelihoods of so many people in so many places, as travel and tourism. No other global industry is better able or as well located to influence and deliver environmental quality at destinations and to communicate and educate both residents and visitors to its importance – changing consumer and business attitudes and

behaviour identified as fundamental to achievement of AGENDA 21.

Critics of tourism development should state what global economic resources and international marketing energy they identify to provide employment and achieve sustainability for the countries to whose growing populations they would deny the opportunities of tourism development. They should explain what other equivalent source of communication is available universally to promote sustainable environment messages. They should indicate what financial resources are available to combat the negative impacts of other, non-tourism sources of global change and environmental damage, from which no community is any longer immune. Such resources will not come from fishing, agriculture, logging or mineral extraction, and for most communities it will not come from shipbuilding, iron and steel, manufacturing industry or financial services industries. As Inskeep (1994) noted: 'Tourism is only one source of change in Society' (p. 35). To identify all environmental negatives under one visible issue – tourism – is weak argument based on poor scholarship.

Above all, modern travel and tourism is built upon a powerful dynamic capable of being moulded and channelled to sustainable goals. We endorse the view of Arden-Clarke of WWF International that 'sustainable development requires that markets be based on prices which ensure that the full environmental and social costs of economic activities are borne by those who benefit materially from them' (*The Economist*, 1993). Only a marketing perspective can deliver and maintain that requirement, adapting as necessary to market conditions. The cases and illustrations in this book, and they are now replicated all over the world, point to an exciting and achievable future in which sustainable goals are at the centre of policy, not at the periphery or as an afterthought. Our vision of marketing is of a massive global source of energy, innovation and change, and a set of tools or management techniques that can work best where it matters most – at local destinations in proactive private sector – public sector partnerships.

Appendix I

Select glossary of environmental, tourism and marketing terms

This selective glossary is offered to readers as a quick guide/aide-mémoire to some of the more commonly used terms and some of the leading international organizations associated with tourism, sustainability and marketing. The intention is to indicate the main meaning but not to provide definitive dictionary coverage of each of the terms noted below. Recommended dictionaries for further reference are contained in the Select Bibliography under Medlik (for tourism and hospitality), Gilpin (for sustainability), and Hart (for Marketing).

Acid rain Abnormally acidic precipitation especially associated with energy production and consumption and the emissions of heavy industrial processes, which can fall as rain, snow, mist, dew, or dry particles. Carried by prevailing winds this form of pollution easily crosses national frontiers, damaging trees and eroding stonework as it falls, causing major problems for forests and heritage structures such as cathedrals, sculptures and monuments.

Adventure tourism Defined as a holiday which contains an element of personal challenge through controlled risk, daring and/or excitement, often in a relatively inaccessible (wilderness) environment. Adventure holidays embrace a spectrum which ranges from 'soft' (e.g. hot-air ballooning in France) through to 'medium' (safaris in Tanzania), to 'hard' (e.g. trekking in Nepal). Activities include canoeing, white-water rafting, sailing, rock climbing, walking, trekking, caving, expeditions, hang gliding, ballooning, mountain biking, horse riding, scuba diving, cross-country skiing, etc. (Adapted from Ogilvie and Dickinson, 'Market segments – the UK adventure holiday market' in *Travel & Tourism Analyst*, No. 3, 1992, EIU, London).

AGENDA 21 The comprehensive programme of recommended actions intended to lead to sustainable development in the twenty-first century, developed over 1991/2 and adopted by 182 governments at the United Nations Conference on Environment and Development – the Earth Summit at Rio de Janeiro in 1992. Sets out an internationally agreed framework for action by governments, their agencies and the private sector relevant to all forms of economic activity, including travel and tourism. Sometimes referred to as a *blueprint* for securing a sustainable future, it comprises some 40 chapters and 115 programme areas but the progress achieved in practice between 1992 to 1997 has been disappointing. AGENDA 21 was interpreted for travel and tourism by WTTC, WTO and the Earth Council in 1996 (see Select bibliography).

Alternative tourism   Forms of tourism product considered not to form part of mainstream, especially so-called *mass tourism* holiday provision. For the most part, these products are considered (or claim) to be more environmentally friendly and culturally less damaging than others.

Best Practical Environmental Option (BPEO) The best possible approach for the environment although it may not always coincide with the best economic option. In some countries, BPEO is an established principle but most identify BATNEEC as a more pragmatic alternative.

Best Available Technique Not Entailing Excessive Cost (BATNEEC)   Concept accepted in law in many countries to minimize pollution, intended to ensure that companies select technologies and techniques in their day-to-day operations which abate or minimise pollution, without incurring excessive costs which may make the business uneconomic.

Biodiversity   The existence of a wide variety of natural environments and plant and animal species that make up the biosphere.

Biosphere   The part of the earth's surface and atmosphere which is inhabited by living things.

Blue Flag campaign   The campaign is an award scheme funded by the European Union, national governments and fees paid by participants. Targeted primarily at local authorities the campaign began in the mid-1980s as a means of encouraging local authorities in European countries to provide clean and safe beaches and marinas. The award is given annually to inspected beaches and marinas that meet specified criteria for environmental quality. It has developed from the focus on individual beaches since 1994, with wider objectives to improve understanding and protection of the coastal environment and it is targeted also at the tourist industry and the general public as visitors and users. In 1996, WTO, UNEP and the Federation for Environmental Education in Europe (the organizers of

the European scheme) were examining ways to develop this programme for global application beyond Europe.

Brundtland Commission   The popular name for the World Commission on Environment and Development created by the UN in 1983. Its report, *Our Common Future*, was completed in 1987. Chaired by Gro Harlem Brundltand, then prime minister of Norway, the report explored many of the issues developed by UNCED for the 1992 Earth Summit, especially concepts of sustainable development.

Buyer behaviour   Means the decisions that buyers make in relation to their purchases. Buyers may be heavy users of the environment – in terms of energy used to reach and enjoy a destination, activities at the destination based on environmental resources such as coral reef diving, off-road driving on fragile tracks, careless disposal of wastes and so on. Light users may consciously moderate their behaviour to respect environmental values at the destination.

Carrying capacity   An important concept for sustainable tourism, capacity is a measure of the tolerance of a site or building to tourist activity and the limit beyond which an area may suffer from the adverse impacts of tourism. Carrying capacity has four major facets – physical carrying capacity, social, economic, and psychological carrying capacity. Methodologies to measure and rank the relative importance of these capacities have been extensively debated, and in some places pilot tested, but have yet to be developed as reliable tools. This makes the overall tourism capacity of an area difficult or impossible to assess. Conceptually straightforward, carrying capacity is difficult to define in practice because tolerance will vary, for example, according to the time of year, the characteristics of the site and the complex interactions between tourists, residents and their environment. When capacities are measured, they nearly always refer to physical capacities at specific location, or to facilities available, such as the number of beds or car parking spaces (WTTERC, 1995).

Climate change   A term related to the effects of global warming accelerated by human intervention, especially economic development.

Codes of Environmental Conduct for Travel and Tourism   The development and publication of guidelines variously aiming to influence the environmental activities of companies, government departments with responsibility for tourism, trade associations, residents, or tourists themselves. The implementation of such guidelines or codes of conduct is usually undertaken on a voluntary basis – although management tools (such as manuals or examples of good practice) may be provided. Adherence to agreed codes of conduct may in future be made a requirement for membership of some trade associations and professional bodies.

Conservation   Protection and management of natural resources, buildings and/or the environment, for their intrinsic values and for posterity, not excluding some forms of sympathetic development.

Cost–Benefit Analysis (CBA)   A well-established measurement technique which can be applied to environmental decisions to assess the relative economic and other costs of a proposed development and weigh this against the projected benefits. The technique has some methodological difficulties when applied to the natural or cultural environment, because of the difficulties associated with ascribing values to naturally occurring assets such as mountains, or wildlife species.

Database marketing   Greatly facilitated by the speed of developments in information technology the term denotes the widespread development of sophisticated computerized databases since the late 1980s containing details of individual buyers and their transactions, and the use of such databases for core marketing activities such as customer research, market segmentation, media targeting and evaluation of marketing efficiency measured in costs to reach and influence customers.

Deforestation   The large-scale destruction and loss of forest areas around the world as a result of population growth and economic activities. Although commonly associated with the Amazon rainforest, deforestation occurs the world over. The process is estimated to have accelerated since 1992, notwithstanding international concern.

Desertification   The expansion of desert areas, largely as a result of population growth and economic activities, especially associated with poor water management practices, deforestation, destruction of vegetation, and poor agricultural practices. Desertification threatens or affects a large proportion of the world, including areas of the USA, Spain, sub-Saharan Africa, and Australia.

Direct response marketing   Utilizing databases to communicate with customers in ways designed to encourage a response to the producer rather than via an intermediary. Usually associated with highly developed segmentation using geo-demographic analysis, such marketing may use direct mail, house-to-house leafleting and telephone sales, as well as closely targeted media advertising with coupons and phone numbers designed to elicit the direct response.

Earth Summit   The popular name for the United Nations Conference on Environment and Development held at Rio de Janeiro in 1992.

Ecolabels   Trademarks or logos which have been developed to indicate the environmental credentials of a company, product or service to its clients. Such labels are usually sought by companies because they are perceived as communicating a particular approach to the conduct of business products which may also lead to a more advantageous market position. Examples in tourism are Green Globe (WTTC), Green Leaf (PATA), Green Key (Denmark), and Green Suitcase (Germany). See also **EMS** and **ISO**.

Ecosystem The complex range of interactions within and between living organisms and the non-living world that surrounds them.

Ecotourism In its broadest definition, ecotourism can include all forms of tourism in which the enjoyment of nature and/or the culture of the area visited is a primary reason for the visit. The Ecotourism Society define it as 'purposeful travel to natural areas to understand the cultural and natural history of the environment, taking care not to alter the integrity of the ecosystem, while producing economic opportunities that make the conservation of natural resources beneficial to local people'.

Environment Traditionally used to mean the physical and biological resources of the planet upon which human communities depend for their survival, the term is often used more broadly in a tourism context to include the cultural and social resources of communities.

Environmental audit A systematic, regular and objective evaluation of the environmental performance of an organization or area, its plant, buildings and processes. Much like financial audits, environmental audits can provide a measure of the environmental performance of a company as regards management procedures, resource use, waste production and disposal, etc., and usually specify ways in which this performance can be improved.

Environmental Impact Assessment (EIA) The process of predicting and evaluating the impacts of specific developments or actions on the environment. Associated with the development planning processes found in most countries, the conclusions of the EIA process are used as a tool in decision making. The purpose of an EIA is to prevent environmental degradation by giving decision makers better information about likely consequences that development actions could have on the environment. It cannot, in itself, achieve that protection. The EIA process involves reviewing the existing state of the environment and the characteristics of a proposed development; predicting the state of the future environment with and without the action or development; considering methods for reducing or eliminating any negative impacts; producing the environmental impact statement that discuses these points (for public consultation); and after a decision is made about whether the action should proceed or not, possibly monitoring the actual impacts of the action. In its initial conception it was envisaged that EIAs would be applied to programmes, policies and plans, but in reality in tourism, it has been applied only to large development projects (such as marinas and airports).

Environmental indicators Systematic quantified measures of the state of environmental resources. Measures for acid rain, water pollution, atmospheric pollution and noise, for example, are relatively easy to define and monitor. Measures of tourism impact on the environment are far more difficult to define because tourism is typically only a minor part of the total impact of human actions upon environmental resources. Currently being researched by the World Tourism Organisation, there are no internationally agreed indicators for tourism activity at the present time.

Environmental Management System (EMS) The systematically applied processes adopted by management decisions, through which the impacts of an activity or company on the environment are continuously assessed, measured and monitored, targets for action are devised, and programmes implemented. Environmental auditing and impact assessments are examples of an environmental management systems. EMS may be voluntary or monitored and recognized by independent parties. The European Union introduced its own Eco-Management and Audit Regulation in 1993 known as EMAS. It is a voluntary scheme encouraging companies to set environmental targets and management systems and operate to specified standards, with external auditors verifying compliance. A label can be used by companies fulfilling the requirements and meeting the standards (EMAS) but not on specific products. The Scheme started in 1995. See also **Ecolabels**.

Framework convention A type of international agreement which sets a precedent, rather than rigid rules. Countries which sign up to the convention then devise their own ways for meeting the provisions of the convention. Relevant to tourism, the primary example is the Framework Convention on Climate Change agreed at the Rio Earth Summit.

Global Warming An accumulation of carbon dioxide, nitrogen oxides, methane and chlorofluorocarbons in the atmosphere which allow incoming solar radiation to penetrate and heat up the earth's atmosphere, but prevent outgoing heat from escaping. In principle a naturally occurring phenomenon, the warming process is accelerated by economic and other human activity. Also known as the 'greenhouse effect'.

Green tourism A widely but loosely used and much debated term, 'Green Tourism' is seldom defined and may be used to refer to any tourism activity which is undertaken in a natural area, on which the primary focus is a natural resource, or tourism which is considered to be 'environmentally responsible' in nature.

Green Globe An international initiative launched in 1994 by the World Travel & Tourism Council to promote and recognize good environmental practice in the industry. All sizes of business in all sectors of travel and tourism are invited to join Green Globe as a declaration of their intentions and willingness to work towards establishing EMS. Green Globe confers a logo for members and a wide range of guidelines, manuals and advisory information is available.

Hazardous Waste Term which is defined in law in some countries but for which the definition may vary. In general, hazardous wastes are substances which pose a threat to human health and/or the environment if disposed of incorrectly. Typically byproducts of industrial and agriculture-related processes, they include toxins, carcinogens, corrosive agents, etc. within their scope.

Integrated resorts Facilities built specifically for the purpose of tourism and which include all the elements required for a staying visit on a single site and within a single plan. Such resorts often include shops, restaurants, accommodation, sport and leisure facilities and car hire outlets within their scope. Examples are Club Mediterranée villages, Sandals and Center Parcs.

Inter-governmental Organizations (IGOs) Organizations which have been officially established to represent the interests of a number of government authorities. Invariably governments make some form of financial contribution to belong to such organizations. In tourism, the World Tourism Organization (WTO) and International Civil Aviation Organization (ICAO), are examples.

International Civil Aviation Organization (ICAO) ICAO, established in 1947, is an intergovernmental organization and a special agency of the United Nations. It is responsible for all matters concerning civil aviation and is the main coordinating agency for international aviation standards under the Convention on International Civil Aviation (the 'Chicago Convention'). ICAO's objective with regard to environmental protection, as stated in its Strategic Action Plan, is to minimize the environmental impact of civil aviation in a manner that is acceptable on a global basis. ICAO has a Committee on Aviation Environmental Protection (CAEP) whose work programme was substantially revised in 1992. While CAEP continues to seek improvements to reduce aircraft noise and the impact of aircraft emissions near airports, it is now placing particular emphasis on determining the contribution of engine emissions to problems in the upper atmosphere and to identifying appropriate solutions to these problems.

International Hotels Environment Initiative (IHEI) Group of thirteen international hotel companies which developed a partnership in the early 1990s from which to promote the benefits of good environmental practice to the hotel sector globally. Commencing with an environmental manual developed for Inter-Continental Hotels and Resorts and coordinated by the Prince of Wales Business Leaders Forum, IHEI have been active through publications, seminars and workshops in promoting the concepts of sustainability for hotels and sharing examples of leading-edge practice (see the Select Bibliography).

International Union for Conservation of Nature and Natural Resources/The World Conservation Union (IUCN/WCU) A voluntary international body, originally founded in 1948 with the objective of ensuring the perpetuation of nature and natural resources throughout the world, with membership of NGOs and research institutions in more than 120 countries world-wide. Known originally as IUCN, the organization changed its name to WCU post Rio and has worked closely with WWF and UNEP with whom it has developed and published some highly influential environmental strategies (see Select Bibliography).

ISO Founded in 1946 the widely respected International Organization for Standardization (ISO) is an NGO specializing in communicating standards in most technical and non-technical fields. ISO has national equivalents (British Standards – BS in the UK). ISO 9000 established international quality management standards (see also TQM). In 1996 ISO introduced a set of environmental management guidelines known as ISO 14001 that can be adopted by organizations in most sectors of the economy, including travel and tourism. Organizations successfully meeting the standards as verified by qualified auditors achieve certification and can use the ISO logo.

Life-cycle assessment An assessment of the environmental implications of a product or service which takes full account of the entire life of the product from initial resource extraction and manufacture to final disposal (cradle to grave). Increasingly applied to manufactured products such as automobiles and consumer electrical goods, the term has not yet been systematically applied to tourism products although British Airways has undertaken some pioneering work in the Seychelles and St Lucia.

Limits to growth Name given to environmental thinking that became popular in the 1970s postulating that there are definitive limits to the level of economic growth that the world can sustain and that overriding these limits will bring economic and environmental catastrophe. One of the major works on this theme used a complex computer model known as *World 3* to predict the limits to growth for the planet. (See Meadows *et al.*, 1972.)

Marketing From an environmental standpoint the 1991 Kotler definition included in Chapter 1 offers the most useful resource-based approach. 'The organization's task is to determine the needs, wants and interests of target markets and to deliver the desired satisfactions more effectively and efficiently than competitors in a way that preserves or enhances the customers' and the society's well being'.

Market mechanisms A combination of fiscal, regulatory and economic tools which can be used by governments and their agencies or on a self-regulatory basis by industry itself, to influence what would otherwise be the free market price of goods and services. Market mechanisms are used to reflect the environmental costs of using resources, manufacturing and service operations, recycling and disposal of waste materials.

Marketing mix The set of variables used to influence buyers to make a purchase which are influenced directly or controlled by the decisions of marketing people, including product capacity, design and delivery, price, distribution and promotion. Marketing mix decisions are the focus of corporate marking and determine the capacity and profitability of an operation, reflecting the best market knowledge available to a business at any point in time.

Marketing motivation The attitudes and desires of consumers in relation to products available to them which determine their buying decisions. Motivations reflect the personality, experience and relative affluence of buyers and they may be influenced by marketing mix decisions.

Marketing objectives Reflecting corporate goals and mission statements, these are mostly quantified as to the number of buyers by type that are targeted to purchase the available range of products over a specified period of time. Marketing objectives typically include associated targets such as share of market and profitability and are specified as monthly as well as annual targets but may also be for longer periods ahead.

Marketing perspective A corporate standpoint or approach to the conduct of business which is forward- and outward-looking to the needs and interests of markets – and how to influence them. Alternative perspectives for the conduct of business may be a community approach, a resource approach, a religious approach, or even a sales approach. A marketing perspective will aim to deliver the society benefits of marketing identified above under *Marketing*.

Market segment A closely identified sub-group within a total market which makes it possible to design, price, promote and deliver purpose-designed/adapted products best calculated to deliver maximum customer satisfaction and profitability at least possible cost – within the overall constraints of the marketing definition noted above.

Mass tourism A term commonly but loosely applied to a popular form of leisure tourism pioneered, for example, in South European, Caribbean and North American destinations in the 1960s and 1970s. It involves the movement of a large number of people on nominally standardized packaged tour holidays to resorts that are mostly purpose-built or adapted for the purpose. Such tourism is often associated with high volume and low prices (*pile it high and sell it cheap*) as opposed to alternative tourism and ecotourism which is often associated with higher prices and low volume. *Mass tourism* is also often used as an elitist expression of contempt for the participation of the bulk of the population in holidays and leisure travel.

Mission/policy statement A carefully constructed statement of overall company intent/purpose. Typically one or two sentences in length, most publicly quoted companies publish their mission statement in their annual reports and a growing number adopt the statement or define it for specific issues, such as the environment.

National Tourism Administration (NTA) NTAs are typically created by government decisions and funded primarily by the public sector – although this is not the case in all countries – and they may be a ministry or other arm of government. Traditionally, NTAs have been responsible for marketing and planning inbound and domestic tourism to a country, and advising central government on travel and tourism issues including aspects concerning the environment. Increasingly, governments are looking to the private sector to increase their funding of NTAs. Also known as National Tourism Organisations (NTOs)

Niche marketing A niche in marketing terms identifies a particular product or products associated with a particular operator or place which have some highly specific advantages that are not easily copied by others. Whale-watching operations, Grand Prix motor racing circuits, or the Tour de France occupy specific market niches that attract identifiable groups of customers for whom it is possible to design and market wholly specific product offers. The quality of the environment in many places provides a route for identifying and marketing niche products.

Non-governmental organizations (NGOs) Organizations which are independent of national governments. Usually such organizations are funded by charitable funds, trade, or public donations and subscriptions. NGOs are not directly answerable to ministers of the government of any state, but usually are answerable to the public or companies which fund their existence. NGOs are prominent players in environmental issues and in tourism. They include internationally active pressure groups such as Friends of the Earth and Greenpeace, and trade or special interest bodies such as the World Travel & Tourism Council and the National Trust.

Ozone depletion Deterioration of the thin layer of gases which form the protective ozone layer around the earth. Although not scientifically measured before the 1980s, this thinning has been occurring over a number of decades and has now resulted in the formation of a 'hole' in certain parts of the world. It is a process believed to be accelerated by the effects of a growing world population and emissions generated by some manufacturing and transport processes.

Ozone layer Thin layer of oxygen related gases in the upper part of the atmosphere known as the stratosphere approximately 25 km above the earth. The ozone layer effectively acts a sun-screen for the earth, filtering ultra-violet radiation from the sun (UV-B) while allowing other radiation through.

Partnerships In the context of this book, partnerships means business orientated voluntary co-operative groupings between interested parties with the aim of defining and achieving common goals and objectives. Such partnerships are usually forward-looking based on perceptions of mutual benefit and may take place between companies – for marketing purposes, for example, or to improve health and safety of travellers, or to achieve agreed goals for sustainable development and protection of the environment. Modern forms of partnership identified in this book are between the public sector and private sector, created to define and achieve sustainable forms of tourism development, especially at local destinations.

Polluter Pays Principle (PPP) Accepted by the OECD as a principle in international law, the Polluter Pays Principle requires that those emitting damaging wastes to the environment should bear the full costs of rectifying that damage or containing the damage within acceptable limits according to national environmental standards. The principle is often implemented through the use of market mechanisms.

Pollution Contamination by harmful or poisonous substances resulting from human activities that deteriorates the natural resource quality of the earth, sea, rivers, lakes and atmosphere.

Precautionary Principle Principle established in law in some countries that, in the absence of precise scientific evidence, a cautious approach shall nevertheless be taken to developments and processes and, if there is evidence of potential environmental damage, the activity or process shall be changed to prevent that damage from occurring.

Preservation In environmental terms, preservation often refers to keeping an asset or attribute in its traditional form and character, so far as possible preserving existing uses. Preservation in these terms is often seen as more restrictive than conservation, which also seeks to retain a resource in its natural state, but not necessarily to prevent development and some change of use.

Product 'A bundle of or package of tangible and intangible components based on activity at a destination. The package is perceived by the tourist as an experience available at a price' (Middleton, 1994). It should be noted that 'package' in this context does not imply the product of a tour operator as all travellers within the definition of tourism – including business visitors and those visiting friends and relatives – also put together a package conceived as a bundle of separate elements.

Quasi-Autonomous Non-Government Organizations (QUANGOS) Organizations which, although funded by governments, technically have autonomy in their day-to-day management procedures because they are not directly responsible to either ministers or parliament, although they may be funded by public sector money. QUANGOs in the UK include the national tourist boards and Councils for Countryside, Sport and the Arts.

Regulations (for the environment) Legal and other tools and procedures developed by international and national governments to compel companies to adopt strategies to protect the environment and/or human health and safety in the areas in which they operate. In most cases companies failing to comply with national regulations may be penalised by having their development permits withheld, permission or licence to operate retracted, costs imposed, or in some cases their directors fined or imprisoned.

Relationship marketing Typically associated with database marketing and direct response marketing, the essence of relationship marketing is the building up of a continuing, ideally long-term mutually beneficial relationship between buyer and sellers over a series of purchases. The opposite of treating each purchase as a simple transaction, relationship building is

widely used in airlines and hotels to promote repeat purchase by current and potentially loyal buyers.

Risk assessment (for the environment) At its simplest level, an assessment of the financial risk associated with a certain path of action and its projected impact on the environment. Insurance companies are increasingly utilizing risk assessment methodologies to assess the viability of investments, or the potential for such investments to result in environmental or cultural liabilities.

Self-regulation/voluntary industry-led initiatives Programmes, usually developed by trade associations or individual companies, which aim to ensure more responsible and ethical management of products and processes from the point of view of health and safety for clients and staff, and for broader protection and sustainability of the environment. Such programmes are often influenced by existing or prospective international and national regulatory procedures, or by the desire to move faster in a chosen direction. Self-regulation is often guided by the development and communication of charters and codes of conduct. It may extend also to the membership criteria imposed by trade associations and professional bodies.

SERVQUAL A particular model for measuring the specifics of customer expectations of a service product and their satisfaction with all aspects of its delivery. By incorporating expectations as well as the tangible and intangible aspects of the experience, the model advances the traditional overall approach to measuring customer satisfaction practised for decades in the more sophisticated businesses operating in the travel and tourism industry. The model was initially developed by Parasuraman, Zeitholm and Berry in the USA in 1985.

Soft tourism A term sometimes used to denote green or alternative tourism. Hard tourism is usually associated with developed resorts for so-called mass tourism, complete with infrastructure and superstructure for hotels and transport.

Social Impact Assessment (SIA) Although the cultural or social implications of a development, including tourism developments, are often implicit in an environmental impact assessment, some commentators believe that they are neglected. Social impact assessment is thus the process of examining the likely impact of a development on the social and cultural environment of an area, and developing appropriate mitigation measures for any negative impacts judged to be excessive.

Strategic Environmental Assessment The formalized, systematic and comprehensive process of evaluating the environmental impacts of a policy, plan or programme and its alternatives, including the preparation of a written report on the findings of that evaluation and using the findings in publicly accountable decision making.

Sustainability Impossible to define or measure with precision, sustainability implies a state of equilibrium in which the activities of the human population coexist in broad harmony with their natural, social and cultural environments. Generally attributed to the Brundtland Report, sustainability in tourism is generally an aspiration and a goal rather than a measurable or achievable objective. In nature, of course, the environment is in a constant state of change and evolution and sustainability cannot, therefore, logically be identified with attempts to prevent change.

Sustainable development Development that 'meets the needs of the present without compromising the ability of future generations to meet their own needs' (Brundtland Commission). A concept endorsed as Principle Three of the Rio Declaration, it implies improving the quality of human life for all the world's population while living within the overall renewable carrying capacity of supporting ecosystems. At least in

theory, if an activity is sustainable, for all practical purposes, it can continue indefinitely.

Sustainable tourism Applying the logic of the previous two terms sustainable tourism development meets the needs of present visitors, tourism businesses and host destinations while protecting and where possible enhancing opportunities for the future. It is envisaged as leading to the management of resources in such a way that social, economic, and aesthetic needs can be fulfilled while maintaining cultural integrity, essential ecological processes, biological diversity, and life support systems.

Target marketing The focus of the marketing mix on market segments (see above). Also associated with niche marketing.

Three Rs The basic three R's of Reduce, Re-use and Recycle are the mantra for many promoting environmental management. See Chapter 11 for a view of the Ten Rs relevant to tourism.

Total Quality Management (TQM) Commonly identified with leading market-orientated companies in service industries, TQM is a term applied over the last decade to a systematic, whole business approach to appreciating customer needs, developing and maintaining facilities and service processes that satisfy those needs, and conducting all service processes to specified (written) standards. Based on forms of auditing and production of service manuals, several airlines and hotels have adopted the procedures which may also qualify for national and international recognition and certification by organizations designing, promoting and monitoring standards. See also **ISO**.

Tourism management Also known as visitor management and the foundation for any approach to sustainable tourism, tourism management involves a comprehensive, systematic planning process which assesses and estimates the current and probable future levels of tourism supply and demand activity within a region, or local destination area. It establishes goals and objectives for targeted types of tourism and their associated behaviour patterns (volume and characteristics of demand) and targeted types of product (capacity and characteristics of supply). Very much dependent on the ability to measure tourism efficiently at local level, visitor management objectives have to be quantified and supported with programmes and budgets required to achieve them. The techniques or tools for visitor management lie in the hands of both the public and private sector and are only fully effective when operated through joint sector partnerships. See also Chapters 8 and 9.

Tourism   Comprises 'the activities of persons travelling to and staying in places outside their usual environment for not more than one consecutive year for leisure, business and other purposes' (WTO, 1993).

Tourist area life-cycle   A theory which describes the evolution of tourist resorts adapted from the classic curve presented by Polli and Cook for all products. Much debated by tourism academics, the concept was proposed by Richard Butler in 1983 who noted that tourist destinations undergo a simple pattern of development with three basic phases: development; growth; and decline, stagnation, or rejuvenation. The theory supports the view that destination managers can arrest or change this 'normal' development pattern by the management strategies that they adopt.

Trade association   For tourism, an association or trade body which has a voluntary membership comprised mainly of travel and tourism companies in the private sector, and represents the views and interests of this membership to all its members and to other groups which are commonly commercial or political in orientation. Through their choice of criteria for membership, and the rigour with which they monitor and implement them, trade bodies may have a significant impact on the attitudes and activities of their members, especially members categorized

as small or medium-sized enterprises (SMEs). By operating marketing programmes and other services for members, trade bodies may stipulate additional criteria for participation, including environmental practices. See also Epilogue.

United Nations Environment Programme – Industry and Environment Programme Activity Centre (UNEP IE/PAC)   Created by the Stockholm Conference on the Human Environment in 1972 UNEP is the UN body responsible for environmental issues, especially as they relate to industry sectors, including travel and tourism. UNEP is committed to implementing and developing the outcomes of the UNCED conference, specifically AGENDA 21, through its future programmes. The environmental policy of the organization is to provide a platform to bring together industry, government, and NGOs to work towards environmentally sound forms of industrial development. To this end UNEP IE/PAC seeks to help in the formulation of policies and strategies for sustainable industrial and tourism development, to facilitate their improvement, and to stimulate the exchange of information. UNEP undertakes and sponsors technical reports, publications, seminars, forums, and training and demonstration projects. UNEP works with specific industry sectors to develop appropriate programmes; for instance, it is working with UNESCO and WTO to develop guidelines for the management of World Heritage Sites.

Vacation   US term for holiday. For the purposes of this book the two terms are interchangeable.

World Travel & Tourism Council (WTTC)   A global coalition of more than seventy chief executive officers from all sectors of travel and tourism, including transport, accommodation, tour operation and travel agencies, visitor attractions and aircraft manufacture. Although relatively few in number the companies involved are leaders in their sectors and all operate on a multinational or global scale and between them are responsible for hundreds of millions of tourism-related purchases a year. WTTC has three key aims within its mission: (1) to convince governments of the strategic economic importance of travel and tourism; (2) to raise barriers to tourism growth and development; and (3) to promote environmentally compatible development. WTTC took an active involvement in the issues of sustainable development in 1991 and lobbied actively at the Rio Earth Summit. It sponsored the foundation of the World Travel & Tourism Environment Research Centre (WTTERC) and its numerous publications at Oxford Brookes University in 1991, and launched the Green Globe programme in 1994 which subsequently took over the role of WTTERC. With WTO and the Earth Council (an NGO formed post-Rio), WTTC was responsible for analysing AGENDA 21 from a tourism perspective (see Select Bibliography).

World Tourism Organization (WTO) Is an inter-governmental agency established in 1975 as a UN specialized agency to replace the non-governmental International Union of Official Travel Organizations (IUOTO) founded in 1925. Representing some 124 member states and 234 affiliate members, the aim of the organization is to promote and support tourism development globally. In environmental terms, WTO works closely with UNEP and has established an environment committee to assist the travel and tourism industry to develop sustainable policies to ensure long-term growth. It organizes and supports seminars, workshops, and events and produces manuals, guidelines, and handbooks to assist in the education and training of tourism employees, and to assist in networking with other groups involved in travel and tourism.

World Wide Fund for Nature (WWF) A highly respected and leading voluntary NGO in the environmental field, WWF has some 28 affiliate offices around the world. Its objectives are global in scope and it aims to preserve genetic species and ecosystem diversity and it runs its own scientific research and practical conservation projects. WWF's work is closely linked with other leading international organizations, especially UNEP and WCU, and it has taken a specific interest in tourism development.

Visitor management See **Tourism management**.

Appendix II

Environmental regulations, market mechanisms and self-regulatory codes influencing the tourism industry

Table A.1 Environmental regulations, market mechanisms and self-regulatory codes influencing the tourism industry

Issues covered	Major international treaties	Implications for national regulators	Tools used to achieve ends	Implications for travel and tourism operations
Global warming; energy consumption	United Nations Framework Convention on Climate Change[a]	(i) Development of targets to reduce emission of CO_2, (ii) management provision for new and protection of existing 'sinks' to absorb CO_2, (iii) provision of environmentally sound technologies which minimize CO_2 emissions, especially in developing countries	(i) Energy taxation at source, (ii) energy taxation on end user, (iii) incentives to install energy efficient equipment, (iv) taxation/incentives for the use of 'cleaner' fuels, (v) positive promotion of energy efficiency	(i) Change in the relative consumption of different fuels; (ii) potential increase in prices of certain fuels; (iii) emphasis on reduction of use of certain modes of transport (aircraft and international shipping are omitted from the current monitoring system); (iv) emphasis on transferring appropriate technologies between facilities in developed and developing countries; (v) emphasis on efficient use of energy

Table A.1 *(continued)*

Issues covered	Major international treaties	Implications for national regulators	Tools used to achieve ends	Implications for travel and tourism operations
Ozone depletion	Montreal Protocol on Ozone Depleting Substances and its London and Copenhagen Amendments	(i) Elimination of the manufacture of CFCs and carbon tetrachloride by 1996 and halons by 2004. Developing countries have deferred elimination schedules	(i) Taxation on CFC/ODS products; (ii) ban on production of ODS[b] manufacture with financial or legal penalties for those who fail to comply; (iii) increase in market price for recycled ODSs, (iv) incentives for the development and use of alternatives	(i) Increase in price of certain ODSs; (ii) change in refrigeration and fire retardants to favour non-ODS varieties; (iii) increased in level of fines for companies that dispose of ODS's irresponsibly; (iv) increased pressure for good maintenance of existing ODS technologies
Biodiversity and habitat loss	United Nations Framework Convention on Biological Diversity; Convention on International Trade in Endangered Species (CITES)	(i) Development of strategies for the conservation of biological diversity; (ii) integration of biological diversity into planning procedures; (iii) introduction of regulations to protect endangered species; (iv) establishment of procedures to control the risks from biotechnology; (v) encouragement of public participation through, for example, EIA procedures; (vi) prohibition of the introduction of certain alien species; (vii) restriction of the import of goods made from certain species, for example tortoise shell, tiger bone, ivory	(i) incentives/subsidies for certain activities that conserve natural environments; (ii) prevention of development activities in certain environments; (iii) restrictions on species which can be used for, for example, landscaping in certain environments; (iv) tightening of planning laws as regards some activities, e.g. EIAs; (v) confiscation of some goods purchased on holiday at customs points	(i) Subsidies/preference within the planning system for types of tourism which can provide an economic incentive for environmental protection; (ii) increased requirements for EIA procedures and in some countries SEA; (iii) greater requirement for public participation within the planning process; (iv) pressure to utilize raw materials such as wood from sustainable resources; (v) greater awareness among customers of products to avoid and 'boycotting' of some activities, such as poaching

(continued)

Table A.1   *(continued)*

Issues covered	Major international treaties	Implications for national regulators	Tools used to achieve ends	Implications for travel and tourism operations
Desertification/ water depletion	United Nations Framework Convention on Desertification	(i) Protection of fresh water resources; (pollution prevention, especially of groundwater resources); (ii) adoption of measures to encourage water saving; (iii) encouragement of indigenous technologies which preserve water resources	(i) Increase in the costs of fresh water consumption and waste water disposal in some countries; (ii) emphasis in planning procedures to favour water efficient uses; (iii) subsidies for installation of water saving devices	(i) Increased pressure for thorough EIAs which consider water issues; (ii) increased penalties for pollution (through poor disposal or extraction practices) of fresh water resources; (iii) subsidies and incentives for companies to install water-saving devices; (iv) requirements for companies in some areas to install waste water treatment plant and possibly make this available for resident use; (v) possible implications for new golf course applications and other water-intensive uses
Noise	International Civil Aviation Organization (ICAO) Chapter III Aircraft Regulations (Annex 16); National and regional noise regulations	(i) Reductions in noise from flight operations; (ii) restrictions on noise from, for example, generators or discos	(i) Financial penalties for those who exceed noise limits; (ii) withdrawal of licence to operate from persistent offenders	(i) Increasingly stringent specifications for aircraft operations, especially during the night; (ii) increased resident opposition to new airport and tourist facility development in some areas
Emissions	Regulations relating to transboundary pollution, e.g. the 1985 Sulphur Protocol on Long Range Transboundary air pollution and the 1988 Protocol on NOx	(i) Reduction in emissions of specific pollutants at source; (ii) reduction in demand for certain materials; (iii) development and installation of technologies to prevent or limit pollution (e.g. catalytic converters for cars)	(i) Financial penalties for those who infringe emission limits; (ii) increased use of emission quotas and limits; (iii) subsidies or incentives to select low emission technologies; (iv) public-awareness programmes to reduce use of cars, etc.	(i) Increasing costs for certain products and services that have high emissions associated with them; (ii) potential increases in air fares as companies seek to purchase less polluting technologies; (iii) increased drive to use transport more efficiently, install energy saving and pollution prevention devices

Table A.1   *(Continued)*

Issues covered	Major international treaties	Implications for national regulators	Tools used to achieve ends	Implications for travel and tourism operations
Water pollution	EU Bathing Water Quality Directive; US and Canadian Bathing Water Standards Regulations; UN Regional Seas Programmes	(i) Development of national standards for water quality supplemented by standards and regulations governing the level and nature of effluent discharges permitted to rivers; (ii) some attempts to change land use practices especially as regards agricultural fertilizers and chemicals which affect water quality	(i) Increased charges for effluent disposal; (ii) increased penalties for emission of potentially damaging materials without prior treatment; (iii) incentives to install waste water treatment technologies	(i) Increased costs for the disposal of effluent; (ii) increased pressure to install waste water treatment facilities especially in biologically diverse and sensitive environments (for example, coral reefs) ; (iii) in some areas increased emergency preparedness procedures to deal with red tides, algal blooms and chemical spills; (iv) increased consumer pressure in some areas for cleaner water
Use of potentially hazardous substances	Various UN and national agreements regarding the manufacture, use, transport and disposal of potentially hazardous materials	(i) Reduction in the range of substances which are considered acceptable for use by companies; (ii) fines for companies that use or dispose of such materials inappropriately; (iii) increased public liability for companies which damage human health and/or the environment through the use, transport or disposal of such materials	(i) Increased charges for the disposal of such wastes; (ii) increased pressure on some developing countries to import such materials; (iii) incentives to encourage the purchase of environmentally benign alternatives to certain substances; (iv) stringent penalties for those who disregard the law	(i) Increased personal liability for managers who dispose of potentially hazardous wastes inappropriately; (ii) escalating costs for hazardous waste disposal; (iii) escalating insurance costs for the users of such products; (iv) increased subsidies for the development and use of environmentally benign alternatives (v) increased difficulties in selling on land on which such substances have been used because of the liabilities associated with purchasing contaminated land

(continued)

Table A.1 *(Continued)*

Issues covered	Major international treaties	Implications for national regulators	Tools used to achieve ends	Implications for travel and tourism operations
Heritage conservation	UNESCO Convention Concerning the Protection of World Cultural and Natural Heritage	(i) Identification of World Heritage Sites which are overseen (and in some cases funded) by the World Heritage Committee. Such sites are often tourist attractions and authorities in signatory sites are obliged to preserve them from damage	(i) Development of a fund to preserve World Heritage Sites; (ii) development of visitor management strategies for some sites; (iii) some site operators have introduced permit, licence or fee systems to protect their sites from the impacts of tourism	(i) Increased role for the tourism industry in providing funding for the protection of such sites; (ii) increasing restrictions on access and freedom to visit such sites; (iii) increased requirement for visitor management of such sites
Land use planning; building control	National/ Federal/local planning regulations. In Europe, the 1985 Directive on the Assessment of the Effects of Certain Private and Public Projects. In the USA the 1979 Environmental Protection Regulations (EPA)	(i) Identification of large-scale projects which require the preparation of an Environmental Impact Statement as a part of an Environmental Impact Assessment procedure	(i) Regulations to ensure that relevant environmental Impact Assessment procedures are carried out prior to development; (ii) in the longer term strategic environmental impact assessment procedures may also be required	(i) Increased requirements for lengthy EIA studies especially for large projects; (ii) increased necessity for post-development implementation studies; (iii) should SEA become the norm, increased cooperation between tourism facilities within an area to ensure compatible developments; (iv) growing role of local authorities under the umbrella of AGENDA 21
Aviation Standards	Chicago Convention (Annex 16 – 1968)	(i) International agreement confirming that air space above sovereign territory lies within the jurisdiction of that sovereign country and defined the so-called freedoms of the air. (ii) Established ICAO as the UN designated body for all issues regarding civil aviation	(i) Development of more stringent regulations regarding acceptable aircraft noise levels in and around airports; (ii) financial penalties on those companies that fail to comply; (iii) possible development of permissible emission levels; (iv) possible prohibition of some types of older and noisier aircraft landing in some areas	(i) Introduction of newer and quieter aircraft by some airlines to avoid financial penalties; (ii) possible restrictions on NO_x emissions which could increase fuel consumption and thus prices of air travel

Table A.1 *(Continued)*

Issues covered	Major international treaties	Implications for national regulators	Tools used to achieve ends	Implications for travel and tourism operations
Product Standards	International, national and regional trading standards; International Standard ISO 14001; EU Eco Management and Audit Regulation	(i) Enshrinement in law that products must meet certain criteria and match the claims of manu-facturers (aerosols that claim not to contain CFCs must, therefore not contain such substances). In some countries such as Germany these standards have been developed for specific environmental claims as represented by the Blue Angel pro-gramme; (ii) establishment of an internationally accepted and independently verified standard for environmental management systems (ISO 14001); (iii) establishment by the EU of a regulation specifying the procedures and performance measures that must be in place for companies to qualify for EMAS recognition	(i) Fines for companies that fail to meet criteria specified by trading standards; (ii) pressure from consumer groups on products that fail to meet criteria or standards; (iii) pressure from consumers and suppliers for companies to adopt and apply the universally accepted standard for environmental management systems	(i) Increased pressure from consumers and suppliers to adopt universally accepted management standards such as EMAS or ISO 14001; (ii) increased pressure from consumers to match promises of clean seas and uncongested streets made in brochures with reality

[a] See *AGENDA 21 for the Travel & Tourism Industry – Towards Environmentally Sustainable Development*, WTTC, 1995, for a summary of the implications of this document.
[b] ODS = ozone-depleting substances.

The travel and tourism industry has re-sponded to the increasing regulatory framework which could – in the eyes of some operators – reduce its ability to respond to market forces in an increasingly competitive market by develop-ing codes of conduct to govern its own practices and illustrate its willingness to government to act in a responsible manner. More than 100 such codes have been developed in the last five years to help the industry govern its own practices or change the behaviour of visitors. Table 2 provides a brief summary of the main codes of conduct that have been developed by the industry and their implications. (For a detailed examination of the codes of conduct that have been developed by the industry, the reader is directed to the UNEP IE/PAC publication of 1995 which examines the range of codes available in some depth.)

Table 2   *Summary of Some Key Codes of Conduct for the Travel and Tourism industry*

Originating organization	*Code*	*Main recommendations*
World Tourism Organization	Manila Declaration on World Tourism	States should recognize tourism as a phenomenon which has social and environmental impacts as well as economic benefits
World Tourism Organization	Tourism Code and Tourism Bill of Rights	Develops the role that the tourism industry should play in developing the legal and institutional framework for international tourism
World Tourism Organization/United Nations Environment Programme	Joint Declaration on Tourism	Details an agreement between UNEP and WTO based on the preamble that 'the protection, enhancement and improvement of the various components of man's environment are among the fundamental conditions for the harmonious development of tourism'
International Chamber of Commerce	Charter on Environmentally Sustainable Business Practices	First code of its type, which urges all companies to operate in a sustainable manner. The code was the basis for the WTTC guidelines
Pacific Asia Travel Association	Code for Environmentally Responsible Tourism	This code aims to encourage and assist in the development of the travel industry in Pacific Asia in a manner which recognises the urgent importance to practise an environmental ethic that supports responsible conservation and restoration of Pacific Asia's unique combination of natural, cultural, and social resources
World Tourism Organization	Hague Declaration on Tourism	Developed with the aim of defining the nature of tourism and to emphasize the importance of developing tourism that meets the social, environmental, and economic criteria of nations
World Travel & Tourism Council	Recommended Environmental Guidelines	Guidelines developed for tourism companies to assist them in the management of elements of their business. Recommendations relate to operational areas such as energy efficiency and waste management. The guidelines are supported by the Green Globe environmental management programme
World Wide Fund for Nature	Principles for Sustainable Tourism	Ten principles developed for tourism companies to encourage efficient resource use, consultation of local communities and responsible planning for tourism developments
Alliance International de Tourisme/ Federation International de la Automobile	Charter of Ethics for Tourism and the Environment	Charter which aims to help motorists and tourism companies to protect the environment in which they operate

Table 2   *(Continued)*

Originating organization	Code	Main recommendations
International Hotels Environment Initiative	Charter of Environmental Action for the Hotel and Catering Industry	Charter signed by the thirteen members of IHEI which serves as a mantra for the organization and also the longer-term development of environmental programmes for the hotel and catering sector
International Association of Tour Managers	Position Statement – The Tour Manager	Charter outlining the duties and responsibilities of tour managers with regard to the environment
European Tour Operators Association	Environmental Guidelines	Guidelines which offer recommendations to both tour managers and visitors to help them protect the cultural and natural environment of the destinations they visit
World Tourism Organization	Charter for Sustainable Tourism	An 18-point action programme agreed at an international conference as a way of bringing about more sustainable forms of tourism development
World Travel & Tourism Council/ World Tourism Organization/Earth Council	AGENDA 21 for the Travel & Tourism Industry	Interpretation of AGENDA 21 into a targeted action programme for travel and tourism companies and national and regional tourism authorities. The agenda specifies twenty action points and achievements will be monitored through the Green Globe initiative to the year 2005

Select bibliography

Australian Tourism Indstry Association, *Ecologically Sustainable Working Groups: Final Report – Tourism*, Australian Government Publishing Service, Canberrra, 1991.

Beaumont, J.R., Pedersen, L.M. and Whitaker, B.D., *Managing the Environment*, Butterworth-Heinemann, Oxford, 1993.

British Airways, *Environmental Report*, BA Environment Branch, London Heathrow, 1996.

Baker, M.J., *Marketing: An Introductory Text*, 6th edn, Macmillan Business, London 1996.

Boers, H. and Bosch, M., *The Earth as a Holiday Resort: An Introduction to Tourism and the Environment*, SME Institute for Environmental Communication, Utrecht, 1994.

Boniface, B.G. and Cooper, C., *The Geography of Travel and Tourism*, 2nd edn, Butterworth-Heinemann, Oxford, 1994.

Boo, E. (ed.), *Ecotourism: The Potentials and Pitfalls*, WWF, Washington, DC, 1990.

Burkart, A.J. and Medlik, S., *Tourism: Past, Present and Future*, 2nd edn, Heinemann, London, 1981.

Butler, R.W., 'Tourism, Environment, and Sustainable Development', *Environmental Conservation*, **18**, No. 3, 1991.

Butler, R.W., *Tourism and Sustainable Development*, Dept of Geography, Iniversity of Waterloo, 1993.

Butler, R.W. and Pearce, D. (eds), *Change in Tourism: People, Places, Processes*, Routledge, London, 1995.

Cairncross, F., *Costing the Earth*, The Economist Books and Business Books Ltd, London, 1991.

Carribean Hotel Association, *Environmental Management Toolkit for Carribean Hotels*, 1995.

Charter, M. (ed.), *Greener Marketing: A Responsible Approach to Business*, Greenleaf Publishing, Sheffield, 1991.

Charter, M. and King R., *Greener Management*, Greenleaf Publishing, Sheffield, 1994.

Cohen, E., 'Alternative Tourism – A Critique,' *Tourism Recreation Research*, **12**, No. 2, 1987.

Commission of the European Communities, *Towards Sustainability: A European Community Programme of Policy and Action in Relation to the Environment and Sustainable Development*, [Com(92)23], Brussels, 1992.

Commission of the European Communities (CEC), *European Community Environmental Legislation*, CEC (DGXI), Brussels, 1992.

Commonwealth Department of Tourism, *National Ecotourism Strategy*, Canberra, 1994.

Cooper, C., Fletcher, J., Gilbert, D. and Wanhill, S., *Tourism Principles and Practice*, Pitman, London, 1993.

Countryside Commission, and Rural Development Commission, *Green Audit Kit: The DIY Guide to Greening Your Tourism Business*, Cheltenham, 1995.

Croall, J., *Preserve or Destroy: Tourism and the Environment*, Calouste Gulbenkian Foundation, London, 1995.

Davidson, J.H., *Offensive Marketing*, 2nd edn, Penguin Books, London, 1987.

Dawkins, R., *The Selfish Gene*, Oxford University Press, Oxford, 1989.

Doganis, R., *Flying Off Course*, HarperCollins Academic, 2nd edn, Routledge, London, 1991.

Earthscan Publications, London – A range of published environmental contributions from the late 1980s, too numerous to mention separately. See also Pearce, D.W. (1989, 1993).

Eber, S. (ed., for Tourism Concern), *Beyond the Green Horizon*, World Wide Fund for Nature (WWK-UK), Godalming, 1992.

Economist Intelligence Unit, *The Tourism Industry and the Environment* (Special Report No. 2453), EIU, London, 1992.

Economist Intelligence Unit, *Managing Europe's Environmental Challenge*, EIU, London, 1994.

Ekington J., *Green Consumer Guide*, Victor Gollancz, London, 1988.

Elkington, J. and Hailes, J., *Holidays That Don't Cost the Earth*, Victor Gollancz, London, 1992.

English Tourist Board (ETB), *The Green Light: A Guide to Sustainable Tourism*, ETB, London, 1991.

English Tourist Board (ETB), *Tourism and the Environment: Maintaining the Balance*, ETB and Department of Employment, London, 1991.

Environment Strategy Europe: The Way Forward After Maestricht, Campden Publishing, London, 1994/5.

Environment Strategy Europe, Campden Publishing, London, 1996.

European Travel Commission (ETC), *Europe's Senior Market*, ETC, Paris, 1993.

Federation of Nature and National Parks in Europe, *Loving Them to Death: The Need for Sustainable Tourism for Europe's Nature and Natural Parks*, Grafenau, 1993.

Forsyth, T. (for Tourism Concern), *Sustainable Tourism: Moving From Theory to Practice*, World Wide Fund for Nature (WWF-UK), Godalming, 1996.

France, D., *Auditing: A Practical Perspective: Proceedings of Environmental Audits, Trends and Practice*, Institute of Environmental Assessment, London, 1991.

Gilpin, A., *Dictionary of Environment and Sustainable Development*, John Wiley & Sons, Chichester, 1996.

Gunn, C.A., *Tourism Planning: Basics, Concepts, Cases*, 3rd edn, Taylor and Francis, Washington, DC, 1994.

Hall, P., *Urban and Regional Planning*, 2nd edn, Routledge, London, 1992.

Hamele, H., *The Book of Environmental Seals and Ecolabels: Environmental Awards in Tourism*, German Federal Ministry for the Environment, Nature Conservation, and Nuclear Safety, Berlin, 1996.

Hart, N.A., *Marketing Dictionary*, 5th edn, Butterworth-Heinemann, Oxford, 1996.

Hawkins, R., 'Tourism in the Wider Caribbean and its Impact on Marine and Coastal Ecosystems', paper to a Conference of the Advisory Committee on the Protection of the Seas, Mexico City, 1995.

Heath, E. and Wall, G., *Marketing Tourism Destinations: A Strategic Planning Approach*, John Wiley, New Jersey, 1992.

Hughes, P., *Planning for Sustainable Tourism: The ECOMOST Project*, International Federation of Tour Operators, London, 1994.

Inskeep, E., *Tourism Planning: An Integrated and Sustainable Development Approach*, Van Nostrand Reinhold, New York, 1991.

Inskeep, E., *National and Regional Tourism Planning*, Routledge, London, 1994.

Inter-Continental Hotels and Resorts, *Environmental Review*, ICHR, London, 1996.

International Hotels Environment Initiative, *Environmental Management for Hotels: The Industry Guide to Best Practice*, Butterworth-Heinemann, Oxford, 1993.

International Hotels Environment Initiative, *Environmental Action Pack for Hotels*, IHEI, London, 1995.

International Hotels and Restaurant Association and UNEP, *Environmental Good Practice in Hotels: Case Studies*, UNEP, Paris, 1996.

International Union for the Conservation of Nature (IUCN), *World Conservation Strategy*, IUCN, Geneva, 1980.

International Union for the Conservation of Nature (IUCN), *Caring for the Earth: A Strategy for Sustainable Living*, IUCN (with UNEP and WWF), Geneva, 1991.

Josephides, N., 'Managing Tourism in a Recession', *Tourism Management*, **14**, No. 3, 1993.

De Kadt, E. (ed.), *Tourism: Passport to Development*, Oxford University Press, New York, 1979.

De Kadt, E., *Making The Alternative Sustainable: Lessons From Development for Tourism*, Institute of Development Studies, University of Sussex, 1990.

Kirk, D., *Environmental Management for Hotels: A Students' Handbook*, Butterworth-Heinemann, Oxford, 1996.

Kotler, P., *Marketing Management: Analysis, Planning, Implementation and Control*, 8th edn, Prentice Hall International, Hemel Hempstead, 1994.

Kotler, P., Bowen, J., and Makens, J.C., *Marketing for Hospitality and Tourism*, Prentice-Hall International, Hemel Hempstead, 1996.

Kotler, P., Haider, D.H. and Rein, I., *Marketing Places, Attracting Investment, Industry and Tourism to Cities, States and Nations*, Free Press, New York, 1993.

Krippendorf, J., *The Holidaymakers*, Heinemann, Oxford, 1987.

Laws, E., *Tourist Destination Management*, Routledge, London, 1995.

Lewis, R.C., Chambers, R.E. and Chacko, H.E., *Marketing Leadership in Hospitality*, 2nd edn, Van Nostrand Reinhold, New York, 1995.

Lindberg, K., *Analysis of Tourism's Contribution to Conservation and Development in Belize*, WWF and Ministry of Tourism, 1994.

Lovelock, J.E., *Gaia: A New Look at Life On Earth*, Oxford University Press, Oxford, 1979.

Manning, E., *et al.*, *A Practical Guide to the Development and Use of Indicators of Sustainable Tourism* (for World Tourism Organization, Madrid), 1995.

McIntyre, G., *Sustainable Tourism Development: A Guide for Local Planner*, World Tourism Organization, Madrid, 1994.

Meadows, D.H., Meadows, D.L., Randers, J. and Behrens, W., *The Limits to Growth*, Universe Books, New York, 1972.

Meadows, D.H., Meadows, D.L. and Randers, J.,

Beyond The Limits: Global Collapse or a Sustainable Future? Earthscan, London, 1992.

Medlik, S., *Dictionary of Travel, Tourism and Hospitality*, 2nd edn, Butterworth-Heinemann, Oxford, 1996.

Medlik, S. and Middleton, V.T.C., 'Product Formulation in Tourism', *Tourism and Marketing*, **13**, AIEST, Berne, 1973.

Middleton, V.T.C., *Managing Tourism Flows*, Tourism Society Lecture Series, The Tourism Society, London, 1979.

Middleton, V.T.C., *Marketing in Travel and Tourism*, 2nd edn, Butterworth-Heinemann, Oxford, 1994.

Middleton, V.T.C., 'The Tourist Product,' in Witt, S.F. and Moutinho, L. (eds), *Tourism Marketing and Management Handbook*, 2nd edn, Prentice Hall International, Hemel Hempstead, 1994.

Middleton, V.T.C., 'The Marketing and Management of Tourist Destinations,' in *Tourism Research*, published papers of the 44th Congress of AIEST (Vol. 36), St Gallen, 1994.

Middleton, V.T.C., 'Sustainable Tourism: A Marketing Perspective,' in Stabler, M.J. (ed.), *Tourism and Sustainability*, CAB International, Oxford, 1997.

Middleton, V.T.C. and Hawkins, R., 'Practical Environmental Policies in Travel and Tourism,' Parts I and II in *Travel and Tourism Analyst* No. 6 of 1993 and No. 1 of 1994, Economist Intelligence Unit, London.

Murphy, P.E., *Tourism: A Community Approach*, Methuen, New York, 1985.

Naisbitt, J., *Global Paradox*, Nicholas Brealey, London, 1994.

New Zealand Ministry for The Environment, *Business and the Environment: A Developing Partnership*, New Zealand, 1993.

New Zealand Ministry for the Environment, *Company Environmental Policies: Guidelines for Development and Implementation*, New Zealand, 1993.

Nicholson, M., *The Environmental Revolution*, Penguin, London, 1972.

Pearce, D., *Tourist Development*, 2nd edn, Longman, New York, 1989.

Pearce, D. and Turner, K., *Economics of Natural Resources and the Environment*, Harvester Wheatsheaf, London, 1990.

Pearce, D.W., *Blue Print for A Green Economy*, Earthscan Publications, London, 1989 (see also other *Blue Prints* by same author in subsequent years).

Pearce, D. W., *Economic Values and the Natural World*, Earthscan Publications, London, 1993.

Pearce, F., 'Dead in the Water', *New Scientist*, 4 February 1995.

Poon, A., *Tourism,Technology and Competitive Strategies*, CAB International, Wallingford, 1993.

Porter, M.E., *Competitive Advantage: Creating and Sustaining Superior Performance*, Free Press, New York, 1985.

Porter, M.E., *The Competitive Advantage of Nations*, Macmillan, London, 1990.

Ryan, C., *Researching Tourist Satisfaction*, Routledge, London, 1995.

Ryan, C., *The Tourist Experience, A New Introduction*, Cassell, London, 1996.

Seaton, A.V. and Bennett, M. (eds), *Marketing Tourism Products: Concepts, Issues, Cases*, International Thomson Business, London, 1996.

Smith, V. L., *Hosts and Guests: The Anthropology of Tourism*, University of Pennsylvania Press, Philadelphia, 1977.

Smith, V.L. and Eadington, W.R. (eds), *Tourism Alternatives: Potentials and and Problems in the Development of Tourism*, University of Pennsylvania Press, Philadelphia, 1992.

South Australia Tourism Commission, *Ecotourism – A South Australian Design Guide for Sustainable Development*, Australia, 1994.

Taylor, G., 'The Community Approach: Does It Really Work?' *Tourism Management*, **16**, No.7, 1995.

Theobold, W.F. (ed.), *Global Tourism: The Next Decade*, Butterworth-Heinemann, Oxford, 1994.

Toffler, A., *Power Shift*, Bantam Books, London, 1990 (and *Future Shock*, 1970, *Third Wave*, 1980, and *Creating a New Civilisation*, 1995).

Toffler, A. and Toffler, H., 'What Exactly is a Third Wave Information Society?' Paper delivered at an International Conference on Tourism and Heritage Management, held at Yogyakarta, Indonesia, October 1996.

Tourism Council for the South Pacific (TCSP), *Guidelines for the Integration of Tourism Development and Environmental Protection in the South Pacific*, TCSP, Suva, 1990.

Turner, L. and Ash, J., *The Golden Hordes: International Tourism and the Pleaure Periphery*, Constable, London, 1975.

UNCED, *AGENDA 21: A Guide to the United Nations Conference on Environment and Development*, UN Publications, Geneva, 1992.

UNEP, 'Sustainable Tourism Development', *Industry and Environment*, **15**, No. 3–4, Paris, 1992.

Urry, J., *The Tourist Gaze: Leisure & Travel in Contemporary Societies*, Sage, London, 1990.

Witt, S.F. and Moutinho, L. (eds), *Tourism Marketing and Management Handbook*, 2nd edn, Prentice Hall International, Hemel Hempstead, 1994.

World Commission on Environment and Development, *Our Common Future* (The Brundtland Report), Oxford University Press, 1987.

World Tourism Organization (WTO), Madrid, *Government and Business: Partners in Tourism*, December 1995 (WTO News); *Guidelines for the Development of National Parks and Protected Areas for Tourism* (with UNEP and IUCN), 1992; *National and Regional Planning Methodologies and Case Studies* (1993); *Round Table on Planning for Sustainable Tourism Development* (Bali), 1993; *Integrated Approach to Resort Development*, 1995; *Tourism Carrying Capacity* (with UNEP), 1992; *What is Ecotourism?* May 1995 (WTO News); *Global Tourism Forecasts to the Year 2000 and Beyond* (Paci), 1994; *Indicators for the Sustainable Management of Tourism* (Manning), 1993.

World Travel & Tourism Council (WTTC), London, *Travel & Tourism's Economic Perspective* (Global estimates to 2005), 1995; *AGENDA 21 for the Travel & Tourism Industry: Towards Environmentally Sustainable Development* (with WTO and The Earth Council), 1996; Green Globe includes a series of published guidelines for environmental good practice in the main sectors of the travel and tourism industry, since 1995.

World Travel & Tourism Environment Research Centre (WTTERC), Oxford Brookes University *Travel & Tourism: Environment and Development*, Annual Reports for 1992, 1993, and 1994; *Environment and Development*, Series of Newsletters published between 1992 and 1995.

WWF/Tourism Concern, *Beyond the Green Horizon*, WWF, Godalming, 1994.

WWF/Tourism Concern, *Sustainable Tourism: Moving from Theory to Practice*, WWF, Godalming, 1996.

Young, G., *Tourism: Blessing or Blight?* Pelican Books, London, 1973.

Index